D1552811

WAYS OF THE WORLD

WAYS OF THE WORLD

THEATER AND
COSMOPOLITANISM IN
THE RESTORATION
AND BEYOND

LAURA J. ROSENTHAL

CORNELL UNIVERSITY PRESS
Ithaca and London

Copyright © 2020 by Cornell University

All rights reserved. Except for brief quotations in a review, this book, or parts thereof, must not be reproduced in any form without permission in writing from the publisher. For information, address Cornell University Press, Sage House, 512 East State Street, Ithaca, New York 14850. Visit our website at cornellpress.cornell.edu.

First published 2020 by Cornell University Press

Library of Congress Cataloging-in-Publication Data

Names: Rosenthal, Laura J. (Laura Jean), 1960– author.
Title: Ways of the world : theater and cosmopolitanism in the Restoration and beyond / Laura J. Rosenthal.
Description: Ithaca [New York] : Cornell University Press, 2020. | Includes bibliographical references and index.
Identifiers: LCCN 2020016156 (print) | LCCN 2020016157 (ebook) | ISBN 9781501751585 (hardcover) | ISBN 9781501751592 (epub) | ISBN 9781501751608 (pdf)
Subjects: LCSH: English drama—Restoration, 1660–1700—History and criticism. | Theater—England—History—17th century. | Cosmopolitanism—England—History—17th century. | Cosmopolitanism in literature. | Literature and society—England—17th century.
Classification: LCC PR695 .R67 2020 (print) | LCC PR695 (ebook) | DDC 822/.409—dc23
LC record available at https://lccn.loc.gov/2020016156
LC ebook record available at https://lccn.loc.gov/2020016157

For Jerry, with love

✆ Contents

List of Illustrations   ix

Preface   xi

Acknowledgments   xv

Introduction   1

1. All Roads Lead to Rhodes: William
   Davenant, Ottomanphilia, and the
   Reinvention of Theater in
   the Restoration   19

2. Travesties: William Wycherley, the
   Fop, and the Provincial Girl   54

3. Indian Queens and the Queen Who
   Brought the Indies: Dryden, Settle,
   and the Tragedies of Empire   88

4. Restoration Legacies: Tragic
   Monarchs, Exotic and Enslaved   129

5. "Have You Not Been Sophisticated?":
   The Afterlife of the Restoration Actress   152

6. Histories of Their Own Times:
   Burnet, Cibber, and Rochester   181

   Epilogue: Mr. Spectator, Adam Smith,
   and the New Global Citizenship   214

Notes   241

Selected Bibliography   287

Index   299

🎶 ILLUSTRATIONS

2.1. Pierre Mignard, *Louise de Kéroualle, Duchess of Portsmouth*, 1682   66

3.1. Benedetto Gennari II, *Catherine of Braganza*, Queen Consort
of Charles II (1638–1705), 1678   92

3.2. Statue of Catherine of Braganza by Audrey Flack, 1998,
and the Vasco da Gama Bridge, Park of the Nations,
Lisbon, Portugal   93

3.3. Stump-work box featuring Charles II and Catherine of
Braganza, circa 1662   94

3.4. Panel from a table carpet showing the Four Continents,
the Seasons, and Four Planets, between 1662 and 1680   95

3.5. Panel from a table carpet showing the Four Continents,
the Seasons, and Four Planets, between 1662 and 1680   95

3.6. From Elkanah Settle, *The Empress of Morocco*   120

3.7. From Elkanah Settle, *The Empress of Morocco*   123

3.8. From Elkanah Settle, *The Empress of Morocco*   125

3.9. From Elkanah Settle, *The Empress of Morocco*   127

4.1. Mrs. Litchfield as Zara in William Congreve's *The Mourning
Bride*: "When I feel these bonds, I look with loathing on
myself" (act 1), 1807   130

4.2. Anne Bracegirdle as the Indian Queen, by William Vincent,
circa 1689   136

4.3. Sarah Siddons as Zara in William Congreve's *The Mourning
Bride*, by John Raphael Smith, circa 1783   148

4.4. Sarah Siddons as Zara in William Congreve's *The Mourning
Bride*, act 5   149

5.1. Mrs. Abington as Miss Prue in *Love for Love* by William
Congreve, by Sir Joshua Reynolds, 1723–1792   157

5.2. William Hogarth, *The Beggar's Opera*, 1729   165

❧ PREFACE

Restoration theater, energized by perfor-
mances of sophisticated pleasures, dangerous passions, and exotic encounters, embraced, troubled, and inspired an elite cosmopolitan culture. This
book aims to reframe that development in ways that will change the way we
think about this moment in theater history in the context of the nascent British commercial empire. As a preface, I begin with a brief glance at another
such attempt. In 1944, Kathleen Winsor created a lively and fantastical version of Restoration culture, including its theater, in her wildly popular novel
Forever Amber (1944). This international best seller and later film tells the
scandalous story of a young girl from England's countryside who falls in love
with a dashing cavalier passing through town on his way to restore Charles II
to the throne.[1] *Forever Amber* skillfully captures key myths about Restoration
culture that *Ways of the World* will explore, complicate, and sometimes
explode. After a brief romantic interlude, the cavalier leaves Amber, pregnant
and alone, in London to pursue his own adventures at sea. However, she will
not be defeated so easily, and scratches her way out of multiple predicaments
through seduction and wiles. She works her way through several husbands
and lovers, collecting houses, land, and titles and eventually becoming one
of the mistresses of Charles II. Winsor adroitly Photoshops Amber into the
Restoration court, where she competes with Barbara Palmer for the attentions of the king, pities Queen Catherine for her inability to produce an heir,
and struggles to outmaneuver the Duke of Buckingham.

It is the theater that provides Amber with the opportunity to make the
leap from poverty to glamor. She learns that actors, as servants of the king,
cannot be imprisoned for debt, and so approaches Edward Kynaston about
the possibility of an audition, which he easily arranges because the theaters,
having recently been commanded by the king to fill women's parts with
women rather than boy actors (like Kynaston himself), stood in great need
of attractive actresses. Soon Amber is performing regularly, basking in the
admiration of a higher class of men, and brawling with Rebecca Marshall
over costumes and lovers. By becoming an actress, Amber pulls herself out

of London's underworld and its grubby sleeping quarters and progresses to the much finer bedchambers of dukes, earls, and eventually Charles II.

The novel was publicized as historical fiction in the wake of *Gone with the Wind* (1936), but some contemporary critics attacked it as pornography. Winsor reported spending "1,303 hours of research reading (356 books, many of them 2 or 3 volumes)" and "380 hours of indexing notes."[2] She advised her publisher, Macmillan, to market the book to "students of the seventeenth century." Macmillan editors even had the book vetted for anachronisms by a "Yale specialist of the Restoration period."[3] Indeed, the author sprinkles the novel with delightful lesser-known details about the period and vividly depicts crucial historical events, such as the ravages of the plague and the fire of London.[4] When Amber plays the role of Cleopatra on stage, it is clearly in Dryden's *All for Love* rather than Shakespeare's *Antony and Cleopatra*. Some reviewers nevertheless condemned the novel as trashy, a "product of a sick society."[5] Macmillan received a flurry of angry letters from members of the Catholic Church and from Boston's Watch and Ward Society.[6] The novel was banned in Australia.[7] In the twenty-first century, *Forever Amber* has enjoyed a minor feminist revival, winning praise from Elaine Showalter for the heroine's courage and Winsor's arresting portrayal of the period. "It may be time," Showalter wrote in *The Guardian* on August 9, 2002, "to recognise *Forever Amber* as a classic, and to appreciate Kathleen Winsor's special brand of feminine genius."[8]

Forever Amber entertainingly captures Restoration cosmopolitanism, but tends to remain silent on the geopolitics behind the court's luxury. Amber's personal journey from naïve curiosity to urban sophistication reiterates, as we will see, the comic tension in Restoration comedies between country bumpkins and city schemers, as well as the audience's insatiable appetite for witnessing the transformation of rustic girls into city ladies. Her journey toward sophistication—a word that in the seventeenth century meant "adulteration" but, by the eighteenth, had begun to suggest a welcome complexity—also recapitulates biographies, real or contrived, of Restoration and eighteenth-century actresses who began life as naïve but became sophisticated in both senses of the term. *Forever Amber* takes place mostly in London, which reveals itself as more and more of a global city the higher the heroine climbs. Bruce Carlton, her cavalier, gives Amber a topaz necklace from the East Indies and later oversees a plantation in America. Amber's dressmaker is French, and her hairdresser newly arrived from Paris. One of her creepier husbands, the Earl of Radclyffe, collects Italian art. Amber declares that in her lodgings "Everything's in the latest style—and nothing's English."[9] Lord Carlton returns from Jamaica with a very special kind of exotic gift: "Some of the nobility owned black servants, but Amber had never seen one of them at close range before and she examined him as though he were some small inanimate object or a new dog."[10] Tansy, as this small child is named, stays with Amber for the rest of the novel, mostly in the background, although he becomes a point of contention between Amber and the nasty virtuoso, the Earl of Radclyffe, who suspects his wife of a lascivious relationship with Tansy and forbids the young African from his wife's dressing room. Winsor uses the figure of the enslaved African child in ways reminiscent of Charles II's own iconographic strategy, posing several of his mistresses in affectionate proximity to a young black boy or girl.

Forever Amber's Restoration London, then, is glamorous, exotic, and dangerous at the top and grubby, frightening, and desperate at the bottom. Amber first wants to escape the boredom of the country and then to escape the nightmare of urban poverty. But once she establishes herself through her acting career, her ambition becomes boundless (although always complicated by her enduring love for Lord Carlton). The novel luxuriates in the splendor of the court, the delicacy of the silk dresses, and the craftsmanship of the imported porcelain, revealing the author's careful research into cherished seventeenth-century imports. But while Amber delights in her human gift from Bruce's sojourn in Jamaica (and even defends Tansy, as noted, against the Earl of Radclyffe's cruelty), and while the other royal mistresses in the novel are also trailed by black servants, *Forever Amber* only gives readers a vague sense of the violence behind the arrival of exotic people and objects. We can surmise that Lord Carlton must be a slave master, as by the end of the novel he owns a flourishing plantation. We also know his ownership of this property was a result of some kind of arrangement with the king. Tansy is a sample from this other world beyond the pages of the novel; within it, he is decorative, evocative, and slightly indicative of the miscegenational potential of imperial practice. Readers learn about wars and other violent conflicts over trade routes because Bruce Carlton returns from them, but Bruce only tells Amber about his financial successes and excitement about colonial possibilities, shielding her ears—and ours—from the atrocities on which they depended. These two halves of the novel—Amber's world of wit, seduction, and scheming at court and Bruce's hidden world of slavery and war capitalism—[11] only come together sporadically when the lovers meet for passionate interludes. The two main characters never marry each other, and in the end Amber's enemies at court send her on a wild goose chase to America on the fabrication that Lady Carlton, Bruce's lovely New World wife, is dead. It is as if the author could not imagine these two crucial parts of the period happening at the same time. In this, she is not alone. Kathleen

Winsor offers a compelling picture of the Restoration, but it is one that has
been filtered through centuries of obfuscation, beginning with eighteenth-
century writers seeking to preserve this period's brilliance while downplay-
ing its brutality.

My goal in *Ways of the World* is to finally bring Amber and Bruce together,
at least metaphorically, with what can be glimpsed of Tansy's story, as they
play out on the Restoration stage. If Amber represents the sophisticated
glamor and dangerous scheming of the era's court and theater cultures,
Bruce, mostly absent, represents the war capitalism, New World genocide,
and transatlantic slave trade that enabled it. Tansy appears briefly as a bridge
between these worlds. I will suggest, however, that while the forces these
characters represent have only been pulled asunder in retrospect, in the
period's theater, the glamor, brutality, and exploitation were all considered
together, and that the Restoration stage itself depicted geopolitics much
more darkly than does *Forever Amber*, and more than criticism generally has
recognized. I make the case that this darkness becomes visible through the
emotional intensity of the stage, an aspect missing from Winsor's novel, which
depicts Restoration performances as too stilted to generate feelings—a myth
about the period that persists. For all of *Amber*'s truly gripping forays into
the plague, urban poverty, and debtor's prison, the novel offers little sense
of ethical or emotional response to the exploitation it depicts, to the fallout
from exotic luxury of the court, or to the violence on which it depended.
Throughout *Ways of the World*, I suggest that Restoration theater confronts
the moral complications of Stuart imperial ambitions in ways that are often
overlooked because they are expressed through structures of feeling, to borrow Raymond Williams's term, that we no longer share and that demand
careful excavation. These confrontations can also be subtle and, in some
cases, strategically encoded in ways that preserve deniability. In the introduction, then, I turn to one of the most memorable examples of this kind
of encoding from the Restoration stage in which exchanges probably mean
what you think they mean, but that, in a pinch, the author could—and did—
suggest that the second meaning was all in your head.[12]

❧ Acknowledgments

This book has benefited from the support and encouragement of many people and institutions. I am grateful to the Folger Shakespeare Library for a short-term fellowship in 2016 and to the librarians and staff during that period, as well as before and after. The Graduate School at the University of Maryland provided me with two different fellowships at key moments in the project, which proved crucial to its completion. I am also grateful to the many resources available at the British Library and to support over many years from the University of Maryland that allowed me to travel to those collections. The librarians at the University of Maryland, especially Pat Herron, have been very helpful as well in responding to requests and advocating for the acquisition of books, journals, electronic databases, and collections of primary sources. The American Society for Eighteenth-Century Studies has provided both a warm and supportive community and a vibrant professional structure for testing possibilities and learning about new ideas. I am also grateful for the opportunity to have presented many different versions and aspects of this project at St. John's University, the University of Alabama (as part of the Hudson Strode Lecture Series), Simon Fraser University, Neumann University, the University of Pennsylvania, and Southern Methodist University, and as keynote addresses at the British Women's Writers Conference and the conference "The Authenticity of Emotions: Skeptical and Sympathetic Sociability in the Eighteenth-Century British Public Sphere" at the University of Adelaide in Australia. Part of my epilogue was previously published as "Adam Smith and the Theater of Moral Sentiments" in *Passions, Sympathy and Print Culture: Public Opinion and Emotional Authenticity in Eighteenth-Century Britain*, ed. David Lemmings, Heather Kerr, and Robert Phiddian (Basingstoke: Palgrave Macmillan, 2015), a volume that came out of the latter conference. I am grateful to the editors for including me in this project, and to the publisher for their policy to grant permission to reprint. An earlier version of part of chapter 5 was published as "Eighteenth-Century English Actresses: From Rustic Simplicity to Urban Sophistication" in *The Palgrave Handbook of the History of Women on Stage,* ed. Jan Sewell and Clair Smout (Basingstoke: Palgrave Macmillan, 2020). A small part of chapter 4 appeared in an article called "*Oroonoko*'s Cosmopolitans" in *Approaches to Teaching Behn's "Oroonoko,"* ed. Cynthia Richards and Mary Ann O'Donnell (New York: MLA, 2014); those passages are reprinted by permission of the copyright owner, The Modern Language Association of America. I am grateful to the Folger Shakespeare Library for digitizing several images that appear here, and to Elizabeth Selby, Director of Collections and Public Engagement, Dorset County Museum, who tracked down an image for me even when the museum was closed for renovation.

Over the years, many colleagues have provided support, critiques, and patient listening. There are too many to name, but they include Misty Anderson, Paula Backscheider, Vin Carretta, Tita Chico, Theresa Colletti, Helen Deutsch, Tom DiPiero, Laura Engel, Julius Fleming, Marcie Frank, Alexandra Hultquist, Catherine Ingrassia, Eugenia Zuroski Jenkins, Tamar LeRoy, Kathleen Lubey, Robert Markley, Elaine McGirr, Felicity Nussbaum, Bridget Orr, Joseph Roach, Rajani Sudan, Charlotte Sussman, Scott Trudell, Orrin Wang, Kathleen Wilson, and Chi-Ming Yang. Lisa Freeman, Jean Marsden, Dave Mazella, Melissa Mowry, Danny O'Quinn, and Kris Straub have been brilliant and generous interlocutors over the years of building this project. I am grateful for all of the students, undergraduate and graduate, who helped me think about Restoration and eighteenth-century literature and culture. I would also like to remember J. Douglas Canfield for his encouragement at an early stage in this project and his excitement about Restoration drama, and Srinivas Aravamudan for his intellectual generosity. While many colleagues have been helpful and supportive, I want to extend particular gratitude to the members of my writing group at the University of Maryland: Holly Brewer, Jessica Enoch, Kristy Maddox, and Ashwini Tambe, who have read every single word of this manuscript at least once, and also a lot of words from which, thanks to them, you will be spared. Holly has guided me toward resources that I never would have found on my own; Jessica has helped me find the best strategies for the presentation of the argument through shaping and streamlining; Kristy has continually reminded me of the importance of audience, and Ashwini has helped ground my thinking about looking beyond national boundaries. I would also like to thank Holly Brewer for sharing with me in manuscript her game-changing work on slavery. The energy of the group has enabled me to stay on track with scholarship through various administrative appointments. The amazing team who helps me edit *Restoration: Studies in Literary Culture 1660–1700*—Elaine McGirr, Catherine Ingrassia, Tamar LeRoy—has my gratitude as well, as does Misty Anderson for making the transition of the journal from Tennessee to Maryland as smooth as public university bureaucracies could allow.

Finally, I would like to send love and gratitude to my parents, Bernard and Evelyn Rosenthal, and my children, Sophie and Victor, who have sustained me through many years of research and writing. My greatest debt is to my spouse, Jerry Parrott, who provided intellectual and emotional support through the writing of this book, and has been my most important interlocutor.

WAYS OF THE WORLD

Introduction

In William Wycherley's *The Country Wife* (1675), the plot hinges on an offstage cabinet filled with precious porcelain dishes imported from China. The worldly Mr. Horner, as everyone in the play knows, possesses great expertise in selecting these pieces, a fact that offers a compelling reason for the sophisticated ladies of London to visit him and even to retire to his private chambers to inspect this collection. Although he confesses to a limited supply, Lady Fidget emerges triumphantly from his chamber with a very fine sample in her hands.

This scandalous "china scene," as it has come to be called, filled with double and triple entendres around precious porcelain, opens a window into Restoration theater and Restoration cosmopolitanism, a form of cosmopolitics born out of the newly energized merger of vigorous global ambitions with an intensified striving for sophistication—the convergence, we might say, of the risky and the risqué—and on display on stage. Lady Fidget, originated by a woman (Mrs. Knepp) rather than a boy in one of the Restoration theater's cosmopolitan innovations, clutches a piece of china, which functions simultaneously as a figure for a male body part, a sign of her sophisticated taste, and a precious object from a fascinating foreign empire. Her grip performs the cosmopolitan ethos ignited in the Restoration, suggesting the intense interest in, even eroticization of the global, her willingness to violate social norms to get her hands on it, and the importance of the theater in both rehearsing and mocking these cosmopolitan ambitions. In brief contrast, when Diogenes of Sinope, the Greek philosopher who declared himself a citizen of the world, saw a child drinking water out of his hands, he threw away his cup. For Diogenes, becoming truly cosmopolitan meant liberating himself from dependence on luxuries. Just as there is no need to be encumbered by a national identity, there is no need to be encumbered by a cup if you can drink out of your hands. Wycherley's play proposes a world in which a different cup emerges as the object of desire, compelling English yahoos, as Swift would later deem them, to travel three times around the globe to acquire one for their females. Restoration cosmopolitanism came to define sophistication through possession and appreciation of selected treasures, but also the ideas and differences they carry. This conflation of the material and the ideal, in opposition to the Diogenite renunciation, has haunted debates over cosmopolitanism ever since.

Restoration cosmopolitanism, widely acknowledged but less commonly analyzed, emerged in the context of two major factors: first, that the monarch and much of the court had spent many years in exile during the civil wars, and second, that during those years they witnessed ways in which the Continental monarchs and their courts had enriched themselves through trade, aggression, and plunder in Asia, Africa, and the Americas. The Stuart court of Charles II returned to power with empire-building ambitions, but also with a distinct sense of inferiority to their European counterparts. Thus Lady Fidget clutches an expensive piece of china (or a stage-prop version of one) taken from the bedroom of Mr. Horner, who can only succeed with elite women by spreading the rumor that he has become a "eunuch" by way of "the French disease." Mr. Horner has traveled to the more sophisticated nation of France, and he comically adopts the stance of a figure (the eunuch) associated with the Ottoman Empire. Like much of Restoration writing, this scene expresses sensual pleasure, cosmopolitan ambition, and impotence, all in the same moment of performance. We have made a 180-degree turn, as Dave Mazella observes, from the Diogenite notion of world citizenship as freedom from worldly goods to a new kind of cosmopolitanism defined by those goods.[1] But like the ancient philosopher, this scene from *The Country Wife* nevertheless rejects an autochthonous national identity, embracing—even *clutching*—the sign of the foreign.

Ways of the World explores Restoration cosmopolitanism as engaged, critiqued, and embodied by the theater, itself a deliberately cosmopolitan institution at this time. Some of the plays I discuss, such as *The Country Wife*, are familiar, but others, such as William Congreve's *The Mourning Bride*, have attracted less attention. I believe that Restoration cosmopolitanism itself plays a role in the continuing obscurity of popular tragedies of the period. Tensions over sophistication tend to be salient in comedies, with the global surfacing through objects such as Horner's china closet, and functioning as the play's "dark matter," to borrow Andrew Sofer's term for the forces that invisibly hold performances together.[2] *The Country Wife* and other comedies continue to attract pedagogical, scholarly, and theatrical enthusiasm. Specific global investments, however, made the tragedies and heroic plays less accessible and also less popular beyond the period. These non-comedies set in remote locations, although admired at the time, have generated less interest among scholars and even less among theaters. They are rarely, if ever, revived. It is tempting to conclude that they are simply bad scripts, as perhaps only the most specialized of scholars have come to love them. Susan Staves suggests that Restoration audiences admired, but also laughed at the heroes set before them on the stage, an argument picked up and expanded by Michael Neill, who notes that the playwrights themselves do not seem persuaded by their own heroic creations.[3] Both point to the proliferation of satire of the heroic as evidence for this claim. Recent work on the history of emotions, however, suggests that our own affective responses to these plays may not be the best guide to understanding them or how Restoration and eighteenth-century audiences responded, as "emotional regimes" have changed over time.[4] Further, the proliferation of satire does not necessarily indicate a public rejection of the original. It can even suggest the opposite: the off-Broadway success of *Spamilton: An American Parody* attests to the admiration, rather than contempt, for *Hamilton: An American Musical.* I want to suggest that our own suspicion of these plays has been shaped by eighteenth-century suspicions of their global orientation. Part of the eighteenth-century embrace of Shakespeare as the national poet and as a figure for English nationalism, as Michael Dobson has persuasively demonstrated, was also a rejection, or at least an obscuring, of the more globally focused tragedies and heroic plays of the Restoration and early eighteenth century.[5] This remains, I suggest, a factor in our own love of Shakespeare and general head-scratching response to Congreve's *Mourning Bride.* Even when set in remote locations and involving foreign characters, Shakespeare's plays have been taken to say something special about Englishness that bears repeating and implicitly distinguishes them from globally oriented Restoration tragic and heroic plays. Restoration comedies have sometimes been suppressed on related grounds, as they reveal not what is special about being English, but what is particularly embarrassing.

The theater and what I call "theater culture" (in contrast to "print culture," a point to which I will return) was ground zero for Restoration cosmopolitanism; the theater was uniquely positioned as an incubator for new ideas and feelings about global aspirations and sophisticated style. The restored monarch Charles II, periodically fearing the development of conspiracies, shut down coffeehouses and prosecuted publishers.[6] But he loved theater and tolerated in the ephemeral world of the playhouse—to a point—violations of social norms, disrespect for hierarchy, and mockery of the elite. Restoration theater culture generated cosmopolitan ideals and became a space for cosmopolitan exchange, but at the same time revealed the human cost of global expansion in unexpected ways. Through comic satire and tragic pathos, theatrical productions scrutinized Stuart imperial ambitions and absolutist domestic policies. The playhouse confronted national desires to compete with more powerful empires and to draw its audience and its nation, as advocates argued, out of their barbarity.

Theater companies, in short, observed, staged, parodied, and analyzed the uneven national process of becoming a cosmopolitan empire with a privilege unavailable in print culture, and they did so with an influence beyond Drury Lane. The emergence of print culture itself gave theater a distinctive new character, both by contrast and through mutual synergies. The new print culture helped to emphasize the ephemerality of performance. At the same time, as Stuart Sherman has argued, performances endured beyond their original time and space through commentary in print media.[7] Restoration comedies affronted their audiences as they explored newly destabilized identities in which elite status provided an advantage, but not a guarantee of respect, a message repeated ritually through misguided heroes and titled fops, prompting startling mismatches between status and character as sources of unsettling humor.[8] Tragedies and heroic plays suggest the failure of expressed ideals about honor. Not only do the plays themselves explore cosmopolitan ideals and disasters, but the theater experience itself—the nearly unique, mixed-gender public character; spectatorship and self-presentation; the lingering influence through conversation and print; the emotional intensity; chance encounters with strangers; foreign performers, and foreign ideas—offered an enticing but volatile cosmopolitan experience that held meaning beyond the pleasure of the moment. I thus use the phrase "theater culture" as an analogue to "print culture" in order to suggest that stage entertainments had significance beyond their immediate time and place, and to capture the ways in which performance itself pervaded Restoration elite society.

The cultural significance of the stage at this time was by design rather than by accident: a cosmopolitan nation, Charles II and his circle believed, demanded an exquisite theater. Scenic panels now opened and closed; costumes, props, and machines became significantly more elaborate; audience members sported the latest fashions while scanning the crowd for a glimpse of the king, the duke, and the mistresses. The new genre of heroic drama, inspired by Continental romances, complemented traditional tragedy; comedies pushed the envelope on acceptable sexual representation in witty exchanges and outrageous antics; and more plays than ever took place in remote locations or incorporated worldly travelers and exotic commodities, such as those enjoyed on the Continent. Dramatists, players, and designers embraced this cosmopolitan vision: they flattered the elite on whom they depended and took full advantage of their ambitions to create a vibrant theater culture.

Charles II's mandate to replace boy actors with women—perhaps the most important of these changes to the theater—has been read for its profound implications for gender and performance; salient for contemporaries, however, would have been the association between the professional actress and Continental theater and, to a lesser extent but still significantly, with the masque tradition cultivated by Charles II's Catholic mother, Henrietta Maria. The actress, then, became both a key emblem for and a constant reminder of the cosmopolitanization of English theater and, by extension, culture. Well past the reign of Charles II and into the eighteenth century, the female body on stage, I will suggest, was shadowed by her Restoration origins and Continental valence. Attacks on actresses were animated by these cosmopolitan associations.

The courts of Charles II and James II fashioned a distinct version of cosmopolitanism as part of their commercial and imperial strategy. We can see Charles II's ambitions in his strategic marriage to the Portuguese Catherine of Braganza, who changed English culture by popularizing her own nation's taste for tea, porcelain, calico, and cane. Catherine's dowry included Bombay and Tangier, expanded trading rights in the New World and East Indies, and the opportunity to increase participation in the transatlantic African slave trade.[9] The Restoration saw the opening of the first English coffeehouses and new passions for tea, Asian porcelain, Indian textiles, and spices. Charles II patronized the King's Theater. To his brother James, Duke of York, Charles assigned a second theater, and also governorship of the Royal African Company, the nation's first chartered company that traded in enslaved Africans. Out of the theater and the court emerged a new ethos that defined personal sophistication and refinement in terms of the consumption and appreciation of global objects, ideas, and opportunities, built on profits from unspeakable violence and lingering injustice.

In *Ways of the World*, then, I explore Restoration cosmopolitanism as a force, like the Enlightenment itself, with profoundly mixed implications.

It was complex and dynamic, but marked by the Stuart ambition to raise the status of England through two inextricable investments: global traffic (including the slave trade) in the context of more powerful rivals and cultural sophistication in the context of shame over England's perceived relative barbarity.[10] The court set the tone for an intensified global orientation, but interest in looking beyond the boundaries of nation took a variety of other forms as well at this time. Merchants created global networks for profit; some religious groups understood leadership as transnational; and scientists built communities of knowledge.[11] Cosmopolitan ambitions promoted intellectual projects such as the Royal Society and the observatory at Greenwich. Strategic mixing could carry more prestige than purity.[12] Citizens drank Ethiopian coffee from Asian porcelain at Ottoman-inspired coffeehouses. At the same time, Charles II continued Oliver Cromwell's project to compete with the Spanish for dominance in the Caribbean, as Abigail Swingen has shown. Groundbreaking work by Robert Markley, Eugenia Jenkins, Gerald MacLean, and Alok Yadav outlines how English elites envied and even felt humiliated by the more powerful empires in France and Asia.[13] English ambitions to compete on the global stage brought new textiles, tastes, and ideas, but trading vessels featured rows of cannons and military fleets guarded trading posts, leading historian Sven Beckert to suggest that we should exchange the term "mercantilism" for the more descriptive "war capitalism."[14]

The craving for sophistication in this period, so often mocked on the stage, became so frantic in part because traditional forms of access to status had been destabilized. E. P. Thompson has described elite culture of the eighteenth century as a "theater of the great"—that is, performances of taste as a strategy for upholding fragile divisions of rank.[15] Much of this performance style finds its origins in the Restoration. Through the pursuit of sophistication, Britons could incorporate a burgeoning urbanity as well as material and intellectual experiences of the foreign into their own identities. For most of the seventeenth century the word "sophisticated" in English, as noted, meant simply "polluted," but by the end of the eighteenth century it had acquired its modern meaning of a welcome complexity, reflecting at least one strand of thinking about contact with the foreign and the unfamiliar. Cosmopolitanism, then, must remain an unstable term, capturing the amalgamation of the emergent kind of sophistication (urban complexity) with an appetite, for better or worse, for the global. Cosmopolitanism in the Restoration, however, remained a work in progress, as knowledge of and interest in the rest of the globe shifted and expanded.

Ways of the World alters standard narratives about Restoration drama by showing how attention to this highly contested cosmopolitanism, which grew out of the period's most intriguing accomplishments and disturbing atrocities, reveals an otherwise elusive consistency among comedy, tragedy, heroic plays, and tragicomedy; disrupts a generally accepted narrative about early capitalism; and offers a fresh perspective on theatrical performances. Traditionally, critics have seen Restoration drama as aiming to repair disrupted traditions by upholding a waning aristocratic ideology against the interests of emerging merchant and bourgeois classes.[16] Newer research suggests, however, that the Stuart elite were not threatened by mercantile capitalism; instead, they tried to monopolize it.[17] Restoration cosmopolitanism was not nostalgic elitism but the groundwork for ambitions that would shape the British Empire. Theatrical productions held it up for scrutiny: plays echoed the cosmopolitan and imperial ambitions of the court, but nevertheless satirized national envy of other empires (Ottoman, Spanish, French) and the human costs of "war capitalism."

Restoration cosmopolitanism did not end in the Restoration, but rather was baked into the institution of the theater and, to some extent, culture in the eighteenth century and beyond. Scholarship of eighteenth-century literature has explored how both novels and the theater self-consciously rejected Restoration immorality in favor of a new bourgeois identity upholding sexual virtue and English nationalism. While it is true that in the eighteenth century, unlike in the Restoration, nationalist identity competed with cosmopolitanism and both print and theater cultures in some ways rejected the earlier period's exploratory ethos, *Ways of the World* suggests that Restoration cosmopolitanism persisted and "ghosted" the reformed early eighteenth-century stage (to borrow Marvin Carlson's generative term for the way theatrical productions spark memories of earlier performances).[18] The actress, in particular, repeatedly performed the Restoration narrative of the emergence from naïve provincialism (or barbarity) into sophistication. Eighteenth-century theater, with its reformist agenda, explicitly rejected many aspects of the Restoration, but nevertheless found ways to reproduce and preserve its cosmopolitan vitality. The cosmopolitanism of this later period owes much, I suggest, to the Restoration, a moment to which it continually returns for renewal and disavowal. Restoration geopolitics, such as the initial chartering of the Royal African Company and the acquisition of Bombay, and Restoration theatricality, such as the female body on stage and the culture of spectacle, left a lasting imprint on the institution of theater, and on the world.

Ways of the World, while a study of plays, performances, and theater culture, explores dramatic writing and other documents in the context of the period's geopolitics. As a field, Restoration and eighteenth-century literary studies has long welcomed interpretation shaped by historical context, even during the years when historicism fell out of fashion. Given the distinctiveness of performance, theater studies has developed its own kinds of historicisms that differ somewhat from those in studies of the novel, the genre that, until recently, dominated the field. In studies of the period's drama, scholars have looked deeply and specifically into the materiality of performance. Those who pursue the material culture of the theater have attended to the rich archival possibilities, exploring extant play texts, newspapers, diaries, and periodicals, as well as acting styles and the physical properties of the stage.[19] Others have looked at ideological tensions in plays and performances as well as their expressions of party politics.[20] *Ways of the World* benefits from both of these approaches, but focuses less on ideological changes or conflicts between political parties than the dynamics shaped by England's engagement with the rest of the world, either physically or imaginatively. Thinking about the global can illuminate otherwise obscure aspects of Restoration performances that seem overly simplistic or make limited sense in a national context alone. Audience members, I suggest throughout, would have been aware of the national global interests evoked or assumed in performance, but these interests are less apparent beyond the context of the Restoration. I am interested in capturing, to the extent possible, how performances might have resonated politically and affectively at the time—in excavating what might have been apparent to original audiences but seems remote and even puzzling to us now. Like those who read for ideology, then, I focus on reading the lines and reading between them. I am less committed to identifying how each play fits into English political ideological categories, and attempt instead to capture the complex ways in which these performances open up disturbing (and embarrassing) questions for their audiences at a moment when the Stuarts were pushing for greater global networks and imperial expansion. My readings aim to draw out the way these performances simultaneously honor and undermine their patrons, their audiences, and their national leadership.

Ways of the World makes the case for the importance of understanding both dramatic texts and theater culture in the context of, and in dialogue with, shifting global relations and the resulting appreciation for and exploitation of the foreign and the exotic. As noted earlier, other scholars in Restoration and eighteenth-century studies have paved the way. *Ways of the World*, however, looks broadly at England's multiple global connections rather than its relations with a particular region (China, Ottoman Empire, France), and narrowly at theater and theater culture, and even more narrowly at a small group of iconic plays. In exploring the entanglement of theater culture with geopolitics, I do not focus exclusively on imperialism, although this is a central part of the story.[21] I have tried instead to capture, within the limits of time and space, the multiple forms of enthusiasm for the global in this period. I have tried to distill these under the general rubric of "cosmopolitanism." One embedded suggestion, then, is that not all forays beyond the boundaries of nation, both real and imagined, are imperial gestures, and that we might want to stay attuned to these alternative possibilities, however subtle.

For my understanding of these shifting global relations, I have looked at primary materials when possible, but also relied on the research of historians. The result, I hope, is neither "old historicism," with its positivistic confidence, nor entirely "new historicism," with its anecdotal and psychoanalytic bent, although I have gleaned much from this approach. The foundational insight from new historicism that theater speaks truth to power by representationally contorting and displacing both truth and power has become a touchstone for this project. Nevertheless, new historicism, as many have noted, did not necessarily engage the work of historians, but instead explored resonances between literary texts and objects or events not generally read as literary. The goals of this project, however, have demanded some distinctions. While remaining skeptical of any absolute distinction between text and context, and also aware of the crucial corrective emphasis of performance studies, each chapter here focuses on literary texts with a particular claim to cultural resonance and gains insights from attention to political and historical developments underway at the time of the work's performance. The transatlantic African slave trade, for example, is an important part of my story, but tends to be left out of discussions of Restoration drama because it does not often explicitly surface in performance.[22] Yet, as we will see, there are times when it does surface and, arguably, becomes the "dark matter" of the stage, as do other forms of violence taking place in remote locations. Recourse to the history of global engagements in this period helps make this dark matter visible. I have relied on work by historians to help illuminate certain aspects of theater culture that may very well have been much more accessible to Restoration audiences themselves, as they are implied, gestured toward, or assumed rather than explicitly stated. With limited records of audience reaction, some of these connections must be speculative, and speculatively supported by putting together the language of the text with both an imagined performance and alertness to its embedding in a nation set on cultivating its global reach. Some of my claims about the meaning of these performances suggest the development of a modern political unconscious about economics and human differences—that is, political assumptions and structures of feeling that lurk below the surface and would not necessarily have been articulated at the time, but also make some sense of strange connections and obscure material.[23] I also make some claims for *conscious* expressions encoded in performances that have become obscure through time and distance. Restoration drama, after all, is all about coded language and gestures set before audiences to interpret: for Lady Fidget to declare that she visited Horner's chamber for sex would have been far less interesting than elaborate multiple entendres about china. Given the complexity of both the plays and the period's geopolitics, I have chosen to focus on a select group of productions in order to trace their global connections in detail and in their specific context. *Ways of the World* thus does not aim to be comprehensive but rather makes the case for certain plays as representative, and analyzes a combination of comedies, tragedies, and heroic plays in depth and in their contextual specificity in order to excavate some of their subtler implications.

After 1688, some critics and some theater professionals distanced themselves from the exotic tragedies and embarrassing comedies that constituted Restoration worldliness. In the end, however, and in spite of attempts at its erasure, Restoration practices embedded certain kinds of cosmopolitanism into the institution of the English/British theater. Critics may have objected to the scandal of the china scene, but no one seriously proposed returning to the boy actor. The story of cosmopolitanism is not a linear one, but sometimes moves backward rather than forward, persisting and disappearing and popping up again. Similarly, the global connections in the performances are sometimes explicit, but are at other times the "dark matter" that holds the play together. Often this dark matter becomes momentarily visible in key stage objects rather than humans, such as a china cup, or an oversized periwig, or the chains around Zara's wrists in Congreve's *The Mourning Bride*.

Finally, *Ways of the World* is not just about *thinking* beyond the nation, but also, to quote the subtitle of Pheng Cheah and Bruce Robbins' important *Cosmopolitics*, about *feeling* beyond the nation as well.[24] Theater is an emotional business. I have tried to pay attention to ways in which productions communicated the feelings of the figures onstage, and to what sorts of feelings they inspired in the audience. In alignment with recent work in the history of emotions, I avoid the assumption that the feelings generated for a twenty-first-century reader would map onto those generated for a seventeenth- or eighteenth-century audience in any simple way.[25] Beyond historical differences in emotional expression, I have tried to take into account the particularity of the theater experience and its own cosmopolitics. For Charles II, a refined and worldly stage, no less than investments in science and navigation, became an essential sign of a global nation. Restoration and eighteenth-century theatrical productions explored shifting emotional ties, real and imagined, between the domestic and the foreign. That drama theorists of this time focused so intently on the classic unities of time, place, and action suggests how seriously they took the space-travel and time-travel possibilities in the playhouse. These were, it seems, getting out of hand, although recourse to the unities did little to constrain them. These imaginary journeys of time and space played out in front of merchants, tradesmen, ladies, prostitutes, and the king. The cosmopolitics of Restoration drama become visible in other genres as well, but the institution of theater both captured and represented the darkness and the light of a brave new world that had such people in it.

The first legal production after the interregnum closure of the theaters was Sir William Davenant's *The Siege of Rhodes*, initially advertised as a "musical entertainment" in 1656 and then remounted, in expanded form, in 1661. This book's first chapter, "All Roads Lead to Rhodes: William Davenant, Ottomanphilia, and the Reinvention of Theater in the Restoration," explores the reopened theater with particular attention to Davenant.[26] In spite of his own stated goal of creating continuity across the gap of the interregnum, he transformed English theater in significant ways. Restoration theater artists (performers, writers, managers) not only intensified onstage explorations of an increasingly interconnected global network, but also defended the revived theater as more sophisticated than a posited barbaric past. Further, they understood theater, for better or worse, as a mechanism for national refinement. Davenant became the most successful advocate for this vision, arguing for the positive effects of theater through its capacity to help England emerge from its crude provincial past and match the more advanced European and Asian empires. Richard Flecknoe, later ridiculed by John Dryden, made a similar case with less success.

The Siege of Rhodes transformed theatrical possibilities, featuring moveable scenery, a new genre (the heroic), and the professional actress. At the moment of the Stuart restoration after defeat and exile, it also marked the first English stage representation of an admirable Ottoman Empire. Davenant's production flattered, but also revealed the vulnerabilities of the restored monarch's cosmopolitics. Even though the play features the defeat of Christians at the hands of Ottomans, *The Siege* does not promote fear or hatred, but rather *envy* of this empire's sophistication and power. Ottomanphilia became fashionable in the Restoration: for the first time, Ottoman-inspired coffeehouses sprang up all over London, and English proprietors would sometimes dress in Turkish garb to underscore the exotic nature of their commodity. Charles II himself wore Eastern clothing to the opening of his friend Roger Boyle's play *Mustapha*. Davenant's immensely popular *Siege of Rhodes* inaugurated, with the opening of the theater, a new form of cosmopolitanism that promoted the widespread consumption of global objects and ideas as signs of sophistication.

Chapter 2 turns to the comedies of William Wycherley, which have long been taken to epitomize the libertine spirit of Restoration court culture. However, I argue that Wycherley (and others) pushed back against the court. The playwright's close relationship with the monarch enabled this resistance: he enjoyed royal patronage, had an affair with a royal mistress, and even received a personal visit from a concerned Charles II when he fell ill. The connection began before the poet's birth: Wycherley's family lost much of their wealth supporting the Stuarts during the civil wars, which gave William access to the court's inner circle. Such deep connections have often been read to suggest that Restoration plays promoted the aristocratic ideology of the Stuarts. The libertinism in the comedies, Jeremy Webster, Harold Weber, and others have argued, emerged from a libertine court culture, and the scandalous nature of the plays reflected the scandalous experimentation at court.[27] But Wycherley, I will suggest, did not include scandalous scenes to create libertine solidarity; instead, he exploited the leeway created by libertine envelope-pushing to critique royal ambitions with two figures that have entered standard theatrical vocabulary: in *The Gentleman Dancing-Master* (1672), the fop, and in *The Country Wife* (1675), the provincial girl shocked into sophistication. Wycherley immortalized but did not invent these two figures; in different ways they each come to embody anxieties at the heart of many comedies of the period. Wycherley is an outlier for his extremity and wit, but representative in his concerns.

Even before George Etherege, *The Gentleman Dancing-Master* solidified the figure of the Restoration fop as, I argue, a travesty role, defamiliarizing both nation and gender. In Wycherley's play, fops don French and Spanish clothing with non-normative gender implications, engaging in both cultural and gendered transvestism. As Marjorie Garber has observed and as Restoration comedy tends to bear out, transvestism on stage suggests a crisis of category itself, which, I suggest, becomes the key comic function of the fop.[28] This character's gender transvestism is, in Garber's terms, "unmarked": that is, he does not wear petticoats and stays, but he is defined by clothing, accessories, and gestures deliberately outside of gender norms. His national transvestism, however, is more clearly marked and a source of tense comedy as ordinary (non-elite) English men aspire to imitate the worldly ways of the French and Spanish Empires, in implicit contrast to provincial English manners. Possession of a black servant/slave marks Iberian identity in this play, while sophisticated luxury marks the Gallic. Both in key ways satirize the imperial ambitions of the Stuart court. In this play and in much of Restoration comedy, the fop, who aims for worldly sophistication, becomes an enduring comic figure for cosmopolitan failure that satirizes English envy of more powerful empires and nations.

Wycherley's *The Country Wife* takes on the problem of sophistication and worldliness in outrageous and sobering ways. The play revolves around two characters at the opposite ends of the cosmopolitan spectrum: Horner, the sophisticated and well-traveled trickster, and Margery, the comically naïve country wife who must learn the ways of the world. Later playwrights, as we will see, continually return to the provincial girl, who also becomes, as I will show in chapter 4, a figure for the actress herself. The plot of *The Country Wife* hinges on French sophistication, Ottoman polygamy, and Asian porcelain, theatricalizing the pleasures and dangers of female sophistication. The play challenges audiences to consider both the temptations and the costs of the process of cosmopolitanization, a problem echoed by later actress biographies. While *The Country Wife* has been read and appreciated for its complex challenge to gendered and sexual norms, its satire of the monarch and court's "empire envy" (a phrase I adapt from Gerald MacLean to discuss both plays)[29] and aggressive program of global ambitions have attracted less attention. Restoration theaters produced such memorable comedies not because they consistently expressed the court perspective, but because they pushed back against it.

Chapter 3, "Indian Queens and the Queen Who Brought the Indies: Dryden, Settle, and the Tragedies of Empire," returns to tragedy. Bridget Orr, Heidi Hutner, and Joseph Roach have all in different ways noted the spike in exoticism on the Restoration stage.[30] In heroic plays and tragedies, this often took the form of a romance between a European and a non-European character. Critics have generally interpreted this widespread "miscegenation" as revealing distress over an increasing proximity of the "other" and the danger of racial pollution. This chapter, however, explores instead how "mixed marriages" captivated audience sympathies. In their dramas, John Dryden (*The Indian Queen; The Indian Emperour*); Elkanah Settle (*The Empress of Morocco*); Edward Howard (*The Womens Conquest*); and Aphra Behn (*The Rover; The Widow Ranter*) explore intercultural romance as a figure for the benefits and volatility of cosmopolitanization. Often in the plots, *opposition* to affection across boundaries is what leads to disaster.

In the process of exploring these boundaries, Restoration theater culture produced some remarkably powerful exoticized women. I make the case that these dramatic unions between European men and foreign women point in two directions at once. One the one hand, as much scholarship has explored, they work through new questions about race, gender, and identity in a globalized context. The sexual union of two figures from different nations explores the boundaries of identity and of humanity itself. But while transcultural attractions open up these broader questions, at the same time they have a specific referent, I argue, that has attracted less attention. The paradigmatic "mixed marriage" in this period was between Charles II and his olive-skinned Portuguese bride. The various theatrical "Indian queens" evoke the English queen—Catherine of Braganza—who brought Britons the Indies, the East through possession and the West through trade routes, including those that enabled the trade in slaves. Catherine hailed from the European nation that pioneered global war capitalism: the Portuguese were the first Europeans to round the Cape of Good Hope, achieving access to Asia without having to negotiate with the powerful Ottoman Empire, which controlled the Mediterranean. The Portuguese also inaugurated the European transatlantic slave trade. Catherine herself was often described as "swarthy," with the possible implication of her Portuguese blood's having been tainted in the course of long proximity to Moors. Catherine brought in her dowry objects rarely seen before in London: lacquered boxes from Japan, chairs made of cane, inlaid cabinets from India. Her taste for tea and use of a fan folded in the now-familiar style launched previously rare curiosities into fashion trends. Her dowry included Bombay and Tangier, a colony that the English failed to hold and that became indelibly associated with the queen. All of these associations emerge on stage in powerful echoes of the exotic Portuguese bride.

Dryden's and Settle's plays work through broader issues of shifting identities in a globalized context through powerful exoticized women who resonate as figures for the Portuguese queen. These playwrights depict their powerful women as dangerously ambitious. Settle, who eventually aligned himself with the emergent Whig party, creates a relentlessly vicious Empress of Morocco at the height of conflicts over the expense of defending Tangier as an English colony. Dryden, whose loyalties vacillated, offers a more complicated picture. His Indian queens seek power, but also remain vulnerable, particularly to falling in love and suffering rejection and abandonment. They offer a complicated amalgamation of power and vulnerability, evoking Catherine's unhappy treatment at court, infertility, and abandonment by her husband for his mistresses. Bringing their figuration full circle, these abandoned women also evoke the losers of not just love but of history, those peoples left vulnerable by England's cosmopolitanizing ambitions.

Chapters 4, 5, and 6 and the epilogue move into the "Long Restoration," by which I mean the persisting force of Restoration theater and Restoration cosmopolitanism beyond 1688, into the eighteenth century and beyond. Congreve, whose plays I explore in chapter 4, becomes a pivotal figure here. Writing in the Williamite age of reform and in the midst of the paper war sparked by Jeremy Collier's attack on the immorality of the stage, he nevertheless looked back to the scandalous Restoration for his literary models. Contemporaries Richard Steele and Colley Cibber, by contrast, pioneered the reformist theater that laid the foundations for the new sentimental styles. Congreve, however, continually returned to the Restoration theater's exploration of rusticity, sophistication, urbanity, global networks, and cosmopolitanism.

Like Restoration playwrights intrigued by the novelty of the actress, Congreve narrates the process of becoming cosmopolitan through female bodies and performances. Actresses' biographies during this period and into the eighteenth century repeatedly tell stories of a journey from naïveté to sophistication and even worldliness. In Congreve and in the eighteenth-century theater in general, the memory of the actress as an icon of Restoration cosmopolitanism persists: embedded in her body is the cultural memory of her Continental origins, the court performance by Charles I's Catholic wife Henrietta Maria that was attacked by William Prynne, and Charles II's own insistence on the actress's presence at the heart of his revitalized theater.

Chapter 4, "Restoration Legacies: Tragic Monarchs, Exotic and Enslaved," looks at Congreve's enormously popular but now unfamiliar play *The Mourning Bride* (1697) alongside Aphra Behn's play about an Indian queen, *The Widow Ranter*, and her heroic novella about an enslaved African prince, *Oroonoko*. *The Mourning Bride* has become almost invisible in scholarship, but it remained one of the most frequently performed tragedies throughout the eighteenth century and consolidated Congreve's reputation as a serious artist. This tragedy persists mostly through the misquotation "Hell hath no fury like a woman scorned." My discussion focuses on this woman: Zara, a powerful African queen reduced to captivity and humiliated by her European lover (who disguises himself as a Moor), for whom she betrays her nation. Zara echoes the powerful Indian queens created by Dryden. Dryden's Mesoamerican plays first appeared at the beginning of England's entry into the African slave trade in the form of a royal monopoly; *The Mourning Bride* appeared in the midst of a pamphlet war over the fate of the Royal African Company generated by the threat to its monopoly when its governor, James II, fled the country. While *The Mourning Bride* does not depict plantation slavery or the slave trade itself, it nevertheless registers the impact of trafficking in African bodies. Congreve's Zara evokes the exotic queens of the Restoration, but is a more complicated figure who demands respect for her dignity and empathy over her abuse. As I suggest, Zara moved audiences not just as a "woman scorned," but as an African who has been deracinated and, in her own words, "enslaved."

Chapter 5 demonstrates how the figure of the actress in the eighteenth century evokes her Restoration origins and commonly performs roles that demand the transformation of provincialism to worldliness. Congreve's best-known comedy of this period, *Love for Love*, reprises the Restoration by reviving *The Country Wife*'s Margery Pinchwife in the character of Miss Prue. By reaching back to Margery, he created an iconic figure who continued to resonate back to the Restoration in all of her various embodiments. The iconic provincial girls of the Restoration and eighteenth-century stage became closely associated with particular actresses, whose reputed life stories mirrored the character of the rustic girl in her transformation from country naïveté to worldly (and global) sophistication by way of the theater. I explore Miss Prue and her close association with Frances Abington, then look back to Margery Pinchwife and her association with Elizabeth Boutell. I then turn to perhaps the most memorable of these provincials: Polly Peachum in *The Beggar's Opera*, inextricably associated with the life and art of Lavinia Fenton. The character and the actress who played her became so popular that John Gay wrote a sequel called *Polly*, in which the heroine confronts transatlantic corruption as she follows her husband to North America and finds him there transformed into a black pirate, implicitly the globalized version of the Restoration-style rake he had played before. Gay's Macheath thus returns audiences to the Restoration through not just his aristocratic-style libertinism, but the memory of Charles's chartering of the Royal African Company, condemning the Whig capitalism of the eighteenth century but also the war capitalism of the Stuarts. Through performances of female journeys from naïveté to cosmopolitanism in which the role evoked the reputed biography of the actress, these productions rehearsed the originating transformation of women into public performers. Actresses became kinetic links between the reformed eighteenth-century theater, with its new political landscape, and the cosmopolitan ambitions of the Stuart Restoration. Eighteenth-century audiences had not forgotten the role of Charles II in transforming the theater, and if they had, Colley Cibber would remind them.

Cibber, as I explain in chapter 6, became a crucial figure in the preservation of Restoration cosmopolitanism in the eighteenth century, through both his fop performances and his influential *Apology*. As a prominent Whig who was cozy with the Walpole administration, he repudiated Restoration absolutist ambitions. While rejecting Tory politics, he nevertheless embraced Stuart glamor and particularly Stuart theatrical innovations. In ways that would have been clear to contemporary readers but now demand excavation, Cibber, I argue, sets up his *Apology* as an alternative to Gilbert Burnet's ubiquitous *History of His Own Times*, which dwells on the brutality of Stuart rule. (Cibber calls his own work a "theatrical history of his own times.") Cibber shares Burnet's rejection of absolutist politics, but nevertheless recovers the glamor and theatrical innovation of the Restoration by impersonating and exaggerating its fops in repeated gestures of deliberate anachronism that promoted the pleasures of the foppish spirit of national and gendered fungibility.

In a closing epilogue, I turn to Joseph Addison's *Spectator* and finally to Adam Smith, who transformed the theatrical cosmopolitanism of the Restoration into a theory of emotions and cosmopolitics. Mr. Spectator summarizes the new Whig cosmopolitanism in his celebration of the New Exchange in an essay that inspired Adam Smith's vision in *The Wealth of Nations*, in which he proposes an ideal of exchange that transforms the Restoration war capitalism to a mutually beneficial global system. The roots of this vision can be found in Smith's earlier *Theory of Moral Sentiments* (1759), in which he turns to theater for the secrets of human behavior and human possibility. He looks back to the Restoration to warn against the dangerous human tendency to sympathize with social superiors, noting how sentiment for the Stuarts overshadowed the lives lost in the civil wars. The period provides for Smith a negative model of emotional misdirection that leads to political oppression. Traditional tragedy that invests too heavily in a monarch, his writing implies, must give way to a new kind of theater for a new kind of emotionally calibrated culture that will provide the foundation for peaceful exchange. *Ways of the World* ends, then, with the most salient example of this new tragedy about capitalism: George Lillo's *The London Merchant*, which suggests the limits of "sympathizing up" and the tragedy of failing to sympathize more broadly.

Like many philosophers in the eighteenth century, Adam Smith aims to understand both emotions and political economy. In *Ways of the World*, however, I show how these two points of interest were profoundly intertwined in the Restoration. In order to try to understand the significance of this intersection, this book turns, as does Smith, to the theater for insight. Restoration theater has been, I hope to show, underestimated, partly because, to return once more to the preface, the two worlds of Amber and Bruce Carlton have been often read in different contexts and in different kinds of critical projects. While certainly theater audience members of the Restoration period would have had different expectations for comedy, tragedy, tragicomedy, and heroic drama, they nevertheless witnessed them in the same moment of imperial ambition, political turbulence, and cosmopolitan explorations. Restoration plays have sometimes been read as frivolous entertainment or nationalist propaganda, but in what follows I characterize them as more ambitious and more capacious, often too edgy or insufficiently nationalistic for subsequent contexts. I make the case for key theater experiences that were produced with wit, daring, and insight as not expressing the last gasp of absolutist monarchy, but instead engaging some beginnings: of war capitalism, of the embrace of sophistication, of England's entrance into the slave trade in earnest, and of new possibilities for human passions redirected for this expanding world.

🎵 CHAPTER 1

All Roads Lead to Rhodes

William Davenant, Ottomanphilia, and
the Reinvention of Theater in the Restoration

On October 8, 1666, John Evelyn saw King Charles II wearing a new kind of suit:

> To Court. It being the first time his Majesty put himself solemnly into the Eastern fashion of vest, changing doublet, stiff collar, bands and cloak, into a comely dress, after the Persian mode, with girdles or straps, and shoestrings and garters into buckles, of which some were set with precious stones, resolving never to alter it, and to leave the French mode, which had hitherto obtained to our great expense and reproach. Upon which, divers courtiers and gentlemen gave his Majesty gold by way of wager that he would not persist in this resolution.[1]

But persist he did, launching a new fashion trend that dovetailed with a broader Ottomanphilia that gripped Restoration England. This Eastern-inspired style ultimately evolved into the familiar three-piece suit.[2]

That evening, Evelyn joined the court audience for a Whitehall production of the popular tragedy of *Mustapha* (1665), written by Charles's close associate Roger Boyle, Earl of Orrery. The king may have broken out his Eastern attire with this performance in mind. *Mustapha* dramatizes the 1541 conflict between the Ottoman Empire and the Holy Roman Empire for control of Hungary, into which the author inserted the figure of Sultan Suleiman's famous wife Roxolana, who had nothing to do with this particular historical conflict but who fascinated the playgoing and reading public of the seventeenth century.[3] Evelyn identifies Charles II's new look as "Persian," but fashion historian Diana De Marly suggests that "the first likely source of influence" of this long-lasting trend (the waistcoat) was theatrical productions based on Turkish history, particularly Sir William Davenant's *The Siege of Rhodes* (1656 and 1661) and *Mustapha*, with which the court was entertained that evening.[4] Charles wore his trend-setting Eastern attire to attend this performance of a popular play that capitalized on the success of *The Siege of Rhodes*, which, as we will see, inaugurated a new kind of theater in the Restoration.

The enthusiasm for everything Ottoman in which the king heartily participated—as evidenced by his hosting a performance of a play about Ottoman history while wearing the Ottoman-inspired fashions similar to those costuming the actors—was central to the formation of Restoration cosmopolitan aspirations. While England had been the main trading partner with the Ottomans since the 1620s,[5] the Stuart Restoration marked a new level of fascination with this empire. Coffeehouses sprang up during this period; both the venue and the drink were Ottoman imports, a point leveraged to increase their sales.[6] Many coffeehouses, Gerald MacLean notes, "bore names like 'the Turk's Head.' Sometimes proprietors dressed as Turks or Arabs; sometimes these proprietors were Levantines. It was not uncommon to see even English coffee house customers wearing turbans, and indeed, Ottoman headgear became a fashionable alternative to the ubiquitous wigs sported by post-Restoration men of fashion."[7]

The understanding of London coffeehouses as both Ottoman and cosmopolitan spaces sets the stage for Thomas St. Serfe's *Tarugo's Wiles; or, The Coffeehouse* (1668), a play purchased by Margery Pinchwife during her brief shopping spree at the New Exchange in *The Country Wife* (to which we will turn in chapter 2). Tarugo disguises himself as a coffee-server to escape men who pursue him for debt and assures customers that the berries for their drink come from "two Houses of Pleasure four miles from Constantinople."[8] In this play, the coffeehouse serves as a meeting place for scholars, merchants, politicians, and tradesmen. Customers at one table debate painting, while at another two men pore over a celestial globe and then a terrestrial one. Patrons become particularly excited when the coffee-man brings in "fresh news from all parts" in the form of a gazette, with satiric and lurid reports such as how the Dutch ambassador has brought the "Grand Signeur" a "Covy . . . of Boyes" (24). The absorption of patrons in newspaper reports about the Ottoman Empire and physical models of the world in miniature satirizes a modern urban global consciousness taking place over, as the outraged baker's wife puts it, "the abominable liquor of Infidels" (23).[9] As Brian Cowan astutely observes, coffee did not appeal to London consumers *in spite of* its exotic association[10], but *because* "[t]he coffeehouses and bagnios of London encouraged their customers to believe that they could experience the orient through sharing the same consumption patterns."[11] The coffeehouse scene in *Tarugo's Wiles* suggests not just the business's exotic appeal, but Ottoman culture's association for Londoners with cosmopolitanism itself. The Ottoman traders offered not just coffee, but also textiles, carpets, and horses, widely acknowledged to be the best in the world and highly coveted.[12] Crucially, by controlling the Mediterranean, the Ottoman Empire also profited from controlling trade with nations further East.

At court and in the emerging public sphere, the Ottoman Empire was not just a power to be feared but a model to be emulated. In his *Politicall Reflections upon the Government of the Turks*, Francis Osborne advocates for the benefits of the Ottoman model of government. For Henry Blount and some other travelers, the empire provided a model for England's own imperial ambitions.[13] But we can also see that Ottomanphilia was rooted in cosmopolitan as well as imperial aspirations: while certainly sharing the aggression of all empires, the Ottoman Empire had the reputation for allowing multiple communities to thrive within its boundaries. English travelers there admired its diversity, remarking on the wide variety of peoples and cultures.[14] Joseph Pitts, an Englishman enslaved in the Ottoman Empire, reported that seventy-two distinct languages were spoken in Cairo.[15] Travelers also admired the luxuries from the Far East enjoyed there and resold to European trading partners.

Charles II clearly shared this fascination. The Ottoman Empire not only suggested a model for successful expansion, but was also a key part of Charles's geopolitical ambitions. His marriage to Catherine of Braganza brought as part of her dowry the colony of Tangier. As Tristan Stein has argued, this was crucial to the imperial strategy of Charles's administration, but because the English would prove unable to defend it, it was also a key failure, Linda Colley shows, in the "dream of global supremacy."[16] An outpost in Tangier would, in this vision, have given England control of the Mediterranean and also secured them access to the coast of Africa.

It is no accident, then, that for the first legal performance since the closure of the theaters under Cromwell, Sir William Davenant chose an Ottoman-inspired story with his *The Siege of Rhodes* (1656). This musical production, as well as its revival in expanded form in 1661, was a key part of Davenant's reinvention of the English stage. *The Siege of Rhodes* was the first heroic drama, the first English production to use moveable scenery, and the first public performance in which the central female role was played by a woman. All of these practices reshaped theater in the Restoration.[17] *The Siege of Rhodes* was also the first English performance to reject the earlier stereotype of the "terrible Turk" and create a dignified and admirable Ottoman sultan, a shift that launched the notable trend of Restoration stage exoticism.

As we will see throughout this book, many foreign empires and nations fascinated the Restoration monarch, court, and theater culture. This chapter begins with Davenant's attention to the Ottoman Empire, however, because this powerful rival emerged as a model for the cosmopolitan culture and imperial power to which the Stuart monarch in this period aspired. English contact with the empire also played a significant role, as Michael Guasco has asserted, in naturalizing slavery. English readers absorbed with alarm popular narratives of English sailors and merchants captured into Ottoman slavery, a fascination revived in Daniel Defoe's *Robinson Crusoe* (which is set in this earlier period when concerns about enslavement by Ottomans had become salient). Yet England's own slave trade also became a significant economic venture and a crucial point of reference, although often an oblique one, in Restoration performances (as we will see in chapters 2, 3, 4, and 5).[18]

As a playwright and theater impresario looking to reestablish himself even before the lifting of the legal ban, William Davenant devoted much attention to making the case for the value of theater. Crucial to his project for a restored and reformed theater was not just the embrace of the exotic but also an enthusiasm for *sophistication*, suggesting that a well-funded stage would raise the cultural status of the nation and, implicitly, allow the fragmented English people to hold up their heads in the face of Spanish power, Ottoman sophistication, French refinement, and Dutch commerce. Davenant and his contemporaries made the case for theater as a cosmopolitanizing force.[19] In the following pages, I explore how Davenant reformulated the relationship between world citizenship and refinement in his *First Day's Entertainment at Rutland House* (1656). He was not the first to thread these ideals together, but as a successful impresario he embedded this particular cosmopolitan vision into theatrical practice. His original production of *The Siege of Rhodes* in 1656 and an expanded form in 1661 experimented with cosmopolitan possibilities and set the stage for the Restoration's cosmopolitan theater. While later playwrights in this period, as we will see, turned to multiple nations and empires to cosmopolitanize their productions, a crucial part of the story begins with Davenant's decision to look to the Ottoman Empire for inspiration in the reinvention of English performance.

Protheatricality and Sophistication: Civilizing the Stage

In 1668, Richard Flecknoe published *Sir William Davenant's Voyage to the Other World*, which depicted great poets in the afterlife berating the freshly dead laureate for disrespecting them. One, however, had something nice to say:

> Now Davenant's dead, the Stage will mourn,
> And all to Barbarism turn:
> Since He it was this later Age,
> Who chiefly civilized the stage.[20]

A bitter rival to Davenant, Flecknoe here satirizes his rival's claim to the invention of a new kind of theater that transformed the public stage from primitive rudeness to a sophisticated post-Interregnum media experience modeled on the Continental drama and the English court masque. In Flecknoe's account, Davenant boasted that he alone had been holding, Atlas-like, the theater on his back, and that without his formidable wit it would tumble back into native coarseness. This exaggeration has a kernel of truth. Davenant claimed to have polished the theater, and also that the theater would polish the people. While we can find moments of panic over the threat of foreign contamination in this period, for Davenant and others, looking beyond national boundaries had greater aesthetic, ideological, and financial benefits than costs. In his vision, the reformed theater, like the coffeehouse, would not only form a refined, cosmopolitan space, but would also offer a kind of portal to parts of the world in which the nation's elite had developed a keen interest.

Davenant influenced these changes, but he was not the only playwright to hope for a new kind of theater at this time. In the final years of the Interregnum, Richard Flecknoe also tried to position himself as poised to create a reformed, even revolutionized London stage. In spite of their enmity, Flecknoe, now remembered mainly as the butt of John Dryden's satire in *Mac Flecknoe*, and Davenant, who became a successful theater manager, converged on a vision in which a reformed theater would connect a newly cosmopolitan London to a global network of other nations, cities, and cultures. Like many royalists, both men spent time abroad during the Interregnum. Their theatrical visions reflect these travels in their settings, their aesthetics, and their intensified awareness of European commercial and imperial expansion.

The newly invigorated cosmopolitanism evident in Restoration theater, if not always respectful, humane, or sympathetic, reflected the travel

experiences of its artists, the ambitions of the restored monarch, and a volatile combination of curiosity and skepticism that emerged among the intel-
ligentsia in response to England's expanded participation in the competition
for global resources. Strengthened ties between the royalist elite of England
and their Continental equivalents, coupled with the former's desire to claim
greater sophistication than England's barbaric past, promoted an interest in
not just the global but also the refined.[21] Theatrical productions rehearsed
the exigencies of manners and repeatedly dramatized moments of intercultural frisson. They also satirized the fashion for both. Antitheatricalists
characterized the stage as lascivious, frivolous, and politically volatile; pro-
theatricalists proposed that a reformed theater would become a cosmopolitanizing force, in the dual sense of refining English culture and positioning
the nation as a player on the global stage.[22] Debates over the importance of
the classical unities of time, space, and action evidence an anxious desire to
rein in the geographical and temporal expansiveness of a theater eager to
incorporate vast swaths of foreign and exotic spaces.[23]

Cosmopolitanism has been celebrated mostly as an Enlightenment ideal
rather than a Restoration phenomenon.[24] But while Enlightenment thinkers formulated cosmopolitan ideals, cosmopolitan practices appeared much
earlier. In *The Web of Empire*, Alison Games has argued that merchants in the
early modern period cosmopolitanized themselves of necessity, learning to
be flexible in their own identities in order to conduct business in more powerful nations.[25] While they practiced a kind of cosmopolitanism by adopting
the dress, language, and customs of local cultures, cosmopolitan political
structures of the sixteenth and early seventeenth centuries competed with
emerging nationalist visions. In particular, as Brian Lockey has observed, the
Catholic transnational network established a model that was later echoed
in the philosophy of natural law, which held that the laws of nature transcended the authority of an individual monarch. Thus, Lockey suggests, cosmopolitanism formed an alternative political tradition to nationalism, first
religious and then secular.[26]

Like the cosmopolitanized merchants, William Davenant also traveled, although as a soldier and a messenger for the crown rather than as
a trader. (Flecknoe traveled as well, as we will see in chapter 2.) But while
English travelers in the early modern period adjusted their own identities
for encounters at the peripheries of empire, Restoration theaters, commercial venues such as the New Exchange, and the court culture made it
possible for Londoners to encounter the global in their own city through
Asian porcelain, Ottoman-inspired coffeehouses, New World tobacco and
sugar, Indian textiles, and a proliferation of newspapers reporting on world

events. Theaters regularly offered imagined experiences of encounters with the exotic. While earlier English monarchs limited the travel of their subjects by requiring royal permission for journeys outside of the country, in the Restoration travel became highly recommended for those hoping to participate in national leadership. Young men were sent to explore and learn refinement from the courts of Europe in a new social practice called the Grand Tour.[27] Experience beyond the nation became an important qualification for authority at home.

Lockey proposes that we look to the epic for literary expressions of cosmopolitanism in the pre-Enlightenment period.[28] Restoration drama, however, incorporates a flexibility of identity that complicates epic triumphalism even as it shows the influence of this genre. Theatrical performances demand fluidity: audiences watch as performers transform themselves into alternative identities. Further, the model of English conduct documented by Games, in which early modern travelers morphed by adopting the clothing, food, language, and customs of other cultures, also become commonplace at home in the "short eighteenth century," as described by Dror Wahrman in *The Making of the Modern Self*. Warhman identifies the years leading up to 1780 as an ancien régime of identity in which race, gender, class, and even species were understood to be surprisingly fluid, permeable, and performative.[29] Thus the kind of experimentation with identity that we see on the Restoration stage expresses a version of selfhood that had not yet settled into the familiar rigid categories that solidified, in Wahrman's account, in the 1780s.[30]

On the reinvented stage of the Restoration, as Bridget Orr has shown, depictions of nations, cultures, and empires beyond the boundaries of England exploded.[31] Some of these performances were "proto-Orientalist," but others offered a more complicated perspective. Sir William Davenant's *Siege of Rhodes* not only inaugurated a new kind of theater, but also abandoned the earlier stereotype of the Turk as a frightening barbarian. The restored Stuart regime attempted ambitiously to position England more firmly, as we will see, in a European and non-European global context, opening up new opportunities for profit and new possibilities for both understanding and exploitation. Lockey argues that early modern writers negotiated tensions between nationalism and cosmopolitanism that persisted through the seventeenth century in the genre of the epic.[32] Restoration theater explores these tensions but nevertheless also suspends them, instead proposing a global orientation consistent with a new kind of national identity. Restoration performances engaged the desire of Charles II and his court to remake England as a cosmopolitan nation.

Even before the Restoration, Davenant argued that a reformed stage would provide the key medium for the creation of a refined cosmopolitan modernity set to emerge, phoenix-like, from the years of brutal conflict during the civil wars. Rather than dragging spectators into the mire of lasciviousness or rebellion, as antitheatricalists objected, a new theater would open the doors to a world of conciliation, global trade networks, and personal sophistication.[33] Perhaps because of his embrace of a cosmopolitan stage, Davenant succeeded in his theatrical projects where Flecknoe did not.[34] His *Siege of Rhodes* was inspired by court masques, the Continental stage, and the shifting political landscape. It demanded considerable self-conscious reimagining, especially given that this production took place under Cromwell.

Like Flecknoe, Davenant went into exile during the Interregnum and was flexible in his loyalties through challenging times.[35] However, he was a soldier as well as a poet, and enjoyed closer ties to the royal family. He fought under the Duke of Newcastle during the civil wars. He joined Charles I at Oxford and fought with him at Gloucester, earning a knighthood for his efforts. He also worked as an agent for Queen Henrietta Maria, who sold her jewels to raise money for the royal army. He remained with the king when the queen retreated to the Continent. Beginning in 1644, Davenant took on a new job of maneuvering through the Parliament blockade to deliver munitions from the queen to the king's army. Henrietta Maria came to believe that Charles's only hope lay in joining with French and English Presbyterians, and she chose Davenant to attempt to persuade the king, a mission that did not succeed. Later the court in exile appointed Davenant lieutenant governor of Maryland and sent him to defend the colony against Parliamentary forces. He was captured and imprisoned, during which time he worked on his epic poem *Gondibert*. He narrowly escaped execution.[36]

Davenant, then, stayed close to the royal family, for whose court he had written masques in better times.[37] Upon the restoration of Charles II, the crown rewarded him with one of only two theater patents, and from this position he popularized a genre (heroic drama) whose trademark would become its exotic characters and settings. While it is true that heroic plays often exploit these settings for sensationalism, and also that playwrights would use these distant locations to veil commentary on English political tensions, the genre is, as Bridget Orr has shown, more complicated, encompassing plays that represent a wide range of ways to understand empire.[38] Davenant fought for the Stuarts, but he also made the best of the situation under Oliver Cromwell. Both his *The Cruelty of the Spaniards in Peru* (1658) and *The History of Sir Francis Drake* (1659) were designed to flatter Cromwell's ambitions in New World by representing English imperialism as a humane alternative to Spanish brutality. Sir Henry Herbert later wrote disparagingly that Davenant served as "Master of the Revells to Oliuer the Tyrant."[39] Herbert ("Davenant's nemesis")[40] suggested that *Cruelty* was produced to make Cromwell's own ruthlessness appear less severe by comparison. Alfred Harbage argues that Davenant's erstwhile cooperation with Cromwell led Charles II to grant him fewer favors than to the holder of the other patent, Thomas Killigrew, and to keep him permanently outside of the inner court circle. Political allegiances, then, were messy, a complexity reflected in the plays. Michael Neill has gone so far as to suggest that the authors of heroic plays do not seem to believe the ideals that their dramas promote.[41] But while there may indeed be a gap between belief and execution, a closer look at the plays suggests that the ideals themselves may have been more complicated than generally recognized.

Flecknoe also made the case in the reign of Cromwell for the utility—even necessity—of theater to a virtuous, refined, and orderly society. In a "daring move," as J. Douglas Canfield notes, he dedicated to Lady Claypole, daughter of Oliver Cromwell, his play *Love's Dominion, A Dramatique Piece, Full of Excellent Moralitie; Written as a Pattern for the Reformed Stage* (1654).[42] As Canfield suggests, Flecknoe was hoping to use the daughter to sway the father. Elizabeth had protected other writers and appeared to have some influence. In a preface, the playwright argues that the reform of the stage needs to begin with the refining power of love, "being the generall passion of every breast."[43] Love's "abuse," however, has been "most frequent, and most notorious" in the theater, "and therefore 'twas first to be rectified, and first to be reduced to its right Channel, where its overflow and debordment was the most dangerous" (9). Flecknoe sets his play in a special "dominion" ruled by Philostrates, "Love's Sovereign Pontif" (12), in which everyone must fall in love and marry within six months of arrival. The plot concerns the potential breach by Bellinda, beloved by two men; a comic subplot follows the frustrated libertine Pamphilus, who has little success in the dominion of love. While in Restoration drama the libertine would become a contrasting type to the fop, Flecknoe's Pamphilus *is* a fop: "a Cockscomb, Stranger to the Customs of Love's Dominions: in Ridiculous Fantastique Equipage" (12). Flecknoe's Interregnum libertine is foolish and out of fashion where Love rules.

In his dedication, the playwright strategically flatters Lady Claypole as a new but properly virtuous version of Henrietta Maria, encouraging her to exercise moral leadership by supporting theatrical performances.[44] Lady Claypole may have liked the implied comparison: C. H. Firth identifies her as Cromwell's "favorite daughter" and cites contemporary criticism of her pretensions to quasi-royal status.[45] Exploiting these apparent regal aspirations, Flecknoe hints that Lady Claypole could be like the exiled queen, only English and virtuous; instead of encouraging scandal, she would preside over a land of peace, love, harmony, sophistication, and good manners.

Flecknoe insists that theater itself is essential to the creation of such a happy commonwealth. He concedes that theater in the past had sometimes led to the debasement of manners, but that it is nevertheless too powerful a cultural medium to suppress. If it holds the capacity to corrupt manners, it also holds the key to reforming them. Theater does not undermine the church, but can become "a humble coadjutor of the Pulpit, to teach *Morality*, in order to the others *Divinity*, and th' moulding and tempering mens minds for the better receiving the impressions of Godliness. Devotion, (like gilding to matter) cleaving not, nor sticking to rough and unpolish'd minds, unlesse they be first prepared with politeness of manners, and the tincture of good education, for the receiving it; which is best taught on the *Theater*" (5–6). Flecknoe argues that one must first achieve a certain level of sophistication before morality becomes possible. Preaching will be wasted on unpolished minds; a virtuous theater, then, is needed to mold the minds of spectators into politeness. Only once molded in this way can subjects learn virtue from the pulpit.[46] As a visual demonstration of this point, Flecknoe has the unscrupulous libertine Pamphilus appear in unfashionable attire. *Love's Dominion* went unproduced, so we don't know exactly how he might have looked; nevertheless, the playwright suggests the lack of fashion acumen to be a symptom of moral insufficiency. Flecknoe returned to this theme after the Restoration, when he called theater the "School of good Language and Behaviour, that makes Youth soonest Man, and man soonest good and virtuous."[47]

In his *Proposition for Advancement of Moralitie* (1653), Davenant makes a similar argument for reinstating theater, writing that it can polish an unruly population and create harmony through greater sophistication and refinement.[48] But while Flecknoe appeals to Venus, Davenant appeals to Mars; further, while Flecknoe concentrates on sexual virtue, Davenant presents a nationally sanctioned theater as key to successful competition in a global marketplace and global battlefield. Theater is essential to an expansionist mission because of its power to manipulate emotions. Davenant argues that just as military leaders have the responsibility for making their armies civil, so statesmen must "civilize the people."[49] He assures his readers that a higher level of refinement will not produce a nation of fops—also Flecknoe's outcasts in the new cosmopolitan regime—but instead more disciplined subjects: "[C]ivilizing of a Nation makes them not effeminate, or too soft for such discipline or war as enables them to affront their Enemies, but takes off that rudeness by which they grow injurious to one another, and impudent towards Authority" (2). Subjects should receive a good education from the state, he argues, "not by penall Statutes and Prisons, but by Morall Schooles and Heroick Representations at the publick charge" (2). The nation builds authority through "Religion, Armes, and Laws"; most men, however, fail to "digest" these forms of authority (3). Religion "prevailes slowly upon the wicked" (4). Religion, the poet despairs, has failed to bring peace and has only generated additional conflict through internal divisions. (He hastens to add, however, that this is because "the nature of divine doctrine brings in things not easily digested by humane capacity" [4]). At the other extreme, armies lead only through "compulsion" and thus do not truly persuade; they are "obey'd, they are not revrenc'd" (5). Laws constantly change and have become too complicated for most people to grasp; further, there are always those who will get around them, "as some beasts are too wylie for their Hunter" (8). Most people are guided by emotion rather than by reason; "common soules" are impressed by buildings, pictures, statues, and pageants" (10–11). So "[s]ince there hath not been a perfect meanes to retaine the people in quiet (they being naturally passionate and turbulent, and yet reducible) and that Perswasion must be joyn'd to Force, it can be compass'd no other way then by surprisall of their Eyes and Ears" (11).

Rather than confuse people with the abstraction of divinity (12), Davenant writes, the state should support emotionally provocative entertainment, "where their Eyes might be subdu'd with *Heroicall Pictures* and change of *Scenes*, their Eares civiliz'd with *Musick* and wholsome discourses, by some *Academie* where may be presented in a Theater severall ingenious *Mechanicks*, as *Motion* and *Transposition of Lights* . . . without any scandalous disguising of men in womens habits" (14–15). He proposes a reimagined public theater organized around music, which can civilize "a rude people" (16), arresting spectacle to captivate audiences, and women to replace those transvestite men. It is a theater of the senses, persuading through the emotions. Actresses will not feminize the stage because performances will include "famous Battels at Land and Sea" (21); productions will not, "like the softer arguments of Playes, make the people effeminate, but warme and incite them to Heroicall Attempts, when the State shall command them; and bring into derision the present Vices and Luxury" (22). Davenant designs this projected theater for visceral response rather than intellectual reflection;[50] neither men nor women on this stage will be effeminate. Such a theater, he suggests, would create a more refined, less barbaric population. Davenant asserts that government officials should worry less that the people will become too savvy and more that they will remain unpolished, a problem that the new theater will help to solve.[51]

Both Davenant and Flecknoe insist that the significance of drama's usefulness lies in its capacity to cultivate sophistication, without which virtue, loyalty, and peace become impossible. That theorists of drama during this time and in the Restoration emphasize the civilizing effects of the stage has been read as strategy for social control, a reasonable but limiting interpretation of their project. In *The Politics and Poetics of Transgression*, Peter Stallybrass and Allon White state that Dryden used prologues condemning unruliness to help form spectators into a "deferential and receptive bourgeois audience."[52] We might see Davenant and Flecknoe as contributing to this desire for order as well. Indeed, James R. Jacob and Timothy Raynor have made a case that Davenant's *Proposition* is a comprehensive strategy for using theater to establish social control, inspired in part by the playwright's friend Thomas Hobbes.[53] They point out that Davenant's later plea in *Some Observations Concerning the People of this Nation* continues this argument. *Some Observations* drops the *Proposition*'s philosophical reflection and makes two arguments in favor of theater: first, that commercial entertainment will bring much-needed revenue to the city by attracting consumers, and second, in a different kind of argument for the theater's ability to manipulate emotions, that commercial entertainment will diminish the chance of rebelliousness by providing harmless pleasure and taking the edge off the English tendency toward melancholy, which in itself "breeds sedition."[54]

But whether we see Flecknoe and Davenant as royalist ideologues, Hobbesian strategists of social control, or flexible opportunists,[55] both poets argue for theater as a social good that cultivates a more sophisticated population through appeal to the emotions. They advocate for theater to the public, but also to governmental authorities who had antitheatricalist commitments in the Interregnum and some residual skepticism, at least in some quarters, during the Restoration. They both argue that a sophisticated population will cause less trouble than an ignorant one, and that theater can become an engine for this desired refinement. Because one of the main anxieties about theater, as Janet Clare points out, was its potential to foment insurrection through large groups of people gathering together for frivolous or even subversive diversions,[56] Davenant concentrates on assuring government officials that it will have the opposite effect of cosmopolitanizing an unruly population. Both he and Flecknoe propose theater, with its highly accessible aural, visual, and visceral pleasures, as the medium through which a restless, fractured, and fractious population can be inspired, distracted, and unified.

Davenant's more expansive, court-inspired vision nevertheless assumes no relationship between elite stature and civilized behavior; instead, it proceeds under the belief—even the anxiety—that such a relationship cannot be assumed. Rebellion could come from a variety of quarters. In planning for a new theater, then, Davenant made the case that the reformed stage would contribute to the cultivation of a more refined population. This possibility demanded the relentless exploration of the world beyond the boundaries of the nation in search of models as well as points of contrast.

The First Day's Entertainment at Rutland House

Davenant's *The First Day's Entertainment at Rutland House* (1656) was the first work of theater to be sanctioned by the Protectorate government. Both a theatrical entertainment in the form of speeches and an argument for theater itself, it makes the case for the stage as a strategy for improving civility and proposes that its London audience understand drama, as Susan Wiseman observes, "in a European framework."[57] Davenant folded the courtly model of performance he had developed when designing masques for Henrietta Maria into this new kind of production. His masques had featured music, dance, spectacular costumes, and allegorical figures celebrating the reigning monarchs. *Rutland House* pares down the spectacle, as one would expect, but it nevertheless reproduces, in altered form, some of the performative implications of the queen's theatrical project. It revives not just the style, but also the ideological goals of court performance in the reign of Charles I. Performances orchestrated by the queen, in collaboration with the talents of Davenant and others, were meant to harmonize religious differences, integrating her own French Catholicism into the English court.[58] Davenant's later productions echo this possibility of theater as force of harmonization in the face of a fractured audience: like Henrietta Maria, Davenant represents theater as holding the potential to integrate different groups into a peaceful union. In the first half of *Rutland House*, he presents two historical figures who make arguments for and against public entertainment. In the second half, a Londoner and a Parisian each make the case for the superiority of his city. In the first dialogue, Davenant uses the figure of Diogenes to suggest that a new kind of world citizenship must arise, in part through theater, to replace an old ascetic one; in the second, by comparing London and Paris in jocular detail, he implies that Britons need a first-rate theater to compete with their European rivals.

In the first dialogue of *Rutland House*, two figures stand before the audience, each at a rostrum, each in historical costume: Diogenes the Cynic, the citizen of the world, and Aristophanes, the comic playwright. Musical interludes punctuate the speeches. The music introducing Diogenes is "adapted" to his "sullen disposition," and the old philosopher makes a case against theater.[59] Through this performance, Davenant unsettles the cynic's link between cosmopolitanism and asceticism. The image of Diogenes in the early modern period, as David Mazella points out, appears in two forms, "a classical Diogenes whose philosophic powers of reflection, self-control, and freedom from flattery made his speech more effective than that of conventional courtiers, and a vernacular cynic whose unreflective violations of civility and decorum left him a misanthrope railing impotently against his fellow men."[60] While audiences may have expected a wise old man in Diogenes, Davenant gives us a cynic who stubbornly rejects civility. Both the asceticism and exiled status of Diogenes would have had immediate resonances for contemporary audiences: the first aligns this figure with Puritan antitheatricality, but the second with the exiled royalists. As Flecknoe writes in his *Relation of Ten Years Travell in Europe, Asia, Affrique, and America*, a narrative of his Interregnum exile: "I have learnt how wide the world is, and to esteem every place for my Country, where I may live quietly, and without molestation,"[61] a thought that must have crossed the minds of many. Davenant's cynical Diogenes, then, could also stand as a warning against holding on to the bitterness of exile, as many powerful royalists became citizens of the world by circumstance rather than design. If exile helped inspire the choice of this character, however, the philosopher's legendary refusal of luxury contrasted starkly with both the lavish aesthetic of the court masque and the emerging imperial ambitions of the future monarch.

Davenant thus raises, then rejects an older style of cosmopolitanism in order to make room for a new kind. Diogenes opens by warning against the danger of such public gatherings: "Man, when alone, is perhaps not wholly a Beast; but man meeting man till he grows to a Multitude is certainly more than a Monster" (6). He rails at the audience for having spent so much money on ornamenting themselves to appear in public. Meeting for recreation is a waste of time: the elders among them should be beyond mirth, and the young should be on their way to becoming serious. Thus Davenant's audience, surely in fashionable apparel for the occasion, endured the rants of the old philosopher telling them that they should not have gathered in the first place. Diogenes provokes audience skepticism through "antiquated notions of virtue and vice" that leave the old cynic, as Mazella observes, "indifferent to the civilizing pleasures of commercial modernity."[62]

Diogenes and Aristophanes debate the heroic, emotionally evocative theater envisioned by Davenant in his *Proposition*. Representing a virtuous hero on stage will not inspire virtue, claims Diogenes, because the actor will always form a pale shadow of the real thing. Assemblies gathered for the purpose of entertainment indulge the senses in pleasure. Poets live in the realm of imagination rather than reality, having audiences "gaze on imaginary Woods and Meadows . . . on Seas where you have no Ships, and on Rivers where you catch no Fish" (17). Further, while the poetry and spectacle of theater deceive the eyes, the "extasy of Music transport[s] us beyond the Regions of Reason" (16). Such sensual productions lead audience members to the "wildness of dreams" (16), urging their minds toward "the impossible successes of Love" and the "destructive ambitions of War." Musical theater mesmerizes, leaving its audience with fantasies of love, honor, and war, during which their emotions run out of control. Instead of bringing harmony, then, these experiences of pleasure will erupt in chaos.[63]

Diogenes anticipates the argument of his opponent that theater "will introduce Civility" (12), but instead of arguing that it does *not* introduce civility (an assumption Davenant strategically leaves untouched), he instead rails against civility itself. Like theater, civility is essentially a lie: "Would he [Aristophanes] make an Art of external behaviour, and have it read in the Schools? Would he prescribe a certain comely posture in your sleep, and not to wake without a long compliment to your Chamber-Grooms?" (13). The philosopher proposes instead a rigorous honesty. Civility, rather than lack of refinement, endangers: "Let the people be rude still, for . . . by suffering [civility] to be taught in publique we refine their craftiness" (14). With this new widespread craftiness, social distinctions will break down, which will ultimately lead to rebellion. Davenant has Diogenes accept that theater creates greater sophistication in audiences, and that this sophistication is at stake in allowing or barring public theater. At the heart of his argument, then, is a reversal of the fear that theater causes riotous behavior and an insistence, through the rejection of the philosopher, that theater will become the foundation for politeness, and any society desiring to advance in politeness should invest in a few good theaters.

In proposing a worldly and harmonious but also antiascetic model of cosmopolitanism, Davenant puts a distinctive spin on the classical citizen of the world. David Mazella observes that Davenant "was one of the earliest English writers to represent Diogenes as a rude moralist who worried over the political consequences of addressing 'the multitude.'"[64] If earlier English representations had admired the philosopher's rigorous honesty, Davenant's depiction draws out other elements of the ancient Diogenes legend. Diogenes Laertes (no relation; 3rd century BCE) offers a considerably less idealized picture. According to his *Lives of the Ancient*

Philosophers, Diogenes the Cynic was banished from Sinope for coining false money: in a 1702 translation, the cynic "had neither City, House, nor Country, nor certain Livelihood . . . He walk'd in the Snow Barefoot, and try'd (though in vain) to eat raw Flesh"; "being ask'd what Country he was of, he said, He was a Citizen of the World."[65] Scandalously, "He us'd to do every thing in publick view that related either to *Ceres* or *Venus*; arguing, That since there was no absurdity in eating one's Dinner, so there was none in eating it in the Market-Place; and as he polluted himself with Manual Violence in publick view, he would wish he could satisfy his Hunger as easily." Further, he "derided Nobility and Greatness, as the Varnishes of Vice. He said, Women should be common, and likewise their Children" (258) and praised men "who talk of marrying, going to Sea, serving in publick Offices, keeping handsome Boys, and living with great Men, and yet never marry" (259).

In these unflattering accounts, then, Diogenes the Cynic encouraged detachment from people, nations, and things. He relinquished all of his possessions and lived in a tub. "Seeing a little Boy drinking Water out of the hollow of his Hand, and another holding his Broth in a hollow piece of Bread, he threw away his Cup and his Dish, saying, The Boys went beyond him in Frugality" (261). By building the case against this very rude kind of cosmopolitan, Davenant proposes that a different kind of world citizenship might emerge out of the crisis of exile and fracture.

Aristophanes's rebuttal has two components: one challenges Diogenes's attack on luxury and the other his rejection of civility and its inherent theatricality. He defends theatrical performance mainly by insisting on the importance of sociability. Respectable people must become sociable ones because "Nature hath inclin'd mischievous men, as well as Beasts of Prey, to live alone" (23). For Aristophanes, it is not so much that all the world is a stage, but that the stage encompasses all the world: strangers politely mix at the theater and benefit from each other while contemplating the spectacle before them. This kind of flexibility in getting along with strangers, as we have seen in Alison Games's account, became crucial to early British mercantilism. Thus in Davenant and in the merchants studied by Games emerge a paradoxical kind of cosmopolitanism: that particular character of the English, the ability to politely accommodate and even absorb the customs of others (although not *too* much, lest they become foppish, as we will later see). The ancient Diogenite citizen of the world would provide the worst possible model for the new cosmopolitanism, given the old philosopher's hostility to the rituals of politeness, as well as to the material gain for which these English merchants traveled in the first place. Davenant raises this ancient model in order to dispel it. The new cosmopolite must carefully study manners in order to understand which set to practice in each social and commercial situation. The theater provides excellent training, according to Davenant, and Restoration plays thus pay careful attention to the words, gestures, and rituals needed for different social situations, often through comic moments of their violation. They also rehearse imagined cultural interactions in strategic locations all over the world.

Davenant's Aristophanes accuses Diogenes of opposing pleasure: he is "implacably offended at Recreation" (24–25). To follow Diogenes would mean giving up houses for tubs. Developing the suspicions that what the philosopher proposes is opposed to nature (including a subtle reminder of his notorious public masturbation), Aristophanes suggests that Diogenes demands the sacrifice of civilized refinements: "He thinks your dwellings so large as they divert your contemplation; and perhaps imagines that the Creation hath provided too much room; that the Air is too spacious for Birds, the Woods for Beasts, and the Seas for Fish; especially if their various motion in enjoying their large Elements contribute to what he esteems vain idleness, Recreation . . . [Diogenes] would accuse Nature her self to want gravity for bringing in the Spring so merrily with the Musick of Birds" (25–26). He adds that Diogenes objects that theater demands extensive beautification on the part of the audience while he, Aristophanes, argues that good grooming is better than rude behavior and neglect of personal hygiene. Like fashion, polite ceremony might become ridiculous, but both maintain the social distinctions necessary for an ambitious nation: "Can large Dominions be continu'd without distinction of qualities?" he asks (27–28). The elite can only maintain their influence through such theatrical spectacles. Theater also maintains social order by forcing audience members to control their emotions in public, and "those who are not misgovern'd by passion have an instinct to communication, that by vertuous emulations each may endeavour to become the best example to the rest" (23). With this argument, Aristophanes refutes the statement by Diogenes that public theater will undermine distinctions by making refined cosmopolitan identities more widely available. Instead, he insists, this cosmopolitanization will reinforce social order.

Aristophanes clearly wins this debate. Nevertheless, some of the doubts planted by Diogenes linger. If theater does become a school for manners, then might he not have a point in anticipating how such an education could confuse distinctions of rank? Will more people become craftier in their own social performances after learning from the theater? Will they blur distinctions of rank by a careful analysis and imitation of manners? While Davenant works to put to rest such concerns with the extreme negative example of Diogenes, who scandalously rejects all civility, the dialogue nevertheless reveals the slippages that Restoration comedies gleefully exploit, a point that I will explore in the next chapter. This very slippage would come to generate both the pleasure and the scandal of Restoration comedy.

In the second dialogue, in which a Parisian and a Londoner take over the rostrums, the Londoner does not emerge as the undisputed champion. While the first dialogue does not entirely put to rest the suspicion that analyses and public demonstrations of refinement will not destabilize social performances, this second betrays the suspicion that the English are falling behind other nations. To be sure, Davenant gives the local favorite the last word, and he makes fun of French cooking and French ceremony as overly fussy. While the dialogue does not exactly propose harmonic fusion, it nevertheless suggests that both parties benefit from exposure to each other. The Parisian looks down his nose at London, pointing out the irregularity of the streets and houses and the general unfitness for modern life. The watermen are rude, he says; the roofs of the houses are too low; the bread is coarse. Children receive only a limited and often brutal education, although the Parisian praises the wisdom of some English parents for sending their young men to the "school of Europe" (59) for polish. Unfortunately, those young men too often converse with themselves rather than "with us," thus missing the opportunity to absorb true refinement. They return home "over-careful and forc'd," both in their "dress and mind" (60). Thus by not venturing out far enough, they do not acquire the fluidity of identity of the true cosmopolite. The Londoner, however, is able to rebut: French houses may be elegant, but they have large enough windows for wives to catch the attention of men passing under them. Bridges are not well made: while a Parisian may "frisk" over their "gaps," the "heavy Londoner" finds them challenging to cross. The pleasure of elegant interiors is undermined by French garrulousness, lacking the brevity of the English or the "Majestical silence" of the Turk (73). The London advocate also points out the dangers of Paris streets and the proliferation of lackeys who make passage through them so difficult. Finally, he declares that he would happily kiss the hand of the Parisian, for he has learned not a little from the abundant "Civility of Paris" from the example of two "aged *Crocheteurs*" heavily loaded with billets who died under their burdens as a result of the "length of ceremony" (81–82).

Through this final image of this death-match of politeness and throughout his short speech, the Londoner mocks the Parisian excess of ceremony. There is a point at which courtesy becomes absurd and, in this comic closing example, downright life-threatening. But the Parisian accuses young Londoners of the same flaw: by visiting the courts of Europe but not paying proper attention, they only absorb the most superficial gestures of politeness without internalizing true graciousness. The Londoner does not set French politeness against something like English honesty; instead, each accuses the other's countrymen of suffering from foppish errors. Each defends his own countrymen as the ones who display the more refined form of manners. *Rutland House* thus ends with the assertion of urban sophistication as a key value, and a clear message that Londoners should continue to polish their manners through travel to other global cities, but pay better attention. Both debates propose the value of civility, polish, and refined pleasure. By concentrating on theater in the first dialogue and comparing cities in the second, *Rutland House* analogizes theater and travel: both provide training to become the right kind of citizen of the world. Together, they lay out the foundation for a new kind of cosmopolitanism—worldly, sophisticated, refined, curious, globally conscious, and ambitious—that Diogenes the Cynic would have found appalling.

The Siege of Rhodes, 1656: A Global Island

While *The First Day's Entertainment at Rutland House* had theatrical elements (costumes, speeches), Davenant's Ottoman-themed *The Siege of Rhodes* of 1656 was a full-scale operatic production, escaping the antitheatrical prohibition as a musical entertainment rather than a play.[66] Designed, as Brandon Chua observes, to "capture and arrest the senses," *The Siege of Rhodes* incorporates musical interludes and full stage pageantry frustratingly limited, Davenant complains, by the size of the stage.[67] This "total-sensory experience"[68] also featured the first professional female performer on the English public stage: one Mrs. Coleman, "wife of Mr. Edward Coleman," in the role of Ianthe. While critics after the Restoration disparaged actresses for their on- and offstage sexual allure, and while recent scholars have observed how the stage exploited their visual presence,[69] Davenant proposes a very different narrative: that the presence of women cosmopolitanizes the theater and the audience. Women need not be visual objects, *The Siege of Rhodes* suggests, and can be incorporated into—even featured in—a cosmopolitan heroic vision. And while the historical conflict depicted might lead us to expect a performance about the barbaric threat of the powerful Ottomans, Davenant does something different here as well. Instead, the play aims to cosmopolitanize the audience through the paired influence of a dignified Ottoman sultan and a heroic woman warrior.

　The Siege of Rhodes explores England's place in a globalized economy by looking back to the story of the Ottoman attack on the island of Rhodes in

1522, which marked a significant expansion of their territory.[70] At that time, Rhodes was a small Christian outpost in a Mediterranean controlled by the powerful Ottoman Empire at its peak, ruled by Suleiman the Magnificent. Rhodes was occupied by an international European order of knights who frequently skirmished with Ottoman forces. According to historian Daniel Goffman, the siege of Rhodes was a key victory for the Ottomans because the knights had "preyed upon Ottoman ships carrying provisions and monies between Egypt and Istanbul," and its conquest helped secure Ottoman control over the Mediterranean.[71] Caroline Finkel, however, suggests that the Ottomans invaded Rhodes less because of concerns about piracy than out of the objection that the knights "held as slaves many Muslims" captured while making the pilgrimage to Mecca.[72] After the Ottoman incursion, the knights retreated to Malta. Davenant's 1656 production stops short of the Christian defeat and leaves the Europeans weakened but still in possession. The play integrates this military conflict with a love plot between Sicilian nobles Ianthe and Alphonso. When Ianthe hears that Ottoman forces have attacked Rhodes, she sells her jewels and hires a fleet of ships to assist the knights. Solyman's (i.e., Suleiman the Magnificent) general Mustapha, however, intercepts her fleet and brings her before the sultan. Audience members accustomed to early modern depictions of Turks as barbaric and lustful would have feared for her safety. But, impressed with Ianthe's loyalty and courage, Solyman respects her modesty and offers free passage out of the war zone for her and Alphonso. The knights celebrate Ianthe's bravery when she arrives in their camp. Alphonso, however, reveals his unreasonable jealousy when he demands that Ianthe explain her "strange escape" (19), speculating that her beauty has civilized the "barb'rous Foe." Alphonso refuses the safe passage offered by the sultan and unstrategically throws himself into the battle to defend Rhodes; Ianthe enters the combat zone dressed as a soldier. (Thus the first play featuring a professional actress *also* includes a cross-dressing role.) The Ottomans close in, but the Europeans fight heroically, inspired by Alphonso, whose jealousy spurs him on to take ever greater and more reckless risks. The end unites Ianthe and Alphonso, both wounded in battle against a more powerful force. Alphonso regrets his irrational jealousy. The Christians have held off the Ottomans when the opera ends, but Alphonso acted impulsively and passionately rather than wisely, which he regrets.

In his preface to *The Conquest of Granada* (published in 1672), John Dryden argues that heroic drama began with this play and has its foundation in the epic. Davenant's inaugural example of the genre as identified by Dryden, however, leaves the Europeans injured, remorseful, and about to lose Rhodes and thus their small claim to a foothold in the Mediterranean. If the heroic imitates the epic, why did he choose a story about European failure rather than triumph? Part of his inspiration must have been the great interest in everything Ottoman even before the Restoration; a story about their victory acknowledges their continuing significance.[73] The later two-part version of the opera became both a commercial and critical success in the Restoration, and the 1656 version managed not to offend Cromwell's censors. The Ottomans in general and the defeat of Rhodes in particular occupied the early modern imagination on stage, in travel narratives, and, even later, in the novel. In 1679, Dominique Bouhours published *The Life of the Renowned Peter D'Aubusson, Grand Master of Rhodes*, which tells the story of the last Christian holdout of Rhodes against the Ottomans. At the end of the eighteenth century, George Monk Berkeley retold the siege as Gothic romance in his 1789 novel *Heloise: or, The Siege of Rhodes*. The early seventeenth-century stage had featured plays about the adventures of Europeans into the Ottoman Empire and entanglements with Ottoman forces, a trend that continued through the second half of the century.

In addition to general Ottomanphilia, more recent conflicts—as Susan Wiseman points out, the Venetians had in 1655 held out against Ottoman attacks—may have inspired Davenant to compose his opera around this story.[74] In Davenant's *Siege*, the knights complain that the Christian monarchs have abandoned them, which makes the independent actions of Ianthe particularly heroic. Cromwell had chosen not to send troops to help the Venetians and instead turned his attention from the Mediterranean to the Caribbean in his "Western design" project, allying with France against the Spanish Empire for power in the Atlantic.[75] Davenant would follow this production with his anti-Spanish *Cruelty of the Spaniards in Peru*, in which the English and enslaved Africans join together against the barbarous Spanish.[76] The 1656 *Siege of Rhodes*, then, could have served as a subtle reminder not to neglect the Mediterranean in the midst of a campaign for an expanded English stake in the New World. Audiences would also have been particularly sensitive to any parallels with England's own internal conflicts. Given Davenant's royalist sympathies and seventeenth-century depictions of Cromwell as the "Grand Seignior," it would be tempting to see the opera as a covert royalist project undermining the Lord Protector as an Eastern tyrant. But, as Susan Wiseman points out, the figure of the Sultan could equally be aligned with a Western-style monarch with absolutist aspirations, such as Charles I.[77] Indeed, later audiences found the potential analogy between the beheaded king's son, Charles II, and the oriental despot particularly intriguing, a point to which I will return.

While these important political resonances have been explored, the work's departure from epic triumph has attracted less attention: in a world of increasing global circulation, *The Siege of Rhodes* exposes European vulnerability. It dramatizes a moment in which European triumph cannot be assumed and proposes that Ianthe-style diplomacy might offer more advantage than Alphonso-style rage. Alison Games, as noted earlier, argues that the flexibility of the weak gave English travelers in the seventeenth century a particular commercial advantage; we might think of *The Siege of Rhodes* as exploring the possibility of advancing this cosmopolitan trait at the national level. A reinvented theater, Davenant seems to suggest, could help accustom audience members to thinking in cosmopolitan terms without ever leaving London.

The performance opens with an elaborate spectacle of 1522 Rhodes as a figure for Christian cosmopolitanism, presenting "the military Ensignes of those several Nations who were famous for defense of that Island, which were the *French, Germans,* and *Spaniards,* the *Italians, Avergnois,* and *English.*"[78] The stage is further enriched with "Crimson Drapery, whereon several Trophies of Arms were fixed; Those on the Right hand, representing such as are chiefly in use amongst the Western Nations; together with the proper cognisance of the Order of the *Rhodian* Knights; and on the left, such as are most esteem'd in the Eastern Countries; and on an Antique Shield the Crescent of the *Ottomans*" (2). In this description and in the performance we learn about the particular courage of the English; nevertheless, the production emphasizes the convergence of powers from many different nations into two coalitions. This may seem like a familiar pitting of Christians against Muslims, and indeed Davenant draws on those expectations. But the generosity of the Sultan, as well as weakness within the European ranks, complicates this anticipated division.

The Siege takes for granted not just the Catholic cosmopolitanism of the early modern period but also explores, without an obvious conclusion, the extent to which mutual understanding could extend beyond Christian boundaries. Before Davenant, stage performances generally foreclosed this possibility by representing Ottomans as untrustworthy and aggressive. Nabil Matar has argued that while travel narratives before the civil wars commonly represent the Ottomans as complex, prosperous, intellectually appealing, and economically promising, the stage gave the opposite impression, representing them as belligerent and barbaric. He notes that the empire genuinely fascinated Western travelers, but that at home theatrical productions and religious polemics emphasized the divine retribution that would greet Christians interested in these strangers.[79] The figure of the convert, according to Matar, became a flashpoint for this tension, and to the chagrin of many Britons, "Thousands of European Christians converted to Islam in the Renaissance and the seventeenth century, either because their poor social conditions forced them toward such a choice, or because they sought to identify with a powerful empire. . . . The Ottoman Empire in the sixteenth and seventeenth centuries presented a higher civilization than Christendom and offered opportunities to numerous Christians who sought employment and advancement."[80] The unfavorable representation of Ottomans on stage, then, was a reaction to English fears that too many of their own would "turn Turk."

If the plays before 1642 express anxiety over the potential absorption of English travelers into Islam, Davenant's *Siege* works with a more fluid model of selfhood and represents characters that experiment with this fluidity as more admirable.[81] It recognizes the power of the Ottomans, but breaks away from the early modern habit of theatrical depictions, replacing the lustful barbarian with a reflective sophisticate. As an opera, *The Siege* presents all of the characters in relatively broad strokes; nevertheless, Solyman consistently acts with honor and the plot hinges in part on Alphonso's failure to recognize the sultan's dignity. The performance opens with the impending attack on Rhodes and Alphonso's resolve to defend the island against the Ottoman sultan, "His cursed Prophet and his sensual Law" (5), a line echoed by the chorus. The knights lament their vulnerability before the sultan's powerful forces and the lack of assistance from Rome. (Davenant voices anti-Spanish sentiment here too. The knights sing of the lack of assistance from Spain, who leaves her land unplowed to "plough the Main; / And still would more of the old World subdue, / As if unsatisfi'd with all the New" [7]). But while the Europeans sing of the Ottoman "sensual law," Solyman identifies the *Europeans* as the sensual ones: they show military skill and courage, he admits, but drink and commit adultery and indulge every "loud expensive Vice," draining all of their resources on pleasure. Davenant was not alone in making this unfavorable comparison: interestingly, a slave narrative from the sixteenth century reprinted in 1661 called *The Rarities of Turkey* echoes the observation that Christians live luxuriously and riotously on the battlefield, but the Turks have the advantage for their "sobriety, parsimony, diligence, fidelity, and obedience."[82]

Solyman's treatment of Ianthe confirms this revisionist depiction of Ottoman dignity. Mustapha had captured her at sea and brought her before Solyman as a prisoner. This crucial scene early in the opera features the first appearance of a professional actress on the English stage, a moment that Davenant handles with great care.[83] Mrs. Coleman in the role of Ianthe enters veiled, and the audience learns that she had also worn a veil when she defended her fleet from Ottoman attack (11). As a prisoner of war, Ianthe expects punishment, but she extracts a promise from her captors that no man except her husband will remove the veil that covers her face. The initial amazement of Solyman, and by extension the audience, with Ianthe veiled marks the significance of the female body on stage while at the same time deferring the fetishization of female beauty. Ianthe, in fact, had enabled her own participation in the battle by sacrificing the luxury of her jewels and their capacity to enhance her attractions. Her heroic refusal to be looked at awes the sultan, as do her sacrifice and her military prowess. In Solyman's court, she is "the *Cicilian* flower, / Sweeter then buds unfolded in a shower"; at sea, however, she "urg'd their courage when they boldly Fought, / And many shun'd the dangers, which she sought" (11). Thus Davenant carefully negotiates the Puritan and also the prurient assumption of female objectification by insisting on Ianthe's transcendence of the visual and her utter lack of effeminacy. In this first appearance of an actress, then, the actress does not entirely appear. Impressed with her virtue, her self-sacrifice, her courage, and her loyalty to her husband, the sultan gives Ianthe free passage back to her friends in Rhodes.

The knights welcome Ianthe, but Alphonso becomes immediately suspicious of the sultan's generosity. In a jealous rage, he bitterly concludes that Ianthe's beauty "seem'd to civilize a barb'rous Foe" (19). Yet the audience already know that he is wrong, for the sultan controls his emotions better than does Alphonso, who prejudicially imagines that any scene between an Ottoman sultan and a Christian woman will end in seduction. Solyman, however, treats Ianthe with respect; he only regrets that Mustapha had the opportunity to transcend his own virtue when he extended his protection to the Christian lady upon her capture. The audience knows that Ianthe did not "civilize a barb'rous Foe"; instead, she and Solyman bring out the best in each other, a dynamic that shapes the rest of the play. Thus Davenant casts the presence of Ianthe in the narrative and the actress on stage as forces of refinement in the face of objections to the contrary. Alphonso's jealousy suggests unwarranted suspicions of the Ottomans within the plays and also, in the broader context of performance, unwarranted resistance to a female presence on a public stage.

Davenant's founding example of the strange genre of heroic drama points away from unreflective nationalism, then, and insists on performance, the actress, and exploration of everything Ottoman all as positive cosmopolitanizing forces. Davenant proposes a counternarrative to the antitheatricalist insistence that a female body on stage would lead to vice, and shows how Ianthe's presence inspires the virtue and civility of all spectators. (Years later, in 1722, Richard Steele would reprise this argument in *The Conscious Lovers*, when Bevil Jr. insists that a rowdy masquerader will learn civilized behavior merely by casting his eyes upon the lovely Indiana.) Unlike the bloodthirsty Turks in earlier plays and histories, Davenant's Solyman has become weary of war; he only attacks Rhodes because the people demand more and more prizes. Because of their mutual commitment to honor, Ianthe and Solyman come to respect each across the boundaries of nation—a configuration that becomes a trademark of heroic drama. Alphonso, however, cannot get over his jealousy; he cannot believe that Solyman granted Ianthe safe passage innocently and he certainly has no intention of accepting the sultan's offer of protection. Ianthe tries to explain to him that Solyman is not a barbarian: "He seem'd in civil *France*, and Monarch there" (19), she attests. Alphonso, however, endangers himself and his beloved because of his outdated image of the sultan as barbaric and of women as weak. His limitations leave the lovers wounded and in despair. The 1656 production does not end in either European or Ottoman triumph, but instead with sad regret over Alphonso's inability to see past his own prejudices and pathos over Ianthe's heroic sacrifice.

Given Davenant's personal relationship with Henrietta Maria, it is difficult not to see Ianthe as, among other things, the author's homage to this queen in exile, as Susan Wiseman has argued, as risky as that might have been.[84] Henrietta Maria sold her jewels to raise money in support of her husband's cause. Davenant, however, not only honors her by invoking her through Ianthe, but recruits her image in the service of protheatricality and the respectability of women on stage. At the very least, invoking Henrietta Maria with the presentation of the first actress perhaps headed off objections by normalizing the practice. The queen's own court performance, Karen Britland has written, strategically attempted to draw together different religious identities within the same nation.[85] In the opera, Ianthe plays a similar role at the global scale: Just as Henrietta Maria's theatrics united Catholic and Protestant England, so Ianthe serves as the diplomatic hope between East and West. Those who insist that women acting in public will inevitably lead to lascivious thoughts and behavior echo Alphonso, who ultimately regrets making such assumptions. Instead, actresses will contribute to the cosmopolitanizing effect of the reformed stage, for the more dignified sultans in the audience will recognize their value through any veil.[86]

The Siege of Rhodes, 1661: "Ianthe Is the Word"

In 1661, a year after the restoration of Charles II to the throne, Davenant inaugurated his new patent theater at Lincoln's Inn Fields with an expanded version of *The Siege of Rhodes*. For this event the king himself appeared at a public theater for the first time, which apparently ruined the career of the actor playing the eunuch: The sight of "that August presence," John Downes later lamented, "spoil'd me for an Actor."[87] At least one audience member confirms this failure: Samuel Pepys also attended this lavish production, which he deemed "very fine and magnificent, and well acted, all but the Eunuche, who was so much out that he was hissed off the stage."[88] Pepys saw the play again a year later, improved by a new Roxolana (played now by Mary Norton; Hester Davenport, who originated the character, had left to become the mistress to the Earl of Oxford).[89] Aside from Downes, the revival boasted an impressive cast, with Thomas Betterton in the role of Solyman, Joseph Harris as Alphonso, and Mrs. Saunderson—soon to become Mrs. Betterton—as Ianthe. Mary Betterton became so associated with this role that Pepys later refers to her as "Ianthe" in his diary regardless of the play in which she performed.[90] In 1664 Pepys read *The Siege of Rhodes* to his wife and in 1665 he read it with his friend Captain George Cocke, calling it "the best poem that ever was wrote." He read it again in 1666 and saw it performed again in 1667.[91]

The revived *Siege* speaks to a different moment, capturing the Ottoman-philia of the Restoration court, with which we opened, but also suggesting the ways the new administration looked to the Ottoman Empire with a combination of trepidation and desire. For the Restoration productions, Davenant expanded the original version into two parts and added new scenes.[92] These expand the importance of women, taking advantage of this stage novelty but also further complicating the play's relationship to the epic. In the first act (or "entry") of the revised part 1, Ianthe appears with her maids and with two caskets of jewels, expressing her love for Alphonso and her plan to sell her valuable treasures in order to help rescue Rhodes. Her women marvel at this momentous sacrifice, but also express comic skepticism over her romantic idealism. The added scene introduces the actress earlier than the key moment before the sultan highlighted in the 1656 performance. By 1661, the appearance of a woman on the public stage was less remarkable, not only because of Davenant's pre-Restoration production but because of the women players in the rival Drury Lane patent theater. But the additional scene also brings the resonance between Ianthe and Henrietta Maria to the foreground in a more confidently royalist environment. (The queen mother herself returned with the Stuart Restoration and remained in England until 1665, with the exception of a trip back to France in 1661.[93]) In addition to expanding Ianthe's part, Davenant added the new character of Roxolana, the legendary wife of Suleiman the Magnificent. The historical "Roxolana" fascinated Europeans and found many literary incarnations. She was actually named Hurrem but called her now-familiar name by Italian diplomats who thought she was Russian; she was captured into slavery by Crimean Tartars and sold to Ibrahim Pasha, a close friend of the young Prince Suleiman, whose favorite concubine she became.[94] She bore him five sons. In 1533, Suleiman took the highly unusual step of signing a legal marriage contract with Hurrem, thus freeing her from slavery.[95] This marriage provides one of the central storylines in Madame Scudéry's *Ibrahim, the Illustrious Bassa*, translated into English in 1652. In marrying Roxolana, Suleiman defied a long-standing Ottoman custom in which the sultan could not marry for fear that a tie of affection could distract him from matters of state or give an enemy a point of vulnerability. When a sultan died, all of the sons of his concubines except the single heir faced execution in order to avoid conflict over sovereignty.[96] For many Western writers, Roxolana became a figure for Orientalist luxury and sensuality because of her unusual power.[97]

The East in general provided the setting for many heroic plays and tragedies during this period. As Bridget Orr notes, "Between 1660 and 1714, at least forty plays set in Asia or the Levant appeared on the London stage. They were almost all serious, heroic plays or tragedies, recording turbulent episodes in the empires of Persia, Egypt, India, China and Turkey."[98] Thus Davenant's expanded *Siege of Rhodes* tapped into a longstanding European fascination with the Ottoman Empire, but also helped to build the cosmopolitan frame of reference for the revived Restoration theater. To audiences, the figure of the original Roxolana was, on the one hand, an actress, the future mistress of an Earl wearing a colorful turban and an exotic-looking gown. On the other hand, if we take into account Dror Wahrman's insight that people in the "short eighteenth century" understood identity as fluid and sartorial changes as themselves transformational, then we might speculate that Restoration audiences experienced a more palpable sense of global exchange through the figure of Roxolana and other such enactments of alterity than do modern readers of the texts.[99] As Ros Ballaster asserts, "[W]hen an English actor takes the role of Aurangzeb or Mustapha or Muhammad, in his own person he indicates the permeability of a national culture, the possibility that appropriative traffic is never one way: the Orient inhabits him at the same time as he impersonates the Orient."[100] Accustomed to accepting boy actors as women, 1661 audiences would have experienced Roxolana on stage as a *particularly* fluid identity performance. Davenant put more women on stage because, like his colleagues, he understood that men in the audience liked to look at them. But he also advocated female performance as enhancing the cosmopolitanizing effect (and affect) of the stage.

The second part of the revised *Siege of Rhodes* opens with the Christian coalition lamenting their diminishing hopes against the formidable Ottomans. The Rhodians have run out of food and the European armies realize that they need to come to some kind of terms. Both the military leaders and the common people of Rhodes turn to Ianthe for this task: she has been to the sultan before, and also has been granted free passage. In order to rescue the common people from starvation and the knights from the growing discontent on the island, Ianthe agrees to negotiate but, both for the sake of her own honor and out of her respect for the sultan's, refuses to send for free passage and declares her intention to rely instead on virtue and trust. Alphonso lets her go with reluctance and a little suspicion. Meanwhile, Solyman has been quarrelling with Roxolana and come up with a scheme to "check her Pride" (43). Hearing that Ianthe has arrived to plead the cause of Rhodes, he decides to use the ambassadress for leverage in his marital conflicts. Thus he tells Ianthe that he will negotiate with her, but insists that she stay overnight and sends her to lodge with Roxolana. The sultana is outraged and sends a message to Alphonso warning him about her husband's designs on Ianthe (50); she then plots to murder the unwelcome guest in her sleep.[101] Ianthe's own virtue and kindness, however, win her over. But the letter, already sent, has confirmed Alphonso's worst prejudices. He and the knights break their truce with the Ottomans, gather their forces for an attack, and set their own palace ablaze as part of their military strategy. The Ottomans defeat them and take Alphonso prisoner. Solyman turns Alphonso over to Roxolana to decide his fate (as a test of her integrity). After considering the possibility of executing him, she lets him go out of consideration for her new friendship with Ianthe. Alphonso once again regrets his jealous passion, which has caused considerably more damage this time. The sultan, however, honors Ianthe for her trust in putting herself under his power without invoking the right of free passage. For this, he allows them both to return to Rhodes and Ianthe to negotiate generous terms on behalf of the knights and the Rhodians.

The Restoration two-part version, like the earlier performance, proposes a reformed theater defined by sophistication, civility, global citizenship, and a full sensory experience, a vision undoubtedly underwritten by the cosmopolitan monarch and his entourage, and now able to find full expression in the new reign. In his 1663 dedication to the Earl of Clarendon, Davenant insists on theater as a civilizing force, complaining, "Dramatick Poetry meets with the same persecution now from such who esteem themselves the most refin'd and civil as it ever did from the Barbarous," and casting Clarendon as the judge of Solyman's "civility & magnificence."[102]

The rival patent theater, run by Thomas Killigrew, had opened its inaugural season with Shakespeare's Othello; both theaters, then, had selected plays referencing the Ottoman empire for their first productions. Othello clearly influenced The Siege in Alphonso's unwarranted sexual jealousy.[103] The similarities between the plays, however, would also have highlighted the contrast, for while Othello fights the "Great Turk," Ianthe negotiates with him. Further, while Othello wins his battle, Davenant's play tells the story of a significant European defeat and the Ottoman control of the Mediterranean. The Siege also echoes and revises Othello in specific interpersonal tensions. In the added scene to part 1, Ianthe expresses her love for Alphonso and her intention to sell her jewels to support him while her women, much like Desdemona's Emilia, express comic, worldly concerns about the value of such treasures. Like Othello, the plot of The Siege turns on jealousy, especially in the 1661 version, although Davenant has altered the racial dynamic: here, Ianthe loves a fellow European who suspects her attraction to a racialized foreigner. In both plays, the jealousy proves destructive and has no foundation. But while jealousy leads to Othello's personal downfall, in Davenant's play it has immediate political consequences: Alphonso leads the Europeans into a hopeless attack against the Ottomans out of the conviction that Ianthe has been seduced. He even suspects her intentions when she agrees to negotiate with the sultan at the request of the people of Rhodes. Davenant highlights the theme of jealousy by creating a parallel plot with Solyman's wife, in which Roxolana must host Ianthe while she too suspects her husband's intention to seduce her. The obligation to treat this interloper as her guest insults and enrages Roxolana, and she approaches the sleeping beauty with her dagger drawn. Roxolana soon learns, however, that Ianthe loves Alphonso and has no intention of competing with her for the sultan, and the two women become affectionate friends. Thus each side in this conflict has a jealous lover and a nobler, non-jealous lover; East and West mirror each other in the Restoration version.

If the 1656 Siege picks up Interregnum associations between Cromwell and the Grand Seignior, the 1661 version tilts the scales toward associating the Ottoman ruler with the Stuarts, although in this case with Charles II. Casting decisions are revealing here: In 1656, we recall, a husband-and-wife team played the roles of Alphonso and Ianthe. In 1661, however, Thomas Betterton and Mary Sanderson—soon Mary Betterton—played Solyman and Ianthe. The later version, then, emphasizes the potentially erotic pairing of the heroic woman and the sultan, whose domestic and successional troubles could have reminded audience members of their new monarch. Indeed, the image of Charles II as himself a "Great Turk" became a commonplace literary trope in the Restoration and beyond. In her play *Ibrahim*, for example, Mary Pix would cast the Stuart court as Ottomans in utterly unflattering ways.[104] Satirists characterized Charles II as an Eastern sultan because of his sexual escapades; as Felicity Nussbaum observes, "Charles's debauchery . . . connected his reign to Turkish tyranny, his court to a seraglio."[105] Restoration novels, or *romans à clef*, allegorized the court as an Eastern sultanate filled with maneuvering, scandal, and intrigue.[106] The 1661 *Siege* associates the restored English monarch with the sultan, but in a flattering way rather than as satire. In the 1661 version Solyman, after all, leads his empire to victory and possession of Rhodes, a historical destiny that remains strangely unfulfilled in the 1656 performance. Further, Davenant does not depict in his sultan a cold-hearted, lascivious alpha male with a collection of veiled beauties, as do the satires, but rather represents the particular sultan who *broke* with Ottoman tradition and committed himself to one wife, a plot also featured by Roger Boyle in his play *Mustapha*. Even associations with the famous sultanic polygamy might not have satirized a monarch known for his interest in women. While it is true, as Nussbaum points out, that polygamy could serve as the mark of the "other" in the eighteenth century, the alterity of the practice was not entirely a given and would return in debates over succession.[107] Gilbert Burnet thought (although he later retracted this position) that polygamy was not inconsistent with Christianity, and that Charles II should take another wife when it became clear that the queen was not going to produce an heir.[108] With the addition of the Roxolana plot, Davenant links the sultan to Charles II through not just the monarch's well-known sexual proclivities, but fears of the powerful women in his court, particularly his Catholic mistress Barbara Palmer (Lady Castlemaine).[109]

While Roxolana resembles Lady Castlemaine in her power and influence, Davenant's addition to the plot of the marriage of a Charles-like sultan and an exotic former slave also pointed to the impending marriage of the king to a foreigner. In 1661, the same year the play opened, Charles concluded negotiations for his marriage to the Portuguese Catherine of Braganza, the princess favored by his mother, Henrietta Maria. Charles had not yet met Catherine and would send the Earl of Sandwich to escort her to London, drawing criticism for traveling with Lady Castlemaine even after the queen had arrived in England. Those following court gossip could reasonably have anticipated tension between the new queen and the longstanding mistress who appeared to hold a dangerous level of influence over the king. For the most part, Catherine, who had been raised in a convent, had little control over the situation, but she did assert herself at least once: Charles recommended Castlemaine as one of the ladies of her bedchamber, a demand that Catherine resisted, although she eventually backed down.[110] If we take the sultan as evocative of Charles II in the revised *Siege*, then we see a mistress of long standing threatened by a new woman from across the sea. It is also not hard to imagine how Ianthe could have suggested the Portuguese Catherine to theatergoers, as she had so clearly already evoked Henrietta Maria in the 1656 version. The bride may not have personally resembled the heroic warrior Ianthe, but the marriage was a strategic one, intended to help England become a more significant player in the European competition for global territory. This union profoundly shaped Restoration serious drama, a point to which I will return in chapters 3 and 4, but Davenant sensed its dramatic possibilities right away. In that sense, Catherine could have been seen as "rescuing" Charles II from financial difficulties in a way that would have resonated with Ianthe's rescue of Alphonso and the Knights of Rhodes. Thus the meeting between Solyman and Ianthe, galvanized by the offstage attraction between Saunderson and Betterton, flashes between an image of the Portuguese princess arriving in a new country backed by her treasure *and* an eroticized partnership between East and West—not the Orientalist seduction of an otherwise rational male by the feminized East, but a partnership based on honor between a sophisticated and powerful monarch and a heroic warrior woman. The revived *Siege* expresses both hopeful fantasies.

The 1661 revival, then, diminishes the significance of Alphonso: both the text and the casting point to the charged but chaste relationship between the two honorable and powerful figures of Ianthe and the sultan, played by real-life lovers, as structuring the play. Just as Ianthe remains loyal to Alphonso, however, so Solyman remains loyal to Roxolana. He only wants to contain her power, and does so by insisting that Ianthe spend the night in Roxolana's pavilion—a mandate that seems an inverted foreshadowing of the king's demand that his new wife accept his long-standing mistress as a maid of honor. Thus Davenant squares off the love triangle of the earlier version, providing Ottoman and European jealousy plots. Roxolana resents Ianthe at first, but when she learns of her virtue and seriousness of purpose, she comes to admire and feel affection for her European rival. The Eastern jealousy of the Western woman thus dissolves into friendship. The Western jealousy of Ottoman masculinity, however, proves explosive and emotionally uncontainable. Alphonso leads the knights to break their truce and attack their more powerful adversaries; they even set their own palace on fire as a distraction, as if blazing with Alphonso's impotent passion. This pointless maneuver proves to be the knights' last stand in Rhodes, although thanks to Ianthe's diplomacy they leave peacefully, an important detail given the salient fears at the time about English travelers captured into Ottoman slavery generated by multiple published reports of the experience of enslavement.[111]

It seems worth asking why Davenant saw an advantage in squaring off the previous love triangle, and then why, as the squaring emphasizes, jealousy persists in one direction but not in the other. The historical moments of 1656 and 1661 suggest an answer. In 1656, Davenant balanced a romantic tragedy on a political tightrope, with some delicate implications that Charles I had lost the war because he loved his wife too passionately. The marriage of Charles I and Henrietta Maria, although initially a dynastic arrangement, apparently grew into an affectionate relationship, a development that entered public consciousness through the publication of their letters. These were compiled by Parliamentarians and selected to suggest the queen's inappropriate power as well as the king's attempts to negotiate with Catholic armies to invade England. While the book was intended to damage the royalists politically, the letters also revealed the intensity of affection between the king and queen.[112] Davenant's *Siege* hints at an overly emotional Charles I, overwhelmed by nothing worse than too much love for his wife. If Alphonso could in 1656 have paralleled Charles I in his passion, then spectators could conclude that he lost the war not through lack of valor, but out of his uncontrolled passion for Ianthe. This version unsurprisingly tempers its author's royalist sympathies: audience members who identified Cromwell with the sultan would have no reason to take offense at Davenant's dignified and conquering Solyman. Further, in the first version Davenant leaves the historical narrative incomplete by stopping short of dramatizing the defeat of Christians. The 1661 version, by contrast, reflects the restored monarch's greater interest in the Mediterranean, as evidenced by the negotiation for Tangier, which, given to England by Portugal as part of Catherine's dowry, briefly became the only English colony in Ottoman territory. In this augmented version, the more powerful Ottomans pose a greater threat and also a greater attraction than the weaker Europeans, a point emphasized by Davenant's decision to tell the story of the European *loss* of Rhodes. But if this version, as I have suggested, flatters Charles II as the powerful and sophisticated sultan and his soon-to-be-contracted wife as the virtuous foreign princess backed up by treasure, where does Alphonso, the jealous and overly passionate husband, fit in?

Alphonso's character, I suggest, opens up a new anxious space for audience identification. He sets an example for both heroic and excessive actions, but he also becomes a vexing point of identification for the English male spectator, impotently enraged by the powerful sultan who so clearly proves himself the equal of Ianthe while Alphonso himself falls short. He falls into a jealous rage over unwarranted suspicions, grounded in prejudice, of the sultan's violation of Ianthe or her own willingness to exchange sexual favors for negotiating privileges. This kind of malicious jealousy, as emotion researcher W. Gerrod Parrott argues, tends to include envy of the threatening third party: envy and jealousy, while distinct emotions, commonly appear together.[113] Here, Alphonso has much to envy: charm, sophistication, civility, and imperial conquest. Thus, at the root of this play about *jealousy* lies the closely related emotion of *envy*—or specifically, in Gerald MacLean's resonant phrase, "imperial envy." As MacLean explains,

> To the pious among the English, the Ottoman Empire was at once the great enemy and scourge of Christendom, yet to the commercially minded it was also the fabulously wealthy and magnificent court from which the sultan ruled over three continents with his great and powerful army. . . . The Ottomans were not simply foreign "others" but models by which the English learned to frame their own self-representations while seeking and building an empire of their own. Spurred by imperial ambitions, English envy of the Ottomans produced not only political parallels but also some remarkable fantasies of Anglo-Ottoman filiation.[114]

The Siege of Rhodes was one of those fantasies.

In an otherwise gratuitous scene that does little to advance the plot, Roxolana receives emissaries from many Eastern nations: the ambassadors of Persia "seek [her] Favour"; the Armenian cities, a court functionary reports, have paid their tribute, but the Georgian princes request aid; another ambassador brings jewels from the Hungarian queen (41). Roxolana displays her power here (she is "no European Queen," she remarks) by conducting the business of empire, but the scene also reminds the audience of the vast reach and cosmopolitan structure of Ottoman rule. The particular imperial envy expressed in *The Siege of Rhodes*, then, upholds the Ottoman Empire as a model for cosmopolitanism itself: for sophistication, for a vast network of trading partners, and for its mix of cultures.

Given the admiration shot through with fear and envy expressed in *The Siege of Rhodes*, the play's link to the epic might then be more complicated than claimed by John Dryden. This work offers less a mythology of the founding of a nation or a history told by winners, as David Quint suggests of the epic, than it does the impulse toward a more cosmopolitan future, whatever form that may take.[115] In concluding this, I am not suggesting that the playwright necessarily had a more enlightened view of foreigners and should provide a cosmopolitan model. Davenant, after all, in 1638 published a poem called *Madagascar*, a utopian colonialist fantasy in which the poet dreams that Prince Rupert could fly to the African island, conquer it, and make himself master of untold riches. Madagascar held strategic importance and could have served as a way station for English traders on their way to and from India on the model of the Dutch Batavia, which flourished. After more propaganda and much enthusiasm for this project, however, two colonizing attempts failed miserably, leaving hardly any survivors.[116] Thus Davenant's most prominent epic-like celebration of colonial triumph promoted a project that ended in disaster and humiliation by, among other mistakes, overestimating the ease of conquest. The circumstances, both of authorship and empire, were very different, but the experience of Madagascar would have complicated faith in epic triumphalism. Alternatively, *The Siege* documents a failure rather than a success, conquest, or founding of a nation. It does not even fulfill Davenant's own stated purpose of heroic drama— that is, to create inspiring models of heroic action.[117] Alphonso undermines the truce with the Sultan through his irrational and prejudicial jealousy. He leads the knights into a pointless final battle because the Grand Master of Rhodes, in an otherwise gratuitous plot twist, has also fallen in love with Ianthe and joins in the jealous battle-cry, "Ianthe is the Word!" (59). The inspiring actions in this play belong mainly to Solyman and Ianthe, and those actions are diplomatic rather than military. Solyman may be intimidating in his military power, but he earns admiration by his honorable treatment of Ianthe and his generosity toward the defeated Christians. On the European side, Ianthe achieves a level of heroism that contrasts her sharply with the relatively passive Desdemona and the overly emotional Alphonso. Ianthe, more than any other character, models heroic action and heroic values, but unlike in the epic, these emerge as distinct from military prowess. Ianthe *does* fight in battle, but both times she loses: early in the play she battles the Ottoman sea forces on her way to Rhodes and later she enters the war disguised as a man and sustains near-fatal injuries. Clearly her true heroism lies elsewhere: in her initial sacrifice of the luxury of her jewels for the sake of Rhodes, her voyage to help defend the island, and the courage with which she confronts Solyman, first by refusing to remove her veil when captured and later by undertaking the diplomatic mission to secure favorable terms for the knights and the Rhodians. Thus in spite of Davenant's own description of the ideals of heroic drama, his inaugural example departs from the epic model of heroic conquest and the display of admirable heroic action. While some heroic plays that would follow express epic confidence in an expanding trajectory of a British empire, others offer more ambivalent and complicated assessments of global relations. They embrace a newly globalized economy, sometimes expressing distress over contamination but nevertheless seeking the profits, pleasures, and novelties of amalgamation.

❦ CHAPTER 2

Travesties

William Wycherley, the Fop, and the Provincial Girl

> The seat of wit, when one speaks as a man of the town and the world, is the playhouse.
>
> —Joseph Addison

Nothing reveals the significance of cosmopolitan ambitions in the Restoration quite so much as the relentless performance of their failure. The theater embodied this failure in two salient types: the rustic, who is comically bewildered by urban settings and exotic practices, and the fop, who is overly confident of his own cosmopolitanism. Both of these figures continually rehearse cosmopolitan failures for the entertainment of urban audiences: the rustic does not know the town well enough to know the world, and the fop reveals how birth, status, and wealth prove insufficient for cosmopolitan self-fashioning. Through the ubiquitous figure of the fop, Restoration comedies propose by negation a distinct cosmopolitan identity assisted but not subsumed by rank. Cosmopolitan identities, though born of elite ambitions, nevertheless undermine and reshuffle traditional markers of status. The recycling of these two figures in various forms through so many performances points to the high stakes and powerful anxieties over failure or success. Performances reflect, indulge, and generate these anxieties, claiming, on the one hand, that theater can cure cosmopolitan failure and, on the other hand, satirizing their own claims to this salutary function.

Davenant's *The Siege of Rhodes*, as we saw in chapter 1, expressed admiration for both Christian cosmopolitanism and the cosmopolitan Ottoman empire. In this chapter, we will see how comic explorations of worldliness held political meaning beyond the drawing room and the bedchamber.

Comedies, I will suggest, tackled highly sensitive issues with an enigmatic but ingratiating smile: the licensed theater could play the part of licensed fool. Charles II and his administration, as Harold Weber has shown, exerted considerable control over print media, even periodically closing the coffee-houses out of fear of insurrection during the unstable Restoration settle-ment.[1] Performance, however, had a little more leeway: the two licensed theaters, one sponsored by the king and the other by the Duke of York, maintained a close relationship with the court. The actors were their ser-vants. In 1740, Colley Cibber looked back wistfully to the benefits of such royal patronage and the regular appearance of the royal entourage in the audience.[2] The presence of the king and his retinue created a spectacle that could successfully compete with the production: for Samuel Pepys on July 23, 1661, an excellent view of Barbara Palmer, the king's mistress, made up for a mediocre performance.[3] Awareness of this tight interpenetration of politics and entertainment has often led critics to observe how much the plays reproduced the aristocratic ideology and divinity of sovereignty favored by such patrons.[4] But sometimes, I will suggest, this proximity had the opposite effect: closeness to the court offered privileged latitude to joke about not only scandalous sexual antics, but also the expansionist ambitions that fueled the luxurious indulgences of the elite. Thus, as I will show, while certain plays helped to create cosmopolitan ideals by entertaining audiences with cosmopolitan failures, at the same time they satirized the court's ambi-tions and exposed the cost of sophistication.

Fops and provincials provide the engine of humor in many Restoration comedies. In the context of the broad sense of the significance of these figures, I focus on two plays by William Wycherley: *The Gentleman Dancing-Master* (1672) and *The Country Wife* (1675). Wycherley and the handful of other widely anthologized playwrights, as Robert Hume has argued, should not be mistaken as typical, but perhaps we can think of them as differing in degree rather than kind.[5] Indeed, Wycherley was exceptional in both his insider status and his extraordinary skill. His privileged status empowered him, at least for a time, to test the limits of acceptability not just in sexual exploration, but also in political critique. Wycherley's family had contributed money to the royalist cause at a key moment,[6] and he became a court insider with the success of his first play, *Love in a Wood; or, St James Park* (1671). He grew so close to the court that king offered to hire him as a tutor to the young Duke of Richmond. Charles II personally visited the poet when he fell ill.[7] In his prime, Wycherley attracted the attention of the king's powerful mistress, Barbara Palmer, Countess of Castlemaine, and became her lover.[8] Like the Earl of Rochester, he enjoyed the pleasures of the court but did not pay back the king's hospitality with obsequious entertainment; unlike Rochester, Wycherley escaped punishment, perhaps because he embedded his subversion in comedies that allowed for more benign interpretations. In a scene from his final play, *The Plain Dealer*, Wycherley lets the audience in on this strategy when antiheroine Olivia rails against the lasciviousness of the "china scene" in *The Country Wife*, acknowledging the offense in some quarters over his own earlier production. Olivia's cousin Eliza, however, claims to understand nothing but literal china and suggests that the others interpret a double meaning only out of their own salaciousness. Observation of insurrection, then, reveals only the insurrection of the observer.

Wycherley's plays drew attention not just for their insight, wit, and pointed social critique, but also for the way they captured salient issues of the 1670s, engaging the court's cosmopolitan ambitions. George Etherege created the most memorable faux sophisticate in his *The Man of Mode*, but Wycherley had fashioned intriguing versions of this figure before Sir Fopling Flutter. Generally recognized as an edgy but comical exploration of sexuality and class, the fop, along with the rustic, anchors Restoration comedy. In what follows, I begin with the importance and aesthetics of foppery suggested by Dryden's analysis of the stage in *Mac Flecknoe*. I then turn to Wycherley's underappreciated and globally orientated fops in *The Gentleman Dancing-Master*, and end with the explorations of sophistication and global commerce in Wycherley's masterful play about provinciality, *The Country Wife*.

Gender Amphibians

In *Mac Flecknoe* (probably written in 1676 although not published until 1682), John Dryden explores a cosmopolitan ideal through the comedy of its failure. In this poem about the current state of theater, Dryden suggests that his rival Thomas Shadwell reigns as a faux monarch because he, like his theatrical father, creates fop characters modeled on himself. Better writers fashion fops with comic distance:

> Let gentle *George* in triumph tread the Stage,
> Make *Dorimant* betray, and *Loveit* rage;
> Let *Cully*, *Cockwood*, *Fopling*, charm the Pit,
> And in their folly show the Writer's wit.
> Yet still thy fools shall stand in thy defence,
> And justifie their Author's want of sense.
> Let 'em be all by thy own model made

Of dullness, and desire no foreign aid:
That they to future ages may be known,
Not Copies drawn, but Issue of thy own.[9]

Dryden praises Etherege by praising his fops, beginning with Sir Nicholas Cully from *The Comical Revenge* (1664), then Sir Oliver Cockwood from *She Would If She Could* (1668), and finally the memorable Sir Fopling Flutter (1676). The exquisite folly of these fops, Dryden argues, displays the formidable wit of their author. But those drawn by Shadwell will be the genuine "issue" of their author: Shadwell, like his "father," merely portrays himself in his stage fops.

Dryden's hostility toward Shadwell had roots in professional rivalry and political difference. The reasons behind Dryden's selection of Richard Flecknoe as the foolish poet from whom Shadwell descends, however, has remained something of a mystery.[10] Descent from Flecknoe clearly conveys a particular *kind* of insult: Flecknoe apparently reminded Dryden and his readers of the fop figure that had become so popular on stage.[11] Restoration fops aspire to become men of the world but fail comically. They aim for the two key elements of Restoration cosmopolitanism—experience with foreign places and exotic objects combined with sophistication—and their inadequacies, presented for comedy, expose the difficulty of achieving this and the high cost of failure. A brief foray into Flecknoe's writing suggests that he did not, in the eyes of his contemporaries, optimally calibrate this balance: he aimed to present himself as a man of the world, but struck others as a poser, an upstart, or an effeminate sycophant.[12] In his own writing, Flecknoe fashions himself as a world traveler and a ladies' man, but he earned a reputation for "vanity and conceit, and fondness for society,"[13] as a fop who worked relentlessly to "ingratiate himself among the nobility."[14] Dryden thus uses Flecknoe to exemplify a comically misjudged calibration of cosmopolitan performance.

Fops, as critics have recognized, elicit laughter through their foolishness, but also through the way they violate social expectations. Kristina Straub, Thomas A. King, and others have pointed out the fop's particular challenge to the conventions of sexuality and his gender fluidity.[15] Mark Dawson has challenged this view, arguing that the fop generally expresses heterosexual desire and instead reveals the instability of *gentility* rather than gender.[16] But while it is true, as Dawson points out, that the fop commonly seeks to marry, this does not mean that his performance does not violate emerging heteronormative conventions. His self-presentation, as we will see, continually disturbs the boundaries of gender, whatever his marital goals. Straub points out that fops commonly engage in queer flirtation: Thomas Dilke's *The Lover's Luck* (1696), we might add, even ends with the fop marrying a boy.[17] But even when this character does not explicitly desire another man, he takes full advantage of the general fluidity available onstage that characterizes, as Dror Wahrman has demonstrated, the fluidity of personal identity in this period.[18] As noted in chapter 1, Wahrman shows in fascinating detail that print and performance in Britain and France in the years before 1780 reveal a remarkable sense of fungibility in the categories of gender, race, and social rank. The fop entertains audiences by testing these limits. He does this less through the human objects of his sexual desire than, I will suggest, through his clothes.

It is not a coincidence that the particular flexibility in identity described by Wahrman also characterizes early modern cosmopolitans. Alison Games, as discussed in chapter 1, argues that early modern English merchants adapted to their position as emissaries from a weak nation by becoming particularly flexible, at least temporarily, toward local customs. They created networks of trade in part by eating local food and wearing local clothing while abroad rather than clinging to English practices.[19] The fop thus resembles the cosmopolitan merchant in that both embrace fluidity in gender, in social rank, and in national identity. But while the ideal cosmopolite moves smoothly between the identities demanded by different situations and retains an openness to dissimilarity and an appreciation of exotic practices, the fop moves comically and clumsily. The seams show: no matter where his gloves were made, Sir Fopling Flutter still appears to Dorimant and his circle as a "plain bashful English blockhead."[20] While a traveling English merchant looking to expand his network of trade might don an Ottoman vest to improve his chances of gaining trust by appearing familiar, the fop in elite English society dresses to impress but fails through excess. In doing so, he engages in what Marjorie Garber identifies as the "unmarked" kind of transvestism: that is, he sports garments recognized by other characters as crossing social boundaries, particularly—but not exclusively—of gender.[21] Garber describes unmarked transvestites as those who imply gender crossing without actually adopting the other sex's garments; twentieth-century examples include Michael Jackson and Liberace, who wore fabrics and styles marked as feminine or too extravagant for men. While fops reveal their foppery through several related characteristics, such as insufficient wit or the inability to correctly read the status of other characters, they are most saliently identifiable as fops by what they are wearing. The fop engages, then, in the tradition of travesty performance, his clothes marking his comic difference. Other characters in Restoration comedy entertain through their witty repartee, but the fop's performance relies on visual comedy and his own self-consciousness about the performativity of social (including gendered) identity; he is, as Andrew Williams notes, a "one man metatheater."[22] George Etherege's *The Man of Mode* introduces Sir Fopling Flutter by describing his clothes before he even appears onstage: "He was yesterday at the play, with a pair of gloves up to his elbows, and a periwig more exactly curled than a lady's head newly dressed for a ball."[23]

Marjorie Garber further suggests that transvestism not only constitutes a crises of boundaries, but alerts us to a crisis of category that incorporates multiple forms of boundary confusion. Consistent with her observation, gender is not the only sartorial boundary that the fop ostentatiously crosses. Cultural cross-dressing could suggest empowerment (the Ottoman habit worn by the king), commercial authenticity (the turbans worn by proprietors of coffeehouses), or personal refinement,[24] but in the theater it was also played for comic incongruity. In Edward Howard's *Six Days Adventure, or the New Utopia* (1671), the foppish Peacock violates animal/human boundaries: he has ordered his tailor to make him a full suit of feathers to match his name. He loves the way he looks in it. In Joseph Arrowsmith's *The Reformation* (1673), the Venetian Pecheco has traveled to England and adopted "all the fopperies of that Nation, which they borrow from the French." The eponymous *Town-Fopp: or, Sir Timothy Tawdry* of Aphra Behn's play (1676) shares with Sir Fopling Flutter a personal history as a "Countrey Squire" who "Turns wond'rous Gay, bedizen'd to Excess, / Till he is all Burlesque in Mode and Dress."[25] At the other end of the decorative spectrum, Behn's Blunt calls himself an "English country fop" at the end of Act Two of *The Rover*, when he finds himself standing onstage in his underwear. He appears even more ridiculously at the play's end in Spanish clothes, as no English ones can be procured.

Attention to the stage fop's clothing rather than the human objects of his sexual desires also reveals his crucial function in the Restoration's comic exploration of cosmopolitan ambitions. Writing about the Shakespearean stage, Garber observes, "Transvestite theater recognizes that *all* of the figures onstage are impersonators. The notion that there has to be a naturalness to the sign is exactly what great theater puts in question."[26] Charles II ended the boy actor convention by decree, but the popularity of the "breeches part" for women evokes this longstanding theatrical practice and calls attention to the novelty of the female body onstage. Like the transvestite boy actor and the actress in breeches, the fop also highlights the performativity of gender and of identity in general. Thus while the figure of the fop promotes (and also satirizes) the importance of cosmopolitanized identity through his humorous failure to become a genuine man of the world, he does this through his capacity to invoke anxiety, pleasure, and self-consciousness around the fluidity of multiple forms of identity.

Fops comically violate national and cultural boundaries as well as gendered ones, and as such, I will show, they suggest the formation of categories of identity that do not entirely align with traditional notions of rank. "One of the most consistent and effective functions of the transvestite in culture," Garber goes on to argue, "is to indicate the place of . . . 'category crisis.'"[27] The fop highlights the significance of his counterpart, the genuine cosmopolite, and functions as both a warning against and performance of the allure of the excessive blurring of categories. Restoration theater did not invent this character, but he flourished in the category crises on display in Restoration theater and took on new meaning on a stage in which the predominant form of theatrical cross-dressing had been officially banned. Wycherley, as we will see, exploits the fop's indication of category crises beyond gender; he also, like many Restoration playwrights, exploits the disruptive potential of the cross-dressed actress.

Identified by Dryden as the ur-fop from whom the fop-author Shadwell sprang, Richard Flecknoe represents in *Mac Flecknoe* the failed cosmopolitan. Flecknoe presented himself as a well-traveled man of fashion, but Dryden takes it as a given that everyone can see that he is trying too hard. Flecknoe's travels failed to produce genuine understanding; his clothes and affect risk effeminacy. His identity has become *too* fungible. In about 1656, Flecknoe shared his travel experiences by publishing his *Relations of Ten Years Travell in Europe, Asia, Affrique, and America. All by way of Letters occasionally written to divers noble Personages, from place to place.* The civil wars made travelers of many; a Catholic and probably a priest, Flecknoe would have had good reasons for leaving England.[28] He reports finding great welcome among the Catholic elites of Europe. Flecknoe's letters boast of these acquaintances and, for a documentation of exile, seem strangely lighthearted as he evaluates various people and locations by their perceived degree of sophistication, sounding persuasively foppish. He prefers the company of women for their superior refinement, writing, "You wonder I am always amongst the Ladies, and I wonder, you and all men are not so."[29]Among women one learns "nothing but Vertue, high honour and Nobleness," whereas among men one learns only *libertinage* (11). With women there is "no contention . . . but in courtesie; they gently give you their opinion, and let you retain your own" (12–13). Paris is "one of the greatest Cities in the World" (17) and no place has "handsomer Women, better behaved, nor richlier clad, so accostable and free of Company and Entertainment" (19). Flecknoe tells of a voyage to

Genoa, "frighted only a little with Pirats on our way" (21). Italians, however, are excessively provincial (33) and even in Rome, "when you have seen their Ruins, you have seen all here" (34). Constantinople, by contrast, is delightfully colorful: he has never seen "greater gallantry than there, every one wearing such various coloured silks, with swelling Turbans, and flowing garments, as their streets appear just like *Tulipp* Gardens, whilst ours (with so many's wearing black) appear just like *mortuary* houses, all mourning for the dead" (45). Flecknoe enjoys meeting the Queen of Portugal, but notes cattily that she uses "the *Trowel* in painting" (56). While banished cavaliers often note the hardships of this period and characters in Aphra Behn's *Rover* protest Wilmore's seafaring smell, Flecknoe carefully distinguishes between the tastes of different varieties of fish served on board. He describes the thick algae surrounding the ship as a "Garden . . . at Sea" (62), although a dip in the water upon reaching Brazil leaves him "all faintish" (65). The country itself, however, proves a delightful "*Paradise* of Birds," with parrots so colorful as to resemble "a whole Garden of *Tulips*" (73). When his own "Arara" (a kind of parrot) unfortunately drowns on the return voyage, he writes a spontaneous epigram, reminiscent of the fop Sir Benjamin Backbite offering impromptu verses to the ponies of Lady Betty Curricle in R. B. Sheridan's *The School for Scandal*:

> *Since thou so like unto the* Phoenix *wert,*
> *In shape, in colour, and in every part,*
> *That so unlike should be your destiny,*
> *That should by fire, thou should by water die.*
>
> (74)[30]

Flecknoe finds himself overwhelmed with pleasure at the sight of Berseel Castle: "There are certain moments and ravishing Minutes like the divine Extasies of Saints, we should desire might always last" (95), he gushes as he views the castle one day in May, which "had put on its best attire, the *day* its serenest Countenance" with his ubiquitous lute, never "in better Tune" (97).[31]

Flecknoe's prose reflects the persona that would become shorthand for foppery in Dryden's poem: he pays more attention to fine appearances than in the conflicts raging in his home country; he trivializes serious dangers ("frighted a little with Pirats"); he makes rather superficial observations, reducing the peoples of Constantinople to a garden of tulips; he expresses abundant emotion for domesticated animals; he presents himself as delicate rather than intrepid. The salient marker for the danger of excessive worldliness becomes feminization: as Garber suggests, one form of category disturbance points toward others, and Flecknoe is promiscuous in his violation of categories. This image that emerges in the *Relation of Ten Years Travells* contrasts sharply with Andrew Marvell's portrait, which may be why this aspect of Flecknoe's persona has often been overlooked.[32] These letters, however, project excessive politeness, interpreted by contemporaries and by the writer himself as a form of gender fluidity, not visible in the scrawny cleric of Andrew Marvell's oft-cited description of Flecknoe. Discussing his plans for writing a play on friendship, Flecknoe reports choosing "to have personated it in the loveliest sex, and that between two persons of the same sex too, for avoiding all suspect; *Friendship being nothing but Love stript of suspicion of Harm*" (147). He believes himself uniquely qualified to represent this kind of female passion, "having been long Time train'd up & conversant in the Courts of the greatest Queens and Princesses in *Europe*, and consequently not altogether ignorant of personating and presenting them according to their dignity and quality" (147). The plot involves a "Commonwealth of Amazons . . . capable of all the Heroical Exploits you admire of men in Story" (149).[33] Thus Flecknoe embraces female gender fluidity as much as he embraces his own. He declares himself of "that *Amphibean* Gender, with those who are now in one, now in tother . . . all pleasures in this life consisting in a certain change, and vicissitude" (167).

Flecknoe in this correspondence is not just a gender amphibian, but an amphibian of nation as well. In one of the more serious letters in the collection, he reports, Gulliver-like, having to explain the beheading of the king of England to "one of the greatest in this Kingdom" of Portugal (85). Flecknoe bemoans the king's execution, but traces its cause back to the Reformation. Once religious and civil authority became separate, he argues, the monarch would never again be able to hold the same kind of authority, as "that foundation of Monarchy . . . was so shaken and weaken'd, as it has stood wavering and tottering ever since" (87). In Flecknoe's view, conflicts among the monarch, the parliament, and the church will under these circumstances never cease; a unified national identity has been permanently unmoored. He closes by hoping that he may one day return to England if it becomes possible to lead a quiet life there; "if not, I have learnt how wide the world is, and to esteem every place for my Country, where I may live quietly, and without any molestation" (88). The death of Charles I, then, as the culmination of schisms created by the Reformation, has made Flecknoe, and potentially everyone else in England, a citizen of the world.

A Relation of Ten Years Travells, then, proposes a particular kind of cosmopolitanism, the result of turbulent untethering. But travel in itself does not make one a man of the world. The fop, lacking sophistication, absorbs fashion without an internal sense of stabilizing taste. The man of the world, however, is eternally one compliment, one misplaced piece of lace, away from becoming a fop. Flecknoe is not ridiculous for attempting unmoored refinement; he is ridiculous for not, in the eyes of his contemporaries, pulling it off. Flecknoe-like figures would thus become a staple of comedy in the Restoration.

Whatever enmity existed between Dryden and Flecknoe—Flecknoe's insults to Dryden's friend Davenant, his threat as a rival for patronage, the men's political differences[34]—Dryden found in Flecknoe a real-life version of the stage fop. Flecknoe was not only a self-declared gender amphibian, but also showed amphibious tendencies in his national identity. The figure of Flecknoe recalls the category crises that constituted the turbulence of the middle of the seventeenth century, from which the newly restored government struggled, without success, to recover. Richard Flecknoe becomes the perfect origin, then, for bad dramatic poetry: great theater, *Mac Flecknoe* implies, is both threatened by and fascinated with cosmopolitan failure.

The Gentleman Dancing-Master

With his mythologized origins in Richard Flecknoe, the Restoration fop entertains through not just his comically failed cosmopolitanism, but his embodied satire of the cosmopolitan aspirations of the elite and the global ambitions of the monarch. Few theatrical works reveal this as clearly as William Wycherley's second play, *The Gentleman Dancing-Master*. This 1672 performance exposes the global networks scaffolding the comedy of the fop. Critics have tended to dismiss this play as an inferior work, noting also its limited stage run. In its satire of the restored monarch's imperial ambitions, however, it may have failed to amuse in some quarters for its political implications.

The Gentleman Dancing-Master anticipates some of the highlights of *The Country Wife*: Gerrard, a "young gentleman of the town," has fallen for Hippolita, the daughter of Mr. James Formal, "an old, rich *Spanish* Merchant, newly returned home" and "much affected with the Habit and Customs of *Spain*."[35] Wearing Spanish clothes and insisting that everyone address him as "Don Diego," this comically absolutist father locks up his daughter in what he takes to be the Spanish style of parenting. He has arranged for her to marry Mr. Parris, "a vain Coxcomb and rich City-heir, newly returned from *France*, and mightily affected with the *French* Language and Fashions." Monsieur de Paris, as he insists on being called, speaks English with a fake French accent, peppering his phrases with French words just as "Don Diego" does Spanish ones. Monsieur de Paris foreshadows Sparkish in *The Country Wife*: he feels no jealousy and thus unwittingly helps his rival gain access to his mistress. Caught by Don Diego with her lover, Hippolita persuades her father that Gerrard has only come to teach her how to dance at her wedding, a ruse that leads to a series of comic scenes in which Gerrard courts her in front of her father, who prides himself on his patriarchal control. Gerrard wins over Hippolita with a promise to whisk her away in a coach and six, which impresses her because she craves marriage to a gentleman rather than an upstart fop like Parris. Of her competing suitors, only Gerrard can truly claim genteel status. Hippolita decides that she wants him before the courtship begins.[36] Parris is wealthy but only a "City heir"; he also keeps a city whore, who returns to claim him at the play's end. Hilarity ensues when Don Diego demands that Parris give up his French travesty and replace it with Spanish travesty. In compliance, and out of his desire for Don Diego's fortune, Parris drops the French accent and musters the courage to endure Spanish garb.

Criticism of *The Gentleman Dancing-Master* has focused mainly on its intriguing representations of gender and desire, as Hippolita seeks to escape the control of her merchant father and marry a gentleman, in part so she can live in London rather than in the provinces, which might as well be, in her view, "Barbados" (2.466). Thus her own cosmopolitan aspirations equally exclude the peripheries of empire and nation, and she takes charge of her goal of marriage to a sophisticated and wealthy gentleman.[37] Cynthia Lowenthal has suggested that the Iberophilic father and the Francophilic suitor represent past (Spanish) and emerging (French) English fears of powerful rival empires.[38] Further, these two men operate under the "delusion that their nationhood can be taken off or put on as easily as a new set of clothes."[39] The cultural cross-dressing of Mr. Parris and Sir James Formal, however, not only exposes fears of the French and Spanish Empires, but also satirizes English envy, provincialism, and clumsy attempts as cosmopolitanism. Part of the joke here is that Don Diego ultimately lacks Spanish dignity and Monsieur de Paris, French style.

The Gentleman Dancing-Master, then, raises questions about England's own imperial ambitions. Monsieur de Paris imitates the French out of envy for their superiority and shame over his feeble, unfashionable Englishness. Gerrard, by contrast, "has been abroad as much as any man," but he "does not make the least show of it, but a little in his Meen" (1.1.135). He has thus achieved the smooth cosmopolitan grace that eludes Mr. Parris. While Parris adopts French fashions after experiencing the superior splendor of that nation, James Formal has learned to love everything Spanish through a career of doing business with this powerful empire. Parris envies Frenchness, and hopes in turn to be envied by his compatriots for his adoption of the style of this superior nation. Formal admires the Spanish for their mercantile power and hopes similarly to attract admiration at home for his Spanish-style success abroad. Each of these comic rejections of a stable English selfhood is enmeshed in two distinct, but related transnational developments that came to a boiling point in 1672, the year the play first appeared: the Second Dutch War and the chartering of the Royal African Trading Company.

James Formal's family, though now magnificently wealthy from Iberian profits, worked their way up to this current status from humble beginnings with a genealogy noted in the play as follows: a pin-maker, a felt-maker, a wine-cooper, a vintner, and now, finally, a "Canary-Merchant" (5.1.386). "Don Diego," then, admires Spanish culture at least in part because he has made his fortune through the success of the Spanish Empire, without which the leap in status from tradesman to merchant would have been impossible. The Canary Islands, located off the coast of Northwest Africa, were conquered by Spain in the 15th century. These islands became a crucial stopping point for Spanish voyages to the New World, and prospered because of this. Don Diego rides on these coattails and, as the play also reveals, may have been profiting from more than wine.

In the third act, Don Diego makes a grand entrance in full faux-Spanish glory to inspect his future son-in-law, *"walking gravely, a little Black behind him"* (3.1. 117). This moment must have been comically drawn out in performance: Monsieur comments that "by his march he won't be near enough to hear us this half-hour, hah ha ha" (3.1.127–28), contrasting French frivolity with Spanish gravity.[40] The merchant, at his most Spanish moment of seriousness, processes before a (presumably) enslaved black child who appears to follow him for theatrical and decorative effect. The child signifies Don Diego's importance, his commercial success, and his Spanishness, but also reminds audiences of the Formal family's transition from urban commerce to trading at the periphery of empire, where such reinvention becomes possible. What his own daughter Hippolita scorns as desolate, like the English countryside—recall her comment on Barbados—Don Diego proudly parades as the source of his great wealth and his cosmopolitan superiority to his provincial ancestors. His Spanish performance indicates not confusion of national identity, but rather a proud claim to the elevation of his business to global rather than domestic traffic. The "little Black," as accessory to his Spanish costume, drives this point home. While the English theater had long included African characters performed by white actors, this tableau, with its visual display and comic stasis, echoes less the stage tradition of great actors like Betterton blackening his skin to perform Othello than it does the fashion in England and Continental Europe for paintings of elite subjects attended by enslaved black children (figure 2.1).

Don Diego's two-man parade forms such a moving picture. Susan Dwyer Amussen asserts that these portraits were one of the ways in which seventeenth-century English society attempted to process the disruptive

FIGURE 2.1   Pierre Mignard, *Louise de Kéroualle, Duchess of Portsmouth*, 1682, oil on canvas. © National Portrait Gallery, London.

problem of their nation's relatively new Caribbean slave economy, which challenged its self-definition in multiple ways, but particularly in the treasured identification of the English as a free people.[41] She also argues that for this reason, the English at this time generally kept their new identity as drivers of slaves out of visual depictions and theatrical productions. In this scene's echoes of the portraits and in Don Diego's comic hybrid identity, however, it alludes gingerly to the parallels between English and Spanish practices, unlike Davenant's earlier Iberophobic *Cruelty of the Spanish in Peru*, which casts the Spanish as brutal enslavers and the English as humanitarians. In the portraits, Amussen states, the presence of black children—such as the young stableboy in Daniel Mytens's portrait of *Charles I and Henrietta Maria Departing for the Hunt* (circa 1630)—indicates the prestige of the subject. Charles II had several of his mistresses painted with black servants (or slaves), including Nell Gwynn, Mary Davis, Barbara Palmer, and Louise de Kéroualle, the Duchess of Portsmouth.[42] Charles, his queen, and several of his mistresses had black servants.[43] The portraits, Amussen argues, follow conventionalized patterns; nevertheless, the "attendants themselves were not stock figures but rather the actual servants of the portrait's subjects."[44] She also points out, interestingly, that "few English people associated with the colonies where slavery was taken for granted had their portraits painted with slaves."[45] More of these seventeenth-century portraits with enslaved children depict women than they do men. Joseph Roach, following Laura Brown's argument about the feminization of empire in literary images, notes a parallel visual iconography in the Pierre Mignard portrait of Louise de Kéroualle (1682), elaborately costumed and draping her arm over the shoulder of an African child (figure 2.1). The child's pearl necklace echoes the slave collar, transforming it from a mark of brutal possession to an aesthetic enhancement. For Roach, the portrait "suggests the conventions whereby the European incorporation of Africa and Africans may be at once acknowledged as conspicuous consumption and disavowed as the vital business of the nation."[46] This line of argument has been expanded by Simon Gikandi, who argues that eighteenth-century aesthetics originated in the disavowal of the origin of domestic luxuries in the transatlantic human traffic.[47]

The appearance of the "little Black" trailing Don Diego, however, suggests a different relationship between aesthetic production and what historian Sven Beckert has called the "war capitalism" of this period.[48] Given the merchant's spectacular profits in the Canary Islands, the boy functions to avow rather than disavow the nation's business by way of comparison to the Spanish Empire. Unlike the paintings, this performance links the image of paired European and African figures explicitly to a business model.

On the one hand, the performance of this little parade associates slave trading with the Spanish, who are in a sense mocked in the play as old-fashioned
and excessively hierarchical. Don Diego's authoritarian confinement of his
daughter, as well as his insistence on a mercenary marriage, represent presumed Spanish customs as comical in their patriarchal excess. Yet his Spanish
affectation also serves as a parody of this character's own extranational yearn-
ings and envy of the Spanish. By audience knowledge of his true identity as
James Formal, the Spanish affectation further implies the more general, and
thus comical, English envy of the Spanish Empire. Unlike Davenant's *Cruelty
of the Spaniards in Peru*, which explicitly claims English moral superiority
in the face of Spanish power and barbarity, Wycherley's play represents the
Spanish Empire as an object of desire, pursued as comically and absurdly
as any love interest or pair of French gloves but with risible results because
Mr. Formal, the descendant of an English pin-maker, might not be worthy.
While some presumed Spanish characteristics—in particular, the patriarchal
absolutism—come across as undeserving of his envy, the black boy's appearance links Don Diego's ambitions to wealth in general and the transatlantic
slave trade in particular. Don Diego envies the Spanish system and Spanish
mercantilism, but 1672, as noted, was also a crucial moment for the English
slave-trading industry, suggesting that he might not be the only one afflicted
by this envy. As one of his first political acts upon his restoration in 1660,
Charles II brought laborers to his nation and its colonies using an Iberian
business model. As Holly Brewer explains,

> Hereditary servitude . . . became an organizing principle behind the
> king's empire. Charles II's first step was to establish the Company of
> Royal Adventurers Trading into Africa, later the Royal African Com-
> pany (RAC), under the leadership of his brother James, Duke of York,
> and with most of the royal family as members. Promising his gover-
> nors to supply the colonies with "conditional [English] servants and
> blacks," Charles II coordinated colonial policy with the African trade
> by promoting RAC factors, or salesmen, to powerful colonial posts,
> such as Thomas Modyford to the governorship of Jamaica in 1664.[49]

While England had participated in the slave trade prior to this charter,
Charles, as Brewer and other historians have shown, set out to compete sys-
tematically with other European empires in this lucrative business.[50] In 1672,
when *The Gentleman Dancing-Master* first opened, Charles launched a new,
more ambitious gambit for African trade out of the ashes of the Company
of Royal Adventurers, which had foundered, partly as a result of the redirec-
tion of military resources during the Second Dutch War and the loss of slave

forts and colonies to the Dutch, as memorialized in Aphra Behn's *Oroonoko*. Charles named the new company the Royal African Company and placed his brother James at the head of it. James used this resource in part to transport slaves to his colony, "New York." The English "guinea" coin was born of this moment and this ambition.[51]

The slave trade certainly provided opportunities for merchants to exploit the circulation of bodies and resources; nevertheless, the Royal African Company remained under the control of the crown, which profited directly from it. According to Abigail Swingen, James involved himself considerably in project's daily management.[52] Charles, James, and their fellow royalists invested in the slave trade as way to provide labor for the West Indian colonies in a way that did not drain England of its population.[53] Don Diego's absurdly Spanish entrance followed by a black child, then, referenced the monarch's massive recommitment to a previously weak venture, one that greatly fortified the company's infrastructure and expanded its power to exercise martial law in West Africa[54] and that would compete, this time with success born from military backing, against Iberian powers. Thus the comic figure of Don Diego satirizes not just patriarchal excess, but also Charles's own empire envy and, potentially, his Spanish-style imperial and absolutist ambitions.

On the other side of the stage, waiting for his future father-in-law to complete his two-man parade, stands Monsieur de Paris. Just as 1672 was a banner year for England's participation in the transatlantic slave trade, so it also marked a moment of intense Francophobia and the beginning of the Third Dutch War.[55] In 1668 the English had established an alliance with Sweden and the Dutch to defend Spanish possessions against invasion by France, the most powerful European empire at the time, which was widely seen as aggressively expansionist and aiming for universal monarchy.[56] In 1670, however, Charles secretly signed the Treaty of Dover, agreeing to support France in the case of a war with the Dutch, with whom the Spanish remained allied. Much of the Netherlands remained under Spanish possession, although the Dutch Republic was independent. The Third Dutch War was highly controversial in the context of the continually unstable Restoration settlement, with opponents raising objections that Charles intended to impose Catholicism on England.[57] They railed—to the extent that anything like railing was possible given the Crown's tight control of the press—against this war.[58] Much of their opposition was expressed as fear of popery, but as Steve Pincus suggests in *1688: The First Modern Revolution*, religion was only one issue and possibly not the predominant one. Opponents pushed back against French absolutism and the nation's growing colonial powers both within Europe and overseas. Whether or not Charles was a Catholic in his heart, he undoubtedly aligned himself with French-style absolutism and French imperial ambitions. As Sir William Coventry warned about the French, "[S]ince the discovery of the *Indies*, and increase of Trade, Naval strength was the most important of all others, and Navigation and commerce the greatest (if not the only) supporters of it; [the French] first erected and encouraged several Trading Companies, and in the second place they spared no cost, and stuck at no charge or expence, to purchase a considerable Fleet of men of War."[59] The French treatment of the Duke of Lorraine was a "new way of dealing with a Sovereign Prince, not known yet in these parts of the World, and which may give some hopes to *Europe* of seeing e're long the West governed by Bashaws as well as the East."

It might be worth mentioning here that the 1682 portrait by Pierre Mignard of the Duchess of Portsmouth, the mistress of Charles II, which has so often been used to discuss English self-fashioning, was in fact painted in France, and adopts the French fashion of using black children as symbols of wealth. The king embraced this style in a show of not just racism and the abuse of human rights, but also the emulation of the imperial French, with whom he remained secretly allied and from whose king he received considerable funds. These paintings of women with African servants or slaves, then, would have been recognized in the court of Charles II as part of the absorption of French style.

How might this complicated relationship with France in 1672 help us rethink Monsieur de Paris and the Frenchified fops that became one of the cornerstones of Restoration comedy? *The Gentleman Dancing-Master* suggests that these characters are not evidence that the English simply thought the French were silly. Rather, as the expressions of the quoted pamphleteers suggests, many English people feared the French, a fear supported by (correct) suspicions that their monarch was secretly in league with the French king. Mockery and feminization are, in the case of the fop, not responses simply to a belief in French frivolity, but rather to fears of the most powerful military machine in Europe. With this in mind, Mr. Parris's envy of the French fashion looks a lot like the king's apparent envy of French colonialism, French absolutism, and the French slave trade. The play, then, thematizes and satirizes the imperial envy extravagantly performed by Don Diego and Monsieur de Paris; at the same time, it reminds audiences of the global origin of the dowry that makes Hippolita so desirable a wife that Monsieur will pretend to be Spanish and Gerrard will pretend to teach dancing.

If Wycherley captures the imperial envy of Charles II and his court, including their absolutist ambitions and participation in the business of selling enslaved humans, he does not represent it in a flattering light. When

Monsieur de Paris reappears in Spanish dress at the command of Don Diego, he too is now followed by a *"little Black-a-moor"* as a key Spanish accessory (4.1.99). The child presents the *golilla* that Monsieur must wear. This stiff Spanish-style collar must have been greatly comic in production; Hippolita laughs as Monsieur swallows his pride and endures it. It visually echoes the collars with which the court elite decorated the enslaved African children represented in paintings, a gesture we can now see as less disavowal than product placement. Don Diego commands the young attendant to instruct Monsieur in walking and bowing in the Spanish style, which he dutifully carries out. The joke, however, is here on English cosmopolitan desire rather than on the young boy, who embodies the true Spanish style; he castigates Monsieur on his Gallic habit of laughing aloud and demonstrates the proper Iberian gestures of politeness. Thus the young African rather than the wealthy merchant comes to embody the performance of true Spanish dignity. In training Monsieur, the "Black" (as he is referred to in the text) also parallels Gerrard, as they both teach others to move with proper grace, an equivalent that draws comment from the other characters in the play and by Monsieur himself. (In the opening lines of Act 5, Monsieur equates the two by calling the attendant Gerrard's "little black brother" and a "little black master.") Gerrard disguises himself as one who teaches others to move in a genteel fashion, and yet he panics when Hippolita's father and aunt want to watch the lesson because he does not dance particularly well—something that helps the aunt see through his disguise. So the genteel suitor reveals his pretense as a master of gentility by the insufficient gentility of his movement. While Formal and Parris mimic the imperial manners of France and Spain in ways that reveal the gaps between the aspirants and the real thing, Gerrard imitates the desires of the English to kinetically demonstrate their genteel sophistication. Performance thus explicitly compares the instability of Gerrard's cosmopolitanism to the black child's unquestioned accomplishment in the art of movement.

While the presence of this African youth parades the dependence of European profits on the slave trade, the comportment of the figure himself and his parallel to Gerrard suggest an intriguing fluidity. Just as Hippolita must be trained to dance, national characteristics also involve performance rather than essence. Mr. Formal is a bad Spaniard; the Black, however, has become quite a good one. One can't help wondering who played these youths in productions. It is possible that a white child actor blacked up for the role, although given the relative rarity of roles for children on the Restoration stage, this seems unlikely. (Child actors clearly appeared on the eighteenth-century stage, however. In Colley Cibber's *King John*, a young girl played the role of Arthur.[60]) Returning to Amussen's point that the black children in portraits were based on individuals, and given the prestige of owning an African child as a domestic servant, it seems possible that two of these enslaved youths played the highly kinetic parts of blackamoors onstage.[61] As we will see, black dancers seem to be a part of the performance of Elkanah Settle's *Empress of Morocco*. John Crowne's *Calisto*, written for a court production, ends with singing parts for three "African women" and also an "Entry of Africans," presumably to perform a dance.[62] It seems possible, then, that some of these enslaved Africans performed onstage. In Wycherley's play, was there an inside joke here, with the play itself performed by the Duke's Company, in which all the players, technically speaking, were servants of the duke? A sly reminder of this disturbing royal business and the traffic to New York? Is it a coincidence that the slaveholding Iberophile's English name is James? Either way, Wycherley highlights rather than disavows the imperial traffic that brought new wealth to the court in comic but troubling ways.

After its six-day run, *The Gentleman Dancing-Master* closed, with no record of a revival until 1693, long after the reigns of Charles and his brother. Some critics have attributed the play's short life to its insufficiency, but it offers some potentially hilarious comic roles and a constant stream of metatheatrical humor. Did the play close because these antics failed onstage, or did it instead fail to amuse an audience who were highly invested in the new royal venture of marketing enslaved African labor? Wycherley was indeed a royalist, but his close relationship with Charles II and the court, rather than confining him to repetitions of court ideology, instead may have emboldened him to take on developments that others might have avoided. *The Gentleman Dancing-Master* reveals that the fop galvanized Restoration audiences through not only his comical gender fluidity and transgression, but his ostentatious and satirical displays of imperial envy.

Provincials and Cosmopolites: *The Country Wife*

Wycherley's *The Country Wife* (1675) hinges on a persistently recycled Restoration plot tension: the comic contrast between the provincial naïf and the urban cosmopolite. Of course, satirizing bumpkins had long provoked laughter on the urban stage in not just the English but also the French and Spanish comedies from which Wycherley drew.[63] Restoration comedies, however, rehearse this contrast with striking regularity, as London was expanding as a center of commerce, matchmaking, and global exchange.[64] Wycherley's Pinchwife, in his desire to marry a country girl, reprises the anti-Londonist character type with particular vigor. Both William Davenant and Richard Flecknoe, as we have seen, promoted ambitious visions of the theater's salutary social impact; Restoration comedies revisit this argument in performance in part through the celebration of the theater as a cosmopolitanizing force. In the flourishing theater culture that followed the Restoration, comedies mocked anti-Londonists and country bumpkins, in part as urban self-promotion. In this remarkably self-conscious moment of theater, however, plays sometimes parodied the widespread confidence in the benefits of sophistication.

The Country Wife was one of many plays to explore these tensions. The anonymous *The Woman Turned Bully* (opened 1675), for example, suggests that the manners performed onstage can corrupt as well as refine.[65] In this play, a rustic girl and her maid turn to printed plays as primers on fashionable manners to prepare for their journey to London; they study these plays because they hope to disguise themselves as young gallants in order to escape an unwanted marriage.[66] Rather than learning civilized polish, however, the girls learn crude language and libertine behavior. Betty Goodfield, who does not want to marry a designated country squire with boorish manners, studies plays on the recommendation of her maid Franck, who informs her that "just as some raw poets borrow their scenes from the fop-company they frequent, in the same manner, many raw gallants square their behaviour to their fop-scenes" (1.2.17–20). Thus Franck describes a never-ending circle of influence between the fashionable urban world and the playhouse. Benefiting from the maid's careful analysis of the depictions of masculinity in recent plays, Betty learns that she needs to develop more sophisticated forms of cursing. ("Son of a whore," for example, has become so common as to function as an endearment.) She must also sleep all morning, harass the watch, and serenade her mistress. Betty lards her conversation with decontextualized quotations from plays, to the infinite amusement of the genuine men of the world she encounters. The sophisticated Truman finds her theatrical repetitions risible, although he admits that he/she "raillies well" (2.1.215). Truman's friend Ned Goodfield, Betty's brother, noticing her dramatic fragments, observes "what havock the little rogue made among the plays." Truman agrees: "Aye, like Don Quixote among the romances" (3.1.9–12). In Goodfield's view, Betty has become a gallant the way Don Quixote became a knight, her rusticity apparent from her unsophisticated textual interpretation and her quixotic attempt to impersonate characters not intended to reflect but rather to exaggerate reality. Betty's bullying behavior satirizes the effects of the stage, although her attempt at urbanity, however insufficient, allows her to escape entrapment in an isolating marriage.

Betty and Franck (like Margery Pinchwife) also experiment with the popular *marked* transvestism of Restoration comedy (in contrast to the fop's unmarked kind) that also explores the pleasures and dangers of a cosmopolitan theater. Scholarship on this period has come to call this kind of travesty performance the "breeches part," although this phrase does not seem to have been in common use at the time.[67] This designation, however, has the effect of emphasizing the sexualization of the actress in these roles. Pepys's pleasure in looking at the legs of Mrs. Knepp bears witness, without a doubt, to the use of cross-dressing to spice up theatrical entertainments with sexual allure.[68] These transvestite performances, however, have other kinds of significance as well. Unlike the fop's adoption of gender-inappropriate and national border-crossing garments, Betty and Franck explore London in full male English dress. But in their theater-inspired attempt to become young men, she and Franck end up as "fops." They travel in triple travesty: first as women disguised as men, second as fops making a travesty of masculinity, and third as rustics trying to imitate urbanites. Put another way: the transvestite performance of the actress ignites, like the fop, category crises, implying that urbanization in general, and theater in particular, has destabilized gender identities, while at the same time cultivating the intense allure of this fluidity. Restoration theater insists on the youthful attractions of urban sophistication, and situates itself as its engine. Further, female transvestism on the Restoration stage plays on the recent memory of the boy actor and the Continental inspiration for admitting female actresses on the English stage.

The Woman Turned Bully nevertheless balances the corrupting potential of the theater and the city against the unpleasant figure of Docket, a committed antitheatricalist and anti-Londonist. Docket locks up his niece Lucia to guard her inheritance and also to keep her from "these naughty plays" (1.3.48, 44).[69] He menacingly threatens to take possession of Truman's property in repayment for a loan. Further, he proposes marriage to the widow Goodfield (mother of Betty). All three of these machinations threaten to prevent the play's romantic couplings (Betty's brother Ned to Lucia; Truman to Betty).[70]

The widow Goodfield hates London. As Ned Goodfield reports, "She believes the town spoils all young men that come to it; but for women, she's confident the very air of London meets 'em, and debauches 'em at Highgate" (1.1.168–71). The widow can barely endure the "hideous . . . din" and "ugly smells in every corner" (2.2.102, 110). She eschews urban refinement: she smokes tobacco and drinks ale—specifically country ale, the only kind worth drinking. She is not, however, entirely unappealing; the play even sympathetically contrasts her bracing honesty to the airs of the town. Her character also suggests a generational as well as a geographical difference in sophistication, for better or worse. Truman captures this assumption that manners in the Restoration have recently and suddenly changed, a transformation with mixed results for women: "[W]omen are not now so dull and unapprehensive as in former ages. For just as times and seasons change, so behaviour grows more polite . . . Anciently, girls had such a gross education that most of them knew neither to read (bawdry) nor write (assignations), their parents not caring to improve their judgement to be more capable than to distinguish betwixt their husband's doublet and breeches" (2.1.278–86). Truman praises modern women, but his asides suggest the interchangeability of female sophistication with sexual transgression. The progress of manners has brought libertinism, irreligion (advanced-level cursing), and status inconsistently; here and elsewhere, comedy nevertheless ambivalently embraces this change.

The 1670s saw a string of comedies featuring provincials floundering in urban settings. Thomas Shadwell's *Epsom Wells* (1672) features an extravagant anti-Londonist named Clodpate, "A Country Justice, a publick spirited, politick, discontented Fop, an immoderate hater of *London*, and a lover of the Country above measure, a hearty true *English* coxcomb." Clodpate might express the author's resistance to London's immorality, as Christopher Wheatley has argued,[71] but the play reveals plenty of bad behavior in the country as well. Clodpate's immoderate anti-Londonism leaves him vulnerable to seduction into marriage by the wily Mrs. Jilt, an urbanite who poses as a country girl to catch a wealthy husband. At the other extreme, John Crowne's Sir Mannerly Shallow in *The Countrey Wit* (1676) begins as an enthusiast of everything London, hanging a map of the metropolis in his parlor. His trip to the city, however, leads to a string of comic disasters when crafty cosmopolitans exploit his innocence, after which he almost becomes a Clodpate: "So, I have come up to *London* to a very fine purpose; I have lost my Mistriss, lost my Money, am Marrried to an Apple-womans Daughter, and must keep a Beggar-Womans Bastard; whereas, I thought to have liv'd in *London*, and never seen the Countrey more: I will now [g]o down into the Countrey, and spend all my time in rayling against *London*."[72] Other plays that pit country innocence against urban sophistication include Edward Ravenscroft's *The London Cuckolds* (1681), in which the country girl Peggy echoes Wycherley's Margery; Aphra Behn's *The Rover* (1677), with Blunt's country ignorance of city wiles; and Henry Nevil Payne's *The Morning Ramble; or, The Town-Humours* (1672). A string of anonymous treatises published in 1673 debated the dangers of leaving the country for London, exhorting young men to pay more attention to their family estates rather than dissipating themselves and their purses in the city.[73]

In *The Country Wife*, Wycherley most memorably makes use of this comic obsession, celebrating urban sophistication but also capturing anxieties over the cosmopolitan ambitions of the restored nation. Like *The Gentleman Dancing-Master*, *The Country Wife* confronts the dependence of urbanity on global traffic. The play does not resist the infusion of exotic commodities and practices, but holds up for scrutiny the intensity of desire for them. Empire envy takes a subtle but unmistakable form, woven into social life but nevertheless haunted by violence. Wycherley structures the play around two extremes on the cosmopolitan spectrum: on one end Horner, the traveled man of the world, and on the other Margery, the unspoiled country girl. Horner plans to seduce the elite women who have previously eluded him by spreading a rumor that he has been rendered impotent by a treatment for venereal disease recently contracted in France. Husbands, then, will trust him with their wives, and he will disabuse the ladies to abuse the husbands. In a parallel plot, his old friend Pinchwife, a former rake, has married the country girl Margery in order to secure a wife innocent of London wiles. Horner sees Margery at the theater and resolves to seduce her, partly for her beauty and partly to torment Pinchwife. Pinchwife, in town to marry his sister Alithea to the fop Sparkish, has not heard the rumor of Horner's impotence and jealously guards his wife, insisting that she may only go see the sights of London if she disguises herself by wearing her brother's suit. Pinchwife chillingly threatens violence whenever he suspects Margery's reciprocal interest in Horner, but she ultimately outmaneuvers him. Margery appears in travesty for the key seduction scene; she eludes her husband's watchful eye to meet her lover by wearing the clothes of her virtuous, dignified sister. For all of her experimentation with identity shifts, however, she must return at the end to the country with her abusive husband.

Horner constructs his disguise verbally rather than sartorially. Charles Hart, known for his romantic attractiveness and liaison with Nell Gwynn, created the role; he had also played Celadon in *Secret Love*, Cortez in *The Indian Emperor*, Palamede in *Marriage à la Mode*, Wildblood in *An Evening's Love*, and, in *The Conquest of Granada*, the indomitable Almanzor, who furnished the model for Drawcansir in the Duke of Buckingham's parody *The Rehearsal* (1672).[74] Thus, Hart could play both the sexy male lead and the royal hero. He began his career before the Interregnum as a boy actor and fought for the king in the civil wars.[75] The prompter John Downes noted that "if [Hart] Acted in any one of these but once in a Fortnight, the House was fill'd as at a New Play, especially *Alexander*, he Acting that with such Grandeur and Agreeable Majesty, That one of the Court was pleas'd to Honour him with this Commendation; That *Hart* might Teach any King on Earth how to Comport himself."[76] The role of Horner, then, was created by an actor known for his depth and dignity, but also for personal magnetism and manners so polished that they could train a monarch. When *The Country Wife* opened, Hart had recently played Almanzor, whose adventures as a fiercely independent heroic warrior who later discovers his royal birth repeated a favorite Restoration theme in which the true identity of an exiled monarch is dramatically revealed.[77] Known for creating a role that evoked the trials of the exiled monarch, for sharing lovers with the king, and for his royal deportment, Hart in the role of Horner carried with him a hint of the regal libertine in disguise. When Margery, after her first trip to the theater, tells Alithea that she didn't care for the play "but lik'd hugeously the Actors; they are the goodlyest, proper'st Men, Sister!," she also refers audiences back to Hart/ Horner's alluring self-display.[78] Margery finds the attentions of this fetching man of the world, whose persona echoes the royal libertine on the throne, irresistible.

Unlike Margery, critics have long been divided about Horner: is he a smug, triumphant rake who humiliates his rivals, an emblem of the period's misogyny, a rebellious libertine, a trickster whose plan backfires, or a man ultimately seeking erotic attention from other men?[79] These various arguments suggest the dazzling complexity of Wycherley's script. In light of Hart's reputation and Margery's inside joke, however, I want to explore how *The Country Wife* captures and scrutinizes not just the general theme of worldliness, but specifically the cosmopolitan aspirations of the audience, the court, and the monarch. However we read Horner's social, sexual, and political status, the play positions him as a cosmopolitan figure who negotiates social complexities through superior sophistication in spite of fewer resources and lower status than his rivals.

While Horner occupies the extreme of the cosmopolitan end of the spectrum, Margery begins as the most naïve. Her responses are among the most humorous moments in the play. She blurts out what she thinks without any of the carefully self-regulated social performances of the other characters. She freely admits lusting after actors. She later insists to Horner that he can become her husband because she sees London ladies change husbands all the time. Margery's journey from country to city manners weighs the costs and benefits of the sophistication that she unwittingly observes in others.

The Country Wife defines the other characters by their real or self-delusional place on the cosmopolitan spectrum as well. Pinchwife claims to "know the town," although not as well as he thinks. He has sought an unsophisticated country wife in order to control her. Sir Jasper is worldly in certain ways, but not enough to detect Horner's plot. Quack provides an onstage surrogate for the audience in marveling at the success of Horner's scheme. The comedy of the Fidget plot, in which Horner seduces the wife and relations of Sir Jasper Fidget, lies in how the ladies turn out to be more sophisticated than they first appear, an event that ultimately undermines Horner's sense of mastery.[80] Horner also claims to know the town: his scheme depends on his belief that he can predict how women and men will behave. The rumor of his impotence reveals the sexual truth about women (those who show aversion to him reveal themselves to love the "sport") and allows him to gain the confidence of men. The Fidget ladies, however, ultimately surprise him by revealing their own secret community of sexual adventuring: "I was deceiv'd in you devilishly," he remarks with amazement (5.4.113) when he learns about their ongoing alertness to clandestine opportunities.

Like Pinchwife, then, Horner also does not know the town as well as he thinks, and events in the play threaten to diminish him to "Harry Common." The country wife becomes Londonized and sophisticated, which means absorbing the deceptive strategies of urban women. When trying to figure out how to get out of writing Horner a rejection letter, Margery tries to imagine what a London wife, afflicted by the "London disease," would do. She first manipulates her husband through textual deception, swapping one letter for another. Next, she engages in a more complicated subterfuge when Pinchwife catches her writing a second letter to Horner. By adding a few strategic words at the end while her husband looks over her shoulder, Margery transforms the meaning of the entire document. By the end of the play, she not only manipulates textual meaning, but performs as a London wife by lying outright about Horner's impotence, something she hesitates to do not because of any remaining scruples but because she does not wish to see him insulted. The emotional distancing needed for this moment marks a deeper grasp of social performance than shifting words in a text or wearing her sister's clothes, the strategy she uses to visit Horner. In the play's final scene, she is neither in disguise nor manipulating a document, but acting in ways that nevertheless contradict her impulses. As with Horner, her disguise has now become invisible.

Margery, then, has achieved a new level of sophistication by the end of the play, something that has a different implication for a woman than for a man. The word "sophisticated" itself at this time meant "impure": as late as Congreve's *Way of the World* (1700), Lady Wishfort is shocked that her daughter Mrs. Fainall has been "sophisticated" by her affair with Mirabell.[81] The three seventeenth-century usages identified by the *Oxford English Dictionary* all refer to the purity of a beverage: Thomas Dekker writes, "The drinke . . . they sweare Is wine sophisticated, that does runne Low on the lees of error" (1607);

J. French in *The Art of Distillation* objects that "They . . . have brought a great Odium upon it by carrying about, and vending . . . their sophisticated oils, & salts" (1651); and Prior and Halifax describe how to "give sophisticated Brewings vent" (1687).[82] Wycherley satirizes both Pinchwife's fetishizing of purity *and* Horner's project to sophisticate Margery.

Complexities of purity and sophistication in this play belong not just to sexuality but also to national identity. Theater cures provincialism through sociability and witty dialogue, but also through engagement with the world outside England. Most saliently, *The Country Wife* engages tensions over the court's political ties and cultural attractions to France as the more cosmopolitan nation: a "French–English disaster" has caused Horner's alleged impotence. The elite Fidget ladies disagree over the extent to which Horner has truly been Frenchified: Mrs. Dainty Fidget, observing his "breeding" (1.1.80), cannot believe he has been on the Continent. Lady Fidget, by contrast, charges that he is "too much a French fellow, such as hate Women of quality and virtue for their love to their Husbands" (1.1.82–84). Confirming the second lady's stereotype of Gallic libertinism, Horner apologizes for failing to bring the latest pornography back for them. In Lady Fidget's view when Sir Jasper Fidget reveals the news about their guest's impotence, Horner becomes a "filthy French Beast" (1.1.100). This opening represents the French as the more cosmopolitan nation whose sophistication Horner fails to match, but at the same time a nation of libertines, eunuchs, and pornographers.

Horner's repeated identification as specifically a *eunuch* also links him to the Ottoman and Asian worlds represented by popular plays such as Davenant's *The Siege of Rhodes* and Roger Boyle's *Mustapha*, which, as we have seen, were important to the Restoration reinvention of the stage. In addition to representing the power, wealth, and intrigue of the Ottoman Empire, these plays also theatricalized the widely noted Ottoman custom of hiring eunuchs as palace guards, especially of women.[83] Wycherley presents the Fidget household as a degraded sultanate, a weak English travesty of an Eastern practice: Sir Jasper Fidget consistently appears with an entourage of ladies whose virtue and entertainment have become his responsibility. When Horner shows Quack the affectionate letter from Margery handed to him by Mr. Pinchwife, he reads it with astonishment and declares, "I will henceforth believe it not impossible for you to cuckold the Grand Signior amidst his guards of eunuchs" (4.3.344–47). This comment casts both Pinchwife and Sir Jasper, who are each responsible for the reputations of multiple ladies, as comic mini-sultans, although Horner is so skilled, Quack implies, that he could cuckold the real thing. In the end, Horner sticks with his claim of impotence to avoid violence at the hands of men who suspect they have been cuckolded, but Pinchwife is not persuaded: "An Eunuch! Pray, no fooling with me" (5.4.352). Here, the word "eunuch" takes on dramatic power: it provides the key declaration that can end the play without a bloodbath. The specific use of this term rather than "castrato" or simply "impotent" ties together a running joke in the play about the pathetic sultanic aspirations of Pinchwife and Sir Jasper.

While Davenant's *Siege of Rhodes* suggests that Europeans might aspire to the dignity and polish of Ottomans, *The Country Wife* comically plays out the distance between the genuine sultan and these petty English overlords who cannot contain their women. Sir Jasper remains happily ignorant at the play's conclusion (or, as I have argued elsewhere, he is satisfied to look the other way).[84] Pinchwife, by contrast, desires not just social agreement about the chastity of Alithea and Margery, but genuine control, and the harder he tries, the less effective he becomes. Pinchwife's household absolutism only results in rebellious plotting.[85] He inadvertently foments this rebellion himself: by warning Margery against the delights of urban life, he reveals their temptations. Once he exposes her to the theater—the cosmopolitan heart of cosmopolitan London—he seals his own fate as a cuckold: her beauty, as well as her position seated next to Pinchwife, ignites Horner's interest. Pinchwife attempts Don Diego's patriarchal absolutist practices by locking his wife in her room, although she ultimately finds her way out. Later, when she resists writing a letter of rejection to Horner, Pinchwife turns to more violent menaces: he threatens first to gouge out her eyes, then to carve the word "Whore" on her face with a penknife.[86] But while Sir Jasper may or may not know that his own harem has been violated, Pinchwife at the play's end deliberately backs down to avoid a duel in the face of clear evidence of his wife's infidelity.[87]

Given the global networks through which performance of this play created meaning, I want to suggest that the eponymous "country wife" evokes both: "wives" (a misogynist satire of the uncontainability of female desire, balanced by an even sharper satire of those who would contain them) and also the "country" (a backwater nation working its way into the sophistication of global networks). In this analogy, we find no more nostalgia for a provincial nation than for a provincial wife, but at the same time ambivalence toward the cosmopolitanization of both. Just as Margery moves toward sophistication in spite of attempts to contain her, so the nation moves, for better or worse, toward deeper embedding with a global network that includes Ottoman power and French sophistication. In *Before the Empire of English*, Alok Yadav has persuasively shown that expressions of nationalism at this time functioned less as statements of smug superiority and more as confrontations with the period's anxieties over English provincialism.[88] Yadav points out that literature written in English during this period did not have the same kind of broad influence as French writing, which commanded wider respect. English writers called for the establishment of national identity and a national literary culture so frequently and forcefully because they understood their nation as lacking. These writers thus "continue to feel the need to rehearse the progress of English and to vindicate their claim to having arrived at a metropolitan standing in the world of letters."[89] Attacks on other European literary traditions were less proto-imperialist attempts to globalize English culture than endeavors to establish the cosmopolitanism of English literature and sometimes the provincialism of other traditions (as in Davenant's comparisons between London and Paris discussed in chapter 1). English writers worked so hard to establish their urbanity, Yadav argues, because they worried they were provincial. The comic distance in the play between the English men who cannot control their women and the period's fascinated depiction of powerful Ottoman sultans for the entertainment of a king often satirized for his Ottoman-style aspirations suggest, along the lines of Yadav's logic, intense forms of empire envy.

The most notorious joke in *The Country Wife* exploits and satirizes this empire envy: here, the desire for "china." Horner has Lady Fidget in his arms when her husband walks in. "But is this your buying China?" (4.3.79) Sir Jasper demands, momentarily forgetting Horner's supposed sexual incapacity. Without missing a beat, Lady Fidget insists that yes, she *is* getting china: Horner "knows China very well" (4.3.103) and has an extensive collection and what looks like illicit sex is in fact a shopping expedition. As she slips into the next room in search of her porcelain prize, Horner berates Sir Jasper and all husbands for letting their wives rifle him of his china, then joins Lady Fidget in his private chamber. Lady Fidget emerges triumphant, but Mrs. Squeamish then shows up and demands some china for herself. Horner is now the one who "wants" china: he has none left, but promises her a "roll-wagon" later. Mrs. Squeamish's request exposes both his desire and his lack.

This "china scene," as it has come to be called, has long been recognized as one of the play's most outrageous moments. One classic reading of the metaphorical force of "china" has been that delicate porcelain serves as a trope for female fragility.[90] But while fragility and resilience are indeed at stake in this play, these women actually prove remarkably durable. The Fidget ladies appear to have been visiting china houses for years with little damage, and Margery seems headed toward the same kind of resilience. Elizabeth Kowaleski-Wallace and David Porter have both suggested that the inspiration for this scene comes in part from the Restoration's craze for imported porcelain objects. Kowaleski-Wallace reads china as a trope for not only female commodification, but female desire, prefiguring the ways in which Restoration and eighteenth-century culture positioned women as consumers of frivolous goods.[91] Porter identifies the china scene as a "literary antecedent" for eighteenth-century "sexualized construction of chinoiserie":[92] "a Chinese artifact," he observes, "appears in this exchange as a symbol of extravagant and illegitimate sexuality, a porcelain priapus evoking a vivid scene of rampant cuckoldry and voracious female desire" undermining patriarchal authority through the transformation of potency into pleasure.[93] For Porter, this works at the aesthetic level as well: "Chinoiserie emerges over the course of the century . . . as a token of an emasculating feminine libido that strips art of its classical patrimony in the service of an aesthetic of immediate and irreverent sensual appeal."

In some ways, Wycherley's play fits with and thus prefigures the feminized and delegitimizing aesthetics that, as Porter shows, emerge around chinoiserie in the eighteenth century. At the same time, however, the "china" in this play has a more expansive, more political, and somewhat more slippery meaning when linked to the larger stakes of the Restoration court and ideologies. What does it mean that Horner, who aspired to outwit the social rules, becomes defined by his desire for and, just as significantly, his *lack* of china, a word itself here variously suggesting expensive porcelain; a kind of fruit (China orange—more on that later and again in chapter 5); a far Eastern country; a rare and highly valued global commodity that expresses cosmopolitan taste; sex; and currency used to pay for sex? In the drama surrounding the contestation over china, *The Country Wife* offers a paradigmatic reflection on the costs and benefits of seeking, fetishizing, and/or shaking off provincialism; threaded throughout with anxiety over English inadequacy, the play satirizes Pinchwife's desire for an unadulterated and unsophisticated country girl, follows her own insatiable desire for all exotic urban commodities, and proposes duplicity as the most reasonable solution to the resulting threats of violence and community dissolution. Through Margery's provincialism on the one hand and the circulation of Asian exotica on the other, *The Country Wife* explores the pleasures and dangers of entrance into the scene of global traffic, an ambivalent narrative about the desire to move from provincialism to urban sophistication. "China" here signifies the most powerful and illusive cosmopolitan object of desire of all, outstripping the more ordinary Frenchification.

Among other things, the china scene depends on "china" not as self-explanatory—Lady Fidget names Horner as an expert, yet she's making this up as she goes along—but as a pleasure that several characters compete to define, marking the pinnacle in this play of what Lisa Berglund has called the "libertine language" that distinguishes the cosmopolites from the unpolished outsiders in Restoration plays.[94] But we have even more nuance than an "in" group and an "out" group in this scene, for each of the characters has a slightly different understanding of what is happening, depending on what he or she takes to be the meaning of "china." For Horner, this ultimately deflating moment begins as the most explicit and triumphant fulfillment of his scheme, for here he beds the wife in the next room from the husband. Lady Fidget worries about what Mrs. Squeamish knows, but Horner insists that her rival, like her cuckolded husband, has only a literal understanding (which does not, however, seem to be the case). Horner, then, embraces Lady Fidget's subterfuge and tries to take control of it, identifying himself by his expertise on china. For a fleeting moment, he reaches the social mastery to which he has aspired: "I will now believe anything he tells me," (4.3.231) proclaims Quack, a former skeptic. Lady Fidget, by contrast, can't tell what Mrs. Squeamish means, Sir Jasper and Old Lady Squeamish seem to entirely miss the meaning of china, and Mrs. Squeamish, alas, misses the china itself. Horner thus masterfully infuses "china" with a slightly different meaning in each exchange; he has successfully unlocked the most exotic of commodities.

But even though Horner temporarily controls the meaning of china and seems to be taken as an expert by Sir Jasper, in the end it turns out that he doesn't really have that much of it. His grand expertise, after all, is faked, and his collection remains offstage. It has been generally assumed in criticism that Horner and Lady Fidget disappear into a room holding the rake's cabinets filled with porcelain. Simon Shepherd has suggested that Horner exerts his power in this scene through his bodily absence, leaving Sir Jasper vulnerable to the audiences' contemptuous gaze.[95] But the china itself also remains invisible, with only one little piece emerging onstage in Lady Fidget's hands.[96] Horner's declared lack of china, of course, suggests his sexual exhaustion, and without denying this double meaning it seems entirely possible that his proclaimed "want" implies that he really had only one or two pieces in the first place. Elsewhere, Horner points out that his limited resources had kept him from pursuing the elite ladies:

With your pardon, Ladies, I know, like great men in Offices, you seem to exact flattery and attendance only from your Followers, but you have receivers about you, and such fees to pay, a man is afraid to pass your Grants; besides we must let you win at Cards, or we lose your hearts; and if you make an assignation, 'tis at a Goldsmiths, Jewellers,

or China-house, where for your Honour, you deposit to him, he must
pawn his to the punctual Citt, and so paying for what you take up, pays
for what he takes up. (5.4.135–43)

Here it is the word "honor" that shifts in meaning, suggesting both male
economic credit and female sexual reputation. While the ladies in the scene
disabuse Horner and insist that they never ask for compensation, Horner had
previously believed that they were simply too expensive for him: china in this
speech functions as currency, equal to money, gold, or jewels. It has, presumably unlike female sexual reputation, a high and unstable value, serving as an
exchange equivalent between male and female versions of credit, and even
the slickest of English gentlemen does not seem to have very much of it.

The down-market version of cuckoldry, like Horner's toils among the
elite ladies, also depends on a Chinese gift. The china scene ends with the
arrival of Pinchwife with Margery's letter, the multiple interpretations of
which echo the interpretive instability of "china." To reach this moment of
the enjoyment of the fruits of his seductive labors, Horner had plied Margery
with a less expensive but still luxurious import, the "China orange," sold as a
treat in the playhouse and perhaps the "country wife" equivalent of the fine
porcelain that the other ladies get.[97] While Horner can seduce Lady Fidget
in front of her husband through his claim to expertise in feminized Eastern
commodities while impersonating a feminized Eastern harem guard, Pinchwife's own scheme of cross-dressing Margery as her own brother allows
Horner a similar opportunity. Margery yearns to see the sights of the town
and finally persuades her husband to take her to the New Exchange, a center
of London cosmopolitan activity. But she may only go in travesty, wearing
her brother's suit. What Pinchwife intends as a disguise, however, Horner
sees as an opportunity, kissing the "young man" in front of the older one.
A cross-dressed Margery gets her first exciting sexual experience in the heart
of London's cosmopolitan New Exchange. (We can assume that Pinchwife
does not excite her; in fact, the play leaves open the possibility that Pinchwife
becomes so enraged with jealousy because he cannot properly perform his
conjugal duties, due to age and early excess.) This moment of "category
crisis" marks the turning point in the play for the country wife: she had previously watched a play and heard about London sophistication, but not yet
experienced it. Upon entering the Exchange, she lunges at the first vendor,
demanding ballads, but settles for *Covent Garden Drollery* (a collection of prologues, epilogues, and songs) and two plays. Horner takes this opportunity
to abscond with Margery, and upon returning her declares, "I have only given
your little Brother an Orange, Sir." "You have only squeez'd my Orange,

I suppose," replies the husband, "and given it me again" (3.2.524–27). If the china scene identifies the Fidget ladies with expensive Asian porcelain, the market scene identifies Margery with damaged exotic produce. When forced to confess to her husband what Horner did to her when they were out of sight, she describes his putting the china orange, his tongue, and perhaps also another body part in her mouth. While the Fidget ladies collect pieces of china, Margery takes the exotic Asian fruit into her mouth while dressed as a boy, her body permeable and her appearance transformed.

Like the porcelain and the fruit, the "eunuch" plot would have had Chinese as well as Ottoman associations. In Elkanah Settle's *Conquest of China by the Tartars*, which opened the same year as *The Country Wife*, the king of China keeps a large harem under guard by a team of eunuchs. In heroic drama of the period, eunuchs, like the ones in Settle's play, are often untrustworthy, frustrated, and treacherous. Though sympathetic for his attention to neglected women, Horner nevertheless also, like the stage eunuchs in heroic plays, proves untrustworthy to every man. He professes friendship to Harcourt, but will not help him defend Alithea's reputation.[98] At the end of the play, he must humiliate himself by publicly acknowledging his (albeit false) impotence. Horner, then, becomes in effect what he has pretended to be, unable to join the ranks of respectably married men and forever a sex toy for elite ladies because he is stuck with his eunuch identity. The elite world of Chinese porcelain ultimately remains out of Horner's reach, even if he can afford to squeeze an orange now and then.

Women in *The Country Wife*, as Lady Fidget observes, never have enough china, but her comic expression of this lack suggests not just a nation of insufficient porcelain and insufficient men, but linguistic inferiority before this Asian empire. While eighteenth-century chinoiserie, as Porter as argued, represented a China "given over to an anarchic abundance of disjointed images and delightfully meaningless signs," earlier representations characterize it as a "semiotic universe dominated by hierarchy, historical rootedness, stability, and control."[99] *The Country Wife*, with its constant contestation over the control of language, appeared at the peak of the late seventeenth-century interest in the stabilizing of the meaning of words, a movement Porter suggests led to the cultural fantasy of the Chinese language as the model of transparency. The same artist—John Webb—who designed the scenes for *The Siege of Rhodes* also lionized Chinese as the original language spoken by Adam in *Essay towards the Primitive Language* (1669). Unlike the language of Restoration comedy, the Chinese language, invented by Adam to pass down to his children, forms an exact association of words and things, according to Webb. It was the common language to the whole world before the flood.[100]

From this perspective, then, presumably in China there could be no china scenes; the china scene itself reveals the English instability of language that can produce such manipulations and transform a eunuch into a rake and back again. Although Webb identifies some weakness in Chinese culture, overall he had little but awe and reverence, especially for "their Potters mystery, the manner of their making of *Porcelain* dishes, cups, vases, and the like utensils; which the richest Cabinets of the greatest Princes not of *Europe* and *Asia* only . . . glory to enjoy."[101] While the English would eventually learn to manufacture high-quality porcelain, in the seventeenth century European products were considered no match for East Asian craftsmanship.[102] In 1675, then, China and chinaware had not undergone the trivialization associated with eighteenth-century chinoiserie. Tellingly, the china scene disappears in David Garrick's 1766 adaptation and revival of this play as *The Country Girl*. Clearly a new commitment to propriety prompted this cut; nevertheless, the disappearance of Asiatic infusion that structures the Restoration play but disappears in the later version may also suggest that the "china" of 1675 no longer held the same meaning in 1766.[103]

Elkanah Settle's *Conquest of China*, first produced a few months after *The Country Wife* opened, further suggests this admiration, as well as, once again, the theatrical association of cross-dressing and the exotic. China is not exactly conquered in this play, but unified through a love marriage between the prince of the Tartars and a refined Chinese princess. They find each other on the battlefield. In male disguise, the princess Amavange leads an army to defend her nation. The Tartar prince, who does not recognize her as the woman he secretly loves, gains such great respect for this warrior's military prowess that he proposes to end the war through a one-on-one confrontation. The prince triumphs and believes he has killed him (her), but she recovers and returns just as he is about to kill himself over the loss of his love. The warrior princess in this play recalls the heroic Ianthe, although here the princess dons male disguise not to help out a husband, but to valiantly defend her nation against an invading army. Her closing marriage to the Tartar prince suggests an ideal balance between Tartar might and Chinese refinement: as her new husband says, "Your Milder Presence will auspicious be, / And Civilize my Rougher *Tartary*."[104]

Horner's posing as a connoisseur of "china," then, associates him with desires, mostly unfulfilled, for value, sophistication, and power, a mark of his temporary access to intimacy with the elite but also a sign of his ultimate humiliation, his empty china closet, and his social impotence. In 1675, China had much that the English wanted, but England had little that China wanted: as Robert Markley summarizes, "until 1800, an integrated world economy

was dominated by China and to a lesser extent Japan and Moghul India."[105]
The British consumed Chinese imports at this time with not imperial condescension, but awe for their craftsmanship, distress over English provincialism,
and anxiety over an unfavorable balance of trade. Horner's own attempts at
a kind of sexual-imperial swagger only reveal his own embarrassing "want."

The characters of Margery and Horner, then, each expose national vulnerability. If Horner figures risky and ambivalently represented cosmopolitan desires characteristic of the restored monarch and his court, Margery's
character plays out anxieties over provincialism. Critics have long seen her
closing lie as Wycherley's exposure of the corrupting influence of the cosmopolitan world of London. Nevertheless, it is only the abusive Pinchwife
who prefers that his country wife remain one. The character of Margery
is so compelling not because the audience looks down on her ignorance in
contempt, but because we delight in her comically excruciating movement
toward sophistication. Horner and Margery, each in their own way, perform
the peril of empire envy: in the end, though, it not clear that Margery, filled
with new desires but banished to the country, is better off than when she
started, and the more Horner succeeds, the more he must contend with his
own lack of china.

✿ CHAPTER 3

Indian Queens and the Queen Who Brought the Indies: Dryden, Settle, and the Tragedies of Empire

> Only there was walking in the gallery some of the Barbary company, and there we saw a draught of the armes of the company, which the King is of and so is called the Royall Company—which is, in a field argent an Elephant proper, with a Canton on which England and France is Quartered—supported by two Moores. The Crest an Anchor Winged, I think it is, and the motto too tedious: "Regio floret patrocinio commercium, commercioque Regnum." [By royal patronage trade flourishes, by trade the realm.]
>
> —Samuel Pepys, May 23, 1663

On Wednesday, July 15th, 1663, Samuel Pepys fantasized about the queen of England: "To supper, and then to a little viall and to bed, sporting in my fancy with the Queen."[1] The erotic fascination of male subjects with Queen Elizabeth has become legendary, as has the sexual allure of the mistresses of Charles II for Restoration courtiers.[2] Catherine of Braganza, however, tends to be overlooked, and while she may have inspired fewer sexual fantasies than Nell Gwynn, she nevertheless haunted the theater as much as she did the nocturnal revels of this navy official. As the infanta of the first European nation to reach the East Indies by sailing around the Cape of Good Hope, she also haunted England's imperial ambitions. The marriage between Charles II and Catherine jump-started a new era of global commerce as the Queen's taste in exotic commodities popularized Asian porcelain, Indian cotton, and Japanese lacquer, all of which had been fashionable in Portugal. Before Catherine became queen, few people in England drank tea.[3] The marriage attested to the Stuart ambition to compete with European nations for trade routes, colonial possessions, and the highly profitable transatlantic traffic in enslaved Africans. So while literary scholarship and theater history have tended to overlook Catherine, Restoration culture and dreamers like Pepys kept her in mind.

In this chapter, I argue that the ambitions this marriage represented, the cosmopolitanizing force of the new queen, and the figure of Catherine herself shaped the Restoration stage in ways that have not been fully recognized. The public fascination with the king's marriage emerges clearly in Edward Howard's *The Womens Conquest*, as we will see, and also provides a subtle but crucial point of reference in John Dryden and Robert Howard's *The Indian Queen* (1663) and Dryden's sequel, *The Indian Emperour* (1665). It plays a key role in Elkanah Settle's 1673 *Empress of Morocco* and appears fleetingly in Aphra Behn's *The Widow Ranter* (1689, as described in chapter 4). In the wake of *The Siege of Rhodes*, many serious plays of the Restoration, as Bridget Orr has demonstrated, "narrativized episodes from imperial history, whether that of the Romans, the Ottomans, the Spanish or the Portuguese," an unsurprising fashion "given the huge expansion in colonial activity in this period."[4] As she points out, these plays were "clearly concerned with exploring and defining the history and nature of empire, in order to clarify the imperial possibilities for their own nation."[5] Nancy Maguire and, more recently, Brandon Chua and Elaine McGirr have argued with equal persuasiveness that the Restoration's serious plays, including those set in distant locations, evoked England's own controversies over sovereignty.[6] In reading these plays in the context of the royal marriage, I will suggest that these two points of reference—imperialism and sovereignty—are inextricably intertwined.[7]

These and other "Catherine" plays celebrate the Restoration, but at the same time raise unsettling questions about Stuart imperial ambitions. Many tragedies and heroic plays of the Restoration feature what I will call "mixed marriages" (to avoid the term "miscegenation," which embeds the assumption of an unsanctioned relationship) as points of tension. These romances need to be read for not just their immediate historical reference—the actual relationship between Cortez and a native woman in the case of *The Indian Emperour*, for example—but additionally for the way they evoke the mixed marriage of Charles II and Catherine, widely seen as an alliance that moved England closer to Iberian practices of imperial conquest, and that promised to open up to the English trafficking opportunities that other European nations had long enjoyed. Simmering feelings of discomfort, distress, and even guilt in these plays explode into horrific violence generated by powerful exotic queens who also emerge as victims themselves. The plays by Dryden, Howard, and Settle take place in regions of strategic interest—Mesoamerica and North Africa—but their plots, like many tragedies at this time, mix political struggles with romance. These mixed-marriage plots explore the English participation in an emerging global economy, but they do this in the specific context of the restored monarch's marriage to a princess associated with

Portugal's crucial role in European imperial history.[8] These iconic "Indian queens," I will suggest, invoke the queen who brought the Indies.

"English Arms upon the *Africk* shore": The Portuguese Bride

When Lincoln's Inn Fields first produced Edward Howard's play *The Womens Conquest* (1670; published 1671), one foreign Catholic queen, Henrietta Maria, had just died, and another, Catherine of Braganza, sat on England's throne. The play honors both of these women, and sympathetically dramatizes the story of a queen ignored by her husband at a time when Charles continued to collect mistresses and Catherine had not produced an heir.[9] In *The Womens Conquest*, the king rudely rejects his foreign bride, Parisatis, but, echoing Shakespeare's *The Winter's Tale*, must ultimately learn to love her again. Howard's play, however, accomplishes this renewal of love not through the queen's modest retirement, but through her alliance with an Amazon queen who defeats the ungrateful king in her campaign to revoke the male right, backed by the king, to divorce a wife at will. *The Womens Conquest* thus exploits the Amazonian self-fashioning cultivated by Henrietta Maria in her masques and recycles it for the restored Stuart court, at the same time honoring the alliance between the two foreign queens. As audiences would have known, Henrietta Maria had defended her son's marriage to Catherine. But while Henrietta Maria appears to have enjoyed an intimate friendship with Charles I, the younger Portuguese queen endured the neglect of a libertine husband in Charles II. *The Womens Conquest* joins a number of literary works in gently expressing the hope that the merry monarch would take his conjugal duties more seriously.

One detail about Howard's representation of the foreign bride, who so clearly evokes Catherine, deserves particular attention.[10] When the stage king rejects his wife and takes a new lover, the queen fakes her own death, disguises herself as a Moor, and joins the Amazons; thus the original production's Mrs. Betterton, in the role of Parisatis, spent much of the play disguised as an African. Audiences would have been accustomed to the blackface performances of her husband, Thomas Betterton, who had already smothered Desdemona many times as the Moor of Venice. Blackened roles for women, however, were less common. Mrs. Betterton was, of course, not playing a Moor but instead a queen *disguised* as a Moor, a transformation signified through dialogue and a change of clothes, and possibly also by makeup. Felicity Nussbaum asserts that eighteenth-century actresses, conscious of demand for fair beauty, did not blacken their skin,[11] but the language of this earlier play suggests that Restoration theater may have experimented with such a practice. Disguised as the Moor Zerissa, the queen Parisatis explains to the Amazons that women of her own

... swarthy clime
Cannot boast Nature's Beauties in Rose
and Lilly Cheeks; that gives us there as Daughters
Of the night; or that the kisses of the Sun
Were so unkindly spent, as it alone
Did darken us, and guild the world besides;
Yet we have there bright souls of honour.[12]

The Amazon queen later remarks on the color of Zerissa's skin, noting that her complexion suits her to battle because "the scars, and wounds of arms, cannot / Dig furrows in the fair brow of Beauty, / So dear unto the vainer of thy kind" (58).

Parisatis's disguise not only advances the plot by allowing the discarded queen to travel unrecognized, but it also calls attention to Catherine's exotic tastes, her exotic customs, and the exotic commodities in her dowry. Catherine grew up in an Iberian nation that had long benefited from commerce with Asia as well as Africa, and had itself once been dominated by Moors. It is hard to know what the historical Catherine looked like, given the range of the contemporary depictions, although some described her as "swarthy,"[13] with the possible implication of mixed blood. Some artists painted her with conventionally light skin, but others depict her complexion as dark, framed by dark, curly hair. The portrait painted by the Italian Benedetto Gennari II gives the queen dusky skin and thick black curls (figure 3.1).

Catherine personally patronized Gennari,[14] which might suggest that his image conformed more closely to her own desired self-representations. In viewing the retinue of ladies who accompanied Catherine to the English court, John Evelyn noted the darkness of their skin as well as the unfashionableness of their dress.[15] When artist Audrey Flack created a statue of Catherine in the 1990s, she deliberately gave it a "multicultural" appearance, responding to the legend of the queen's mixed blood (figure 3.2). She reported in an interview that she modeled Catherine on her own biracial cousin, hoping that the statue would inspire ethnic and multiracial women. The work was intended for Hunter's Point in the New York borough of Queens—named after Catherine—but was never completed due to local protests against honoring a queen with ties to the slave trade, a connection to which I will return.[16]

When celebrating the royal marriage, poets in the Restoration lingered over the color of Catherine's skin. Praise for a lady's whiteness had long been conventional,[17] but attention to this queen's complexion takes on a

FIGURE 3.1   Benedetto Gennari II, *Catherine of Braganza*, Queen Consort of Charles II (1638–1705), 1678. Historic Images/Alamy Stock Photo.

particular significance in light of Portugal's role in the Atlantic slave trade and the region's historical dominance by Moors. One poet overcompensates by representing Catherine as whiter than white; so luminous that she threatens the eyes of the spectator:

> Your Mother, sure, upon Elixirs fed,
> The East blew all its perfumes to her Bed.
> Then were you wrap'd in Lilies, which so grew

A Coverture o'er your own whiter hue,
A Whiteness not with safety to be seen,
Which of a skin of Lilies makes a screen,
Wherein array'd you suffer a disguise,
And put on Snow in mercy to our eyes.[18]

Another poet, however, describes both Catherine and her new husband as particularly dark. While England and Portugal had not always been allies, "Our *Prince* in Honour of the Forrain Mayd / Though *Black* himself against the Moors sent Aide."[19] The poem goes on to celebrate "Beloved *Black!*" and hopes "O may your *Likeness* of Complexions find / *Similitude* of Vertue, Temper, Mind!"[20]

Representations of Catherine's "blackness" evoked her physical appearance, but they also proliferated associations of the new queen with her dowry, which included exotic treasures and imperial opportunities. Unlike the Duke of York, Catherine did not hold an administrative position in the business of the Royal African Company; nevertheless, she came to England from the first of the European nations to commodify African people as slaves. In a pamphlet published to invite new subscribers to the Royal Adventurers of England Trading in Africa joint stock company (the precursor to the Royal African Company), Catherine's name appears prominently under

FIGURE 3.2   Statue of Catherine of Braganza by Audrey Flack, 1998, and the Vasco da Gama Bridge, seen from the Tage banks, Park of the Nations, Lisbon, Portugal. Serge Mouraret/Alamy Stock Photo.

FIGURE 3.3   Stump-work box featuring Charles II and Catherine of Braganza, circa 1662. © Dorset County Museum.

a list of founding subscribers, in block letters under that of the king and above the Duke of York, with the rest listed alphabetically.[21] That her name appears separately in this list suggests her significance to this company independent of the king. Iconography around the wedding between Catherine and Charles took note of the entanglement of this marriage with the African trade: an embroidered box created c.1662 celebrating this union depicts Charles as attended by a small black servant or slave (figure 3.3).[22] One of its panels depicts Solomon and the Queen of Sheba, clearly suggesting an analogy between the English monarch and the wise Biblical ruler, but also between Catherine and the exotic foreign queen.

A pair of tapestries created around the same time depict the four continents, with figures of Catherine and Charles representing Europe on the same panel with depictions of Asian monarchs (figure 3.4). The sultan has a black servant, and between the two couples we can see two nude black figures in a small boat, possibly suggesting the participation of both sets of monarchs in the slave trade. The panel representing Africa and America shows a European vessel hovering in the background in the same position as the nude black figures in the small boat in the other panel (figure 3.5). Also of interest in this tapestry is the way the panels parallel Catherine and the African queen, both with parasols over their heads, further suggesting Catherine's particular connection to the trade with Africa. The similarity between the African queen and the famous depiction of Anne Bracegirdle in the role of the Indian queen, which I will discuss in the next chapter (figure 4.2), is also striking, down to the small dark attendant (although, in the tapestry, the African queen holds her own parasol).

FIGURE 3.4   Panel from a table carpet showing the Four Continents, the Seasons, and Four Planets, between 1662 and 1680. Metropolitan Museum of Art. Gift of Irwin Untermyer, 1964. Creative Commons.

FIGURE 3.5   Panel from a table carpet showing the Four Continents, the Seasons, and Four Planets, between 1662 and 1680. Metropolitan Museum of Art. Gift of Irwin Untermyer, 1964. Creative Commons.

The Portuguese themselves were not shy about—literally—parading their business with Africa: the nation celebrated the marriage between Charles and Catherine with a grand procession led by figures representing Ethiopian kings. Historian Lorraine Madway points out that in the middle of the seventeenth century, Portugal's "trade with its empire shifted from Asia to Brazil and Atlantic Africa." The iconography of the wedding parade reflected this, and also celebrated "the national collective memory that the Portuguese imputed to their 'discovery' of the West African coast." This costly and violent series of ventures "provided the basis for subsequent claims of possession on land and sea."[23] Catherine, then, hailed from the nation claiming the original European trade with Africa, mapped during their pioneering navigation around the Cape of Good Hope for access to the Indian Ocean, which avoided the Ottoman Mediterranean. Whether or not she personally owned slaves (the point of conflict in the twentieth-century argument about whether to erect the statue in Queens), Catherine represented African and Indian trade within and outside of Portugal. She invoked, but sometimes also embodied, the exotic; she represented the ethically disturbing practice of human commodification, but at the same time became a kind of victim herself in the libertine court of Charles II. Ethical distress prevented the erection of her statue in the city named after the first governor and largest shareholder of the Royal African Company, James, Duke of York.

Depictions of Catherine's darkness emphasized the significance of the marriage in expanding England's own imperial reach. Charles II had economic motives for choosing his bride: a large promised dowry that included new trading rights as well as possession of Bombay and Tangier. The marriage came to signify both royal and national desire for a more significant place in global networks of trade, but proved controversial, both for the ambitions themselves and for Catherine in particular, who bore the brunt of unease about this Anglo-Portuguese alliance. She spoke no English, practiced Catholicism devoutly, and dressed in strange ways, which provoked disparaging gossip in the fashionable Restoration court. She bore with her the material evidence of Portugal's extraordinary "war capitalism," a successful combination of religious crusading, extraordinary navigation, imperial aggression, and economic inventiveness.[24] If her unfashionable dress sparked ridicule, however, her dowry packed with splendors from all over the world fascinated onlookers. Catherine drank tea, already common in Portugal but rare in England. The queen's responsibility for the British passion for tea has become legendary, but her Portuguese taste for a variety of exotic items, including porcelain, helped spark English Sinophilia and enthusiasm for Asian imports in general. She also brought Indian cabinets from

Portugal for her bedchamber, the likes of which, according to John Evelyn, "had never before been seen here."[25] She brought into fashion the fan folded in the then-exotic Indian style, used for a range of feminine expressions on stage and off. Portugal had established Macao, the first permanent European trading colony in Asia, so Catherine's treasures included stunning Japanese lacquered furniture and fabrics made of Indian cotton.[26] As Gertrude Thomas has shown, Catherine not only influenced European geopolitics, but also English taste through captivating luxuries, previously unheard of or quite rare, but that came to define fashion.

The marriage, however, opened up cosmopolitan possibilities beyond the queen's treasures, because it announced the monarch's commitment to participation in the late seventeenth-century imperializing scramble.[27] Catherine's dowry included crucial trading rights and territorial possessions. Her marriage treaty includes articles dealing with the transfer of Tangier, to take place before the marriage (2); the transfer of Bombay to Charles, who would protect both English and Portuguese trade there (11); the right to trade in Goa, Cochim, and Dio (12); the English right to trade in Brazil and "all other of the King of Portugal's Dominions in the West Indies" (13); and English trading and possession rights of any formerly Portuguese but then Dutch "Towns, Castles or Territories" retaken by the English and the division of the cinnamon trade between the English and the Portuguese (14). In article 16, England agrees to defend Portuguese trading ports from the Spanish and states that the King "will never make a peace with Castile."[28] The treaty also includes a "Secret Article": that Great Britain would "defend and protect all Conquests or Colonies belonging to the Crown of Portugal, against all his Enemies, as well future as present . . . [and] any Towns, Forts, Castles, or any other Places" (336). The "castles" mentioned in these articles refer to the structures built by the Portuguese along the coast of Africa for the purpose of holding and selling people captured into slavery.[29] The "Elephant and Castle"—the source of African ivory with one of these slave castles on its back—became the official icon for the Royal African Trading Company and appears on the coin launched by Charles II, the "guinea."[30]

The significance of this marriage as part of the global ambitions of the restored monarch must have been clear beyond Whitehall, as poets celebrated the event with much reference to the Indies, East and West. In the 1662 *Britannia Iterarum Beata* celebrating Catherine's arrival in Portsmouth, the author ("W. W.") writes:

No Victories o'er the Dutch, do I here sing,
Nor what new Treasures from the *Indies* bring

Our dancing Fleet; but from a Neighb'ring Myne,
What's greater far, the Treasure KATHERINE.
Till now I thought, the *Portuguez* in vain
So eagerly did Plow the Indian Main
In quest of Gold, when his own private Store
Could shew far richer then their Dirty Ore.
But see the Reason, sure, he did intend
To make our *Britain* Wealthy, and to lend
Us *Lisbon*'s All . . .[31]

The poem glorifies Catherine as herself the equivalent of Portuguese treasure from the Indies, brought to enrich the English. In another celebratory poem, signed "J. L.," the author imagines that while England celebrates the thawing of "Rebellion's ice," Neptune travels "to th' Indian shore, searching that Golden Main, / In hopes of some precious *Carcanet* to gain / Some Massie Orient Pearl . . . but all the store / The *Indy's* yields too small." So instead he "tacks about" to Lisbon and collects the more valuable "Gem."[32] Once again, Catherine herself becomes interchangeable with treasure from the Indies. Crouch's "Upon the Approach of the Illustrious Infanta" intertwines the Portuguese princess with another Indian commodity: "From whose prest lips divinest Nectar flowes / An Aire of Spices with her *Motion* goes."[33] Indian spices, as Rajani Sudan has shown, had a staggering markup: a trader could potentially earn a 60,000 percent profit on nutmeg.[34] Catherine both embodies and promises this value. The same poem, improbably, praises the marriage as one founded on love rather than profit, although through analogies that once again associate Catherine with the wealth of the Indies: "Not all the Mynes of *India* should control, / Or *Bribe* the judgment of a generous Soul: / Resolve to Conquer first with slighter pains, / *Indias* whole *body*, with its wealthy *veins!*"[35] Another poem predicts extraordinary wealth from the match: "Heav'ns Blessings more t'unfold / It hails down Pearls and rains down riguous Gold."[36] A year after the marriage, another poet linked Portugal's imperial past to Britain's imperial future in this address to the queen:

Nature had kept her riches yet unseen,
Had not the *Portuguez* such searchers been;
Who to the fame of finding Worlds unknown,
Have shew'd their art in You of making one.
Well might the haughty *Spaniard* interpose
With all his wealth to hinder such a close,
As hoping no success from his Alarms
'Gainst *Lisbon*, when She lay in CHARLES his Arms;

But that to rival all his power, in you
CHARLES would be Master of the *Indies* too.[37]

The poet thus honors the Portuguese as the first explorers and equates the acquisition of exotic treasures with the marriage to Catherine: Charles II has simultaneously become the master of this precious princess and the master of the Indies. A song printed on a broadside sums up this sentiment in more pedestrian terms, offering "some comfort for Poor Cavaleeres" who have set out for Portugal: "They'l fetch a Queen with store of Indian Treasure / Will make old Cavies laugh beyond all measure."[38]

Portugal not only led Europe in trade with the East, but also in developing the transatlantic slave trade. Some of the promised wealth of Catherine's dowry, in fact, arrived not in gold but in the form of sugar,[39] cultivated by enslaved Africans in the Portuguese colony of Brazil. Writing in the early eighteenth century, Daniel Defoe had not forgotten the early Portuguese domination of the slave trade: when the shipwreck leaves Robinson Crusoe on the "Island of Despair" in 1659, he had been skirting the Portuguese monopoly on the slave trade in Brazil by undertaking an illicit voyage to acquire enslaved Africans for his plantation. Portugal owed much of its prosperity to slave trading, a point not lost on English poets celebrating their king's union with Catherine.[40] One develops an elaborate conceit to celebrate the marriage in which the Bride-God confronts the *"Powe'rs of Love,"* Venus and Cupid, complaining that in Spain, "I am *nothing;* no more honour have / Then *Afric Negro,* or poor *Indian Slave.*"[41] The poem looks forward more directly to the imperial possibilities of the match:

Aeneas one *mixt colony* constrain'd;
By *Charles* the *Universe* is best maintain'd
By his *own* men: *Africk, America*
Shall make him write, like *Spain,* &c.
Which *twisted Dragons tayl* shall hurl the *Nations,*
As *Stars* the Dragons did i' th' Revelations.

(7)

Hymen also celebrates the English colonization of America by the force of virtue: "So in America my honour's seen, / Where I can scarce remember to have been, / By benefit of them no manhood want, / But double have, who *conquer* and who *plant.*" The most virtuous monarch will "Seize the quarters of the World; they plant, / And checquer *Africk* with Inhabitant."[42] A later poet writing to comfort Catherine after the death of Charles still remembers the significance of this royal marriage in giving England a foothold in the transatlantic slave trade: "as a Dowry brought to *England* more / Than any Queen that ever came before, / She plac'd the English Arms upon the *Africk* shore."[43]

At the political, cultural, and symbolic level, then, the marriage between Charles II and Catherine of Braganza marked a key moment in England's imperial, mercantile, and cosmopolitan ambitions. Catherine herself, however, attracted suspicions for her pleasure in foreign imports, her failure to produce a Protestant heir, and her Catholicism. Some writers encouraged Charles to divorce her for her infertility. In *The Womens Conquest*, Howard implicitly defends the new queen and depicts the king as insensitive toward his wife and toward women in general. His monarch ultimately regrets his impulsive rejection of Parisatis. The king's tyranny attracts the heroic anger of the maternal but ferocious Amazon queen. Thus just as Henrietta Maria enthusiastically supported her son's strategic marriage that aligned England with France and Portugal over Spain (which campaigned for its own princess as the wife of Charles),[44] so the Amazon queen in Howard's play protects Parisatis.[45]

While literary history (like Charles himself) has paid more attention to the mistresses than the queen, Catherine took an interest in performance: she attended the theater alongside her husband, sponsored productions at court, and exerted, as Gertrude Thomas points out, enormous cultural influence, deliberately or not. Catherine was personally responsible for bringing Italian opera to London.[46] She did not request the production of the exotic-themed plays that flourished in the Restoration; nevertheless, her presence, her tastes, and the imperial and cosmopolitan ambitions that motivated the marriage encouraged this fashion. Her union with Charles represented both an older kind of European cosmopolitanism, in which the elite married strategically across national boundaries, and also the newer sort driven by global traffic and global commodities. Theatrical performances of this period engaged both of these through, as we will see, portrayals of mixed marriages and exoticized queens.

Indian Queen(s)

In 1664, two years after the royal wedding, John Dryden and Sir Robert Howard, brother to the author of *The Womens Conquest*, collaborated on *The Indian Queen*, a play that fed into audiences' curiosity about imperial practices and also celebrated the marriage of Charles II and Catherine of Braganza. *The Indian Queen* has attracted attention in recent criticism for its novel theatrical depiction of the "New World" and for its dramatization of imperial conflict during a time of renewed fascination with the morality, politics, and benefits of such ambitions. Bridget Orr writes that this play and its sequel (*The Indian Emperour*, by Dryden alone) suggest the semisavagery of native Mesoamericans and the brutality of the Spanish and imply that the English will build a more humane empire. Similarly, Ayanna Thompson asserts that both foreign cultures are racialized in the two plays and marked as inferior. Other critics, by contrast, have argued that the Spanish in *The Indian Emperour* stand in for all Europeans, although they draw different conclusions about this connection.[47] I will return to these questions of racial and national identity; for now, however, I want to suggest that while these categories remain crucial, the plays additionally develop key distinctions among characters *within* each community. Dryden ultimately develops a heroic cosmopolitanism in which remarkable individuals bond with other remarkable individuals across cultures and nations and discover more in common with each other than with their barbarous compatriots. Thus, in addition to all of the differences marked by nation, race, religion, and implied degree of civilization, the plays also demarcate differences *within* those categories shaped by, but not reducible to, class and rank. Inspired by the romance tradition, this heroic cosmopolitanism could either glorify or resist Stuart ambitions. The fascination in heroic plays with relationships across cultural divides was inspired by and confronted the royal marriage of 1662 and the opportunities for imperial growth this marriage provided.

The first of many plays by Dryden set in a remote location of strategic interest, and the first full-length English play set in the New World, *The Indian Queen* opened with a lavish performance before the king and queen at Whitehall and later appeared on the public stage. Among other themes, the play allegorizes Restoration turmoil over sovereignty; it opened in the same year as Edward Howard's *The Usurper*, which offers unmistakable parallels to the Stuarts and their challengers.[48] *The Indian Queen* also features a usurpation: before the play begins, Zempoalla had plotted with her lover, Traxalla, to murder the rightful king (her brother); the pregnant queen, Amexia, however, has escaped. But as Bridget Orr suggests, the play is not just a political allegory for divine right but also an exploration of "Europe's most significant modern colonial conquest." As she points out, the prologue links Spanish conquests in the New World to the broader interests of English spectators.[49] It features two Native American children, one warning the other that

> By ancient Prophesies we have been told
> Our World shall be subdu'd by one more old;
> And see, that World already's hither come.[50]

With these words, the boy presumably looks out and perhaps even gestures toward the audience. So even though *The Indian Queen* features no European characters, the prologue promises the significance of the story for European, and specifically English, global empires. In *The Indian Emperour* (1665), the sequel written by Dryden alone, the cast expands to include Spanish conquistadors. It features a romance between Cortez and Cydaria, the daughter of Montezuma. This coupling has attracted much critical attention: Heidi Hutner argues that, with this plot of transracial desire, Dryden reverts to a familiar colonialist strategy of mythologizing a native woman who betrays her people for the love of a European conqueror. For Bridget Orr, it awkwardly exculpates Cortez from the guilt of imperial violence. Joseph Roach proposes that the mixed-race romance of the Indian princess and the conquistador riveted audiences by stirring up the scandal of impurity raised by Britain's imperial ambitions and enslavement of Africans; in a similar vein, Elliott Visconsi argues that the romance between Cydaria and Cortez exposes the hedonism of the conquistador, but that *Emperour* presents a pessimistic view of English national and racial identity through analogies with these Spanish characters.[51] Thompson takes the opposite perspective, stating that these plays promote English racial superiority by distinguishing between the Spanish characters and the English viewers; she suggests that in this way the play helped to construct modern notions of racial alterity itself.[52] *The Indian Queen* and *The Indian Emperour* both raise the specter of amalgamation; they do so, however, in a way deeply embedded in Stuart politics, Stuart ambitions, and a very recent Stuart marriage. As most of these critics suggest, racial and cultural mixing lies at the center of the impact of these plays. This cannot, however, I believe, be fully understood without reference to the amalgamating marriage of Charles II and Catherine of Braganza. *The Indian Queen* explores England's imperial destiny by dramatizing the impact of the exoticized Queen who brought the Indies.

The King's Company initially presented *The Indian Queen* at court not long after the wedding of Charles and Catherine in May of 1662: Thomas Killigrew requested additional money for costumes for "the play called the Indian Queen to be acted before their [Majesties] Jan. 25 1663."[53] The play, while propagating imperialist stereotypes about Native Americans, promotes mixing rather than purity both within the development of the plot and through reference to the amalgamation of Iberian and English interests that the marriage represented. While this sort of union had long been the goal of European royal marriages, *The Indian Queen* additionally explores the opportunities that an alliance with Portugal, with its exotic treasures from long-established trade with the East (the *other* Indies), promised to bring.

By incorporating this more expansive version of this international alliance, the play and its sequel also confront some of the more disturbing aspects of England's bid for a larger share of global traffic.

Thus *The Indian Queen* engages the traditional cultural exchange of European royal marriages, but it also, like the wedding poems, represents this particular royal marriage as the merger that will bring England into the center of European imperial expansion. The mixing accomplished by the marriage, in other words, promises to lead to even greater mixing at the global level. The Indian queens themselves in these plays are at once desirable, terrifying, and tragic. In *The Indian Queen* and *The Indian Emperour*, the category of "Indian" sometimes stands in for global resource opportunities in general: as we have seen, poets associated Catherine with the East Indies because the transfer of Bombay, and the West Indies because of Portugal's competition with Spain for New World possession, as well as its role in the circum-Atlantic trade in enslaved Africans. At the same time that these plays reflect increasingly racialized forms of alterity, as Thompson has argued, they also remain alert to distinctions between English, Spanish, and Portuguese ambitions, posit different interests and alliances within native American communities, and dramatize factions within those communities. *The Indian Queen* represents the New World as both an object of European desire and a haunted land of foreboding, mixing vague anthropological details with invented aspirational, supernatural, and unnatural dramatic action.[54] Subordinating historical and geographical accuracy to theatrical power, these plays depict a world organized by a complicated series of national, racial, and factional distinctions rather than by the very broad division between conquerors and the conquered as depicted in the prologue.

The Indian Queen has often been read as a heroic drama, and one of the founding productions of this genre.[55] Dryden and Howard, however, call it a "tragedy." While certainly both plays resemble the later productions that Dryden would call heroic—Montezuma, for example, prefigures the outsized and much-ridiculed Almanzor of *The Conquest of Granada*—understanding them instead as tragedies realigns a sense of their impact in important ways. The genre of heroic romance would place Montezuma at the center.[56] The play's *tragedy*, however, belongs to the titular Indian queen, who usurps the throne from her brother but then loses it, partly because she falls in love with Montezuma. The plot ultimately reveals the queen's passion as inadvertently incestuous: Montezuma turns out to be her nephew and the true heir to the throne, raised in isolation and ignorant of his royal status, a plot with obvious reference to Charles II's own story of monarchy in exile. At the play's conclusion, the true Queen Amexia returns with the revelation that Montezuma is her son, fomenting a popular uprising and thus installing the rightful heir on the throne.

Dryden and Howard frame the play with a blocked romance between the heroic Montezuma and the Peruvian princess Orazia, daughter of the Ynca king; the play closes with the successful union of these two royal figures. While the conflict between Montezuma and Acacis, the son of Zempoalla, over Orazia provides a significant point of tension, Dryden organizes the crucial dynastic conflict in *The Indian Queen* around two women: the usurping Zempoalla and the exiled Amexia, mother of Montezuma. There are, then, two Indian queens in this play, but only one legitimate one; Orazia will become the third when she marries Montezuma. When the play opened, there were two foreign queens at the court of Charles II: Catherine and Henrietta Maria, who returned to England in 1662. These two English Catholic queens, unlike in the play, supported rather than rivaled each other. Dryden's legitimate Indian queen, Amexia, pays homage to both of them. Amexia resembles Henrietta Maria in raising her son, the true king, in exile; she also leads an uprising to reclaim her nation, a plot turn that associates her with Henrietta Maria's Amazonian alter ego and theatricalization as the heroic warrior Ianthe in Davenant's *The Siege of Rhodes*. Dryden also, however, links Amexia to Catherine and to Portugal through her name. In 1663, Charles II had sent two thousand troops to Portugal to fight the Spanish in the battle of Ameixial, the final conflict in a drawn-out war for Portuguese independence.[57] In exchange for the massive dowry (much of it unpaid) as well as strategic trading rights and colonial properties, Charles II's commitment to Portugal included assisting in the defense of his wife's nation against the Spanish, who had ruled Portugal until 1640.[58] The anti-Spanish sentiment so salient in the second play repeats that of Davenant's *Cruelty of the Spanish in Peru*, written to support Cromwell's western design, but the original *Indian Queen* also evokes this more immediate conflict between England and Spain, fought in and over Portugal. In the Restoration, Charles II continued the project begun by Cromwell of competing with the Spanish for control of the Caribbean.[59] His choice of Catherine broke off alternative negotiations, begun before Charles returned to England, for his marriage to a Spanish princess. Charles had signed a treaty of alignment with Spain, which promised to assist him with retaking the throne in 1656, but the support never arrived.[60] Both Clarendon, Charles's first minister, and Henrietta Maria favored the alliance with Portugal instead. Through her name that evokes the conflict in which Portugal and England united to defeat Spain, then, *The Indian Queen*'s Amexia represents the newly formed political and marital bond between England and Portugal; in her protection of the new monarch and Amazonian valor, she recalls the other foreign queen at court and the mother of the restored monarch.

Through these connections between the virtuous Indian queen and the exotic queens in the English court, *The Indian Queen* celebrated the royal mixed marriage as well as the potential amalgamations enabled by new global flows.[61] Marriage to the Portuguese Catherine not only sealed an alliance between these two nations, but, at least in the optimistic celebrations of poets, it opened the gates to luxuries from the East Indies and enhanced production, by way of enslaved Africans in a trade initiated by the Portuguese, in the West Indies. Further, while many transatlantic Anglophone writers expressed anxieties over miscegenation throughout this period, the court audience in 1663 and the audiences for the public stage production would have understood that European empires had experimented with different policies for sexual regulation in contact zones. In their Asian exploits, the Portuguese government encouraged marriages between mariners and local women as part of their strategy for establishing a stronghold and for cultivating Portuguese/Asian global cities. The Spanish also, as these two plays dramatize, encouraged strategic mixed marriages in colonized territories.[62] In the broad context of European colonial projects, then, "miscegenation" could be the solution rather than the problem. Thus, the significance of the marriage between Cortez and the Indian princess Cydaria that ends *The Indian Emperour* may be more complicated than first appearances suggest. Both plays, as we will see, ultimately support mixing as part of English cosmopolitan aspirations and in honor of the "mixed marriage" between Charles II and his olive-skinned bride.

The Indian Queen begins with a crisis precipitated by the refusal of a mixed marriage: Montezuma, a young warrior of mysterious birth, has helped Ynca, the Peruvian king, to win three victories over his enemy, the Mexicans. In gratitude, the king offers him any requested reward. Montezuma asks for the hand of the king's daughter Orazia, which horrifies the king:

> Thou deserv'st to die.
> O thou great Author of our Progeny,
> Thou glorious Sun, dost thou not blush to shine,
> While such base Blood attempts to mix with thine!
> (1.1.47–49)

This opening attachment to purity by a misguided monarch sets in motion a series of events that lead to tragedy, for Ynca's refusal, clearly unjust in the context of the play, prompts Montezuma to change sides and fight for the Mexicans instead. Only his love for Orazia prevents him from exacting revenge on the Peruvian king. His Mexican friend Acacis attempts to calm his anger. Heir to the Mexican throne by way of his mother Zempoalla's usurpation, Acacis had become Montezuma's prisoner of war, but also, in the spirit of heroic romance, his honored friend.[63] This passionate alliance of affection across national lines provides a properly mixed alternative to the king's refusal: Montezuma liberates his prisoner and promises to fight now for Mexico. Acacis, however, reveals himself as *also* in love with Orazia. So instead of fighting for his own nation (Mexico), Acacis swears to stay and protect Ynca and his daughter. Montezuma then flees to Mexico to revive the defeated nation currently ruled by Zempoalla and her lover Traxalla. This play, presented for "their Majesties," opens with a scene that contemplates purity and mixing, with mixing associated with heroic honor and purity with foolhardiness.

Montezuma, as Nancy Maguire observes, parallels Charles II in his exile; the playwrights thus flatter the monarch as a warrior-king of romance.[64] Women can't resist him. The ending reveals Montezuma as the true heir to Mexico, child of the monarchs illegitimately overthrown by Zempoalla and Traxalla. The play, then, divides sovereignty schematically between legitimate and illegitimate rule, with Montezuma as the hidden true king, Amexia as the true queen mother, and Zempoalla, assisted by her lover, as the illegitimate ruler. As a commoner with aspirations to power, Traxalla recalls England's own "usurper" Cromwell. In a departure from many usurpation plays of this era, however, *The Indian Queen* offers a complicated figure at the center: a powerful and passionate queen. Zempoalla is, on the one hand, a threatening force of wickedness with Gertrude-like sexual guilt; on the other hand, she fights for the throne to ensure that her son Acacis can inherit it.[65] Unlike Gertrude, she does not cut her son off from the throne, but rather burdens him with the guilt of illegitimate inheritance in her excessive maternal enthusiasm. She undermines all of her aspirations, however, through her all-consuming passion for Montezuma. When he triumphs and finally unites with the Peruvian princess, Zempoalla declares that *"Orazia* has my love, and you my Throne: / And death *Acacis"* (5.1.289–90), saving, perhaps, her most intense emotional connection for the last. She disrupts the proper lineage, but she is not entirely unsympathetic.

Zempoalla is an early example—perhaps even a prototype—of the Restoration stage's commanding, passionate, and dangerous woman, inspired in part by the new opportunity to create roles for actresses and enabled by resulting experimentations with gender identity on stage.[66] She was originated by Anne

Marshall—the only cast member who has been identified—who would later create the role of the powerful courtesan Angellica Bianca in Aphra Behn's *The Rover*. Her character is consistent with a general feminization of illegitimate or usurping authority. Not only was the commonwealth rule associated for royalists with the breakdown of gendered hierarchies, but Cromwell's son and (briefly) heir Richard was satirized as "Queen Dick."[67] The fleshed-out character of Zempoalla, however, cannot be reduced to either royalist allegory or symbol of exotic otherness. Unlike several of the other characters in *The Indian Queen*, she has no historical analogue. In the context of the play, she is of course wrong to usurp her brother, replacing a legitimate male ruler with an illegitimate female one. Yet she is also a tragic figure, subject to an Oedipus-like vulnerability resulting from incomplete knowledge, similarly falling prey to incestuous desires.[68] Zempoalla's death by her own hand moves the other characters to pity. They would have spared her: "[T]here lies one," Montezuma concludes, "to whom all grief is due" (5.1.299). Zempoalla violates the orders of both gender and sovereignty. Her grip on power slips when sexual desire distracts her. Her incestuous passion contrasts sharply with the exogamous desires of Montezuma and Orazia, a union finally achieved with Zempoalla's death. The most dangerous passion in this play, then, is not an attraction to an "other," but to one too close to home.

Zempoalla's passion for Montezuma has another meaning as well, which comes to her in a dream. As she reports to Ismeron the conjuror in a masque-like scene,

> I dream'd before the Altar that I led
> A mighty Lion in a twisted thred;
> I shook to hold him in so slight a tie,
> Yet had not power to seek a remedy.
>
> (3.2.28–31)

A dove then appears, coos to the lion, and snips the thread, at which point the lion turns his rage upon the dreamer. As commanded, Ismeron conjures the God of Dreams to interpret, but he only reveals that Zempoalla would be happier if she did not know what the dream predicted.[69] He refuses to elaborate. Ismeron tries to distract the queen by conjuring some dancing aerial spirits, but the queen vows to burn all the altars unless her sorcerer gives her a potion that will move Montezuma to love her. The monarch in disguise, allegorized in dreams as a lion, has charms no woman can resist; Zempoalla desires him for reasons she cannot understand, which turn out to be the ineffable charisma of the true king, which she tragically misreads as ordinary sexual desire. Thus her tragic fall results from a key piece of obscured information and the monarch's own mysterious magnetism.

In the end, the dove rather than the lion usurps the usurper: Amexia, the rightful queen, returns with an army. One Indian queen, then, defeats another. The exiled mother rescues the exiled son, who learns his true identity in this closing scene. Inspired by the returning dove, all the characters pour their heartfelt forgiveness onto Zempoalla, who now understands the significance of her dream. In spite of the abundance of heroic action, the key political tension takes place between two women, uncannily doubled in each other: while one tragically kills herself, the other has saved her country from illegitimacy, incestuous passion, and continuing warfare. When Ynca gives his daughter Orazia to Montezuma, thus joining the two kingdoms, we assume that a third Indian queen will now rule.

Dryden and Howard, then, give their audience three Indian queens, two virtuous and one dangerous but ultimately forgivable. The tragic and overreaching figure of Zempoalla blocks, for a time, Montezuma's union with the rightful Indian queen, his mother, and the new Indian queen, his wife, who unites the two kingdoms through love and marriage. In a play written by royalists, the celebration of the marriage between England's true king and the new queen who brought the Indies seems clear. But what are we to make of the lustful, dangerous, and overreaching Queen Zempoalla, who uncannily doubles the other two? Alex Garganigo raises the intriguing possibility that, as an active, powerful, and sexually assertive women, Zempoalla has resonances with the powerful mistress of Charles II, Barbara Palmer, although he ultimately concludes that she is more of a "Cromwellian usurper than a Restoration courtesan."[70] Nevertheless, we might entertain the possibility that the other characters forgive her inappropriate desire out of recognition of the king's leonine magnificence, even as they honor the dovelike queen mother and the virtuous Orazia, whose marriage to Montezuma cements an alliance between two nations. While the play flatters the restored monarch, it also directs admiration toward the two living queens in the English court, one a grieving widow and the other a foreign princess. Zempoalla could reasonably be seen to figure this flamboyant threat to domestic happiness who nevertheless must be forgiven, for what woman could control herself in the face of such manly perfection?

But the extraordinary Zempoalla also exceeds this reading. While the play celebrates the union of Charles II and Catherine as well as the cultural and military bond between England and Portugal, she in her outsized magnificence also evokes the unpredictability of this alliance, with its promise of ever-expanding global reach. She is the exotic danger, unexpectedly aroused. Zempoalla cannot be contained even by her demise, for she literally haunts the sequel, rising as a ghost to claim her Montezuma and demanding that her daughters avenge her death. She is an uncontrollable and enigmatic force, driven by rapacious desire, who respects neither the codes of the heroic nor the restriction of feminine honor. The play links Zempoalla to Catherine not by any personal similarities, but through the unpredictable consequences of England's alliance with Portugal. We have noted Dryden's debt to William Davenant's *Cruelty of the Spaniards in Peru* for inspiration, and while no one wrote a play called *The Cruelty of the Portuguese in India and/or Brazil*, conflicted feelings over this new English alignment with Iberian conquistadors become visible through the indomitable Zempoalla.[71] Montezuma will marry the good Indian queen Orazia, but the bad Indian queen, who similarly lusts after the rightful monarch, dies for him and haunts the sequel. Zempoalla represents the colonized rather than the Spanish colonists, a point to which I will return, but she also embodies the volatility of this royal alignment and possibly of the queen herself. Audience members may have felt encouraged to distance themselves from the Spanish "other," as Ayanna Thompson has argued, but it would be hard to avoid the fact that they had at the same time allied themselves with an Iberian nation with a highly developed interest in war capitalism and that had functioned until rather recently (1640) as part of the Spanish Empire.

The full significance of Zempoalla as both victim and the bad fairy of imperialism who shows up on the wedding day could only be fully realized in performance. As John Evelyn observed, with this play the King's Theatre brought the lavish spectacle of the masque to the public commercial stage for the first time. He called it "a tragedy well written, so beautiful with rich scenes as the like had never ben seene here, as happly (except rarely any where else) on a mercenarie theatre."[72] Even in the public theater Evelyn associates the play with its court performances; the lavishness of the production was unusual for the "mercenarie" theater but presumably not for Whitehall. Anne Marshall in the role of Zempoalla, we are told by Aphra Behn, wore an authentic native costume in the play's 1668 revival, although from the east rather than the west coast of South America: "We trade for Feathers [with the native Surinamese], which they order into all Shapes, make themselves little short Habits of 'em, and glorious Wreaths for their Heads, Necks, Arms and Legs, whose Tinctures are unconceivable. I had a Set of these presented to me, and I gave 'em to the King's Theatre, and it was the dress of the *Indian Queen*, infinitely admir'd by Persons of Quality."[73] For the court production, the Master of the Great Wardrobe spent £40 on silk.[74]

Other sources suggest that the visual delights, and the feathers in particular, helped to draw in the rest of the crowd as well.[75]

That this work later appeared as an opera further suggests its initial similarity to the court masque. Music and dancing punctuate the play: it opens with a "soft Air" before the prologue. Act 3, a key visual moment in Restoration plays because the footmen and servants waiting outside then shuffled into the galleries, opens with a celebration of the feathered Zempoalla's "Triumph":

> Zempoalla *appears seated upon her Slaves in Triumph, attended by* Traxalla; *and the* Indians *as to celebrate the Victory, advance in a warlike Dance.*

I wish to pause for a moment on this scene, the visual peak of a stunning production, in a tableau that seems to return us to the controversy over Catherine's statue in Queens. Both the prospect of a gigantic sculpture at Hunter's Point in 2011 and an Indian queen riding on the backs of slaves in 1664 focused ambivalence over the business of the Company of Royal Adventurers in Africa on this mysterious royal figure and her marriage to the restored English monarch. The Portuguese royal family invested great significance in their exploits in African coast, which, as noted, they celebrated in their parade honoring Catherine's marriage "[w]ith a magnificence matched only by its lack of subtlety."[76] The pageant "began with figures of two Ethiopian kings on horseback" wearing tight-fitting black taffeta so as to appear nude, but ornamented with crowns, pearls and feathers. Following these were real Ethiopians who were nude, ornamented, and carrying bows and arrows. They were "followed by ten very beautiful black women" pulling the figure of Fame.[77] The triumphant parade in *The Indian Queen* thus echoes Portugal's own celebration of its princess, its legacy, and its future. While we don't know what these stage slaves who lifted Zempoalla looked like or even how performance communicated their enslaved status (they have no lines, but are identified as slaves in the stage directions), the association between the Queen from a slave-trading nation and the stage Indian queen perched on the backs of slaves loomed ominously, and perhaps precariously, over English spectators.

Nowhere is the Indian queen more Portuguese than in this scene. But this moment of triumph for Zempoalla is also her downfall, for in the midst of this celebration, her son enters with his prisoner, Montezuma, whom she later saves from Traxalla's sword for reasons that she does not yet understand. Zempoalla, Amexia, and Orazia each in different ways evoke the queen who brought the Indies. They all love Montezuma. Zempoalla's violence, lack of honor, garish displays of power, and unabashed lust, however, suggest the dread with which some people may have viewed this alliance and its implications. Catherine was not a popular queen and attracted hostility for her Catholicism and her failure to produce a royal heir. The Duke of Buckingham would even suggest that she be spirited away to an American colony, freeing the king to marry a fertile Protestant, and in a sense bringing Dryden's mythologizing of this match full circle by exporting England's queen to the New World.[78] At this early moment in Catherine's reign, *The Indian Queen* performs looming anxieties over Stuart cosmopolitan alliances that would later become explosive, and that Dryden would go on to explore most immediately with *The Indian Emperour*.

The Indian Emperour

In his sequel to *The Indian Queen*, Dryden adds European characters and dramatizes the brutal torture and death of the monarch whose restoration he and Howard had celebrated in the earlier play. *The Indian Emperour* echoes the anti-Spanish sentiment in Davenant's *The Cruelty of the Spaniards in Peru*, in which English mariners align with the Indians against the Spanish. But by only including Spanish and Indian characters, Dryden complicates loyalties for an English audience. While Ayanna Thompson makes a good point in noting that English audiences would have seen Spanish characters as different from themselves, *The Indian Emperour* does not entirely exculpate English spectators by displacing the questionable morality of imperial conquest onto an alien Iberian race: the sequel, after all, follows a play that celebrates an English/Iberian union. (Contemporary audiences would not have elided Spain and Portugal, but they also would have known that the Braganza dynasty had only come to rule Portugal independently in 1640. This led to a war with Spain that ended only in 1668, three years after the play opened.) The sequel moves beyond, but is still shaped by, the marriage that brought the Indies. *The Indian Emperour* develops *The Indian Queen*'s vision of a cosmopolitanism founded in virtue, apparent in the friendship between Montezuma and Acacis, in which honorable characters bond across national boundaries and, as a result, conflict with those of their own nations.[79] One popular figure for this cosmopolitan ideal becomes the mixed marriage, in which amalgamation provides a flicker of hope in the misery of imperial chaos. Drawn from the aristocratic ideology of romance, mixed-marriage plots at the same time unfold in the context of persisting skepticism toward Stuart absolutism.

Dryden insisted that both readers and audiences noted the continuity between these two plays. In performance, this would have been visually obvious, as the production of the second play used the same sets as the first.[80] The author additionally explained the relationship between the two works in a preface, and he might even have handed out copies of this explanation at performances.[81] In *The Indian Emperour*, twenty years have passed. Zempoalla has left three children behind: Almeria, Alibech, and Orbellan, all new characters. The princess Orazia has died, leaving Montezuma, now emperor, with three grown children, Cydaria, Odmar, and Guyomar. The conquistadors arrive and offer peace on the condition that the Indians relinquish their gold and convert to Catholicism, but the Spanish leader Cortez questions the justice of these royal orders.[82] During these "negotiations," Cortez falls in love with Montezuma's daughter, Cydaria; he later befriends her noble brother, Guyomar, thus further complicating his mission. Other alliances form across the Indian/Spanish boundary as well: Odmar joins conquistadors Pizarro and Vasquez, who promise him the hand of Alibech, whom he has lost to his brother Guyomar. In the end, the Spanish defeat Montezuma, but Cortez wants to marry Cydaria and offers to share power with the noble Guyomar, who declines and heads for the hills. Pepys saw this play at least three times; twice he complained that Nell Gwynn, known best for her comic performances, could not handle the gravity of the role of Cydaria. His comment on November 11, 1667 that the play was "good, but not so good as people cry it up" nevertheless points to its popular and critical success. Pepys also records a performance at court in which the Duke of Monmouth acted (January 14, 1668).[83] Amateur performances were rare at court during the Restoration, so the play must have made a particularly strong impression on the royal family.[84]

The Indian Emperour celebrates two mixed marriages: one between Alibech, a daughter of Zempoalla, and Guyomar, the heir to Montezuma; the other between Montezuma's daughter Cydaria and the Spanish Cortez. While most of the Spaniards behave dishonorably and fancy themselves civilized people among savages, Dryden's Cortez is a relativist: "Wild and untaught are Terms which we alone / Invent, for fashions differing from our own" (1.1.11–14). In seeking the "golden Ore" and "silver shower" reserved for the "bravest Nation," the Spanish align themselves, in a rough approximation of the historical Cortez's strategies, with the Traxallans to conquer Montezuma. This sequel gives audiences a Montezuma both darker and more vulnerable than the one they saw in *The Indian Queen*: the opening infamously depicts the sacrifice of five hundred captured enemies in honor of the emperor's birthday. In the earlier play, human sacrifice had been mostly associated with the usurping Zempoalla and her lover Traxalla. Acacis, Zempoalla's son and the loyal friend to Montezuma, objects to the practice:

> Hold, hold, such sacrifices cannot be,
> Devotion's, but a solemn cruelty:
> How can the Gods delight in human blood?
> Think um not cruel; if you think um good.
> In vain we ask that mercy which they want,
> And hope that pitty which they hate to grant.
>
> (5.1.92–97)

But the bloodshed proceeds.

While in the first play Montezuma loved the Peruvian princess, in the sequel he has ignobly fallen in love with the unscrupulous Almeria, daughter of Zempoalla, who has vowed to avenge her mother's death. Dryden creates two other love triangles: Guyomar and Odmar both love Alibech (another, more tractable daughter of Zempoalla), while Orbellan (Zempoalla's son) and Cortez both love Montezuma's daughter Cydaria. Faced with the Spanish invasion, Montezuma consults a high priest to conjure some spirits who will reveal the fate of his empire. One spirit forecasts the Spanish conquest, but another predicts that Montezuma will have one chance to save himself. Then the ghost of Queen Zempoalla appears, revealing to Montezuma that those denied love in life may fulfill their desires in death. She waits for him in the other world, she announces, with open arms. While in the first play Montezuma triumphs, in the sequel the tragedy belongs to him as events move inexorably toward his torture by the Spanish, his suicide, and the fall of his empire.

The play depicts this brutality, but does not celebrate it. It does, however, celebrate one possible outcome of imperial reach: the particular kind of mixing that can result. The transcultural desire between Cydaria and Cortez is supported by multiple and shifting connections between individuals from different nations. Buckingham satirizes this kind of plot, for which Dryden became notorious, in *The Rehearsal* with characters who suddenly change sides for no apparent reason. But what Buckingham satirizes as random changes of loyalty are actually in Dryden a sorting of characters along the lines of heroic cosmopolitanism, suggesting that noble souls from any culture have more in common with each other than with lesser beings from their own land. In *The Indian Emperour*, Guyomar fights a losing battle to save his father, leading to his capture by the Spaniards. Cortez, however, sets Guyomar free out of respect for his honorable deportment in battle, out of the sympathy that men should show for other men in love, and for the sake of his sister Cydaria, thus cementing a friendship between the two men. Thus when Almeria hatches a plot to have her brother Orbellan sneak into the Spanish camp and kill Cortez in his sleep, Guyomar, after some soul-searching, saves his new Spanish friend by warning him of the plot. Cortez catches Orbellan, but spares him.[85] Almeria, however, does not believe that this obligation extends to conquerors. She sneaks into Cortez's prison cell with a dagger, but on first viewing the noble Spaniard she falls in love and cannot destroy him. Almeria's desire across enemy lines echoes the tragedy of her mother Zempoalla, who similarly loved and spared Montezuma in *The Indian Queen*, to her own detriment. Guyomar argues for peace and for preserving Cortez; through the twists and turns of the plot, these characters function as a kind of passionate couple themselves, each rushing to the defense of the other and placing their bromance over nation. Almeria thinks Guyomar has betrayed his people, but the prince places a higher priority on his personal bond with Cortez. Dryden organizes *The Indian Emperour* around not just warring sides, but also outsized individuals on each side with a connection to each other and in tension with their compatriots. This model draws from, but is not limited to aristocratic ideology. Cortez does not in any obvious way belong to a higher class than his ignoble compatriots. Through its fictionalized Cortez, *The Indian Emperour* dramatizes the ethical dilemma of a virtuous soul torn between obedience to a monarch and instructions to oppress and slaughter with limited justification.[86] The play, in other words, calls on its audience to think about what they as a nation are getting into. The ghost of Zempoalla, the ominous side of the royal marriage, will not rest.

The marriage of Cydaria and Cortez, a heroic European and an exotic princess, romanticizes imperialism and even celebrates the English royal "mixed marriage." But to stop there would be to overlook critical undercurrents in the play. Montezuma had evoked Charles II in *The Indian Queen*; here, however, he sacrifices humans, becomes romantically obsessed with a woman who manipulates him, and falters militarily. He is tortured by a foreign power that, interestingly enough, also attempts to force him to convert to Catholicism. With the author's insistence that the audience remember *The Indian Queen*, then, they could not fail to notice persisting parallels between Charles II and Montezuma that suggest the English monarch's cruelty, authoritarianism, and vulnerability. Not only does *The Indian Emperour* raise concerns about the violence, sexual distractibility, and Catholic leanings of the restored monarch, but it also questions the wisdom and morality of imperial ambitions in ways that are not entirely displaced onto the Spanish. Almeria's cry to destroy Cortez before it is too late is not just rash feminine aggression but prophetic: this was, as the spirit had earlier informed Montezuma, the single opportunity to prevent their destruction.

While the sequel ends with the Spanish/European triumph, native resistance claims some attention, mostly by way of the daughters of Zempoalla. This character, as noted, represents not only the bad Indian queen in contrast with the good ones, but in the second play comes to embody the haunting spirit of the destroyed native peoples. In *On Lingering and Being Last*, Jonathan Elmer suggests that the racialized sovereigns in Aphra Behn's New World writing do not provide generic closure with their deaths, but "linger." They are similar to Tarquin in Behn's novella *The Fair Jilt*: "deterritorialized, a lingering remnant, neither living nor dead, neither legitimate nor clearly illegitimate, neither purely body nor clearly abstractable."[87] Although Elmer considers *The Indian Emperour* a more conventional, generically bound work with the marriage of Cydaria and Cortez,[88] there is a case to be made that Zempoalla also lingers. While she does not live to see the Spanish invasion, her spirit persists through her daughters, who work in different ways for Indigenous sovereignty and survival, and of course literally when her ghost rises. Almeria attempts to avenge her mother's death by manipulating Montezuma; she believes that Cortez should be stabbed in the heart to prevent this invading force from subjugating them. Alibech, the other daughter, also resists, but in a softer way. Loved by two men, she promises her hand to the one who will "set [her] country free." She challenges Cortez, characterizing the Spanish negotiation as transparent aggression:

> ALIB[ECH]. Injurious strength would rapine still excuse,
> By off'ring terms the weaker must refuse;
> And such as these your hard conditions are,
> You threaten Peace, and you invite a War.
> CORT[EZ]. If for my self to Conquer here I came,
> You might perhaps my actions justly blame.
> Now I am sent, and am not to dispute
> My Princes orders, but to execute.
> ALIB[ECH]. He who his Prince so blindly does obey,
> To keep his Faith his Vertue throws away.
>
> (2.2.20–29)

She also makes a similar accusation to Guyomar when she later tries to persuade him to make peace with the Spanish against the wishes of Montezuma in order to save their people from starvation. Even though Dryden ethnocentrically projects European conceptions of monarchy onto a non-European

culture, the play leaves viewers with a sense of the violation of native sovereignty that appalls Cortez. When Vasquez reads the *requirimiento* from the
King of Spain, Cortez at that moment is falling in love with Cydaria. Thus
Cortez and Vasquez model two separate codes of conduct: one of aggression that offers peace only, as Alibech points out, through total surrender,
and another that holds out the possibility of a potentially explosive mixture
formed by the attraction of noble figures to each other across national divisions. Restoration audience members had as their royalty a different kind
of mixed marriage—one that offered the potential for new kinds of pleasures and also brutal violence in remote locations. The result of this Anglo-
Portuguese union remained a source of unease, and Dryden probed this
anxiety in these plays. *The Indian Emperour* begins with a bloodbath in which
an emperor ghosted by Charles II takes pleasure in the spectacle of five hundred enemies thrown into a volcano. The play ends with this same monarch's
torture and suicide. In the middle, a spurned Indian queen warns him about
his downfall, and her daughters desperately try to save their native land from
brutal, chaotic, and ignoble invaders from across the sea.

Cosmopolitanism (Un)Settled: Tangier, and a Barren Queen

Dryden mercilessly satirized Elkanah Settle's successful *Empress of Morocco*
(1673), but this rival play clearly echoes *The Indian Queen* and *The Indian
Emperour* in its mixed marriages and powerful women.[89] Settle raises the
ghost of Zempoalla again in his antiheroine Laula, but with escalated cruelty. Laula channels Dryden's Indian queen through her Amazonian power,
but she also, like Zempoalla, conjures England's own foreign queen—in this
case particularly because the former Portuguese outpost of Tangier came to
England as part of Catherine's dowry. In setting his heroic play in Morocco,
Settle flattered the royal couple's doomed ambition to maintain an English
outpost in the Mediterranean. The English would prove unable to defend it.
Tangier was, as Tristan Stein has argued, crucial to the imperial ambitions
of Charles II and his administration, but a key failure, Linda Colley shows,
in the "dream of global supremacy."[90] In this vision, an outpost in Tangier
would have given England control of the Mediterranean and secured them
access to the coast of Africa. Yet the colony rapidly lost money and support
both in London and Morocco. Charles lost an estimated £70,000 each year
to the project as his soldiers skirmished with Moroccan forces and worked
on constructing a mole to provide a safe harbor for trade and military rein-
forcement. According to historian E. M. Routh, this was the most ambitious

engineering project by the English to date.[91] When the English finally abandoned Tangier, they destroyed the mole so no other nation would benefit from this effort. Over the course of the project, colonists and laborers received insufficient food and supplies.[92] Some men deserted to Spain; others talked of joining the Moors. One John Davis caused a stir by announcing that "kings were but men as well as other men, and that the king was but one man and the people of England 1,900,000 and of them 1,899,000 were of his own opinion."[93] Support for Tangier remained fragile at home.[94]

The Tangier project never lost its close association with Catherine. In 1684, its military force was endowed with the title of "The Queen's Regiment."[95] Catherine took particular care to protect the Catholic churches established in that colony by the Portuguese. Portuguese Dominicans at Tangier, according to Routh, "gave a good deal of trouble to successive Governors. Their chief grievance lay in the desecration of several of the churches and chapels which had been maintained by the Portuguese, and which were used for quarters or storehouses by the English. A petition for the restitution of these churches found a sympathetic listener in Queen Catherine," who took personal care to see them supported.[96] She regarded the abandonment of Tangier with "keen disfavor . . . Catherine never forgot that Tangier was her own gift to England."[97]

Both the colony and the queen became increasingly controversial as the former drained the national coffers and the latter failed to produce an heir. The Earl of Clarendon was accused of encouraging the match between Charles and Catherine because he knew that she was barren, thus ensuring that James, who was married to Clarendon's daughter, would succeed Charles as king. One day, Clarendon found a gibbet painted on his gate, with the following verse:

> Three sights to be seen,
> Dunkirke, Tangier and a barren Queene.[98]

During the Popish Plot (1678–1681), Anglican priest Titus Oates accused Catherine of attempting to poison Charles. Buckingham, as mentioned, proposed spiriting Catherine away to one of the North American colonies so that Charles could marry a fertile Protestant bride. Staged before the Popish Plot but after the fall of Clarendon and a decade of royal infertility, Settle's play about dynastic conflict in Morocco could not have avoided casting attention on the increasingly suspect Portuguese queen consort. In an otherwise excellent discussion, Susan Iwanisziw insists that Settle's Morocco plays have nothing to do with Morocco but instead theatricalize Stuart politics.[99] By recognizing the overlooked importance of Catherine, however, we can see how explorations of royal authority could at the same time be explorations of imperialism. Unlike in England's imperial relations with India, in Tangier the English monarchy did not turn administration over to a semi-independent company, but instead retained royal control. Of all of England's imperial projects in this period, Tangier had the most intimate connection to Catherine.

The Empress of Morocco does not take place in Tangier or dramatize England's colonizing efforts; like *The Indian Queen*, the play instead explores violent conflicts between different local rulers in a region of strategic interest. Before the action begins, Muly Labas, the son of the Emperor of Morocco, had visited the neighboring court of Tassaletta and fallen in love with Morena, who is forbidden by her father to marry him because of tensions between the two nations. The opening scene finds Morena and Muly Labas both imprisoned by the emperor of Morocco and condemned to death for their love. The empress Laula, however, frees the young couple with the news that the emperor is dead and Muly Labas has inherited the throne. But we soon find out that that Laula has poisoned her husband, seeking power for herself and her lover Crimalhaz. The plotting couple must first manipulate Muly Labas into destroying the other contender, Muly Hamet, a prince of royal blood, general of the emperor's army, and lover of Mariamne, the empress's daughter, before they can take the throne themselves. Muly Hamet returns from the wars to an elaborate celebration. Yet in the next scene, he accidently discovers the illicit affair between Laula and Crimalhaz, encountering them asleep together. He takes Crimalhaz's sword to document his discovery. Crimalhaz, however, manages to persuade Muly Labas that Muly Hamet had come to the chamber to rape the empress. Thus the virtuous Muly Hamet is banished. Laula and Crimalhaz then plot to kill Muly Labas. For this, the empress sets an elaborate trap that depends on her own production of a court masque about the story of Orpheus and Eurydice. She persuades Morena to play the leading female role, but then warns her that Crimalhaz (in the role of Orpheus) plans to kidnap and rape her, in character, in the masque. The threat will be real and she must kill him to prevent this violation. Morena gratefully follows the guidance of the empress; Laula, however, deviously replaces Crimalhaz in the masque with Morena's beloved husband and her own son, Muly Labas. As instructed, Morena stabs Orpheus. Muly Labas dies in confusion without ever knowing that his wife has been tricked. The empress accuses Morena of murder, and the young queen goes mad. Crimalhaz takes the throne. In gaining this ultimate prize, he reveals his desire for Morena, betraying Laula by condemning her for her son's murder. Laula kills Morena, then herself. In the midst of this chaos, Muly Hamet returns with Tassaletta to defeat Crimalhaz and claim the throne.

The Empress of Morocco was lavishly produced; it was performed twice at court and many times at the King's Theatre. One sign of both the play's success and its visual impact is a printed edition with detailed illustrations. Not only do the plates attest to the care and artistry of the production, but they also suggest a cultural significance granted to few contemporary dramatic texts. Settle most likely gleaned the outlines of the plot from Lancelot Addison's West Barbary, or, A Short Narrative on the Revolutions of the Kingdoms of Fez and Morocco, published in 1671. Addison, the father of Joseph, had recently returned from Tangier, where he had served as chaplain to the garrison. The story from West Barbary that Settle chose was significant because it recounts the eventual rise to power of Er Rasheed II (Tassaletta in the play), which, according to Addison's account, was enabled by internal conflicts. Er Rasheed competed with Abd Allah Ghailan—who was known to the English as "Gayland" and who appears in Settle's later play The Heir of Morocco—for supremacy in Morocco.[100]

Settle's powerful, sexually desiring empress Laula echoes, as noted, Dryden's powerful, sexually desiring Zempoalla and her powerful, sexually desiring daughter in The Indian Emperour. Like The Indian Queen, The Empress of Morocco also includes a sympathetic "mixed marriage" plot: the lovers Muly Labas and Morena are from warring nations. Both playwrights give their powerful empress a plotting, untrustworthy lover with whom she conspires to kill the rightful king; in both cases the queens die at their own hands. The Empress of Morocco, then, repeats some of the major plot lines of The Indian Emperour, but in a different region of imperial interest. Given these significant parallels, the differences are worth noting as well. While Dryden's queen murders her brother in order to ascend the throne, she does so in part to secure the place of her son Acacis in the line of succession. In Settle's play, however, Laula murders her husband and plots not her son's elevation, but his death. The killing is a masterpiece of theatrical cruelty that uses the court masque as an opportunity to trick a loving wife into murder. Both plays and their sequels include scenes of grotesque sadism, but Settle raises the stakes of physical violence, particularly at the play's end, when "the Scene opens, and Crimalhaz appears cast down on the Gaunches, being hung on a Wall set with spikes of Iron."[101] An accompanying illustration shows three nude male figures draped luridly over the beams of some kind of structure for torture, two upside-down and the third on a center diagonal cross-beam, head down, with one leg on the beam and other dangling. On the floor we see several spikes and some bones and pieces of flesh, presumably from previous torture victims (figure 3.6). In this closing scene, one loyal courtier surveys the carnage and, in an ambiguous conclusion, guides us to "See the reward of Treason; Death's the thing / Distinguishes th' Usurper from the king" (70). Is the courtier suggesting that all usurpers will die horribly, or that the contender left alive will take the throne?

This final declaration rather unambiguously ties the usurpation in the play to the usurpation of the Stuarts. Susan Iwanisziw suggests astutely that through this graphic violence, Settle registers his resistance to the brutality

FIGURE 3.6   From Elkanah Settle, *The Empress of Morocco* (London: Printed for William Cademan, 1673). Used by permission of the Folger Shakespeare Library.

of the Stuarts to their internal enemies. Even though the members of the court embraced *The Empress*, no doubt enjoying the spectacle of mangled usurpers, monarchy itself does not play well here overall. An even stronger sign of the playwright's ambivalence, which would later blossom into full-blown Whig resistance, can perhaps be found in the play's depiction of female royalty. In *The Indian Queen* and *The Indian Emperour*, Dryden creates powerful women faced with momentous decisions on which the fates of their nations hang. Zempoalla, however, cannot resist the pull toward Montezuma, a vulnerability that leads to her downfall. Her death does not lead to celebratory triumph but becomes part of the lingering melancholy of the fall of native empires. The abandoned queen haunts the sequel, plaintively longing from beyond the grave.

With Laula, however, Settle creates a bloodthirsty monster with no regrets. In their *Notes and Observations on the Empress of Morocco*, Dryden and his co-conspirators single out this character for ridicule: *"But of all Women, the Lord Bless us from his Laula: no body can be safe from her; she is so naturally mischievous, that she kills without the least occasion, for the mere Letchery of Bloodshed."*[102] While she is not entirely unmotivated, she nevertheless, as these critics suggest, commits a considerable amount of gratuitous violence. First she kills her husband out of ambition for herself and her lover; then she kills her son, allowing him to believe that his beloved wife has betrayed him; finally, when the usurper Crimalhaz decides he loves Morena, she strangles the young queen as well. She blithely participates in the killing of an innocent bystander to hide her affair with Crimalhaz. Settle, then, creates in Laula a figure considerably more threatening than Zempoalla, but who also echoes the Portuguese bride and the imperial projects opened up by the royal marriage. Through the brutality of the exotic queen on stage who conjures the exotic queen in Whitehall, *The Empress* captures ambivalence toward Stuart ambitions. The mixed marriage of Muly Labas and Morena ends in the horrific deaths of both, engineered by the queen who poisoned the king, a plot twist that anticipates suspicions that Catherine plotted to poison Charles. While Settle supported the Stuarts when he wrote this play and would only later turn against them with strident anti-Catholic propaganda, his suspicions of England's Catholic queen is palpable in *The Empress of Morocco*. Both Catherine and the recently deceased Catholic Queen Mother Henrietta Maria presided over court masques, the Empress of Morocco's most nefarious instruments of death.

But what most closely ties *The Empress of Morocco* and its unsuccessful sequel, *The Heir of Morocco*, to Catherine of Braganza is North Africa itself. As noted, the associations of Tangier with Catherine did not diminish in the Restoration. The two Morocco plays describe the dynasties that had the most impact on Britain's colonial project in the region; Morena, we recall, is the daughter of Tassaletta; in the second play, we meet Gayland. Tangier was a mixed community, populated by English, Portuguese, and other Europeans as well as Moors and a significant number of Jews.[103] The English colonists even created for their own entertainment a space for theatrical performances right on the mole. They performed, among other plays, Dryden's *Indian Queen*, perhaps in honor of the queen who brought the Indies. Or possibly they performed it in recognition of the Native Americans sold into slavery by colonists in the wake of King Phillip's War, and who ended up in Tangier. For the construction of the mole the English relied on slave labor, with a mix of enslaved Africans and, unusually, enslaved Native Americans forcibly transported across the Atlantic for this purpose.[104] Thus English soldiers enacted the brutal devastation of one Native American community atop a structure built, in part, by captured and enslaved members of another.

At one level, *The Empress of Morocco* highlights English ambitions in the Mediterranean, gratifying the court before which it was performed. The play represents Moroccans as engaged in treacherous conflicts over sovereignty, with the primary royal lineage imploding through the queen's maniacal grasping for power. While certainly Settle depicts some characters as honorable and heroic, the play implies that political instability in North Africa could open up an opportunity for the English. Further, its lavishly illustrated publication at a time of tight control over the presses, paired with the work's performance at court, indicate that the intended flattery to imperial ambitions did not pass without notice. The play's action punishes the usurper with spectacular violence, making way for the crown to fall on the head of an exiled, unjustly punished prince who returns to power in part through an alliance with a neighboring empire. As in *The Indian Queen*, unwarranted prejudice against a mixed marriage sets the plot in motion and the virtuous daughter of the defeated female monarch (Mariamne) inherits the throne, lending legitimacy to the reconstituted royal family. We can read this drama, then, as confirming aristocratic ideology,[105] the Stuart right by lineage, and even the desirability of an alliance with France, suggested by the assistance of the neighboring emperor who sheltered the unjustly exiled prince. The play makes no explicit mention of Tangier and, as Dryden and his friends delighted in pointing out, makes several geographical errors about Morocco. And yet, Settle's errors might be revealing. In his scathing *Notes and Observations on the Empress of Morocco*, Dryden notes that the second act of Settle's play "begins with the description of a great Fleet coming up a River, and Sailing to *Morocco*, an in-land City, where Ships were never seen."[106] This arrival is presented by a "large Prospect" (8), presumably the set that

Settle reproduces in the illustrated edition of the play, drawn by William Dolle (figure 3.7). Settle *could* have made a mistake, but the image seems quite clearly to evoke the mole in Tangier: the ships are visible, but so is the protective port into which they sail. The engraving even features a boatful of men rowing toward shore, protected by this elaborate structure. Settle

FIGURE 3.7   From Elkanah Settle, *The Empress of Morocco* (London: Printed for William Cademan, 1673). Used by permission of the Folger Shakespeare Library.

gleaned parts of the narrative from Addison's *West Barbary*, although in the dedication to Henry Howard, who served as ambassador to Morocco in 1669, he reports that he owes the story *"to your Hands, and your honourable Embassy into* Africa."[107] If the play's representation of warring empires in North Africa suggests an opportunity, though, this instability also forebodes danger. Most saliently for current purposes, the play offers a darker—in both senses—view of Britain's own exotic queen, the royal mixed marriage, and the imperial ambitions intended to be fed by it. Zempoalla's desire for Montezuma, as argued, proposes the unmistakable charm of royal blood. None of the monarchs in Settle, however, radiate this charm. Dryden objected to the illogic of Laula's action: she has poisoned her husband while her son and Morena languish in prison. If she simply wanted the throne, why not just leave them there? Releasing them, however, provides the drawn-out pleasure of cruel torment. Settle's exotic queen is a sadistic force of chaos with no redeeming Zempoalla-like pathos.

The *Empress of Morocco* most saliently engages Stuart ambitions for control of the Mediterranean, but it addresses their wish to control the African coast as well. In this metatheatrical play, there are two scenes of highly choreographed performance, both illustrated in the printed edition. In the first, the court celebrates the return of Muly Hamet, who has defeated the enemy but spared the life of Tassaletta for Morena's sake. The printed version pictures a huge palm tree at the center, which, according to the stage directions, has been wheeled in by Moors "in several habits." These Moors perform a dance and a Moorish priest and two Moorish women sing a song, "the Chorus of it being performed by all the Moors" (13). The dancers occupy the foreground. In the printed illustration of the performance, the celebrating royal spectators in the back row are clearly played by white actors whose Moorishness is only indicated by their capacious turbans, visually echoed by the spreading palm (figure 3.8).

Unlike these actors, however, the dancers have black skin. It is possible that these were white performers with black makeup spread not just on their faces but on their exposed arms and legs as well. It also seems possible, however, that the dances were performed by enslaved people from the English court— the same young Africans that one sees in so many court paintings—for if the dancers were wearing black makeup, then why wouldn't the royalty from the same region have similarly shaded skin? The contrast between the black and white figures not only suggests the possibility of African performers on the Restoration stage, but also ties this narrative about conflict in Morocco to the court in the audience. The Moors' song celebrates loyalty to the king:

No Musick like that which Loyalty sings,
A Consort of Hearts at the Crowning of Kings:

There's no such delightful and ravishing Strain,
As the Ecchoes and Shouts of Long Live and Reign.

(13)

The Moorish dancers celebrate Muly Labas and the victory of Muly Hamet over Tassaletta. The specter of these black figures dancing before white royalty, however, also proposes the African loyalty to Charles II and the Queen

FIGURE 3.8 From Elkanah Settle, *The Empress of Morocco* (London: Printed for William Cademan, 1673). Used by permission of the Folger Shakespeare Library.

whose own nation celebrated her marriage with a parade of African dancers. This performance brings the Atlantic circuit full circle by linking the slaves at court, the Atlantic slave trade, and the English fort in Tangier, all honoring Charles and Catherine.

This joyful celebration of royal dominion over dark bodies in all three locations, however, metatheatrically goes to Hell. The next illustration takes place in the underworld in a masque within the play in which Muly Labas in the role of Orpheus seeks Morena as Eurydice (figure 3.9). A large tower rather than a palm tree dominates the center; smoke and devils, rather than branches, shoot out from it. As in the earlier scene, well-dressed figures line up near the back of the stage, while dark figures fill the forestage. In this case, however, the dark figures are devils, complete with wings and horns. Their color seems like the effect of shadowing rather than skin color (whether natural or makeup); nevertheless, the resonance is unmistakable. Spectators see European bodies surrounded by darker bodies, who now menace rather than entertain, perhaps suggesting the explosive precariousness of such colonial projects, both in Tangier and in other outposts such as Jamaica.

So while it is possible to read this play as an allegory for legitimate monarchy with faux-Moroccan figures standing in for English ones, it is also possible that performance visualized the descent of English bodies into the darkness of a hellish Tangier that would destroy them. The threats to the English colony included the powerful Tassaletta, whose nonappearance perhaps allowed audiences to imagine him as a Moor like the other dark bodies on stage rather than as an English actor in a turban. In 1664, the Scottish Catholic governor of Tangier, the Earl of Teviot, appointed by Charles II two years before, was killed along with hundreds of English troops outside the fort. English accounts of this massacre, particularly in the numerous elegies for Teviot published in the 1660s, point to the vulnerability of the project, as Adam R. Beach has shown.[108] In an alternative reading made available through performance, we see Charles's already-unpopular imperial project pushed over the edge by a reckless, exotic, and powerful female monarch, as well as ominous dark figures, led by an unseen but powerful Moroccan about to reclaim his empire from invaders.

The image of Catherine of Braganza, then, is threaded throughout colonial discourse in multiple performances of heroic exoticism in the Restoration. Little has been written in English-language scholarship about Catherine herself: We know much more, and have thought much more, about the glamorous mistresses of Charles II than about his wife, beyond her fruitlessness.[109] The marriage between Charles and Catherine, however, provided a crucial opportunity for English imperial ambitions, and

FIGURE 3.9   From Elkanah Settle, *The Empress of Morocco* (London: Printed for William Cademan, 1673). Used by permission of the Folger Shakespeare Library.

Restoration theater points to an awareness of, and profound ambivalence toward her role in this national transformation. The handful of nonscholarly biographies of Catherine describe her as painfully shy and unable to compete with the resplendent women of the Restoration court. While theatrical Indian queens invoke her symbolically as the queen who brought the Indies, there is reason to believe that we may have underestimated her and her influence. According to Edward Corp, "Catherine made a significant contribution to the development of the cosmopolitan character of the English court in the late seventeenth century" through her patronage of Italian art and music.[110] After Charles II died, Catherine remained in England, but eventually returned to Portugal in 1704, where she ruled as regent. The colony of Tangier may have failed, but another one of her gifts—Bombay—shaped global history for centuries to come, as did the increased access to slave trading forts specified in her marriage treaty, some of the consequences of which I will explore in the next chapter.

❦ CHAPTER 4

Restoration Legacies

Tragic Monarchs, Exotic and Enslaved

The genre of heroic drama lost momentum toward the end of the seventeenth century, but news of its death has been exaggerated. Dryden's *The Indian Emperour* enjoyed many revivals in these years and well into the eighteenth century. Further, while many playwrights turned to emerging genres such as domestic tragedy, others looked back to the Restoration for an aesthetic model and to contemplate for a new audience how the period had changed the place of England in the global landscape. In this chapter, I will look at three late-century texts with deep connections to early Restoration heroic drama, particularly on the point of this genre's exploration of the changes brought by the royal marriage, Stuart imperialism, and the Stuart business of trafficking enslaved human beings: Aphra Behn's *The Widow Ranter* (first performed in 1689–1690), which dramatizes Nathaniel Bacon's rebellion of 1676–1677 and creates a fictional tragic romance with an Indian queen;[1] Behn's novella *Oroonoko* (1688), which describes a New World slave rebellion and the resulting death of an enslaved African prince; and William Congreve's *The Mourning Bride* (1697), which tells the story of a romance between children of the monarchs of warring Granada and Valencia, but also of a captured African queen, abandoned and betrayed (figure 4.1). All of these works, I will suggest, absorb the impact of Stuart imperial and cosmopolitan ambitions and reflect on their fallout.

FIGURE 4.1 Mrs. Litchfield as Zara in William Congreve's *The Mourning Bride*: "When I feel these bonds, I look with loathing on myself" (act 1), 1807. Used by permission of the Folger Shakespeare Library.

Behn's career as a playwright was at its peak in the reign of Charles II; when she later wrote *The Widow Ranter* and *Oroonoko*, Charles was dead and his brother had been, or was about to be, overthrown. Congreve was still a young man during the Glorious Revolution: born in 1670, he spent most of his childhood and youth in Ireland, where his father served in the Royal Irish Army. He returned to England after the accession of the Catholic James II made things difficult for Protestant officers like his father in Ireland.[2] Much changed politically and culturally between the early decades of the Restoration and the 1690s. Charles II died in 1685. His brother, James II, held the throne only briefly: in 1688, Parliament invited the Dutch Protestant William of Orange (the nephew of James and Charles) and Mary (the daughter of James) to invade. Steve Pincus has argued that this revolution, even more than the one in the middle of the century, marked a profound transition in English—and soon British—culture. The 1688 revolution represented a conflict between two different models of modernity rather than one about religion alone. James wanted to make England into a commercial empire on the model of French absolutism; the Whigs who opposed him feared French ambitions for universal domination and sought to build a commercial empire based on the Dutch model of tolerance and development.[3] The Dutch model prevailed as the economic and social landscape changed. By the end of the century, the growth of long-distance trade had made commodities such as tea, sugar, coffee, and tobacco available more widely. An established post office aided both personal and commercial communication.[4] Coffeehouses flourished and became places where urbanites could not only gossip, but learn about foreign affairs.[5] Merchants conducted business there. The risk associated with overseas trade encouraged the growth of insurance companies.[6] William and Mary consolidated a national Protestant identity. Religious reform groups, such as the Societies for the Reformation of Manners, sprang up, and the libertinism that had entertained Restoration audiences came under attack.[7]

Theatrical style was changing as well, with sentimental plots gaining traction and cynicism starting to seem wicked.[8] Reformers argued that the theater should offer characters to admire, criticizing the now-embarrassing style of Restoration outrageousness.[9] At the time of the seventeenth century's second revolution, Aphra Behn was at the end of her life, ill and possibly bitter over the implosion of the Stuart monarchy, even if she had been a skeptic. In these circumstances, she wrote her two major works about empire: *Oroonoko* and *The Widow Ranter*, both of which tell a tragic story of an exotic monarch. *Oroonoko* is a novella, not a play (although Thomas Southerne turned it into one in 1695), but I include a brief discussion of it here because it responds so directly to the heroic plays of the Restoration. Much ink has been spilled over whether Behn actually witnessed or elaborated on the events she describes.[10] I accept Janet Todd's conclusion that she most likely traveled to Suriname in her youth, but I also want to consider why she wrote a story about the 1660s in 1688–1689.

Both *Oroonoko* and *The Widow Ranter*, I will suggest, look back to the Restoration and its ambitions, both imperial and cosmopolitan. As a narrative pitched as the author's own memory of her time in Suriname during the very early years of the restored reign of Charles II, the former work engages events safely in the past that nevertheless had meaning for the present. Oroonoko himself has been read as a figure for Charles I or James II;[11] without doubting the power of those allegories, however, it seems additionally significant that Behn recorded one of the few explicit narratives about the Royal African Company at a time when its director, James II, had become so vulnerable. Richard Kroll suggests that Behn wrote *Oroonoko* to warn James of the danger in which his absolutist policies were placing him. Her focus on James in this narrative, according to Kroll, demonstrates that she cannot have been exploring slavery, because it speaks instead to English sovereignty.[12] By now it should be clear, however, that this is a false opposition: Behn clearly understood the importance of the Stuart restoration to the creation of the Royal African Company, with James continuing to serve as its governor during her composition of *Oroonoko*. Thus to embed a political allegory of the Stuarts in a narrative describing the transatlantic slave trade was not random, but rather drew on common knowledge that they spearheaded English participation in this global atrocity. Behn not only associated the restoration of the Stuarts with slavery and slave rebellion, but she also held back from writing about her experiences in Suriname until many years later, after, or on the cusp of, the Glorious Revolution that sent the governor of this company into exile. *The Widow Ranter* also looks back in time, taking place during the reign of Charles II in the middle of the 1670s, with the king settled on the throne but not yet roiled by the Popish Plot and the surge of anti-Catholicism. While sophisticated Restoration audiences of the 1670s were enjoying libertine comedies (including Behn's own *The Rover*) and heroic tragedies about exotic monarchs, one of England's colonies was in chaos. Because it involved some of the same challenges to sovereignty at stake back in England, Bacon's Rebellion attracted much attention, and London audience would likely have associated it with this period.[13] At the end of her life, then, Behn looked back to the reign of Charles II and created plots around English empire-building and the Royal African Company, both linked in her mind with the Stuarts.

Congreve's blockbuster *The Mourning Bride* does not take place during the reign of Charles II; like many of the heroic plays of that period, however, it explores a conflict in a remote location and in the past. Congreve, more than most dramatists after the Glorious Revolution, looked back to the early years of the Restoration for inspiration during his relatively brief career as a playwright. His embrace of Restoration irreverence while his colleagues moved toward reform earned him the particular vitriol of anti-theatricalist Jeremy Collier. While a new generation of playwrights distanced themselves from the earlier period's global extravaganzas, frank exploration of sexuality, and fascination with the artificiality of refined manners, Congreve kept this spirit alive. In the next chapter, I will explore his engagement with Restoration comedy; here, I will suggest ways that his single tragedy recalls Restoration themes, but with a difference. *The Mourning Bride* tells the story of a passionate African queen who is captured by the Spanish in the midst of a military conflict between Valencia and Granada and, in a sense, tricked into "slave" status. Congreve's enormously popular but currently overlooked play drew audiences to the theater for the entire eighteenth century. According to Charles Gildon, it "had the greatest Success, not only of all Mr. *Congreve's*, but indeed of all the Plays that ever I can remember on the English Stage."[14] *The Mourning Bride* looks back to Restoration mixed-marriage plots and keeps alive the memory of Catherine of Braganza's role in England's global ambitions through a powerful and exotic queen similar to those in Restoration tragedies. Contemporaries noticed this play's resemblance to earlier productions: in 1699, Gildon observed that "some will have the whole Play [*The Mourning Bride*] a kind of copy of [Dryden's *The Indian Emperour*]."[15] While Gildon thought these critics were exaggerating, his comment nevertheless suggests that Congreve's audiences understood this play as a kind of revival of Dryden's Mesoamerica plays. But by replacing Native American royalty with African royalty as the characters with whom the Spanish conflict, Congreve turns attention from the conquest of the New World to the Royal African Company's role in supplying forced labor. The repetition of *The Mourning Bride* throughout the eighteenth century performed the memory of the Stuart origins of global traffic and cosmopolitics, but also, as we will see, turned attention to the ongoing human trafficking launched by Charles II. Just as Indian queens galvanized Dryden's stage productions, so an African queen and the women who performed her became crucial attractions of *The Mourning Bride*. Thus rather than concluding, as have many of Congreve's modern critics, that the enthusiasm of eighteenth-century audiences for this tragedy shows that there is no accounting for taste, I will suggest the possibility that those audiences saw—or more precisely, *felt*—something in the performance of this play that has become less accessible to more recent readers and possibly to audiences as well if it were ever produced, although I imagine some of this eighteenth-century sentiment could be captured in performance. Like Behn and Dryden, Congreve understood the Restoration's imperial ambitions; like Behn, he repurposed the somewhat dated heroic form to address the fallout from Charles's creation of the Royal African Company and the public debate over its destiny after its director had fled across the channel.

Aphra Behn's Exotic Monarchs

Decades after John Dryden's Indian queen plays set in the New World, Aphra Behn created another Native American woman who falls in love with a European. In one of her rare departures from comic form, Behn looked back to heroic drama in the tragic plot of her mixed-genre *The Widow Ranter*. This play juxtaposes a noble Native American tribe with English colonists, most of whom comically lack either the heroic or villainous qualities found in Dryden's conquistadors. These colonists are gamblers and fortune-hunters seeking rewards in the colony of Virginia that had eluded them in England. Behn names one of them after a radical commonwealth religious sect, and her title character embodies the English New World colonization through her dubious past, her blatant opportunism, and her indulgence in a crucial New World product—tobacco—associated in its raw form with the lower classes, although it could also be pulverized to make the snuff favored by the elite. Unlike snuff, most of the English characters in this play are distinctly unrefined. As Elliott Visconsi points out, Aphra Behn uses colonial spaces to expose the tenuousness of any posited national civilizing ambitions on the part of the English.[16] Writing at the end of her life and the end of the Stuart reign, she looks back to Restoration heroic drama with the play's invented romance between the elite Englishman Nathaniel Bacon and the Indian queen, Semernia. In Behn's play, however, Bacon does not marry his lover, but instead accidentally kills her on the battlefield, deceived by her cross-dressing as a warrior. Behn thus declines the sliver of optimism offered by the mixed marriages in Dryden's heroic plays.

Playwrights in general turned away from the heroic after the 1670s, when the political landscape changed and the drama of usurpation held less immediate fascination. Behn's Indian royalty, however, echo the exotic nobility embraced by early Restoration theatergoers. Like Dryden's heroic cosmopolitans, her Indian king regrets the gulf dividing him from the seminoble but unpredictable Nathaniel Bacon, yet at the same time he is "sensible of injuries; and oft [has] heard my grandsire say—that we were monarchs once of all this spacious world, till you an unknown people landing here, distressed and ruined by destructive storms, abusing all our charitable hospitality, usurped our right, and made your friends your slaves."[17] The English colonists, rather than the Spanish conquistadors or a rival native monarch, have become the usurpers. Instead of marrying into a Native American empire, Bacon loves Semernia, tragically, across a political divide. In her Amazonian cross-dressed guise, Semernia pays homage to warrior women like Ianthe, triggering memories of Henrietta Maria as well. An image that might depict Anne Bracegirdle in the role connects this figure not just to Dryden's theatrical Indian queens, but also back to Catherine of Braganza, the queen who brought the Indies (figure 4.2).

In this well-known depiction, an umbrella handle bisects a full-length image and frames the presentation. In the seventeenth century, the umbrella remained an exotic object; Gertrude Thomas traces its appearance in England back to Catherine of Braganza's dowry.[18] Richard Flecknoe offered a pre-Restoration image of Portuguese umbrella-use with striking similarities to the depiction of Semernia, writing that "the *Portuguez* men having a Negro carrying a *Parasol* or *Umbrella* to shadow them from the Sun, whilst the Women are shadowed and defended from publique sight, by some rich coverture thrown over the *Hamatta*, with two Negro Maids going by their sides."[19] Bracegirdle's highly prominent parasol revives the spirit of the exoticized Catherine, as does the actress's gesture of picking up her dress to reveal her feet. According to Pepys, Catherine created a stir in the English court over foot exposure: "Here they talk that the Queene hath a great mind to alter her fashion, and to have the feet seen, which she loves mightily— and they do believe that it [will] come into it in a little time."[20] Catherine also participated in the court fashion of women dressing in men's clothes, a trend echoed throughout the period on stage but a key part of Behn's tragic plot. Finally, the small African servants who hold the umbrella clearly have nothing to do with Native American practices, but echo the court fashion in the reign of Charles II of black servants in general and perhaps the Portuguese use of black slaves as umbrella-bearers in particular as reported by Flecknoe.

Behn's own New World drama revives the spirit of Dryden's heroic cosmopolitan ideals but creates, to borrow a phrase from James Clifford, "discrepant cosmopolitanisms," revealing, as does Clifford, the variety of people who travel and the variety of their motives, with the genre-disturbing decision of putting them in the same play and holding up their differences for

The Indian Queen

J. Smith ex.   W. Vincent fe.

FIGURE 4.2   Anne Bracegirdle as the Indian Queen, by William Vincent, circa 1689. Used by permission of the Folger Shakespeare Library.

reflection.[21] Most of the English rabble in this play have traveled to escape some dubious situation. They are a mixed collection, and Behn represents some with more good humor than others. But unlike earlier tragicomedies that switch between two related plots, Semernia, Cavarnio (the Indian king), and even Bacon seem to belong to a different play. The odd juxtaposition of high and low signals skepticism toward the particular model of cosmo-politics forged in the early Restoration. Behn returns to this model with an Indian queen who echoes those of Dryden: she falls in love with an invading enemy; she consults spiritual forces for advice; she wears beautiful feath-ers, pearls, and a dress that shows her ankles. Her costume, if Behn can be trusted, echoes authentic accessories from the era that popularized heroic plays, back when England had not yet lost Suriname to the Dutch and when the young author visited this New World colony in the early years of the Res-toration. Her Indian queen displays exotic Portuguese luxury and an aestheti-cized version of the Portuguese slave trade, but unlike Dryden's treatment, the mixed marriage plot tragically fails. Semernia loves Bacon, but remains torn between desire and honor,[22] in heroic drama a predicament generally reserved for men. The romance fails because the English reveal themselves as unpolished barbarians.[23] Bacon may rise above the rabble for his commit-ment to honor, but he nevertheless wages a genocidal war against the native Americans. With a nod to Restoration heroic drama, *The Widow Ranter* raises, then dashes the possibility of cross-cultural attraction. On one side of the conflict, the colonists reveal their incapacity for refinement through their cowardice; on the other, Bacon's passionate violence leads to the death of his Indian queen. The play never entirely dispels the suggestion, raised by the other English characters, that Bacon only pursues the Indians so relent-lessly and violently out of personal desire to possess Semernia. Audiences raised on classic heroic plays would have noted the spectacular failure of heroic cosmopolitanism in this plot.

Thomas Southerne noticed a similar failure in Behn's short fictional nar-rative *Oroonoko*. In his preface to his stage adaptation of 1695, Southerne promises to correct Behn's refusal to create a mixed-marriage plot, but he also starts a rumor that the narrative actually *has* such a plot, although sub-merged, in the author's attraction to the title Coramantien prince.[24] While *Oroonoko* represents the slave system through a complicated tangle of con-tradictions that continue to provoke lively debate,[25] there is one division to which Behn returns with consistency in this narrative: the cosmopolitan and the provincial. In the novel's implied comparisons between English war capitalism and Coramantien absolutism, neither system emerges as particu-larly admirable. As in *The Widow Ranter*, the English colonists are hopelessly barbaric, with no respect for Oroonoko's beauty, dignity, or honor. On the other side of the Atlantic, the aging monarch in Coramantien destroys hope for the future of his nation through his impotent sexual greed. Against the backdrop of these two locations, however, several figures emerge who tra-verse them and who do not fit comfortably into any community. Trefry remains at odds with the other settlers. Imoinda is caught between Oroonoko and his grandfather in Africa; in Suriname she both resembles and stands apart from the other enslaved Africans. But the two characters most at odds with their communities are Oroonoko and the narrator. Behn emphasizes the former's anomalous status: a slave himself, Oroonoko nevertheless had traded in slaves; he is captive to, but also looks down on the Englishmen in Suriname. The men and women he sold into slavery now bow down before him as their leader but lack the military spirit that he admires. These anomalies also define the strained friendship that develops between the royal slave and the young Englishwoman who accepts the job of distracting the prince from his bondage. Before his capture, Oroonoko was already anomalous. In a polygamous society, he has fallen in love with one woman. This monogamy sets all of his adventures in motion: it leads to the conflict with his grandfather, to his eventual capture into slavery, to his rebellion against his captors, and to his gruesome death. Oroonoko is not just monogamous, but heroically so: he could have selected several other wives in Coramantien, avoided conflict with his grandfather, and, presumably, inherited the throne. Oroonoko also has a broad base of knowledge: he knows all about the political situation in England; he has read about the lives of the Romans; he has learned languages from his tutor. This intellectual engagement leads to his capture when he befriends the English slave trader because he wants to learn about navigational technique. While another kind of narrative might tempt a hero with women or money, here the captain draws Oroonoko on board through intellectual exchange. Oroonoko has distinctly cosmopolitan inclinations.[26]

In *Oroonoko*, then, a very small group of characters, including the young narrator, Oroonoko, Trefry, and Imoinda, emerge as witty, educated, openminded, literary, and curious about the world against the background of nationalists, of a sort, on both sides. Just as Oroonoko breaks with the supposed Coramantien conjugal custom and also comes to disdain Africans who do not share his outrage at enslavement, so the narrator has nothing but contempt for the other English colonists, whom she depicts as crude and self-serving. Overly provincial themselves, they do not recognize Oroonoko's character, rank, or authority. Thus, in advance of Southerne's adaptation, Behn's *Oroonoko* develops a transcultural synergy between the narrator and the royal slave in their mutual, vexed relationship to cosmopolitanism. One central tragedy of this novel, then, lies with the failure of a cosmopolitan community to emerge, except in brief moments. Between the recognition of Oroonoko's importance and his rebellion, the narrator feeds his intellectual curiosity and indulges her own. They discuss religion and trade stories. They visit the native Surinamese, something that the other colonists seem never to have attempted. When the rebellion fails, Oroonoko immediately worries about Imoinda's vulnerability. He intends to preserve Imoinda from sexual abuse, but his destruction of the woman he loves leads to his own rapid emotional disintegration that ends in his self-mutilation and that echoes practices already tagged as uncivilized.

In *Oroonoko*, Behn looks back to the early years of the Restoration and reflects on England's imperial ambitions and the chartering of a slave-trading company; in this context, she creates cosmopolitan figures who encounter both the promise and the tragedy of new global networks. In doing so, *Oroonoko* engages not just Dryden's Mesoamerican plays, but also in interesting ways echoes Davenant's *The Siege of Rhodes*. In his relentless sense of honor, Oroonoko resembles Davenant's Solyman, held up to English audiences for admiration and envy. Like Solyman, he establishes a chaste friendship with a Christian woman; both Oroonoko and Solyman pursue one woman monogamously in the face of polygamous societies. Both surpass all of the other characters in their sophistication. As I have shown, Solyman's triumph in Davenant's account expressed and fed the growing English imperial envy of the Ottomans. In *Oroonoko*, however, the royal slave dies brutally. If we extended this parallel, then, we would read his death as the triumph of the English and the power and promise of their newly chartered Royal African Company, for the local colonists, in spite of their many inadequacies, succeed in putting down Oroonoko's rebellion and the captain of the English slave-trading vessel manages a successful voyage in spite of his royal cargo. The plot in many ways supports this reading, but the graphic violence and cruelty of the English undermine confidence in any wholehearted embrace of this system. In spite of the relative sophistication of the captain, *Oroonoko* ultimately places this Stuart corporate enterprise in an unfavorable light, suggesting that it profits by unethical and dishonorable practices. Behn's vision of Restoration cosmopolitics here is embittered, rejecting the slight optimism visible in Dryden: for the narrator and for Oroonoko, travel and intellectual exploration lead to sophistication that puts them uncomfortably at odds with their own societies, but at the same time does not give them the tools to form a new one in the poisonous miasma of colonial Suriname.

An African Queen Enslaved: Congreve's *The Mourning Bride*

William Congreve produced his first play a few years after the death of Aphra Behn. This future member of the Whig Kit-Cat Club raised and educated in Ireland on the surface has little in common with Aphra Behn. She supported, albeit skeptically, the Stuarts her whole life; Congreve's family, by contrast, embraced the Glorious Revolution. Congreve and Behn likely would not have met, although Congreve must have known about her writing, at the very least from all of the performers and playwrights they knew in common. Congreve is now mostly remembered for his brilliant comedies, which I will address in chapter 5; first, however, I will discuss his tragedy *The Mourning Bride*, the work for which he was best known in his lifetime. The context of Behn's late writing on empire helps us to see the stakes of Congreve's tragedy, for like Behn, Congreve looked back to the style of heroic drama. Taking note of the way Behn looked back to the reign of Charles II and the Portuguese Catherine at the end of her life to write about New World imperialism and the African slave trade provides both a context and a clue for thinking about Congreve's single tragedy, the story of an African queen enslaved.

John Dryden hailed William Congreve as the standard-bearer for a new generation of playwrights because he took up the Restoration project of refining what was once a crude English stage:

> WELL then, the promis'd Hour is come at last;
> The present Age of Wit obscures the past:
> Strong were our Syres, and as they fought they Writ,
> Conqu'ring with Force of Arms and Dint of Wit:
> Theirs was the Giant Race before the Flood;
> And thus, when Charles Return'd, our Empire stood.
> Like Janus, he the stubborn Soil manur'd,
> With Rules of Husbandry the Rankness cur'd:
> Tam'd us to Manners, when the Stage was rude,
> And boistrous English Wit with Art indu'd.[27]

Dryden claims his own generation as the original beneficiaries of Charles II's cosmopolitanism, but identifies Congreve as the heir:

> In Him all Beauties of this Age we see,
> Etherege his Courtship, Southern's Purity,
> The Satyre, Wit, and Strength of Manly Wycherly.

Dryden places Congreve in the tradition of Restoration comedy, and the younger man's single tragedy shows the influence of his mentor and admirer. Eighteenth-century audiences could not get enough of *The Mourning Bride* (1697), and some of the century's greatest actresses—Elizabeth Barry,

Mrs. Porter, Hannah Pritchard, and Sarah Siddons—made the part of Zara, the captured Moorish queen, a signature role.²⁸ In contrast to newly popular domestic tragedies, *The Mourning Bride* revisits the global expansiveness of the Restoration stage in a different political moment. Congreve's Zara is, like the (anti)heroines of *The Indian Queen* and *The Indian Emperour*, passionate, exotic, and in love with a man who does not return her affection. Osmyn, the object of her desire, instead loves Almeria, the princess of Granada. Zara's ardor and her complexion also recall Elkanah Settle's African queen in *The Empress of Morocco*. Like these pre-1688 alien queens, she dies at her own hand over romantic devastation. Because she recalls these well-known figures so clearly, however, audiences would have also noted her differences. Congreve creates an exotic queen who is more vulnerable and more sympathetic. Upon her rejection by her lover, she pronounces the best-known lines from the play:

Heav'n has no Rage, like Love to Hatred turn'd,
Nor Hell a Fury, like a Woman scorn'd.

(3.8.44–45)

This memorable couplet captures Zara's distress, but also her pathos. Zempoalla, her daughter Almeria, and Settle's Laula would not have identified themselves as "wom[e]n scorned"; they would have found this admission beneath their dignity.²⁹ Not only does Congreve create a more sympathetic exotic heroine, but he also introduces ethical ambiguities that make her outcry resonant. While Montezuma never encourages Zempoalla's passion and while Laula is ultimately betrayed by a lover with whom she shares illegitimate political ambition, Zara suffers rejection from a man who had once pretended to love her and who later expresses remorse for strategically encouraging her attentions. Unlike the Indian queen and the Moroccan empress, the African queen is not a usurper. She falls in love with Osmyn, a supposed prince of Fez, before she knows he is married to someone else. Zara certainly violates sexual propriety: she has an affair with Osmyn; she encourages her husband to attack the enemies of her lover; and when captured she strategically lets the king of Granada think she might return his affections. She does not, however, seek illegitimate power. Instead, Zara endures a sudden and startling loss of stature and freedom because she trusts Osmyn and places this love before other interests.

The Mourning Bride revives Restoration tragedies in one other significant way as well: a mixed-marriage plot. Almeria, daughter of Manuel, the king of Granada, has secretly married Alphonso, the son of the king of Valencia, with which her kingdom is currently at war. The couple are shipwrecked on the same day as their secret wedding. Separated from his bride, Alphonso washes up on the African coast, where Zara finds him, rescues him, and falls in love. He passes himself off as a Prince of Fez named Osmyn, and spends much of the play disguised as a Moor. Thus, Congreve constructs a transracial love triangle, with Osmyn/Alphonso as both Moor and Spaniard, and as the object of desire for both the Spanish princess Almeria and the Moorish queen Zara. While noting that the success of the play owed much to "Congreve's vivid characterization of Zara" and that "Vital and dynamic, Zara controls much of the action of the play," Jean Marsden nevertheless reads Osmyn/Alphonso's rejection of the African queen as the predictable degradation of the sexually assertive woman.[30] To be sure, no spectator in 1697 would have expected Osmyn/Alphonso to leave the Spanish Almeria, played by the lovely Anne Bracegirdle, for the passionate royal Moor, played by the more experienced Elizabeth Barry, and we can certainly read Zara's death as punishment for her excessive passion.

Yet, as Marsden also confirms, the tragedy belongs to Zara: just as in Dryden's Mesoamerican plays, so in Congreve's African-Spanish play the passionate heroine does not entirely deserve her fate. Her death brings tears and pity. She was in fact scorned, and Alphonso/Osmyn exploited her attraction to him, albeit in a moment of desperation. By Restoration codes of honor, his actions were less than heroic: he knowingly took advantage of the Moorish queen's attraction to him. With this combination of power and pathos, Zara became the role coveted by the star actresses of the eighteenth century, one that carried the emotional drama that drew audiences. Even in the play's debut, Zara unexpectedly dominated over Almeria, as Anthony Aston, in his supplement to Colley Cibber's *Apology*, explains: "*Mrs. Barry* outshin'd *Mrs. Bracegirdle* in the character of ZARA in *The Mourning Bride*, tho' Mr. Congreve design'd Almeria for that Favour."[31] Congreve probably did write the role of Almeria for Bracegirdle, with whom he was in love, but he would also have understood Elizabeth Barry's prodigious theatrical power in creating Zara for her.[32] Whichever figure he intended to have prominence, audiences were drawn to the magnificent figure of Zara. After Barry retired, her protégée Mrs. Porter took the role. According to William Chetwood, "her just Action, Eloquence of Look and Gesture, mov'd Astonishment!"[33] Horace Walpole thought that this player surpassed even David Garrick in passionate tragedy. By the 1720s, "Mrs Porter was established as the foremost tragedienne in London," and Zara one of her signature roles.[34] *The Mourning Bride* enjoyed continued popularity into the 1750s, when Hannah Pritchard became the African queen and David Garrick played Osmyn; Sarah

Siddons would immortalize the character at the end of the century. Performance records collected in *The London Stage* suggest that actresses often chose *The Mourning Bride* for their benefit performance.[35] The play was frequently performed "at the request of Several Ladies of Quality"; according to Thomas Davies' *Dramatic Miscellanies*, it was "a favorite play, especially with the ladies."[36]

Critics have long identified the proto-feminism in Congreve's comedies: *Love for Love* renders the patriarchal Sir Sampson an object of ridicule, and Millamant, in an innovative scene of marital negotiation in *The Way of the World*, demands several concessions before she will "dwindle into a wife." *The Mourning Bride* shows some similar antipatriarchal tendencies, which may account in part for its popularity with women. The unsympathetic King Manuel oppresses his daughter Almeria and refuses to accept her love for Alphonso. He reveals his own weakness in his passionate desire for Zara. In a fleeting Othelloesque moment, Manuel rages when he finds out that his daughter has been visiting the captured Moor in his prison (although the audience knows that the Moor is actually Alphonso). Further, as Bridget Orr points out, Congreve represents the imperial ambition of King Manuel as destructive and overreaching.[37] Clearly Almeria, the eponymous "mourning bride," would have provided a powerful point of empathy for female spectators, as she endures the anger of an unjust father and suffers the loss of her beloved husband. The reunion between the young couple at the tomb of Alphonso's father, killed in the war, was praised as particularly moving.[38]

Nevertheless, Zara fascinated audiences and actresses, partly for her majesty, but also, I believe, for similar reasons that Zempoalla, her daughter, and Laula mesmerized audiences in the Restoration: these foreign monarchs suggest the attraction, danger, and cruelty of imperial projects. Congreve, however, was writing for a different moment: rather than exploring the force of a royal marriage, he creates a spectacular African queen who is captured and degraded, in a decade when the fate of the Royal African Company had entered public debate, a point to which I will return. Dryden reserves sympathy for his Indian queens; Congreve, however, demands even greater feelings of pity, evoking with Zara's plight the abandonment of Dido[39] and even perhaps the Didoesque tale of Inkle and Yarico, not yet recycled by *The Spectator* but already published in Richard Ligon's *A True and Exact History of the Island of Barbadoes*.[40] This story offers a striking parallel in which an Indian "princess" rescues the English Inkle, who later sells her into slavery. Alphonso does not sell Zara, but he similarly exploits and abandons her. Nor does Congreve dismiss Zara and other Africans as undeserving barbarians, distinct from Europeans.[41] In Zara's complaint to Osmyn/Alphonso, she notes that:

> Thou hast a heart, though 'tis a Savage one;
> Give it me as it is; I ask no more
> For all I've done, and all I have endur'd:
> For saving thee, when I beheld thee first,
> Driven by the Tide upon my Country's Coast,
> Pale and expiring . . .
>
> (2.9.37–42)

She urges her husband to attack Granada to please the adored stranger. This decision, inspired by illicit desire, loses her everything: her husband dies in the war, and she becomes, tragically, a captive "from Empire fall'n to Slavery" (2.9.69).

Congreve's play rejects Stuart absolutism and Stuart patriarchalism, representing the Granadian King Manuel's imperialist ambition to conquer Valencia as parallel in its injustice to his attempts to control his daughter Almeria.[42] But in rejecting Stuart-style absolutism, the play implicitly challenges Stuart-style imperialism fueled by royal monopolies on trade, including the Royal African Company—most salient to a play about a captured African queen. The Glorious Revolution, however, profoundly altered the circumstances of this venture. James II, the brother of Charles, we recall, was the director of this company, but its monopoly became vulnerable when he fled to France after his "abdication" in 1688. Even though no one else in England was legally empowered to trade with Africa, "interlopers" conducted illegal voyages before 1688. (This is how Robinson Crusoe ends up on the Island of Despair: by joining an illegal slave-trading venture.) With James gone and the leadership of the Royal African Company in doubt, these interlopers and others pressed Parliament to open up the trade. Parliament essentially ended the Royal African Company's monopoly in 1698, which ultimately enabled an increase in English slave-trading, as William Pettigrew has shown. The resulting growth under this deregulation laid the groundwork for Britain's eventual dominance of the trade.[43]

The Mourning Bride debuted in 1697 as slave-trading activity was increasing and, perhaps more importantly, in the midst of a public controversy over the status of the Royal African Company's monopoly. Treatises and pamphlets regularly appeared arguing for one side or the other. For example, in his 1695 *Essay on the State of England, and in Relation to its Trade,* John Cary "esteem[ed] none to be so profitable to us as that we manage to *Africa* and our own Plantations in *America*."[44] Cary argued vigorously for opening up the trade, which would provide the opportunity to supply the plantations with more enslaved Africans and encourage traders to penetrate beyond the coast.[45] By contrast, the anonymous *Considerations relating to the African bill Humbly submitted to the honourable House of Commons*, published in 1698, asserts that the Royal African Company should have particular rights over the slave trade because the company has long maintained the "forts and castles" at its own expense.[46] In *Considerations humbly offer'd to the Honourable House of Commons, by the planters, and others, trading to our British plantations, in relation to the African Company's petition, now before this Honourable House*, however, the anonymous authors, presumably planters, argue that because the Royal African Company charges a duty for maintenance of these forts and castles, others should be able to trade in areas along the African coast that have no such structures.[47] In 1690, one William Wilkinson, claiming to speak for the mariners, enumerated the commercial injustices of the Royal African Company and insisted that opening up the trade to other companies would be highly profitable to the nation.[48] Thus, the debate over the company's fate did not just take place in law courts, but in public print culture as well, with multiple interest groups staking their claims. The legal status of "negro servants," however, was also challenged in this decade. In 1677, under Charles II, in the case of *Butts vs Penny*, the Court of the King's Bench ruled that captured Africans could be considered property, especially because they were heathens, a decision repeated in another case in 1677 and again in 1694. In 1696, however, Lord Justice Holt ruled that although Africans could be bought and sold in the colonies, they could not be enslaved in England. As Holt later put it in 1701, "as soon as a negro comes into England, he becomes free, one may be a *villein* in England but not a slave."[49]

In crafting a play about a captured African queen shortly after the debut of Thomas Southerne's *Oroonoko* and during the decade of these high-profile debates about the Royal African Company, Congreve, it seems, is not only presenting a moving tragedy of loss and betrayal, but also setting these emotional dynamics against the backdrop of contemporary tensions around who counts as a person. The precise relationship of *The Mourning Bride* to the transatlantic slave trade is certainly not straightforward: the play does not represent chattel slavery and it does not tell the story of captives destined for forced labor. Further, Zara is a Moor from the north of Africa rather than the sub-Saharan coast. Valencia and Granada, the two warring Spanish kingdoms, were in their early history Moorish cities and continued to bear that influence. Granada only became entirely Christian-ruled in 1492. But as D. F. McKenzie notes, "The exact time and historical background [in Congreve's play] are left vague."[50] Nevertheless, internal evidence suggests that the Granadians in this play view the Moors as racial "others" and a group distinct from the Spanish. In reporting on King Manuel's victory over Zara and her nation, Gonsalez reports, "Five hundred Mules precede his solemn March, / Which groan beneath the Weight of Moorish Wealth" (1.3.8–9) and "Prisoners of War in shining Fetters follow; / And Captains of the Noblest Blood of *Africk*" (1.3.16–17). Later, Manuel fumes upon learning that his daughter has visited the captured Moor Osmyn (actually her husband Alphonso) in prison: "[T]hat Foreign Dog . . . I'll have him rack'd, / Torn, mangl'd, flay'd, impal'd" (4.7.43 and 49–50), a response that clearly suggests his sense of Spanish racial distinction from and superiority to Africans. Congreve's tragedy also needs to be read in the context of theatrical practices of the Restoration. The most familiar stage Moor—Othello—was unquestionably understood as black and racially "other" in Restoration performances. Further, as noted earlier and discussed by contemporaries, Congreve clearly evokes Dryden's Mesoamerican plays, in which the Spanish in some sense stand in for Europeans in general (see chapter 3).[51] Congreve even names one of the heroines—Almeria, the "mourning bride" herself—after Zempoalla's daughter and the love interest of Montezuma in *The Indian Emperour*, possibly in honor of his mentor and close friend Dryden. So while *The Mourning Bride* does not tell a story of chattel slavery, it nevertheless engages and explores emotions raised by contemporary debates regarding the Royal African Company by repeating tensions made familiar by Dryden between the Spanish and another exploited people.[52]

While contemporary scholarship has neglected this tragedy, eighteenth-century audiences found it infinitely absorbing. It is worth thinking about this difference. Contemporary critical response to the play was a little more mixed,[53] but Samuel Johnson judged some lines in this play as superior to anything written by Shakespeare (much to the chagrin of David Garrick).[54] I want to suggest that one subtle form of political engagement, more detectable in performance, contributed to its success: The play galvanized audiences through the bravado performances of charismatic actresses in the role of Zara. To this day, we remember that Hell hath no fury like a woman scorned, but less visible out of context is the full implication of what she is furious *about*. *The Mourning Bride* looks back to heroic plays, and not only does Alphonso, as mentioned, fall short of heroic romance ideals, but his guilt over his treatment of Zara becomes a persistent theme in the play, culminating in his grief over her death. Alphonso's character radiates not heroic triumph, but shame, confronting English audiences with their own complicity in a tragedy featuring an African queen who becomes, in her own description, a "slave." We first meet Zara when she enters, in chains, with other prisoners of war. King Manuel has defeated a coalition of Valencians and Moors, who entered the fray at Zara's urging to please her lover Osmyn (Alphonso), also captured. Met with a "Symphony of Warlike Musick" (1.4, stage direction), audiences witness the entrance of "Files of Prisoners in Chains, and Guards, who are ranged in Order round the Stage." It is difficult to imagine that such a display would not have evoked England's highly visible debates over the Royal African Company and, later in the eighteenth century, the increasingly familiar images of black bodies in chains. This evocation is displaced quickly, but not quite persuasively, into the language of romance: King Manuel has fallen in love with the beautiful Zara, and declares himself *her* slave. "When I feel," she replies,

These Bonds, I look with loathing on my self;
And scorn vile Slavery, tho's doubly hid
Beneath Mock-Praises, and dissembled State.

(1.6.14–17; see figure 4.1)

On the one hand, the play pits a Spanish (white) virtuous romance (Almeria and Alphonso) against a Moorish (black) illicit one, as Zara is a queen, married, and attracted to a stranger. Osmyn / Alphonso exploits her attraction to him, first for his survival and later to supply military assistance, ultimately rejecting, although not without intense pity, the woman who saved his life. The Alphonso-Almeria romance preserves racial, although not national, purity. On the other hand, the play's appeal to eighteenth-century audiences was clearly more complicated. As noted, Zara moved viewers and became a signature role for star actresses. The play does not reduce Zara to a victimized female body, but elevates her to a royal tragic heroine. John Raphael Smith's portrait shows the power and dignity of this character, albeit later in the century, capturing the combination of anger and majesty in Sarah Siddons' performance (figure 4.3). Another image shows Zara about to drink the poison when she thinks that Osmyn is dead, suggesting a figure of distress to be pitied, in spite of her violent intentions (figure 4.4).

As an African queen who falls, by her own account, into "slavery," Zara conjures the transatlantic commercial slave trade consolidated by the Stuarts, in part through her echoes of Restoration-style exotic stage queens, who themselves invoked the queen who brought the Indies. Yet Congreve revives the figure of the powerful foreign woman with a difference. Zara's plaintive and chilling cry as a woman scorned, widely quoted and misquoted, lies at the emotional heart of this play, and the performance rehearses a cultural unconscious of guilt, fear, and visceral horror.[55] Although Alphonso

FIGURE 4.3 Sarah Siddons as Zara in William Congreve's *The Mourning Bride*, by John Raphael Smith, circa 1783. The Print Collector/Alamy Stock Photo.

can hope for a peaceful future through his marriage to the daughter of his nation's enemy, he nevertheless achieves this at the expense of Zara—literally, over her dead body. Love is notoriously sacred in the formula of heroic drama. Heroes may sometimes have to sacrifice their love for the sake of their nation ("honor"), but sleeping with women on false pretenses is generally left to rakes. Audiences experience Zara through her passion, but also through Alphonso's guilt, something that intensifies the emotional

Act V. MOURNING BRIDE. *Scene 2.*

Stodhard pinx.   *Publish'd May 5.th 1789, by T.&W.Lowndes.*   *Collyer sc.*

M.^{RS} SIDDONS *as* ZARA.

(O friendly draught! already in my heart.)

FIGURE 4.4 Sarah Siddons as Zara in William Congreve's *The Mourning Bride*, act 5. Chronicle/
Alamy Stock Photo.

experience of the play as a lightning rod for collective guilt over a burgeoning national industry in the enslavement of Africans.

This suggestion makes no claim for *The Mourning Bride* as an explicit form of resistance. Instead, it is a play about, as the title indicates, *mourning*. It opens with Almeria lamenting the death of her Alphonso. Act 2 takes place in a graveyard, where Alphonso/Osmyn has come to mourn the death of his own father. Almeria and Zara both gravitate toward the tomb. The play ends with a series of deaths, not atypical but perhaps more graphic than most. King Manuel figures out that Zara loves Osmyn/Alphonso, so he disguises himself as the supposed Moor to trap and seduce her. Manuel has promised his daughter Almeria to Garcia, and so Garcia plots to kill Alphonso because he stands in the way of this highly advantageous marriage. Gonsalez stabs the man he thinks is Alphonso and kills the king. In order to hide this death from the soldiers, Alonzo ("Creature to Gonsalez") then cuts off the head of the dead king, setting it up to keep the troops inspired. Meanwhile, the dead, headless body dressed as Osmyn lies on the floor. Zara encounters the body, and her murderous intentions turn to suicide. In rage and grief, she stabs her eunuch, who dies before he can tell her that Osmyn still lives; she then drinks a cup of poison. Almeria enters and sees the dead body in the clothes of her husband. In despair, she reaches for the cup. But when she bends down to kiss her dead husband one last time, she finds a headless body and drops the fatal chalice in surprise. Alphonso discovers this bloody scene, and the play ends with Almeria lamenting the death of her father and Alphonso the death of Zara.

Dryden's Zempoalla earns the pity of the other characters upon her fall, but Congreve's Zara has some claim on this emotion before her tragic demise. She was betrayed. She was scorned. Alphonso exploited her passion and led her to believe that he returned her affection in order to gain her protection and the military force of her empire. Thus Congreve's Whig version of this classic Tory plot complicates enthusiasm for Alphonso's heroism. Even the superficially salient dichotomies between black and white, Moor and Spaniard, civilized and savage threaten to collapse in Congreve's version of the mixed-marriage plot. Zara refers to her own "savage breast" (3.1), and yet it is Almeria who opens this play by listening to music and proclaiming, in a much-quoted line, that music "has Charms to sooth a savage Breast" (1.1), referring to her own inner turmoil. Osmyn, according to Zara, has a heart, but only a "savage" one. Thus all three characters in this love triangle fall victim to versions of savagery. Alphonso operates, apparently with success, as a Moor as well as a Spaniard. Congreve, then, chips away at binaries between African and European, creating in Zara neither a fragile victim nor an incomprehensible "other," but instead a tragic heroine, an African woman cast into slavery as a result of betrayal by a European man. This complexity made Zara, rather than Almeria, the coveted role.

Jeremy Collier's response to this play, though hostile, supports the possibility that audiences had their hearts broken by Zara. In his *Short View of the Prophaneness and Immorality of the English Stage*, published two years after the debut of *The Mourning Bride*, Collier reserves particular hostility for Congreve for his undermining of class distinction, or "levelling," as Collier puts it. His greatest objection, however, is that the play encourages "self-murder." What is worth noting about this objection is that, in making it, Collier assumes that audience members will identify with and tragically follow the example of Zara, or at least feel the pain of an African queen degraded into slavery, the only character to commit suicide. Congreve builds sympathy for Zara at this crucial historical moment of the transformation of the slave-trading industry from the royal domain of Stuart kings to an openly competitive capitalist operation, and Collier's objection reveals the emotional impact of this play as capacious in its demand for sympathy in a way perhaps less visible to modern eyes. Through Congreve's script and through the passionate performances of a series of star actresses, the relentless productions of *The Mourning Bride* in the eighteenth century recalled Restoration cosmopolitanism, a Stuart imperial project, and the recent turn it had taken.

In his *Specters of the Atlantic*, a study of the notorious incident of the *Zong* (1781), in which enslaved Africans were thrown overboard so that a ship owner could collect insurance money, Ian Baucom traces two strains of history: one, an "abstract, hypercapitalized modernity," and another "recognizably romantic counterdiscourse; a melancholy but cosmopolitan romanticism" that sets itself against "the tide of modernity."[56] This "tide of modernity" includes the Kantian, liberal version of cosmopolitanism. We might think of *The Mourning Bride*, which achieved great popularity in the romantic era with the legendary Sarah Siddons bringing audiences to tears over the fate of the captured African queen, as part of, or at least prefiguring the melancholy romantic kind of cosmopolitanism. The foreign queen remains, no doubt, an exotic "other." By filling *The Mourning Bride* with such unrelenting *mourning* and by setting before audiences an African woman scorned, betrayed, and shackled, Congreve nevertheless conjures the furies unleashed by a hellish industry.

CHAPTER 5

"Have You Not Been Sophisticated?"

The Afterlife of the Restoration Actress

Early in Frances Burney's 1778 novel *Evelina*, a novel about a girl from the country who confronts urban sophistication, the eponymous heroine attends a production of William Congreve's *Love for Love* (1695) and concludes that "tho' it is fraught with wit and entertainment, I hope I shall never see it represented again; for it is so extremely indelicate,— to use the softest word I can,—that Miss Mirvan and I were perpetually out of countenance."[1] The seduction scene between the naïve Miss Prue and the urbane Tattle particularly distresses Evelina, especially when the foppish Lovel hints at her own resemblance to the "rustic girl" on stage.[2] This horrifies Evelina: Burney invokes Congreve's popular comedy to highlight her heroine's awkward transition to London life. These clashes between provincialism and urbanity became popular in other eighteenth-century plays as well, although with more subtle sexual implications than the ones that shock Evelina: Peter Teazle marries a country girl in Richard Sheridan's *The School for Scandal* (1777) with Pinchwife-like hopes of spousal simplicity; in Oliver Goldsmith's *She Stoops to Conquer* (1773), the fashionable heroine pretends to be a country housemaid to get her man; and in Hannah Cowley's *The Belle's Stratagem* (1780), the heroine impersonates, alternately, a stunningly naïve country bumpkin and a cosmopolitan demi-rep.[3] All of these plays find comedy in a young woman's cosmopolitanization, a comic narrative popularized in the eighteenth century by Congreve's *Love for Love* but with deep roots in Wycherley's *The Country Wife*.

The impact of this Restoration-inspired theatrical comic predicament of the rustic girl confronting London sophistication depends, I will suggest, on the novelty of the actress: it was in the Restoration that onstage performance of female identity, whether sophisticated or naïve, first became the task of women. Acting—the capacity to impersonate an imagined character persuasively—is itself a form of sophistication, and Restoration culture's anxieties about women's professional capacity to do this leaks out in the proliferation of plots about women who gain the ability to shape their self-presentation. While the suspicions of female deceptiveness that we see in these plots certainly rehearse longstanding misogynistic preoccupations, in the Restoration and into the eighteenth century the actress herself became inseparable from—even iconic for—narratives about becoming cosmopolitan: moving from country to city, from naïveté to sophistication, from the local to the global.[4] In this period, performances of female naïveté and sophistication both echoed the still-fresh invention of the professional actress.[5] This actress / character pairing around cosmopolitanization echoes throughout the century, reaching peak form in Polly Peachum from John Gay's *The Beggar's Opera*. In his sequel *Polly*, Gay, as we will see, exposes the broader analogy that the cosmopolitanization narrative of the actress / rustic girl encompasses: the movement of the nation itself out of provincialism. In *Polly* and in other plays, the actress thus becomes an admired and suspected icon for the journey from a posited pre-imperialist purity to a globalized sophistication. In mid-century, David Garrick would set up Shakespeare as the towering figure who represented a mythical unadulterated Englishness that flourished under Elizabeth.[6] The professional actress was a Stuart invention inspired by Continental theater and alien to English tradition. Restoration plays recycled on the eighteenth-century stage, like the performance of *Love for Love* witnessed by Evelina, reminded audiences of the nation's global ambitions, cosmopolitan tastes, and sexual indelicacy launched the century before. In this chapter, I trace this ingénue / actress pairing from her roots in Wycherley and Congreve through her iconic and ironic treatment by John Gay to suggests that the actress on the eighteenth-century stage embodied not only both the pleasures and terrifying costs of war capitalism, as we have seen in the Indian queens and in Zara, but also became a figure for the process of cosmopolitanization itself.

Evelina's shock at Congreve's play reminds us of the significance of Restoration theater to eighteenth-century anxieties about becoming more

worldly. Emerging forms of nationalism rendered Restoration-style cosmopolitanism suspect: intriguingly exotic objects became naturalized or rendered shocking; domesticity triumphed over worldliness. Gerald Newman
has argued that the cosmopolitan culture of the Restoration gave way to
nationalism in the eighteenth century with the erosion of the system of
rank.[7] In *A Taste for China*, Eugenia Zuroski Jenkins elaborates on this narrative by suggesting that the fascination with China—which, she argues,
epitomized the cosmopolitanism of the Restoration—changed in the late
eighteenth century to sinophobia and ultimately orientalism.[8] A new kind
of poetic tradition emerged, Katie Trumpener has demonstrated, in which
an ancient bard—discovered or fabricated—could became the unique voice
of a nation.[9] Yet Restoration cosmopolitanism did not disappear. This chapter and the next explore its persistence in the context of these nationalist
impulses. Much scholarship has taken notice of how eighteenth-century
theater helped to consolidate British nationalism through degrading, comic,
and sinister stereotypes of foreigners of various kinds.[10] Through all of this,
however, it continued to bear the marks of its reconstitution in the cosmopolitan experimentation of the Restoration. The most important of these
experiments was the actress herself.[11]

Theatrical performances of this era, drawing on the memory of
Restoration innovations, created parallels between the star actress, commonly represented in popular biographies (as we will see) as a naïve young
thing in the process of confronting London sophistication, and the roles
created for her as an unsophisticated young lady who must transform herself into a woman of the world. This narrative trajectory of provincialism
to worldliness recapitulates the story of English theater itself established
in the Restoration, from a crude regional effort to one that could compete
with the refined theater of France, and an even larger narrative of England's
entrance upon the global stage. Just to be clear: I am not proposing that
pre-Restoration theater *was* crude—only that many critics and playwrights
represented it that way, in contrast to their own new age of polish. The
playwrights who reworked Shakespeare's plays in the Restoration, for example, characterized the bard as capturing nature, but in an unrefined way.
The prologue to Nahum Tate's 1681 adaptation of *King Lear*, for example,
describes the Restoration-era adapter as rearranging a disordered handful
of Shakespearean flowers:

> But he that did this evenings treat prepare
> Bluntly resolv'd beforehand to declare
> Your Entertainment should be most old fare.

Yet hopes, since in rich Shakespeare's soil it grew,
'Twill relish yet with those whose tasts are true,
And his ambition is to please a few.
If then this heap of flow'rs shall chance to wear
Fresh beauty in the order they now bear,
Ev'n this Shakespeare's praise; each rustic knows
'Mongst plenteous flow'rs a garland to compose,
Which strung by his coarse hand may fairer show,
But 'twas a pow'r divine first made 'em grow.[12]

We might think of William Congreve's naïve but curious Miss Prue as a fulcrum between the cosmopolitan theatricality of the Restoration and later, often suspicious responses to this attitude in the eighteenth century. Rumored to have been in love with the actress Anne Bracegirdle,[13] Congreve created powerful roles for women—Miss Prue, of course, but also Millamant in *The Way of the World* and Zara and Almeria, as we have seen, in *The Mourning Bride*. His post-Restoration plays resemble those of Wycherley and Etherege more than the reformist drama coming into fashion. *Way of the World* (1700), however, includes one character who regrets her own risk-taking: Mrs. Fainall wistfully remembers her younger self before she loved "imprudently" and became "sophisticated." The ambivalence embedded in performances of becoming worldly is revealed in the changing meaning of this term. While "sophistication" now is used mainly in a positive sense, in the seventeenth and eighteenth centuries it could just as easily mean polluted, as in: "don't drink that water: it is sophisticated."[14] When Lady Wishfort accuses her daughter Mrs. Fainall of having been "sophisticated," she is not admiring her complexity of thought. Miss Prue becomes a broadly comic version of the danger of sophistication: the provincial girl, exploited by worldly men, who reveals her desires because she doesn't yet know that she is not supposed to have them. She could easily become sophisticated. In *Evelina*, Burney thus creates a heroine struggling to avoid becoming the Restoration-style character on stage; Miss Prue haunts her awkward and humiliating experiences as she struggles to become sophisticated in the modern sense.

In Congreve's post-1688 career, the Restoration ethos emerges as a radical alternative and constant threat: a return to Restoration politics, in the form of Jacobitism, remained a viable hazard until the middle of the eighteenth century. The decade before the debut of *The Way of the World* saw Jacobite rebellions in the form of the Ailesbury plot (1691–1692), the Fenwick plot (1695–1696), and a plot to assassinate William III.[15] At the same time, the Restoration reinvention of theater endured beyond the life of Charles II: English people may have rejected French style absolutism and Catholic Stuarts, but theater managers continued to embrace the Restoration's cosmopolitan aesthetics. The most important theatrical innovation—the actress—became increasingly central to performance culture. Indeed, Felicity Nussbaum has argued that in the eighteenth century, many members of the audience came to see their favorite actresses rather than a particular play.[16] While we may no longer associate actresses specifically with 1660, eighteenth-century audiences were close enough to remember the change. Writing in 1740, Colley Cibber continued to marvel at the stage's display of "real, beautiful women,"[17] thanks to the cosmopolitan tastes of Charles II. In the eighteenth century, then, the body of the actress bears the problem of cosmopolitanization: the professional actress was born in the cosmopolitan moment of the Restoration, embodies its contradictions, and holds them in her DNA. She is the direct result of a worldly monarch's desire to enter his nation more fully into global networks of exchange, and to compete with more refined European tastes, aesthetics, and patterns of consumption. The cosmopolitics of the reign of Charles II thus shaped the reception of the actress, and plots created for her confront the costs and benefits of entrance into the ways of the world.

Miss Prue and Mrs. Pinchwife

Love for Love's Miss Prue is a comically exaggerated version of the credulous young woman that Mrs. Fainall from *The Way of the World* perhaps once was. In *Evelina*, Lovel celebrates Miss Prue as "the first character in the piece" (81). Burney may with this remark indicate Lovel's underdeveloped critical thinking skills, but Miss Prue became for many audience members the play's salient attraction. When Evelina saw *Love for Love*, Miss Prue would have been played by Frances Abington, who became identified with the role. When Joshua Reynolds painted Abington, he captured her in this role looking naïve, curious, and desiring (figure 5.1).

This painting, as James Evans and Martin Postle suggest, merges the actress with the character. Reynolds suggests, according to Postle, "that like Miss Prue, Miss Abington is a woman with an appetite for sensual pleasure, and that her success in the role was allied to her own personality."[18] Central to gossip around Abington was her rise to stardom from humble origins as the daughter of a cobbler.[19] Thus, the inside joke goes, the character of Miss Prue, who comically learns the ways of urban sophistication, parallels the life of the actress who portrayed her: both transform in public from

FIGURE 5.1 Mrs. Abington as Miss Prue in *Love for Love* by William Congreve, by Sir Joshua Reynolds, 1723–1792. Artokoloro Quint Lox Limited/Alamy Stock Photo.

provincial ambition to urban sophistication. This pairing echoes Congreve's inspiration for Miss Prue in Wycherley's Margery Pinchwife, created onstage by Elizabeth Boutell, one of the first actresses of the Restoration, who fascinated audiences with her (performance of) raw sensuality. Just as Congreve's Zara revived the Restoration figure of the "Indian queen" for a post-1688 world, so his Miss Prue revives a Restoration type: the provincial girl with desires she does not yet realize are wrong. The character's comic naïveté highlights the continuing novelty of the female performer: the actress, new to the stage, and the theatricalized rustic girl, new to the city, perform the process of cosmopolitanization, and the provincial girl's journey to sophistication becomes an in-joke about the career of the actress who plays her. Further, the individual country girl and a country self-consciously new to the ways of the world transform themselves, as we will see, in parallel.

Congreve's Miss Prue also, however, revisits the Restoration specifically by echoing Wycherley's Margery. When Tattle tries to seduce her, he explains the difference between country manners and city manners, which, as *The Country Wife* makes clear, means learning how to lie—or, we might say, learning to *perform*. Tattle explains to Miss Prue that she must, like a London lady, pretend not to like him:

MISS PRUE: Why, must I tell a Lie then?

TATTLE: Yes, if you would be well-bred. All well-bred Persons Lie—Besides, you are a Woman, you must never speak what you think: Your Words must contradict your thoughts; but your Actions may contradict your Words. So, when I ask you, if you can love me, you must say no, but you must love me too—If I tell you you are handsome, you must deny it, and say I flatter you—But you must think your self more charming than I speak you:—And like me, for the Beauty which I say you have, as much as if I had it my self—If I ask you to kiss me, you must be angry, but you must not refuse me. If I ask you for more, you must be more angry,—but more complying; and as soon as ever I make you say you'll cry out, you must be sure to hold your Tongue.

MISS PRUE: O Lord, I swear, this is pure!,—I like it better than our old fashion'd Country way of speaking one's mind;—and must not you lie too?

TATTLE: Hum!—Yes—But you must believe I speak Truth.

MISS PRUE: O *Gemini*! well, I always had a great mind to tell Lies—but they frighted me, and said it was a Sin.[20]

In this comic epitome of this subplot, Tattle identifies performance as the condition of urban femininity. In doing so, Congreve tips his hat to Wycherley, who created an iconic and influential version of this figure whom we must now briefly revisit. In *The Country Wife*, the fate of many of the characters depends on Margery's learning to lie like a London lady. On stage, country girls say what they feel and describe what they see, but city women strategically reshape themselves and filter information for public presentation. Margery receives her first lesson in London refinement at the theater, as mentioned in chapter 2:

ALITHEA: But how did you like the Play?

MRS. PINCHWIFE: Indeed I was aweary of the Play, but I lik'd hugeously the Actors; They are the goodlyest, proper'st Men, Sister.

ALITHEA: Oh, but you must not like the Actors, Sister.[21]

Margery's fascination with these actors ignites her curiosity, and she pines for more of the city. When she finally persuades Mr. Pinchwife to take her to the New Exchange safely, her husband believes, cross-dressed as her own brother, she heads to a book vendor and attempts to purchase *Tarugo's Wiles* and *The Slighted Maid*. In *The Slighted Maid*, savvy theater fans would remember, the eponymous heroine spends the play dressed as her own brother. In her attraction to *Tarugo's*, Wycherley signals Margery's limited taste; Pepys called it "the most ridiculous, insipid play that I ever saw in my life."[22] But Wycherley also implies her curiosity about the ways of the world. *Tarugo's*, like *The Country Wife*, features a worldly trickster.[23] Tarugo courts his lady in various exotic disguises. He first gains admission to her chamber dressed as a tailor with a (fake) colorful backstory who learned his trade in the West Indies: "I was . . . taken by a *Muscovite* Man of War, going to *Alexandria*; he sold me to a Jew, who brought me to the Southern parts of *America*, where to the Queen of *Amazons* Taylor I was barter'd for an old Petticoat, there I was instructed." Tarugo next disguises himself as a coffee master, who assures his customers that his coffee was grown at "two Houses of Pleasure four miles from Constantinople."[24] In the fourth act, he disguises himself as an Indian from Mexico, as if he were a character from Dryden and Howard's *Indian Queen*. Horner's cosmopolitanism has a more limited scope than Tarugo's— he has just returned from France and has a taste for Asian porcelain—but through Margery's purchase, the playwright points to Horner's more exotic precursor. While the refined London ladies compete for the most exquisite piece of china, Margery lunges for a play about a trickster in exotic disguises that centers on one cosmopolitan institution, the coffeehouse, which she buys in another, the New Exchange.

It is the theater itself, however, that initially expands Margery's desires and ultimately, for better or worse, her horizons. While the Fidget ladies have settled comfortably into a double life of exterior virtue and secret pleasure, Margery's story comically explores the process of coming to an appreciation of both theater and theatricality. Many of her funniest lines come from her unfiltered observations. Even Mr. Pinchwife admits that if she freely declares her attractions to the actors, she must not be plotting. She later expects Horner to marry her; every day, she reports, she sees women in London leaving their husbands and choosing new ones. Margery eventually learns to refine her performance. When her husband demands that she write a letter rejecting Horner, she wonders "Can one have no shift?," then, "ah, a *London* woman wou'd have had a hundred presently" (4.2.147–48). Trying out this urban performance style, Margery writes a second letter when Mr. Pinchwife briefly leaves the room, and then handily switches them. This proves good practice for switching herself: with the help of the servant Lucy, she dresses as Alithea, and in this disguise is delivered by her husband into Horner's arms. The climax of the play hangs on Margery's willingness to bear (false) witness to Horner's impotence.

As Congreve repeats in his creation of Miss Prue, consciousness of the actress creating the character shapes Margery's role throughout the play. Her arrival at the New Exchange in her brother's suit theatricalizes the novelty of the actress, looping back to a time in the audience's living memory when all female roles would have been played by boys. Thus her transvestism conjures not just the boy actor, but the *girl* actor as well, and one girl actor in particular. Elizabeth Boutell, who created the role of Margery and for whom the part may have been written, played more of these roles than any other actress of her time.[25] In Wycherley's *The Plain Dealer* (1676), Boutell would spend the entire performance cross-dressed in the part of Fidelia. As Kirsten Pullen observes, this player, who was maligned as a whore by satirists and was the victim of an oft-repeated rumor that she was stabbed by another actress over an accessory, nevertheless enjoyed a successful career and benefited from a financially advantageous marriage.[26] I cannot agree with Pullen, however, that Margery's cross-dressing in this play "exists solely for the enjoyment of Pinchwife, Horner, and the audience,"[27] for it highlights the embodied presence of the actress. It reminded audiences that cross-dressing had become optional rather than mandatory; it offers a metatheatrical moment proposing a parallel between the character learning the art of performance and the women in the early Restoration who took the opportunity to do the same. As a rumored petulant whore (although most likely, as Pullen argues, actually neither) who specialized in cross-dressing roles, Betty Boutell is the quintessential early actress, the woman who had to learn theatricality from scratch, and whose boyish presence summarized one crucial contribution of the Restoration stage.

Thus, while the actress of this period served as kinetic memory of the Restoration moment in which her profession began, Margery Pinchwife, as created by Betty Boutell, retained a distinctive connection to this originating moment. Similarly, the Boutell/Margery innocence-to-experience by way of the category crisis of travesty performance rises repeatedly, as we will see, transporting audiences of the time briefly back to the moment of reinvention of a new kind of theater marked by the female body and a new fascination with the ways of the world. The performance of Congreve's Miss Prue time-warps audiences back to the Restoration as it embeds a finely layered past that bears with it the weight of its original context. The country wife figure as scripted by Wycherley and performed by Boutell persists into the eighteenth century as an originating moment of female professional performance itself, binding subsequent actresses to Restoration cosmopolitan ambitions and the cosmopolitan imagination that made their professional incarnation possible. Audiences had not yet forgotten that actresses performed because of their exiled monarch's European sojourn and the childhood influences of his French Catholic masque-loving mother.

Thus, when Congreve presents Miss Prue, the country girl who must learn to lie, he revives not just Margery Pinchwife, but the quintessential Restoration transvestite performances of Betty Boutell, recalling how the reinvented theater, with its central innovation of the female performer, was part of the Stuart cosmopolitan vision. In watching Frances Abington in the role of Miss Prue, Evelina blushes at not just the predicament of a rustic girl's high potential for error, but also the urban cosmopolitan challenge of learning to behave in ways contrary to impulse. The scene at the theater, disconcertingly, reminds Burney's readers that there are women who do this for a living. Evelina blushes, we might say, at the Restoration's cosmopolitan vision that embraced the actress.[28] Margery, Miss Prue, and Evelina all explore the problem blurted out by Lady Wishfort when she demands of Mrs. Fainall, "Have you not been sophisticated?" The actress thus bears with her the problem of Restoration cosmopolitanism itself: its corrupting influence and brutal injustices, but also its risky pleasures and its relentless fascination with the ways of the world.

Polly Peachum

Just as Betty Boutell created the role of Margery Pinchwife and became indelibly linked to her, so the actress Lavinia Fenton created Polly Peachum, an enigmatic character who becomes most comprehensible through the memory of Margery and Miss Prue. *The Beggar's Opera* owed its spectacular success in part to Fenton's talents,[29] but also, as we will see, to its revival of Restoration style. Rarely has a role been so conflated with a performer. A 1728 biography capitalizing on the play's success makes this obvious in its title: *The Life of Lavinia Beswick, Alias Fenton, Alias Polly Peachum.* Throughout, this anonymous biography refers to its subject as simply "Polly Peachum." As Cheryl Wanko observes, this narrative, like so many of the early actress biographies, emphasizes the heroine's erotic adventures rather than fine points of performance.[30] Actress biographies, as Wanko and others point out, exploit the sexuality of their subjects; they are, however, also narratives of *sophistication*, in both the eighteenth-century sense of adulteration and the emerging sense of cosmopolitanization. *The Life of Lavinia Beswick* begins with the heroine's loss of virginity and sexual escapades, as if these are necessary steps to prepare for a career on stage. Perhaps the most memorable conflation of sexual and theatrical initiation is the oft-repeated story of Elizabeth Barry, who supposedly failed miserably at her first dramatic attempts. According to *The History of the English Stage* (1741), the Earl of Rochester whisked her away to his estate on a bet that he could return her as an accomplished performer. Whatever went on while she was alone with the earl (the *History* remains discreet on this point), Barry returned with a newfound ability to deeply move audiences, well on her way to becoming the greatest tragedienne of the Restoration. She returned, in other words, more *sophisticated*. Biographies of male actors generally do not link artistic accomplishment to sexual experience. Actor biographies tell stories of triumphs and of limits. Actress biographies narrate Margeryesque experiences of personal transformation through sophisticating experiences.[31]

Like Margery, Lavinia Fenton, according to contemporary legend, embraced city life. Spurning a lucrative offer that would have required sequestration in the country, Fenton reputedly penned the following poetic rejection of a suitor and his estate:

> *Vain Fop, to court me to a rural Life,*
> *Let him reserve that Usage for a Wife.*
> *A Mistress, sure, may claim more Liberty,*
> *Unbound by Nature, and by Law she's free.*
> *Monster! thy Country Cottage I disdain,*
> *In London let me live, and let me reign;*
> *The Seat of Pleasure, where we, unconfin'd*
> *Delight the Body, and improve the Mind.*
> *To Park we range, where Youth and Beauty shines,*
> *There we Intrigue and manage brave Designs.*
> *Give me a Play, a Ball, or Masquerade,*
> *And let who will enjoy your lonesome Shade,*
> *Lavinia, for more noble Ends was made.*[32]

This celebration of city life opened the door to a new career: the poem happened to fall into the hands of a certain nobleman who, convinced the author had "Wit and Spirit,"[33] determined to find her an opportunity to perform onstage. The poem connects "delight[ing] the body" to theatrical ambition; its additional claim of the heroine "improv[ing] the mind," however, was also an important feature of the actress's transformation. Margery, as we see, becomes worldly in ways beyond sexual knowledge: she learns about the theater; about cross-dressing and disguise; about how people can say one thing and mean another. A broadside biography of Fenton—*The Whole Life of Polly Peachum*—reminds readers of the Restoration origin of the professional actress by casting the *Beggar's Opera* star as a reincarnation of Nell Gwynn. The *Life* reports that Fenton got her start by selling oranges in the theater, where she won notice and employment. The author marvels poetically as Fenton's supposed price for her favors:

A hundred Guineas for a Night's Debauch
Outdoes Don-John *or* Earl of Roch.[34]

An eighteenth-century biography of Nell Gwynn reports that she lost her virginity to the Earl of Rochester after catching his attention in the theater, where she was selling oranges.[35] Other actresses, as well, lived in the royal mistress's shadow: the career of Ann Catley, according to her biographer, "when compared with that of the celebrated Nell Gwynn, exhibits many incidents of strong similitude."[36] If Betty Boutell's fame faded with history, Gwynn haunted the actress biography throughout the eighteenth century, less because of her talent (which must have been considerable, but was also rivaled by Boutell, Barry, Bracegirdle, and others) or even because of her scandalous reputation (again, rivaled by many others), but for her direct association with Charles II, and thus the Restoration itself and the invention of the professional actress as part of the Stuart cosmopolitan vision. The Earl of Rochester became, in the words of Matthew C. Augustine and Steven N. Zwicker, the "poster boy" for the Restoration, a point I will explore in the next chapter.[37] The case could be made that Nell Gwynn, at the nexus of royal intimacy and the reinvented stage, became the "poster *girl*."

Just as Lavinia Fenton's eighteenth-century biographies take readers back to the glamorous Restoration court by conflating her with Nell Gwynn, so Polly Peachum's story within *The Beggar's Opera* and *Polly* offer a Margeryesque narrative of female sophistication *and* a glimpse into the imperial ambitions that underwrote the pleasures of the Stuarts. Neither audiences nor critics have missed the way that *The Beggar's Opera* turns away from the ascendant fashion for sentimental drama (associated with, but not limited to Whig reform) and revives the now-retro Restoration-style comedy of manners. Gay's reanimation invigorates both plays, exploring how the scaffolding of the Stuart past gives shape to the Walpolian present. Gay notoriously exploits the mythology of the highwayman with his antihero,[38] but he molds Macheath in the fashion of the sexy Restoration rake rather than the ruthless outlaw: irresistible to women, Macheath marries for social advantage but desires with minimal discrimination.[39] Polly's father, a notorious fence, catches him—twice—because he cannot resist visiting whores. Gay glamorizes the libertine Macheath, but only to a point; he saves his most bitter satire for Peachum, who recognizes no authority higher than money. Gay places Peachum in the structural position of the patriarchal, blocking father of comedy, but, in a dark revision, this father intends to turn his daughter's beauty into a renewable source of income and will support whichever side of the law helps him profit. Thus, he is no Don Pedro from *The Rover*, exhausted from guarding the honor of the women in his family, but instead a diabolical bookkeeper looking to improve his balance sheet regardless of honor or morality. The wicked but compelling Macheath, by contrast, enjoys the drinking, whoring, and gambling lifestyle of the Restoration rake.

Eighteenth-century audiences could not get enough of *The Beggar's Opera* and of Polly Peachum. This character has nevertheless proven perplexing to modern critics.[40] She seems absurdly out of the place in the criminal underworld into which she was born. Further, if we believe in Polly's deservedness, can we truly want to see her paired with Macheath?

William Hogarth's painting of a scene from the play places Polly slightly off center, but so luminous in white that the figure draws the spectator's gaze (figure 5.2). Many pairs of eyes fix on Polly, who kneels before her father, handkerchief ready to dry her tears. Lucy also pleads, but has her back turned. Polly Peachum is not technically a rustic, having been raised in the midst of urban corruption and violence. And yet, if Macheath's character echoes the Dorimants, Horners, and Willmores of the Restoration, Polly's evokes the country wife in her comic naïveté and contrast with London ladies who understand more about the ways of the world. Her guileless belief in Macheath's love, in contrast to the machinations of the wily whores and the relatively cynical Lucy, constitutes her central comic absurdity, but also her undiminished appeal to audiences. She remains comically and improbably unsophisticated.[41] The performance of the country girl in *The Beggar's Opera* is, like everything else in the play, cleverly askew, and invigorated by the specter of Restoration theater.

FIGURE 5.2   William Hogarth, *The Beggar's Opera*, 1729, oil on canvas. Yale Center for British Art, New Haven, CT. Alamy Stock Photo.

Erin Mackie has objected to the way that audiences and critics tend to forgive and even admire Macheath, who makes his living with a pistol in his hand. Historical highwaymen, she points out, brutalized their victims.[42] Yet this affection for Macheath, evident in the play and clearly felt by audiences, emerges not just from his highwayman status, but also out of his propulsion of Restoration cosmopolitanism, askew through its placement in a criminal underworld but still reminiscent of Stuart violence, into the eighteenth-century present.[43] Macheath, like the Stuart brothers but unlike their father, escapes execution, and instead enjoys the attentions of the innocent Polly and a bevy of other ladies as well. He stands "like a Turk," as did Charles II when he attended the theater appareled in the Eastern-style vest that he made fashionable (see chapter 1). Like Charles, Macheath impregnates his mistresses, but not his declared wife. If this character provides an irresistible model for libertine Stuart masculinity, complete with Hibernian valences, he also propels this model into the eighteenth-century context. In James Boswell's fantasies, he morphed into Macheath, hoping similarly to stand like a Turk among his doxies.[44] But while Macheath offers a powerful model of masculine swagger and libertine exuberance, Polly anchors the play.

Polly, like Margery, engrossed attention as the naïve outsider unable to fully understand the actions of the other characters. Polly/Lavinia Fenton attracted the largest fan base, which might seem odd given the blandness and simplicity of the character. But the play would make no sense without her. Her astonishing naïveté, rendered particularly comic by her childhood in a crime family, sets the corruption of the other characters in high relief. Thus, her parents can express shock at her simplicity in assuming that she will survive on "the Industry of my husband" and characterize her as putting on airs when she declares her desire to marry for love.[45] Gay uses the country girl figure in a kind of double reversal: she innocently observes a corrupt social world, but the corrupt social world of the play is already inverted as a criminal underground, which itself satirically resembles the world of respectability.[46]

Polly's naïve assumptions, however, do not mean that she lacks desire. This is the other scandal of the rustic girl that makes Evelina blush and that Margery and Miss Prue express so unequivocally. Polly, after all, has fallen in love with a notorious highwayman, a rake oozing with sexual potency. As J. Douglas Canfield points out, although Macheath and Peachum both seek illicit gains, Macheath charms through his love of pleasure while Peachum repels as the embodiment of a new kind of desiccated commercial type with no time for enjoyment.[47] But while Canfield reads this as a split between traditional absolutism and an emergent capitalism, Macheath, we should note, is not indifferent to profit. Like the Stuart brothers, he charmingly demands gold, backed up by the force of arms; then he spends the gold on drinking, gambling, and whoring with his crew. Peachum makes life-and-death decisions as well, but with a bookkeeper's sang-froid. While the theater by this point has trained audiences to sympathize fully with women who want to choose their own husbands,[48] the Peachums, like Horner and the Fidget ladies, have a more accurately calibrated sense of how the social world operates. The genius of this play, then, lies partly in its extreme exaggeration of the Restoration comedy of manners: Polly, like Margery, fails to recognize sexual transgression. But while Margery doesn't understand that London women who live with men other than their husbands violate propriety, or that Horner also sleeps with other married ladies, Polly does not see that Macheath spends his money on whores, has married several other women, and uses Lucy strategically in the same way that he uses Polly herself. Further, if Margery does not think it proper to send letters between people in London because letters only travel between London and the country, Polly fails to recognize that her father condemns to death men who fail to steal enough for him. Gay places Polly between two kinds of criminals: the bourgeois accountant capable of reducing human life and stolen pocket watches to the universal equivalent of cash and the violent, swaggering adventurer who takes what he wants at gunpoint.

Gay's Tory loyalties are well known; further, as J. Douglas Canfield and Clement Hawes have in different ways argued, he clearly attacks emergent capitalism.[49] This does not mean, however, that he advocates for a Macheathean Stuart alternative. Macheath's pardon, after all, mocks not only operatic style, but also the system of justice that would forgive him and restore him to his power and pleasures as a Grand Turk. When critics in the eighteenth century attacked *The Beggar's Opera* for immorality, the figure of Macheath often emerges as a source of concern for his combination of criminal behavior and charm. To take one example: in *Thievery A-la-mode: or, The Fatal Encouragement* (1728), a young man who has recently suffered a financial setback attends a production of *The Beggar's Opera* with his friends. The house is packed; one friend boasts that he has seen the play forty times. Millefont (the young man) finds the play "too low to afford any Pleasure to an elegant Taste."[50] The next day, however, he sees in a picture shop "Prints of Captain *Macheath* and *Polly Peachum* hanging in the Window with those of the first Quality of both Sexes in the Kingdom."[51] At an evening gathering, he notices that every lady present has a fan or snuffbox with a picture of "the agreeable Highway-man and his two Doxies."[52] Worn down by these ubiquitous representations of Macheath and Polly in high society, the young man sets up "for Captain *Macheath's* Profession"[53] to solve his financial troubles. After a good run (including robbery of the friend who had originally invited him to the play), he dies of a wound received in one of his adventures. In this story, the patriarchal image of the fashionable polygamous icon etched into boxes that hold a refined version of one quintessential New World commodity produced on slave plantations persuades the young man to follow suit, even if the play itself disgusts him. The admiration for Macheath by the elite, linked to celebrity, luxury, and overseas profits, and not the plot of the play itself, persuades the young man to follow in his footsteps. Millefont does not find the prospect of fencing stolen watches particularly tempting; instead, elite glamor, libertinism, and luxury underwritten by New World goods draws him into the criminal world. Popular culture in the eighteenth century, then, connected Macheath to the insatiability of an imperious and imperializing elite, ghosted by the libertine Stuarts.[54]

The Restoration also haunts the character of Polly, as we have seen; this particular stage tradition of country wives turning urban becomes a figure for the nation coming upon the global scene in a historical moment associated with theatricality itself. Thus, later in the century, when the theater-mad rustic girl Miss Kitty Sprightly in Isaac Jackman's *All the World's a Stage* (1777) extracts a promise from Sir Gilbert Pumkin (whose ward she is) to put on a play, she chooses *The Beggar's Opera*, with the role of Polly reserved for herself. For Kitty, the character embodies theatricality and captures her own position as a naïve girl about to become more sophisticated. Charles Stanley, an officer in the army and nephew of Sir Gilbert, plays the role of Macheath to gain the opportunity to court Miss Kitty. (Can it be a coincidence that the author names him *Charles*?) Sir Gilbert tries to stop the play because "a red coat may spoil my project of marrying her myself,"[55] acknowledging the unstoppable appeal of this young man, especially as Macheath. Sir Gilbert warns Charles about Kitty, saying that "she's always imagining herself to be either Helen, Cleopatra, Polly Peachum, or some other female of antiquity, that made a noise in the world" (13). Like another theatrical red coat—Captain Clerimont in Richard Steele's *The Tender Husband* (1703)—Charles wins Kitty by indulging her literary fantasies. In *Tender Husband*, Biddy Tipkin has read too many romances, fancies herself a heroine (she demands to be called Parthenessa), and only responds to courtship in the style of romance heroines. In Jackman's updated theatrical version, the girl imagines herself as Polly. Like Miss Prue and Margery, Kitty blurts out scandalous information without any sense of its impropriety. When Sir Gilbert allows Charles to lead Kitty out, he declares: "Fear not my government"; to which Kitty responds: "That's what the black man says in the play" (18), declaring, in an aside, her great pleasure at his impersonation of Othello. *All the World's a Stage*, then, parallels three love plots: Charles and Kitty's; Macheath and Polly's; and Othello and Desdemona's, with the first pair a farcical version of the other two romances between an innocent girl and a darkly compelling man. Gay's sequel *Polly*, as we will see, literally turns Macheath black, but this exchange suggests that audiences may already have been making this connection in *The Beggar's Opera*. The play hints at the rustic heroine's attraction to dark men when she expresses her great pleasure in acting out scenes from *Othello* with the servant Cymon. Kitty proudly reports that she told Cymon "to go into the barn, and get by heart the speech, where the blackamoor smothers his wife, and I had not been in bed ten minutes, when he came into the room, and repeated every word of it" (23). This intimacy with a servant shocks Charles, but Kitty continues blithely that Cymon looked "charmingly fright-ful" in blackface. "He laid down the candle, and came up to the bed-side, and said—'one kiss and then'" (23). "What then?" Charles nervously asks. Kitty, in her Margery/Miss Prue-esque naïveté, takes his question as an unfortunate admission that he does not remember the end of the play. A black mark on her cheek left by Cymon/Othello's kiss betrays her impropriety. But just as

Mr. Pinchwife concludes that Margery would only express her appreciation of the player men out of ignorance, so Charles concludes that Kitty exposes only her simplicity. Jackman rewrites the romance-mad girl from Steele into the theater-mad Kitty: play-acting, like romance, both stereotypes and empowers women. *All the World's a Stage*, as the title suggests, blurs onstage and offstage performances, but it does so by invoking the figure of Polly, ghosted by Miss Prue and Margery. When Charles and Kitty announce their stolen marriage at the in-house performance of *The Beggar's Opera*, confusion ensues when audience members accuse Polly and Macheath of starting at the end of the play rather than the beginning.

Like Kitty, Polly marries but does not become sophisticated. Gay, however, was not finished with her, and he gives her a chance to learn the ways of the world in the sequel. In spite of eager anticipation for this performance, it never took place: two weeks before its opening, the Lord Chamberlain, acting on half of Sir Robert Walpole, banned *Polly*. The Duchess of Queensbury responded by encouraging Gay to publish it, defying the king, who had, according to Lord Hervey, "forbid [*Polly's*] being recited." The king banished the duchess from court for her defiance.[56] *Polly* thus attracted attention without a production until 1777 (in a version rewritten by George Colman) by becoming a public scandal and a political cause.[57] Colman's version may have inspired Jackman, whose play about playing Polly debuted in the same year. As a figure in a printed text rather than a performance, the eponymous Polly loses her immediate connection to an actress. Nevertheless, the character was written for performance and in some ways evokes the Restoration invention of the actress even more than does *The Beggar's Opera*.

In the original play, Polly comically retains a degree of innocence in the midst of a corrupt world. In the sequel, she encounters a different kind of corruption and experiences a new level of worldliness, as she leaves London to travel across the Atlantic in pursuit of Macheath. But in spite of her unprotected exposure to an even more dangerous world, Polly still does not become sophisticated. In fact, Gay's determination to retain her innocence makes for a disconcerting ending: Cawwawkee, a noble Indian prince, proposes marriage to Polly, and while she clearly admires him, she still needs time to mourn for Macheath (who has been hanged). She examines her own attraction to the prince for evidence of social climbing: "Frail is ambition, how weak the foundation! / Riches have wings as inconstant as wind."[58] Cawwawkee parallels Polly as a virtuous figure encountering a corrupt world: like her, he finds European dishonor puzzling. The comic tension between the degraded London commercial landscape and Polly's romantic optimism in *The Beggar's Opera* shifts in the sequel to the search for the possibility of virtue anywhere in the world. In *Polly*, Gay moves from one Restoration theater narrative—the comedy of the rustic heroine facing urbanity—to another: the mixed-marriage plot. By joining these in sequence, Gay links the pleasures of the European metropole to violence across the Atlantic. Elizabeth Dillon has argued that in *Polly*, the playwright retreats from his earlier satire of capitalism.[59] Through the play's repetition of Restoration theater and theatricality, however, we can see that instead Gay turns his attention from one style of capitalism to another: from Peachum-style urban corruption to Macheath-style violent conquest for profit, or what Sven Beckert calls "war capitalism."[60]

As part of its glance back to Restoration theatricality, *Polly* includes not one but two cross-dressing plots: Polly spends most of the play dressed as a young man and Macheath disguises himself as an escaped African slave.[61] While the performance of *Polly* would have exploited the comic eroticism of the breeches role, Gay's heroine also revives the heroic warrior women of the Restoration stage, such as Ianthe from *The Siege of Rhodes*.[62] The heroine has pursued Macheath across the Atlantic after her father's death and Macheath's sentence of transportation. Initially, she falls into the hands of the bawd Diana Trapes, also resettled in the New World, who sells her to Mr. Ducat, the owner of a plantation. Mrs. Trapes has been working to persuade Mr. Ducat to indulge himself more to better resemble elite Britons, and a white mistress would be part of this expense: "Though you were born and bred and live in the *Indies*," she tells him, "as you are a subject of *Britain*, you should live up to our customs. . . . [T]he richest of our Lords and Gentlemen, who live elegantly, always run out. 'Tis genteel to be in debt. Your luxury should distinguish you from the vulgar" (1.1.1–11).

Ducat, as Robert G. Dryden argues, can be seen as a commercial type in the tradition of Peachum, extending Gay's Tory critique of capitalism.[63] Polly falls from one form of heartless commerce to another. But this speech suggests something more: Mrs. Trapes is persuading Ducat that he belongs to the landowning class of "Lords and Gentlemen"—or at least that he should imitate their vices, something that Peachum, for all of his flaws, avoids. Mrs. Trapes does not treat Ducat as a capitalist who should manage his resources for the highest possible profit; rather, she persuades him that he belongs to a class of men who accumulate debt through excessive indulgence. Ducat, who welcomes Mrs. Trapes' suggestions and her offer of Polly, is not a bloodless accountant but rather an aspirational Macheath-like Stuart imperialist, expanding absolutist landholding by conquest. He boasts, "Nobody throws himself into the extravagancies of life with a freer spirit. . . . in most of my expences I run into the polite taste. I have a fine library of books that

I never read; I have a fine stable of horses that I never ride: I build, I buy plate, jewels, pictures, or any thing that is valuable and curious, as your great men do, merely out of ostentation" (1.1.3–8). With Ducat, as with Macheath in *The Beggar's Opera*, Gay satirizes Stuart war capitalism. He also, of course, satirizes Whig capitalism, which he consistently characterizes as heartless and corrupt. But he does not do this with an uncritical embrace of the Tory legacy, and it is only through the recognition of this complexity that we can make sense of *Polly*. Gay turns to the edgier Restoration playwrights not just for their aesthetic, but also for their leveling impulses.

In Restoration tradition, Gay explores the process of cosmopolitaniza-tion through the figure of the naïve young girl. The sequel exposes Polly to more of the world, including the Atlantic traffic that enabled the circulation of luxuries in London, but she still, improbably, does not become *sophis-ticated*. Polly's exposure has been a sad experience: while in London, she looked past her lover's multiple infidelities, but in the New World, his full betrayal cannot be denied. Macheath's new identity as an escapee and black-face pirate—blackening, he explains, as a way to avoid previous mistresses and commit himself to Jenny Diver—further ties this character to the Stu-art regime. West Indian piracy flourished in the reign of Charles II after England took Jamaica from the Spanish. The pirate Henry Morgan became an English hero, knighted by Charles II and granted the governorship of Jamaica.[64] In *Polly*, Macheath's men dream of taking more and more terri-tory from the Spanish. In *The Beggar's Opera*, Gay had established the reso-nance between Charles and Macheath through the rake's libertine charm and swagger. In *Polly*, he theatricalizes Charles's nickname—"the black boy," for his dark hair and complexion—and also his close ties to the Royal African Company in Macheath's blackface performance. While the monopoly of the Royal African Company had ended, the continued circulation of the guinea, with Charles's face on one side and the "elephant and castle" on the other, would have kept this connection between Britain's stake in the trade and the merry monarch alive.[65] As John O'Brien has argued, the English slave-trading industry not only bore this persistent reminder of its Restoration origins and entrepreneurial support by Charles II, but came to model the corporation for the eighteenth century.[66] Gay does not satirize corporations in particular, but he vilifies both Peachum and Ducat for, in different ways, turning people into things.[67] Peachum determines the life or death of his thieves by balancing their take against the reward value for turning them in. Ducat follows similar logic, shocked at Mrs. Trapes' charge for Polly as he "could have half a dozen negro princesses for the price" (1.6.26). Mrs. Trapes turns the heroine into cash by selling her to a planter who profits from the slave trade and whose very name is a kind of money. Thus, the connection between Charles Stuart and black skin was not simply one of mythologized shared nobility or warrior culture, but a more direct and literal association with one of the main commodities of Stuart war capitalism. Charles II's originating sponsorship of an English slave-trading corporation continued to associate the monarch himself with the black bodies from whom he profited and with whom he traded. Thus Gay not only suggests the parallel between urban corruption and colonial greed, as Robert G. Dryden has argued, but he also specifically links urban cosmopolitanism to the version of commercial/imperial expansion launched in the Restoration.[68] Polly rejects both by refusing to become sophisticated; she provides a counternarrative to the supposedly whorish Betty Boutell. She is a Margery whose male disguise succeeds, an Elizabeth Barry who declined the invitation to Rochester's estate.

Thus, if we think about Gay as less pitting tradition against modernity than satirizing two different models of commercial modernity (the Whig Peachum-like embrace of profits over people *and* the romanticized Macheath-like Stuart rapaciousness), then *Polly* makes more sense. Like the courtiers surrounding Charles II, the other pirates under Macheath's command complain that his attention to Jenny Diver distracts from business. As Hacker puts it, "He is too much attach'd to his pleasures. That mistress of his is a clog to his ambition. She's an arrant *Cleopatra*." His comrade replies: "If it were not for her, the *Indies* would be our own" (2.2.68–70). As the discussion escalates, however, the men come to blows over how to divide Mexico, Peru, and Cuba among themselves, stopped only by the entrance of Polly, dressed as a boy. A diminished version of Charles II, Macheath similarly undermines his ability to expand his global empire through his weakness for women.

Polly explicitly echoes Dryden's *The Indian Emperour*, still popular in the eighteenth century, as part of its engagement with the Restoration. Morano/Macheath has captured the Native American prince Cawwawkee and—in a reprisal of Dryden—the comically proud English rabble threaten to torture him for information:

MORANO: Torture shall make you squeak.

CAWWAWKEE: I have resolution; and pain shall neither make me lie or betray. I tell thee once more, *European*, I am no coward.

VANDERBLUFF: What, neither cheat nor be cheated! There is no having either commerce or correspondence with these creatures.

JENNY: We have reason to be thankful for our good education. How ignorant is mankind without it!

CAPSTERN: I wonder to hear the brute speak.

LAGUERRE: They would make a shew of him in *England*.

JENNY: Poh, they would only take him for a fool.

CAPSTERN: But how can you expect any thing else from a creature, who hath never seen a civiliz'd country? Which way should he know mankind?

JENNY: Since they are made like us, to be sure, were they in *England* they might be taught.

LAGUERRE: Why we see country gentlemen grow into courtiers, and country gentlewomen, with a little polishing of the town, in a few months become fine ladies.

JENNY: Without doubt, education and example can do much.

POLLY: How happy are these savages! Who would not wish to be in such ignorance. (2.8.53–76)

Gay satirizes in two directions at once: Morano and his comrades, in contrast to their claims of superior education, clearly lack polish, but the play also satirizes the goal of sophistication itself. They cast Cawwawkee as a kind of rustic, but advise that with proper education he could join them in polite society. Not only does the prince reject this goal, but so does Polly. Also like *The Indian Emperour*, *Polly* ends with a projected mixed marriage. But while Dryden has the conquistador Cortez marry into the native elite, in Gay it is the unsophisticated girl who finds a partner in Native American royalty. Thus, by switching the genders of the lovers from Dryden's popular play, *Polly* implies that the single remaining virtuous European (Polly) has no choice but to integrate herself into the imagined Indigenous alternative.[69] In spite of this paradox, and in spite of play's Eurocentric stereotyping of Native Americans as noble savages, *Polly* challenges the stakes of sophistication. Gay, however, does not so much reject cosmopolitanism as return, in spite of his satire, to a version of Dryden's heroic model, once again considering the fleeting possibility of connection across boundaries.

Sophisticated Ladies: *The Way of the World*

Finally, we return to Congreve's most admired play in our own time, which does not tell the story of the sophistication of a provincial girl (this had happened, as mentioned, before the play began), but takes the problem of worldliness as its central tension. Just as *The Mourning Bride* looks back to the Restoration through tragedy, so *The Way of the World* does something similar through comedy. Congreve constructs a Restoration-like plot, in which a rakish male schemes to get what he wants. Mirabell has devised at least four plots: first, he had tried to elope with Millamant before the play begins, but was foiled by Mrs. Marwood; second, he tries to get access to Millamant by pretending to court Lady Wishfort; third—the one that takes place during the time frame of the play—he disguises his servant as "Sir Rowland" so the servant can court Lady Wishfort and then threaten to embarrass her with this unequal romance; and finally, in the only plot that works, he secured Mrs. Fainall's money by contact before the play began to protect her from the husband he compels her to marry in order to disguise their own affair in the case of pregnancy. Lady Wishfort, insufficiently schooled in the most recent ways of the world, keeps a copy of Jeremy Collier's infamous attack on Restoration drama in her closet; she recommends it as reading for Mrs. Marwood (3.59).[70] At the moment when the nefarious scheming comes to a crisis and Mr. Fainall threatens to reveal his wife's illicit sexual activity, Lady Wishfort looks at her daughter (Mrs. Fainall) with horror and demands, as noted above: "Have you not been sophisticated?" (5.138). (She invokes the earlier "contaminated" or "polluted" meaning of the term, as consistent with her old-fashioned character.) Mrs. Fainall's entrance into the ways of the world has been both refining *and* contaminating. Indeed, the changing aspirations to sophistication between the Restoration and the post-1688 world are central to *The Way of the World*.[71]

Congreve's engagement with Restoration cosmopolitanism explains some of the seemingly frivolous aspects of the play's complicated plot. Both Witwouds, for example, with their Restoration-style charactonyms, display doomed cosmopolitan ambitions as objects of derisive humor. Sir Willful Witwoud, Lady Wishfort's nephew, has come to town "to Equip himself for Travel"; he is about to undertake a Grand Tour, but at the ridiculous age of forty, a prospect that Mirabell and Fainall turn into a comic figure for the international balance of trade:

> FAINALL: No matter for that; 'tis for the Honour of *England*, that all *Europe* should know we have Blockheads of all Ages.
> MIRABELL: I wonder there is not an Act of Parliament to save the Credit of the Nation, and prohibit the Exportation of Fools.
> FAINALL: By no means, 'tis better as 'tis; 'tis better to Trade with a little Loss than to be quite eaten up with being overstock'd.
>
> (1.5.12–18)

Sir Willful, like Lady Wishfort, peaked in an earlier era. The impending visit of this gentleman horrifies his half-brother Witwoud, who despises

Willful's country manners and lives in fear that he will expose some familial lack of urban polish. Witwoud's friend Petulant is also comically hypersensitive about his urbanity: he takes such care of his reputation that, to create an illusion of popularity, he pays people to call for him at coffeehouses. Sir Willful later outs his foppish cousin by mentioning that Witwoud had originally come to London as an attorney's clerk, barely escaping an apprenticeship to a feltmaker. Sir Willful himself plans to learn "a spice of your *French*" (3.15.103).

MRS MARWOOD: No doubt you will return very much improv'd.
WITWOUD: Yes, refin'd, like a *Dutch* skipper from a Whale-fishing.

(3.15.107–8)

While both Witwouds strive for cosmopolitanism, Lady Wishfort remains baffled by how the ways of the world have changed since her coquettish youth in the Restoration. She is a comic version of Zara and Zempoalla: a powerful older woman with an inappropriate interest in the play's attractive hero. In his courtship of Lady Wishfort, the fake Sir Rowland calls her his "pearl of India," recalling the extravagant praise of the Restoration's Catherine. In a particularly insightful reading, Robert Erickson suggests that as much as the play treats Lady Wishfort as an object of ridicule, it nevertheless reserves sympathy for her poignant vulnerability—perhaps a comic version of the fear and pity that the defeated exotic queens arouse. Sir Willful's public drinking and Lady Wishfort's surreptitious indulgence in ratafia—a weakness not shared by the younger characters—link them both to the dated debauchery of the court of Charles II. As with Zara and Zempoalla, Lady Wishfort's vulnerability lies in her sexual passion: speaking of Mirabell, who pretended to court her, she confesses that "when I did not see him, I cou'd have brib'd a Villain to his Assassination; but his Appearance rakes the Embers which have so long lain smother'd in my Breast" (5.10.44–46). Yet the character remains a comically diminished version of the earlier queens. Her world is constricted and prejudicial rather than expansive. When Willful shows up drunk, she declares him a Turk or a Saracen. She similarly gives Mr. Fainall a foreign label when he reveals his brutal plot: "This is most inhumanly savage," she remarks, "exceeding the Barbarity of a *Muscovite* husband." The more worldly Mr. Fainall runs with it: "I learn'd it from his *Czarish* Majesty's Retinue, in a Winter Evening's Conference over Brandy and Pepper, amongst other Secrets of Matrimony and Policy, as they are at present practis'd in the Northern Hemisphere" (5.6.24–26). This provincialism on Lady Wishfort's part extends to the education of her daughter. In shock over learning of Mrs. Fainall's adultery,

Lady Wishfort insists that she had gone to great lengths to keep her from becoming sophisticated:

> I promise you, her Education has been unexceptionable—I may say it; for I chiefly made it my own Care to initiate her very Infancy in the Rudiments of Virtue, and to impress upon her Tender years a young Odium and Aversion to the very sight of Men.—Ay, Friend, she would ha' shriek'd if she had but seen a Man, till she was in her Teens. As I'm a Person 'tis true—She was never suffer'd to play with a Male-Child, tho' but in Coats; Nay, her very Babies were of the *Feminine Gender*.— O, she never look'd a Man in the Face but her own Father, or the Chaplain, and him we made a shift to put upon her for a Woman, by the help of his long Garments and his sleek Face, 'till she was going in her Fifteen. . . . I warrant you, or she would never have born to have been catechiz'd by him; and have heard his long Lectures against Singing and Dancing, and such Debaucheries; and going to filthy Plays, and profane Musick-meetings, where the lewd Trebles squeak nothing but Bawdy, and the Basses roar Blasphemy. O, she would have swoon'd at the Sight or Name of an obscene Play-Book—and can I think after all this, that my Daughter can be Naught? What, a Whore? And thought it excommunication to set her Foot within the door of a Play-house. O my dear friend, I can't believe it, no, no. (5.5.2–27)

The theater would have provided an alternative schooling in the ways of the world, but Lady Wishfort kept all such entertainment away from the future Mrs. Fainall, who grows up to make, by her own admission, exceptionally bad choices. Her greatest of these was Mirabell.

The affair and continuing friendship in this play between Mrs. Fainall and Mirabell, who pursues Millamant for marriage, has remained a persistent problem for criticism.[72] Had Mirabell only been out to capture a fortune like any respectable Restoration comic hero, he could have simply married Mrs. Fainall. Had he been unscrupulous, he could at any time have taken possession of her money, which she had already signed over to him. Mrs. Fainall, although she seems to love Mirabell, nevertheless helps to advance his cause with Millamant. The persistent sense in the play that Mrs. Fainall is somehow not good enough for him cannot be explained by any difference in her fortune or social status. Nor can it be explained by the fact that she is not a virgin: while this might be a barrier in another genre, rich widows make excellent mates in Restoration comedy. Rather, Mrs. Fainall, in spite of Lady Wishfort's accusation, is *insufficiently* sophisticated. Her mother has kept her from the world in general and the theater in particular, a cosmopolitan institution providing glimpses into parts of the world inaccessible to most members of the audience. Lady Wishfort's bookshelf filled with moralists and antitheatricalists further reveals the limits of her daughter's education: *"Quarles* and *Prynne,* and the *Short View of the Stage,* with *Bunyan's* works" (3.4.21–23).[73] Although in some ways Mirabell has exploited Mrs. Fainall's ignorance, this man of the world tries to school his lover in the ways of the world when she has trouble containing her loathing for her husband:

> MRS FAINALL: While I only hated my Husband, I cou'd bear to see him; but since I have despis'd him, he's too offensive.
> MIRABELL: Oh, you shou'd hate with Prudence.
> MRS FAINALL: Yes, for I have lov'd with Indiscretion.
> MIRABELL: You shou'd have just so much Disgust for your Husband as may be sufficient to make you relish your Lover.
>
> (2.4.3–8)

Like her mother, Mrs. Fainall suffers from an excess of passion and has not learned to control her feeling and actions; she must be guided by Mirabell.

If Mrs. Fainall ultimately proves too provincial for Mirabell, Millamant risks being too cosmopolitan. Mirabell describes her as a ship in "full sail" (2.5.1). He worries about her capacity to transform herself through foreign commodities, as he makes clear in one of his demands in their marriage negotiation:

> *Item,* I article that you continue to like your own Face, as long as I shall: And while it passes current with me, that you endeavour not to new Coin it. To which end, together with all Vizards for the Day, I prohibit all Masks for the Night, made of Oil'd-skins and I know not what—Hog's-Bones, Hare's-Gall, Pig-Water, and the Marrow of a roasted Cat. In short, I forbid all Commerce with the Gentlewoman in *what-d'ye-call-it* Court. *Item,* I shut my Doors against all Bauds with Baskets, and penny-worths of Muslin, China, Fans, atlasses, &c.
> (4.5.88–97)

The last item that Mirabell forbids her to purchase could be a "a silk-satin manufactured in the East"[74] or a map of the world. Both meanings suggest his efforts to rein in her cosmopolitan impulses. Everything the bawds have in their baskets, in Mirabell's scenario, comes from the East. (Catherine of Braganza, we recall, made the folding fan fashionable, as it had been in Portugal through Asian trade routes.) Mirabell, however, concedes to his bride the right to other global imports and, crucially, to the dominion of the tea table, "but with *proviso*, that you exceed not in your Province; but restrain your self to native and simple *Tea-Table* drinks, as *Tea, Chocolate* and *Coffee*" (4.5.106–10). Stronger drink he will not allow. Mrs. Fainall, with her limited education and limited ambitions, cannot compete with this ship in full sail, this sinophilic empress of the tea table.

If a limited education ultimately damages Mrs. Fainall and Millamant threatens to sail too far away, Lady Wishfort, at the play's heart, misses the boat entirely. Her misperceptions, however, create comedy out of the performance of femininity, and in doing so call attention back to the Restoration origin of the actress. At fifty-five in 1700, she would have been fifteen in 1660—just the right age to be taken to London in search of a husband—and seems in painfully comic ways to be stuck in that moment. Perhaps this is why the text of *The Way of the World* is so precise about her age. She has become unmoored in the postrevolutionary world of 1700. She thinks of herself as a young girl who can attract the rakish attentions of Mirabell and the marriage proposal of "Sir Rowland" (who is actually Mirabell's servant set up to trap her into an embarrassing engagement); either of these men would in theory help her reconstitute a patriarchal family. The new world of contractual machinations baffles her, and she cannot protect herself and her daughter from Mr. Fainall. She does not recognize the deviousness of Mrs. Marwood. Mirabell manipulates Lady Wishfort by playing along with her own delusions, first by trying to court her and then by disguising his own servant as "Sir Rowland." If she agreed to marry Sir Rowland, in the ill-devised plan, Mirabell would step in and "rescue" her. Lady Wishfort does not see this coming: her antitheatricality, which she tries to pass down to her daughter, leaves her vulnerable to such performances.

But in spite of her enthusiasm for Jeremy Collier, Lady Wishfort, more than any other character in this play, conjures the Restoration creation of the professional actress. Most of the characters at some point play within the play: Mirabell pretends to desire Lady Wishfort; both Mirabell and Millamant try to act as if they do not love each other; Mrs. Marwood pretends to be loyal to Lady Wishfort; Waitwell plays the role of Sir Rowland; Mr. Fainall feigns all. Lady Wishfort is the only character who visibly prepares for her performances, practicing her self-presentation in front of the mirror. First performed by Elinor Leigh, the daughter of an actor (James Dixon) and wife to another (Anthony Leigh), Lady Wishfort both performs and is performed by an aging actress who had her start in the reign of Charles II.[75] She looks at herself in the mirror with the critical eye of an actress: "Let me see the Glass—Cracks, say'st thou? Why I am arrantly flea'd—I look like an old peel'd Wall. Thou must repair me, *Foible*, before Sir *Rowland* comes" (3.5.71–73).[76] As Sir Rowland approaches, she considers the posture and gestures with which she will greet him, blocking out her movements with great comic effect:

> Well, and how shall I receive him? In what Figure shall I give his Heart the first Impression? There is a great deal in the first Impression. Shall I sit?—No I won't sit—I'll walk—aye I'll walk from the Door upon his Entrance; and then turn full upon him—No, that will be too sudden. I'll lye—aye, I'll lye down—I'll receive him in my little Dressing-Room, there's a Couch—Yes, yes, I'll give the first Impression on a Couch— I won't lye neither but loll and lean upon one Elbow; with one Foot a little dangling off, jogging in a thoughtful way—Yes—and then as soon as he appears, start, ay, start and be surpriz'd, and rise: to meet him in a pretty Disorder—Yes—O, nothing is more alluring than a Levee from a Couch in some Confusion.—It shews the Foot to advantage, and furnishes with Blushes, and re-composing Airs beyond Comparison. (4.1.19–24)

With an aging diva at its vulnerable center, *The Way of the World* plays the Restoration invention of the actress for comedy. The play declares, on the one hand, the end of the Restoration, as Lady Wishfort's social and political perspective has become comically dysfunctional and misaligned with a new generation that rejects such a strange combination of theatricality and antitheatricality. On the other hand, Lady Wishfort persists. Millamant wins the love of Mirabell (and so many others) not because she rejects Restoration cosmopolitan values, but because she masters them skillfully, especially in comparison with her theater-deprived cousin, Mrs. Fainall. Whether toying with fops or demanding empire over the tea table, Millamant reveals herself as a highly skilled performer who, in a pinch, proves herself willing to sacrifice marital happiness to rescue her aunt. While Lady Wishfort, Mrs. Fainall, and Mrs. Marwood all reveal their comic and tragic lack of sophistication, Millamant emerges through this family crisis relatively unscathed for her superior understanding of the ways of the world.

The Way of the World thus organizes characters along a spectrum of sophistication. Mirabell ultimately outmaneuvers Fainall, with his superior understanding of the post-1688 world, a point that has been widely recognized. By turning to the women in the play, however, we have seen how these are the characters through whom Congreve maps out these differences in the greatest detail. We can also see how the play takes advantage of the continuing cultural association of the actress with her birth in the Restoration. Much discussion of the introduction of women onto the professional stage has focused on the shifting dynamics of gender that it produced and reflected. Congreve's play and many others nevertheless also suggest that those closer to this theatrical innovation were both galvanized and troubled by actresses, not just for their nontraditional gender performances, but for the ways they embodied and were produced by the cosmopolitan aspirations of Charles II.

❦ CHAPTER 6

Histories of Their Own Times

Burnet, Cibber, and Rochester

In 1799, Edward Jerningham hoped to entertain
audiences with a play about the court of Charles II called *The Peckham Frolic:
or Nell Gwyn*. Jerningham's literary career never took off, although he published several sentimental poems decrying social injustices and had produced
three plays before writing this one. His friend Richard Sheridan satirized him
as Sir Benjamin Backbite, the foppish gossip-monger in *The School for Scandal*. *The Peckham Frolic* never made it to the stage.[1] However, I introduce it
briefly into this chapter about historians and memoirists of the Restoration
for insight into the period's afterlife. Jerningham sets the action in Peckham
Manor House, where Charles II, in the fiction of the play, kept Nell Gwynn.[2]
Sir Oliver Luke, "a formal knight who was created by Cromwell,"[3] has come
to Peckham with a petition to present to the king. Hearing that Sir Oliver has
money but no wife, Nell schemes to marry the visitor to her dear friend Anne
Killigrew.[4] In this historical fantasy of reconciliation between rebel and cavalier through marriage, Nell's impish plot succeeds. Comedy ensues, however,
when Sir Oliver cannot understand the cosmopolitan banter of the rusticating
courtiers. Several times, he asks them to repeat themselves in simpler terms.[5]
The cavaliers also flaunt their sexual dalliances, but Sir Oliver takes this in
stride and marries the single virtuous woman in the mix.

In the titular "frolic," Nell persuades the Earl of Rochester to impersonate the king so he can approve the marriage between Sir Oliver and Anne

Killigrew: the Restoration's most notorious libertine, then, stands in for the monarch. Rochester fears the king's disapproval, but Nell assures him that Charles will see the comedy in the situation (and no, she tells him, the frolic does not extend to sleeping arrangements). The sudden entrance of the real king in the midst of this joke alarms the company. But Charles quickly detects the ruse and plays along; he is so amused that he keeps Rochester on the throne through the wedding dinner, at which point he shocks Sir Oliver by claiming that he will overthrow the king. The comic resolution distressingly baffles the bridegroom: "[D]amn these Peckham jokes," he laments, "I don't comprehend them" (30).

With this play, Jerningham romanticizes the Restoration with an even hand, giving Sir Oliver a happy ending, a virtuous wife, and only moderate humiliation. But he clearly encourages audience members to align themselves with the worldly courtiers, a notable choice given Jerningham's antislavery and anticolonialist expressions in his poetry. His "The Fall of Mexico" (1775), which distinctively echoes Dryden's *The Indian Emperour*, laments the brutality of colonialism; his "Yarico to Inkle" (1766) turns this well-known tale of love and betrayal into an explicit abolitionist plea. In Jerningham's version, Yarico is an African princess who kills herself to prevent her baby's being born into slavery.[6] *Peckham*, however, detaches the Restoration court from imperialism, the slave trade, and the threat of absolutism; it features the "Protestant whore" rather than any of the Catholic mistresses (or the Catholic wife) and reduces the differences between commonwealth men and cavaliers to personal sophistication, ready cash, sexual values, and tolerance for theatricality.

In distinguishing commonwealth men and cavaliers this way, Jerningham captures two key points of reference in subsequent depictions of the Restoration. First, Rochester becomes, to borrow the words of Matthew Augustine and Steven Zwicker, the Restoration "poster boy."[7] Indeed, no figure has come to represent the period quite like Rochester. Jerningham, however, also captures Rochester's imagined interchangeability with King Charles II: in the play, he literally stands in for the king; in the eighteenth century and beyond, he stands in for the entire period. Rochester represents the libertine cosmopolitanism that epitomizes the charm and scandal of the court, as if he is not just the king's substitute, but his alter ago. The Restoration becomes fascinating for intertwined impulses for libertinism and theatricality, both of which baffle Sir Oliver and which continue to define our understanding of the period. As we have seen, there is good reason for this: the Restoration reinvented public theater, and Rochester and some contemporaries tested the boundaries of sexual representation.[8] Yet the issues that galvanized debates about this period in the early eighteenth century—tyranny, absolutism, state violence—and those that occupy Jerningham's sentimental poetry—the transatlantic slave trade, imperialism—drop out of this portrait.

Certainly, the intriguing literary experiments with sexual norms in the Restoration continue to deserve attention. The libertine court culture, as Jeremy Webster has argued, included not just writing plays and attending theatrical productions, but also the cultivation of personal theatricality in a way particular to the Restoration.[9] This culture also had a dark side. James Grantham Turner has argued that it produced an elitist, violent, and misogynist culture. Pat Gill, Peggy Thompson, and others have shown how this misogyny found its way into theatrical performances.[10] At the end of the eighteenth century, however, *The Peckham Frolic* treats Charles's sexual adventures as a lighthearted romp. The play represents, albeit in exaggerated form, a picture of the Restoration—a time of wit, playfulness, sexual experimentation, and theatricality—that still has considerable force. Recent scholarship on the writing of this time sometimes seems to split the period in two, into the Restoration of sexual/theatrical experimentation (comedy) and the Restoration of empire-building, exploitation, and absolutism (tragedy, tragicomedy, and heroic plays). This is perhaps mostly starkly suggested by J. Douglas Canfield's publication of two separate volumes about these genres and their political meaning.[11]

Early-eighteenth-century writers noticed and registered their objection to the sexual frolics of the Restoration court, but other political controversies loomed larger for them. One particularly popular and controversial account of the Stuart court was Gilbert Burnet's *History of His Own Time*, which condemned Charles and James as brutal tyrants rather than rascally rakes. Burnet is familiar in literary studies mostly for his self-reported deathbed conversion of Rochester (a story to which I will return). Burnet, however, would not have chosen Rochester as the "poster boy" for the Restoration; instead, he might have nominated Judge Jeffreys, who sent political opponents of the Stuarts to the scaffold. Burnet's account, admired by Whigs and reviled by Tories, has less to say about court libertinism than it does about state violence. When he did write about the king's libertinism, he connected it to his imperious rule and neglect of state business. But while Burnet wrote a damning account of the monarchs as tyrants, absolutists, and war capitalists, he may have contributed inadvertently to the romanticizing of the Stuarts. If we take into account Rochester's odd interchangeability with Charles II, on display in *The Peckham Frolic* and elsewhere throughout the period, we might also suggest that the famous rake's conversion, as described in detail by Burnet, may have implied the King's ultimate goodness to some readers. Rochester's renunciation of his youthful indiscretions could become a proxy for forgetting (and thus for peeling off from the period) the cosmopolitan violence so relentlessly plumbed, as we have seen, in Restoration theater. Thus, instead of reading Rochester's outrageous poems as narratives of war trauma, as Cynthia Richards has done so insightfully, we can see them as scandalously comic; instead of the period that provided the foundation for eighteenth-century war capitalism and British dominance in the slave trade, Jerningham and others can reframe those years as the period of wacky cavaliers who created sophisticated frolics beyond the comprehension of clueless Cromwellians, all in good fun.[12]

Burnet's damning memoirs of life in the Restoration court attracted considerable attention in the eighteenth century, and yet depictions like Jerningham's eventually came to dominate. Many writers contributed to this rebranding of the Restoration, but in this chapter I single out Burnet's conversion narrative of Rochester, and also Colley Cibber, who was particularly influential through his plays, his persona, and his personal account of the relationship between the theater and the Restoration court recorded in his *Apology*. Here, Cibber represents a larger movement for which he cannot entirely be credited. Gilbert Burnet ends his history of the reign of Charles II by comparing the English ruler to Tiberius, a far cry from the fun-loving monarch who changes places with Rochester in the *Frolic*. Cibber, I will suggest, played a crucial role in making the comic interchangeability of Rochester and Charles possible in the wake of the conversion. Cibber, like Burnet, found the politics of the Restoration period repulsive, but he embraced, advanced, and profited from its reinvented theater.

In order fully to understand Cibber's account of the Restoration in his *Apology* and implicitly in his performances, however, we must first look at Burnet's *History of His Own Time*, a narrative, I will show, to which Cibber directly responds. The bishop offers an eyewitness account that differs from Cibber's depiction and that has attracted less interest, perhaps because of his disapproval of both the court and the entertainment it inspired. In the reign of Charles II, Burnet reports, "the stage was defiled beyond all example"; Dryden in particular was "a monster of immodesty."[13] But while post-1688 drama turned away from Stuart absolutism, it was difficult for even the most committed Whig not to appreciate the powerful ways in which the court of Charles II had left its mark on theater. Cibber grasped this tension. He rejected Tory politics and aligned himself with Whig ideals, a position that, as his enemies never stopped pointing out, helped him to achieve the laureateship. At the same time, however, he and many of his contemporaries admired the cosmopolitan aesthetics of the Restoration court. Throughout his career, Cibber negotiated these tensions, and he used the stage and his *Apology* to overwrite the violence of the period documented by Burnet and others. I borrow the term "overwrite" here from William Warner, who uses it to suggest how mid eighteenth-century novelists make use of earlier, less virtuous novels that they spurned, "disavowing but appropriating; tossing out but recycling."[14] Cibber's relationship to Restoration theater and court culture was similar, in sharp contrast to Burnet's excoriating critique. Signaling his comic revision of the bishop's very serious work, Cibber refers to his *Apology* as a *"theatrical* history of my own time" (emphasis added), offering his career narrative as a thespian alternative to Burnet's well-known political one. Through his comic repetitions of Stuart excesses, Cibber wears down the political edge that Burnet records as sharp and jagged. It is in part because of Cibber, I will suggest, that the abolitionist and anti-imperialist Edward Jerningham can make Peckham the scene of a frolic and the Restoration into a moment in which Rochester might as well have ruled.

Gilbert Burnet's Restoration

With the fall of the Stuarts and despite the military, psychological, and ideological threat they continued to pose from across the water in the eighteenth century, British nationalism gained momentum. In *Britons: Forging the Nation 1707–1837*, Linda Colley argues persuasively that Britons consolidated a national identity out of several distinct cultures through the common thread of Protestantism, persistently in tension with Stuart-inflected Catholicism.[15] Gilbert Burnet (1643–1715) died before this full consolidation took place; nevertheless, he played a crucial role in its prehistory, which he represented as the virtuous and just alternative to Stuart cosmopolitanism. Personally, Burnet had as good a claim as anyone to a cosmopolitan identity: he spoke several languages, he traveled widely, and he even wrote a travel narrative later praised by Joseph Addison.[16] Born in Scotland, Burnet became Bishop of Salisbury after a distinguished but turbulent career. He wrote prolifically on theological and political topics and published several works of history. Burnet knew Charles II personally and maintained a close friendship with the Duke of York, although they ultimately fell out. Yet in spite of (or perhaps because of) his extensive exposure to the cosmopolitan court and his own broad knowledge of the world, Burnet helped lay the groundwork for Protestant nationalism, the proponents of which became skeptical of Restoration cosmopolitanism and, unlike their predecessors, saw inherent tensions between it and national identity. Burnet laid out the parameters of this Protestant nationalism in his *History of the Reformation* (published in three volumes in 1679, 1681, and 1714), and also in his *History of My Own Times*, published posthumously in two volumes in 1724 and 1734. Burnet's *History* began as "secret history," handed around in manuscript but never published in his lifetime. According to historian Martin Greig, Burnet reshaped his book at the end of his life for broader consumption, removing some of the personal material and turning the work into a political history of England, Scotland, and Ireland under Charles II, James II, and William and Mary, with a glance back in the beginning at Charles I and then Cromwell.[17] After the bishop's death, his oldest son saw the *History* into print. These fascinating volumes offer the narrative of an insider and a player—albeit an oppositional one—in Restoration politics.

The Restoration court of *The Peckham Frolic* would have been unrecognizable to Burnet. Unlike this play or Colley Cibber's blithe theatrical *Apology*, to which we will turn next, Burnet's *History of My Own Times* records this period of English history as tragic and violent. His prose, though often disparaged, skillfully dramatizes some of the horrific events of the period. In Burnet's account, Charles began his reign as a rather careless and inattentive monarch, but grew into a murderous tyrant. He paints a bleak picture of the Restoration; the monarchy and the court created an atmosphere that bordered on tyranny, with English freedom and interests sold out to French luxury and French Catholic absolutism. Unlike Jerningham, Burnet did not find the king's attachment to Nell Gwynn, or to any other mistress, amusing. In the wake of the Popish Plot, the bishop fled England after watching some of his closest friends die on the scaffold. He remained in exile during the reign of James II and, by his own report, began negotiations with William and Mary for their rescue of Britain from Catholic absolutism. He takes personal credit for persuading Mary to resign her own authority to that of her husband, thus making the Glorious Revolution possible.[18]

Burnet's *History* outraged Tories for the way its author disparaged the Stuarts.[19] He reports that the nation suffered greatly in the years between Queen Elizabeth and 1688 and identifies the influence of foreign Catholic women as a force undermining the English political system. In a quick historical retrospective of politics before his "own time," Burnet calls the reign of James I "inglorious" and writes that "no king could die less lamented" (vol. 1, 26, 29). Charles I and Charles II did not naturally possess admirable characters, but any glimmer of decency was crushed by the powerful influence of foreign Catholic women. The reign of Charles I "was a continual series of errors." He had too high a view of regal power and "was unreasonably feeble to those whom he trusted, chiefly to the queen" (vol. 1, 81). When Charles I came to the throne, Burnet writes, the people hoped that he would be more favorably disposed toward the Puritans. During his reign, however, the influence of Queen Henrietta Maria expanded. The French-born queen loved intrigue, Burnet reports. She was lively in her discourse, and the combination of her charisma and her bad advice was largely to blame for her husband's tragic fate (vol. 1, 46, 54, 55). Burnet does not spare Charles himself, reporting that he "loved high and rough methods" and "hated all that offered prudent and moderate counsels" (vol. 1, 52). But his overreliance on his Catholic bride brought down his reign. Burnet was not alone in suspecting Henrietta Maria and disparaging her apparently excessive influence.[20] She was never even officially coronated because a Catholic crowning ceremony was not permitted. Henrietta Maria violated Burnet's sense of appropriate behavior for women: he suspected her of manipulating political outcomes behind the scenes. But as much as his description of her relies on stereotypes of women, gender ideology alone does not account for his animus. Other powerful women earn praise in the *History*: Elizabeth led the nation to glory; Queen Mary offers a positive counterpoint to Henrietta Maria in her resignation to her husband. Henrietta Maria combined violations of gendered propriety with French Catholicism, which Burnet consistently understood to be opposed to English, Scottish, and Irish national interests.

Henrietta Maria caused even more damage by her influence over her sons, Charles and James, by raising them as Catholics and immersing them in French rather than English culture. The latter included the court masque, a form that Henrietta Maria embraced and that would ultimately influence Restoration public theater by way of key figures who survived the civil wars. In her own time, the queen consort was criticized for her sponsorship of these masques, in which she and her women acted. William Prynne's denunciation of actresses in *Histriomastix* (1632) was widely understood to be an attack on her, suggesting the popular association of the queen with theatrical performance. Burnet does not specifically discuss Henrietta Maria's theatrics, but elsewhere he registers his disapproval of court masques (vol. 1, 24). Henrietta Maria patronized William Davenant, who would at the Restoration honor her, as we saw in chapter 1, through the character of Ianthe in *The Siege of Rhodes*.

In a sense, Burnet saw the vivacious and theater-loving Henrietta Maria as the root cause of England's troubles that were finally addressed in 1688: her influence led to the downfall of her husband, the sympathies of her sons toward French culture, and the Catholicism of her son James II. Only another woman, her Protestant granddaughter Mary, whose modesty compared so favorably to Henrietta's flamboyance, could finally cure this infection. Burnet did not explicitly blame the theater, but he nevertheless aligned court masques, lively women, Catholic extravagance, and vicious executions on one side, and on the other pious, introspective women (such as all three of his wives), Protestant restraint, due process, and the rights of subjects. For Burnet, the Stuart father and son differed mainly in that while Charles I lost his way under the influence of a single charismatic foreign woman, Charles II fell prey to a series of them. His mother could be included as the first of these: after the Restoration, Henrietta Maria returned to court and, according to Burnet, gave bad advice to her son just as she had to his father. Charles's sister, also named Henrietta but known as Minette, belongs to this pantheon of bad influences: she arrived at court in 1671, and Charles could "deny her nothing" (vol. 1, 551). According to Burnet, she persuaded her brother to form an alliance with France against the Dutch, then returned to her home in France, where her husband poisoned her in the wake of rumors of her promiscuity in London (522–24).

Burnet, unsurprisingly, reviled the Catholic Countess of Castlemaine (Barbara Palmer), writing, "She was a woman of great beauty, but most enormously vicious and ravenous; foolish but imperious, very uneasy to the king, and always carrying on intrigues with other men, while yet she pretended she was jealous of him. His passion for her, and her strange behaviour towards him, did so disorder him, that often he was not master of himself, nor capable of minding business, which, in so critical a time, required great application" (vol. 1, 171). Castlemaine interfered in politics, to Burnet's dismay, although the French Louise de Kéroualle, later the Duchess of Portsmouth, replaced her in the king's affections and became even more powerful. According to Burnet, the Duke of Buckingham had proposed to Louis XIV that the only way to control Charles would be to send him a mistress who would manipulate him as desired. The plan, in Burnet's view, succeeded: by 1671 Charles divided his time between Louise de Kéroualle and Nell Gwynn,[21] "but he was so entirely possessed by the duchess of Portsmouth, and so engaged by her in the French interest, that this threw him into great difficulties, and exposed him to much contempt and distrust" (617).[22]

Burnet's Charles II thus little resembles the jaunty cavalier found in eighteenth-century fiction and drama. The future bishop certainly took notice of the sexual irregularity of the court, but did not interpret it as merriment. In his account, Charles hated business but loved pleasure (vol. 1, 170); he secretly practiced Catholicism (169); he was quick-witted but cold-hearted; his entire court "delivered itself up to vice" (470). The licentiousness of the theater contributed to corruption (495). Charles and his courtiers gave themselves up "to all extravagance, and to the wildest frolics that a wanton wit could devise" (485)—frolics, we suspect, that little resembled the one depicted at Peckham in Jerningham's play.

For Burnet, the vulnerability of powerful men to such sophisticated women was a symptom of absolutism. Libertinism did not grow out of insufficient respect for women, but of granting them—especially charismatic, Catholic, and/or theatrical French ones—too much power. In the case of Louise de Kéroualle, the French king, assisted by Buckingham, deliberately exploited the English monarch's sexual susceptibilities. These women, in turn, influenced political decisions. But a closer look at Burnet complicates any simple alliance between sexual freedom and Stuart monarch on one side and Puritan or low-church restraint on the other.[23] Sexual impropriety in itself was not serious enough to ruin a character in his account. He admired William III, who was not faithful to his queen. Burnet had a reputation as a ladies' man himself: he benefited greatly, as his enemies often noted, from his three unions to elite heiresses, all of whom married beneath their social rank when choosing him. Further, he was rumored to have carried on an affair with the charismatic opera singer Catherine Tofts. Tofts' parents both worked in Burnet's household. In a lightly disguised version told by Delarivière Manley in her *Memoirs of Europe*, Burnet first seduced the mother, and then later the daughter. Olive Baldwin and Thelma Wilson point out that the rumors of this affair could have been politically motived, as Burnet had become the "*bête noir* of the Tories and the High Church faction"; nevertheless, Catherine's father left her only five shillings in his will, which may indicate some coolness in their relationship caused by the scandal.[24] Burnet's early twentieth-century biographers note the suspicious circumstances of Catherine's departure from Burnet's household and the response of the "Tory-Jacobite gutter-press": "[T]he virulence of Jacobite libel upon Burnet almost exceeds belief."[25] Notoriously, Burnet once argued that the Bible did not forbid polygamy, presumably proposing polygamy or divorce as reasonable options for solving the problem of the infertility of Catherine of Braganza, although he later retracted this position.[26] The problem with Charles was, for Burnet, less about sexual transgression than the threat of political absolutism and the growing power of the French empire. He characterizes Charles as irreligious and sexually indulgent, but most powerfully, in an element that has tended to be detached from debates about court libertinism, as politically brutal.[27]

In Burnet's *History*, Charles was less the merry monarch than an absolutist who became a murderous tyrant. Absolutism appealed to him in part because he lacked money ("scandalous and poor," as Rochester put it), and did not like relying on Parliament for funding. He began his reign as a bully. Sir John Coventry, who sat in the House of Commons, was among those who resisted the king's persistent demands for funds from Parliament.

Hitting the king where he lived, Coventry proposed a tax on the playhouses, which, in Burnet's view, "in so dissolute a time, were become nests of prostitution" (vol 1, 495). The court opposed this tax because "it was said, that the players were the king's servants, and a part of his pleasure. Coventry asked, whether did the king's pleasure lie among the men or the women that acted," a rather clever insult that could be taken in a number of ways. The monarch was not so merry at this. Although the Duke of York, according to Burnet, tried to dissuade his brother from rash action, Charles had Coventry beaten, and the assailants "cut his nose to the bone" (vol. 1, 495), which created a "furious uproar" in the House of Commons. By 1673, it had become apparent that the king intended to rule on the "French model" (vol. 2, 2). He dissolved Parliament and ruled with a small cabal of ministers. The Popish Plot followed, in which Titus Oates accused the queen and other Catholics of plotting to murder Charles. Burnet implies that scandals raised by this crisis provided Charles with the opportunity to eliminate his enemies. A string of executions followed: "Every execution," Burnet writes, "like a new bleeding, abated the heat that the nation was in; and threw us into a cold deadness, which was like to prove fatal to us" (225).

Burnet offers a particularly riveting account of the execution of his friend Lord Russell, accused of participating in the Rye House plot, in which a group of opposition members, including the Duke of Monmouth, was suspected of planning to kill Charles and his brother to pave the way for the invasion of William of Orange. Lord Russell maintained his innocence. The power of Burnet's account emerges from his talent for biography,[28] but also as part of a narrative the *History* develops about the increasing violence of the monarch, culminating in a string of executions ordered by Judge Jeffreys in response to the Exclusion Crisis. Burnet begins his description of "the tragical day, in which I lost the two best friends in the world" with the death of Lord Essex, also suspected in the plot, sent to the tower, and later found with his throat cut (vol. 2, 375). Burnet accepts the explanation of suicide, as his friend had fallen under "a great depression of spirits" (373), although he also reports the rumors that Charles II had him murdered. While some of the other accused conspirators hoped for a fair hearing, "Lord Russel, from the time of his imprisonment, looked upon himself as a dead man, and turned his thoughts wholly to another world" (370). His friends did what they could to save him; they petitioned the king and the duke; they even offered money to the Duchess of Portsmouth in an attempt to win her influence (380). But Lord Russell's "whole behaviour," according to Burnet, "looked like a triumph over death" (381); he remained cheerful in prison, regretting only the sins of his youth. He parted with his wife with a "composed silence"; when she took her final leave of him, he said that "the bitterness of death is passed" (383). On the day of his execution, Burnet reports, Lord Russell wound up his watch, put it down, and said, "now he had done with time" (386).[29]

Burnet's story offers a moving account of his friend, colored by his own sense of loss. Without a doubt, he wrote this passage, later expanded to a memoir, to commemorate a man he understood as having suffered death in spite of his innocence. At the same time, the story's significance to the *History* also lies in its characterization of an increasing autocratic administration. Burnet reports that he recorded Lord Russell's last hours at the request of his wife, but he also read his journal entry, upon command, before the king and the duke, who "expressed himself so highly offended at me, that it was concluded I would be ruined" (vol. 2, 391). The passage destroyed any remnants of his friendship with the duke. Burnet then fled the country, persuaded that his life was in danger.

Burnet, inspired by standing before a statue of Tiberius, ends his history of the reign of Charles II with a comparison of the English monarch to the notorious Roman leader. The men's physical resemblance does not surprise him, given their likeness of character: "His [Charles's] hating of business, and his love of pleasures; his raising of favorites, and trusting them entirely; and his pulling them down, and hating them excessively; his art of covering deep designs, particularly of revenge, with an appearance of softness, brings them so near a likeness, that I did not wonder much to observe the resemblance of their face and person." (vol. 2, 482) "Few things," Burnet observes of Charles, "ever went near his heart" (488).

With the death of Charles, the nation went from bad to worse (vol. 3, 1). Burnet saw James, unlike his brother, as brutal from the start. He depicts the new king's libertinism as tawdry: according to Burnet, his mistress Catherine Sedley (daughter of the playwright and courtier Charles Sedley) hoped to become another Duchess of Portsmouth, but never attained any of the influence or status of her predecessor (13–14). Monmouth's rebellion features prominently in the discussion of James. Burnet saw this event, in which this illegitimate son of Charles tried to take the throne, as foolish and ill-conceived, but not to be regarded without sympathy. Monmouth went too far: he charged the new king with having burned London, with the Popish Plot, with the murder of Essex, and with having poisoned his own brother to gain the crown (46). Burnet disagrees with these charges, but nevertheless depicts Monmouth as a martyr, and the reaction against his rebellion as a symptom of the ruthlessness of the Stuart brothers. When Monmouth was brought to the block, "[t]he executioner was in great disorder, trembling all over: so he gave him two or three strokes without being able to finish the matter, and then flung the ax out of his hand. But the sheriff forced him to take it up: and at three or four more strokes he severed his head from his body" (56). After this gruesome scene, Burnet remembers Monmouth as "soft and gentle, even to excess." So, while he does not endorse the rebellion, he nevertheless contrasts the harshness of the execution with the mildness of the "unfortunate young man."

With merciless violence against the rebels, the new king, in Burnet's view, squandered the opportunity to create good will, a choice that would come back to haunt him. Two of the king's agents exemplify James's tendencies toward absolutism and the bloodbath of his short reign. Burnet describes each of them as barbaric and foreign, and one as tainted by his time in Morocco. The military commander Colonel Percy Kirke, on orders from the king, relentlessly hunted down the fugitives:

> Kirk, who had commanded long in Tangier, was become so savage by the neighbourhood of the Moors there, that some days after the battle, he ordered several of the prisoners to be hanged up at Taunton, without so much as the form of law, he and his company looking on from an entertainment they were at. At every new health another prisoner was hanged up. And they were so brutal, that observing the shaking of the legs of those whom they hanged, it was said among them, they were dancing; and upon that music was called for. (vol. 3, 58–59)

The other is Judge George Jeffreys, who sent so many of Burnet's friends and associates to the block in the reign of Charles:

> Jefferies [sic] was sent the western circuit to try the prisoners. His behaviour was beyond anything that was ever heard of in a civilized nation. He was perpetually either drunk or in a rage, liker a fury than the zeal of a judge. He required the prisoners to plead guilty. And in that case he gave them some hope of favour, if they gave him no trouble: otherwise, he told them, he would execute the letter of the law upon them in its utmost severity. This made many plead guilty, who had a great defence in law. But he shewed no mercy. He ordered a great many to be hanged up immediately, without allowing them a minute's time to say their prayers. He hanged, in several places, about six hundred persons. The greatest part of these were of the meanest sort, and of no distinction. The impieties with which he treated them, and his behaviour towards some of the nobility and gentry that were well affected, but came and pleaded in favour of some prisoners, would have amazed one, if done by a bashaw in Turkey. (vol. 3, 59–60)

While Kirke learned his brutality from the Moors in Tangier, Jeffreys outdoes a Turkish bashaw in his imperious cruelty. Rhetorically, then, Burnet aligns James, Charles, Kirke, and Jeffreys as non-English, as fundamentally foreigners: they are French; they are North African; they are Turks. His implicit defense of the purity of Anglo-Protestant identity gathers particular energy for exploiting the opportunity to remind readers of the investment and loss by Charles II in Tangier, brought to England by his Portuguese Catholic wife, as well as the Ottomanphilia popular in his court. His rhetoric sets up the rights and virtues of English roots and English purity against the cosmopolitan reign of the Stuart brothers and their Catholic women. Burnet, then, cultivates an English, and ultimately British, nationalism defined against Stuart cosmopolitanism.

Burnet's unabashed Whig version of history attracted much attention upon publication, fomenting anger from both directions. Tory luminaries, including Delarivière Manley and John Dryden, attacked him for his harsh depiction of the Stuarts.[30] Jonathan Swift excoriated the bishop in the margins of his copy of the *History of His Own Time*.[31] Fellow Whigs, however, also attacked Burnet, suspecting that the bishop's insider status had led him to turn a blind eye to even worse Stuart outrages. Some, for example, castigated him for exculpating the king for the death of Lord Essex. Burnet accepted the official explanation that Essex killed himself in the tower, but others believed that Essex had been murdered on the order of the king. While Burnet's *History*, then, remained significant—albeit controversial—well into the eighteenth century, by 1799 Edward Jerningham could, on the one hand, passionately lament the injustices of slavery and colonialism, but at the same time depict Charles II as a fun-loving companion blessing the marriage of Sir Oliver and switching places with the Earl of Rochester. The *Frolic*, like so much of the afterlife of the Restoration, recalls the sexual irregularity of the monarch, but forgets the state violence, the entrance into the transatlantic market in human captives, and the imperialist policies.

In literary criticism, Burnet's *History of His Own Time* has been overshadowed by accounts more sympathetic to the monarchy: we tend to rely more on the lively Pepys than the dour bishop for a sense of the Restoration court. One work of Burnet's, however, has found a secure place in the canon: *Some Passages of the Life and Death of John Wilmot, Earl of Rochester* (1680). In this narrative, Burney tells a version of Rochester's life story based on a series of long conversations with the man himself. The bishop claims that he personally converted the atheistic Rochester to Christianity on his deathbed. While some contemporaries challenged this claim, the *Account* nevertheless offers an intimate narrative that could only have emerged from some level of confidence. These two men seem at first glance a strange pairing: the libertine Rochester would have had little in common, either personally or politically, with the "officious" churchman, even one who had an affair with an opera singer. However, the two men shared disgust with the policies and behavior of Charles II. What Burnet painted in prose, Rochester captured in obscene verse:

> I' th' isle of Britain, long since famous grown
> For breeding the best cunts in Christendom,
> There reigns, and oh! long may he reign and thrive,
> The easiest King and best-bred man alive.
> Him no ambition moves to get renown
> Like the French Fool, that wanders up and down
> Starving his people, hazarding his crown.
>
> . . . .
>
> Restless he rolls about from whore to whore,
> A merry monarch, scandalous and poor.[32]

The phrase "merry monarch" is often detached from this poem, but it is bracingly ironic here. Burnet would have found the language offensive, but sympathized with the critique. If Rochester bitterly describes a royal whoremaster, Burnet presents a paranoid tyrant with a broken moral compass.

Just as Burnet's *History* anticipates the Protestant nationalism that emerged in the eighteenth century as the key for many people to British unity, so his account of Rochester anticipates the "reformed rake" plots that would become so popular in the plays and novels of the eighteenth century. Rochester had already had an impressive theatrical presence during his short life. Some audience members saw more than a hint of the famous libertine in George Etherege's Dorimant in *The Man of Mode* and Aphra Behn's Willmore in *The Rover*. Behn links her Rochester figure closely to Charles II, for during the play Willmore seeks adventure on a brief shore leave from his job of protecting the heir to the throne aboard his ship. Her play thus also recalls Rochester's father, who distinguished himself in battle fighting for Charles I. In some ways, we can see the court libertines as indulging in wine, women, song, and random violence with implicit permission from Charles; their raucousness could be seen as a small-scale version of the monarch's own rough justice.[33] Burnet saw the rakish Duke of Buckingham as a key influence in the corruption of Charles: raised alongside him from boyhood, Buckingham, in Burnet's account, introduced the future monarch to fleshy temptations during their exile together. But even in Burnet's anti-Stuart account, some forms of libertinism could go too far for the king, who rejected Buckingham's plan to send Catherine to the American colonies so that he could take another bride. Rochester and the unruly court libertines, as Michael Neill has argued, rebelled against authority just as much, in their own way, as the Puritan radicals.[34] So while libertines misbehaved with implicit royal permission and also exploited their own class and gender privilege, libertinism could alternatively function as a form of resistance. Rochester satirized the king with increasing boldness throughout his career; twice, Charles sent him into exile. Both before and after his death, Rochester became iconic for outrageous language that nevertheless captured something distinctive about the moment.

Burnet's account of Rochester's life, conversion, and death became one of his most popular and most enduring works. While on opposite sides of the political fence, the bishop shared with Rochester personal antipathy toward Charles and disgust with his vulnerability to the political influence of foreign and/or Catholic women. Burnet must have recognized their commonality on this point, and he expresses considerable sympathy for the dying debauchee. He accounts for Rochester's wild behavior by the "natural heat of his fancy." [35] In Burnet's narrative, Rochester had become an atheist when, in the terrors of battle, he made a compact with a friend that if one of them died and if an afterlife existed, whoever arrived first would return to visit the other. A cannonball tore his companion into pieces in the midst of a sea battle while Rochester stood next to him, leaving the young nobleman shocked and covered with his friend's blood. The friend did not return from the land of the dead, as previously agreed, erroneously leading Rochester to atheism. Rochester then began to pursue pleasure with abandon.[36] By his own account, Burnet ultimately persuaded Rochester that he "had made himself a Beast, and had brought pain and sickness on his Body, and had suffered much on his Reputation" (35). He also convinced him of the existence of God, in spite of the loss of his friend, by guiding Rochester toward the path of reason. Burnet explained that libertinism undermines civil order, as every seduction violates the property that another man maintains in a daughter or wife: "God intended our brutish and sensual Appetites should be governed by our Reason, as that the fierceness of Beasts should be managed and tamed, by the Wisdom and for the use of Man" (40).

Following Rochester's death and for years after, many readers challenged the sincerity of the conversion and the validity of Burnet's report, suspecting self-interest.[37] But whether real, performed, or fabricated, "Rochester's conversion" by Burnet, as Nicholas Fisher observes, "was an event that achieved national significance."[38] Given the close association between Rochester and his king, I want to suggest that in Burnet's conversion narrative, and perhaps echoing similar reformed rake plots on stage and in novels, Rochester stands in for his monarch, just as he does in Jerningham's play: the conversion in Burnet's narrative offers a literary and political fantasy of retroactively converting Charles II. In this fantasy, Rochester expiates his sins on behalf of the entire libertine era, purging the influence of foreign practices and foreign women, and turning wild beasts back into men. Religious transgression, in the form of secret Catholicism, constituted for Burnet the most serious violation of decency by the monarch, but the offense had more to do with policy and politics than with eternal damnation. In *Some Passages* Burnet teaches Rochester about God not through faith, but through reason. The dead friend did not return from the next world, Burnet explains, because the creator limits souls from moving across the boundary between life and death. In his explanation, the seduction of women leads not to damnation, but to civil disorder and the violation of property. People with reason should regulate themselves, and then in turn regulate others who lack sufficient intellectual capacity. In Burnet's logic, then, Charles brought disorder to his nation not only by neglecting duty through sensual indulgence, but by refusing to recognize the ability of individual men to hold property in individual women, and, as Burnet's extensive discussion of unjust executions suggests, even hold property in their own bodies.

Burnet's account of the Restoration leaves both a paradox and a problem for the history of cosmopolitanism. The paradox is that for Burnet, only Protestant nationalism will secure the rights of the subject, which can then ultimately become conceptualized as universal rights.[39] Thus he makes the case for a kind of nationalistic purity, but at the same time for human rights within that context. The emphasis on nationalism in *History of His Own Time* also presented a challenge for the next generation of theater professionals. William and Mary brought with them an age of reform that had significant consequences for the stage.[40] In 1698, Jeremy Collier initiated a furious debate about the morality of contemporary plays. While critics disagree over the extent to which eighteenth-century theater truly reformed,[41] playwrights were aware of new pressures to clean up the stage as part of the push to create a more virtuous nation. They strategized about how to address the larger goal even if they did not entirely eliminate rakish onstage antics.[42] In spite of this movement toward nationalist Protestant reform, however, both theater managers and audiences continued to embrace the cosmopolitan aesthetics introduced by Charles and his court. *The Spectator* and others criticize audiences for loving this aesthetic too much, and for flocking to shows with elaborate pyrotechnics and dubious sexual displays.[43] At the same time, no one seriously proposed banishing actresses or relinquishing moveable scenery. If anything, the commitment to theater as a full sensory experience flourished.

In the next section, I will turn to the ways one important theater professional—Colley Cibber—helped to pave the way for incorporating, revising, and repurposing Restoration cosmopolitanism for a new generation of theatergoers, while at the same time registering political skepticism toward the reign of Charles II. Cibber, I will suggest, made a career out of reconsidering the Restoration through performance. Both the brilliance of the period's aesthetics and the venality of its politics fed Cibber's creative energy.

Colley Cibber's W(h)ig Cosmopolitanism

Cibber's *Apology for the Life of Colley Cibber* (1740) melds multiple genres, but the narrative's engagement with Gilbert Burnet's *History of His Own Time* offers particular insight into the laureate's rebranding of Restoration cosmopolitanism. In his opening, Cibber apologizes for his *Apology* (1740) and the audacity of writing so much about his own place in history:

> [Y]ou may reasonably ask me of what Importance can the History of my private Life be to the Publick? To this, indeed, I can only make you a ludicrous Answer, which is, That the Publick very well knows, my Life has not been a private one; that I have been employ'd in their Service, ever since many of their Grandfathers were young Men; And tho' I have voluntarily laid down my Post, they have a sort of Right to enquire into my Conduct (for which they have so well paid me) and to call for the Account of it, during my Share of Administration in the State of the Theatre. This Work, therefore, which I hope, they will not expect a Man of hasty Head shou'd confine to any regular Method: (For I shall make no scruple of leaving my History, when I think a Digression may make it lighter for my Reader's Digestion.) This Work, I say, shall not only contain the various Impressions of my Mind, (as in *Louis the Fourteenth* his Cabinet you have seen the growing Medals of his Person from Infancy to Old Age,) but shall likewise include with them the *Theatrical History of my Own Time*, from my first Appearance on the Stage to my last Exit.[44]

Cibber's invocation here of Burnet by echoing his title—he will tell the "Theatrical History of my Own Time"—concerns us most in this passage, and I will return to this point.[45] His need to defend writing the *Apology* at all is worth notice as well, for his defensiveness also points to the stakes of the project. Cibber offers defenses against a choice that he rightly predicted would infuriate his adversaries, who attacked him for their surely sincere belief in his artistic inferiority, but also out of political partisanship. While

Alexander Pope had not yet crowned Cibber as king of the Dunces, he had already for many years expressed his contempt for the poet laureate. Pope may have been the superior poet; nevertheless, many of the attacks on Cibber came from Tory writers who felt that the laureate gained his powerful position through political opportunism. Cibber's anticipation of attack, then, recognizes not just authorial rivalries, but also a critical readership alert to factional loyalties. Further, autobiography itself as a genre had not become common enough to pass without suspicion of excessive authorial egotism.[46] Cibber's particular contribution to this genre, however, addresses more than his own personal justification, for he positions his *Apology* as holding *national* significance, a claim that demands more defense than would a personal confession. He offers a narrative about national history to set up next to, and in some ways against, Burnet's, both recounting histories of their own times.

Cibber apologizes for displaying himself in print by pointing out to readers that his private life has never been private. As a theater manager (but also in his capacity as an actor and a playwright and poet laureate), he has been working for the public, and the public has the right to see his literary account books. Cibber represents the theater as a national institution and a kind of national service: he provides, as many readers have noticed, little information in this book about his family, or much of anything that might now qualify as "personal." He briefly mentions the fecundity of his wife, but only as a humorous parallel to his own productivity in playwriting (146). The *Apology* tells us virtually nothing about these offspring; by contrast, we find considerable detail about Cibber's relationship with fellow theater managers. Its series of theatrical anecdotes, opinions, and vignettes, as Brian Glover has pointed out, resembles similar patchwork accounts of lives in the theater published in the eighteenth century as new forms of celebrity emerged.[47]

Cibber, however, does not take notice of this genre as a precedent. Instead, he offers two artistic models for his creation: a series of medals issued by Louis XIV, thus implicitly comparing himself to the French absolutist monarch, and the "Theatrical History of my Own Time, from my first Appearance on the Stage to my last Exit," positioning his *Apology* as a thespian version of Burnet's controversial volumes. Like the medals, Cibber promises, the *Apology* will display a series of impressions rather than form a continuous narrative. His hat-tip to Burnet underscores that the author, like the bishop, has served his nation, and also that his account tells a story about what he learned in this service. Cibber, after all, does not claim to recount his personal life story but a "theatrical history" from his first entrance upon the stage to the last—a narrative of a career rather than a life, much like Burnet's, that will nevertheless include significant observations about his "times."[48] His invocation of

Burnet, like his claim of a life lived in public service, invites readers to think about the author's own volume as a similar national story revealed through an individual in the eye of the storm. In creating national memory through the institution of theater, Colley Cibber aligns the history of his own theatrical times with Burnet's foundational Whig version of history.

Cibber's invocation of Burnet is thus more than incidental. Cibber aligns their histories as a strategy for overwriting the bishop's disturbing narrative with one that recuperates Restoration aesthetics and neutralizes its politics. Burnet's *History* stirred up furious controversy for the author's depiction of the Stuart brothers, defining the Restoration court culture as dissipated, violent, and constantly on the verge of French-style absolutism; he depicts Stuart cosmopolitanism as a brutal and corrupt moral failure. He describes the theatrical productions of the time as shockingly debauched; violently opposed to the Jacobite Jeremy Collier on theological matters, Burnet nevertheless praised his *Brief Account of the Immorality and Prophaneness of the Stage* (1698) for its critique of the theater.[49] Readers in Cibber's time would undoubtedly have recognized the laureate's comparison of his own history to Burnet's; they also would have understood the significance of this comparison. While the bishop's very dark view of the Restoration court might make his *History* seem like a strange choice for Cibber's inspiration, the invocation signals the seriousness of Cibber's purpose in spite of the sprightliness of his tone.

Cibber shares with Burnet a fascination with the court of Charles II and a sense of its significance: for both writers, it looms large in their interpretation of the political conflicts that emerged after the Glorious Revolution. Out of conviction or as an entertainer's finger on the pulse of a nation, Cibber aligned himself with Whig ideals and the reformist agenda.[50] However, he found the theater and theatricality of the period, even with its Stuart foundation, exciting and professionally productive. In the *Apology*, London theater essentially begins in the Restoration. Certainly Cibber admired Shakespeare: one of his own greatest theatrical successes was his adaptation of *Richard III*.[51] He praises Thomas Betterton's performances as Hamlet and Othello at length. Writing before the full impact of David Garrick's Shakespeare revival,[52] however, Cibber, like many of his contemporaries, portrays the bard as a great talent, but one born into an unpolished age with an unsophisticated theater. So while he admired Shakespeare, he did not admire early modern stage practices; instead, he valued the aesthetic pleasures and the commercial potential of Restoration theatrical innovations and their Continental inspirations. Cibber began his career in the 1690s, on the cusp of what historians Neil McKendrick, John Brewer, and J. H. Plumb have called the "consumer revolution."[53] As an actor, Cibber specialized in performing the fop—the effeminate man who enters, as argued in chapter 2, the "transvestite continuum" and who conspicuously consumes luxurious products, many of them foreign.[54] Cibber's fops evoked not only the risk of male overdressing, but also revived the elite figures of the Restoration court who indulged in imported lace and poufy wigs. The fop figure in Cibber's time, then, bore the additional burden of a dated look; of men who had not received the memo about the "great male renunciation" of personal decoration.[55] The lively debate developing about the dangers of luxury provides another index of this shift: Rochester and Burnet complained about the indulgence of the court, but early-eighteenth-century moralists objected to the luxury spending that permeated, in their view, the entire culture.[56] Thus, as we will see, it comes as no surprise to see one of Cibber's fops comically anticipating Bernard Mandeville's defense of luxury spending as an economic stimulus.

I will return to the complicated Restoration revival performed in Cibber's fop roles. For now, I want to suggest that by its implied comparison with Burnet's *History*, the *Apology* takes part in a larger Whig project of detaching cosmopolitan taste from the Stuarts and reclaiming it for a Protestant commercial nation. Cibber was not the only early-eighteenth-century writer engaged in this project, but as an actor, manager, and playwright, he may have been the most self-conscious. Instead of evading, renouncing, disavowing, or working around the Restoration court culture and the signature, highly visual Restoration theatrical aesthetic, he wallowed in it, although not without irony. By fashioning himself as a living reembodiment of George Etherege's Sir Fopling Flutter, tweaked and comically updated, Cibber made a spectacle of not just himself, as Kristina Straub has shown, but also his theater's origins.[57] While for David Garrick, British theater as a national institution would come to have its roots in Shakespeare, for Colley Cibber it began in the Restoration.[58] In fact, we might read Garrick's emphasis on Shakespeare as part of the ongoing project to distance eighteenth-century theater from the cosmopolitan period. As Michael Dobson has shown, Garrick elevated Shakespeare to the position of the national poet, launching the enduring belief that "the Bard of Avon" represents something special about British national identity. By contrast, Restoration tragedies, as we have seen, explore the permeability of these boundaries and tend, whatever their politics, to suggest the instability of national identity. Restoration comedies, as mentioned in the introduction, come to represent not what is special about being English, but what is particularly embarrassing about it.

Cibber begins his life story with memories of Charles II. As Joseph Roach has argued, Restoration and eighteenth-century actors retained a unique relationship to monarchy: initially degraded but emerging, fitfully, as celebrities by the end of the period, actors became surrogates for the monarchs they represented on stage.[59] The frequent embodiment of royalty demanded by the plays called attention to their own humble existence, but at the same time lent them a special mystique.[60] Cibber played many monarchs in his career, perhaps most famously the Richard III of his own adaptation.[61] But he cultivated a particular association with another one: Charles II, with whom the timeline of his *Apology* begins. It might be argued that Cibber, rather than placing any particular importance on the Restoration, instead records events as they happened in his life. It is true that he and Burnet lived in approximately the same era, and that both would thus remember the Restoration as a formative period. But there is reason to look for more meaning in Cibber's time frame. First, as discussed, autobiography was not a fully established genre. Indeed, Kristina Straub has identified the *Apology* as the first such telling of a life story by an actor.[62] Something about the Restoration, perhaps, inspired this genre in progress. Second, neither Cibber's life nor his career are coterminous with the events he describes. Born in 1671, he would have been five years old when *The Man of Mode* first opened in 1676; Charles II had been on the throne for eleven years.

Cibber tells us little about his childhood, but, significantly, remembers a great deal about the king. He recounts attending the Free-School of Grantham in Lincolnshire, where he was "the same inconsistent Creature I have been ever since!" (9), and recounts the death of Charles in February 1685 as a formative event. He records his adolescent grief over the king's death, but he also communicates his skepticism about Charles to his 1740 readers, writing that "his Death made a strong Impression upon me, as it drew Tears from the Eyes of Multitudes, who look'd no further into him than I did" (21). He explains to his contemporary readers the emotional impact of a king's death in a community with an outdated faith in divine right: "[I]t was, then, a sort of School-Doctrine to regard our Monarch as a Deity; as in the former Reign it was to insist he was accountable to this World, as well as to that above him. But what, perhaps, gave King *Charles* II this peculiar Possession of so many Hearts, was his affable and easy manner in conversing; a Quality that goes farther with the greater Part of Mankind than many higher Virtues" (21–22). Cibber praises Charles and distances himself from the monarch at the same time; he explains the king's powerful emotional appeal while hinting at his flaws by implying his lack of higher virtues. He expects his readers to recognize the particular failings to which he refers, as they go unspecified. The common people adored Charles, Cibber proposes, when they watched him playing with his dogs and feeding his ducks. But for Cibber, their observation of these simple pleasures led the people to "overlook in him, what, in a Prince of a different Temper, they might have been out of humour at" (22). If Gilbert Burnet, then, lingers over the heartbreaking execution of Lord Russell and the grotesque suicide of the Earl of Essex, both victims in his account of royal paranoia and despotism, Cibber masters the sly, understated judgment. Affable and easy manners, after all, became his own stock in trade, in contrast to Gilbert Burnet's lifelong pursuit of the higher virtues and blunter truths.[63] His critique of Charles is subtle and paired with an appreciation for the king's theatricality.[64]

The divergent representations of Charles's secret Catholicism in both books make this point as well. Throughout the *History*, Burnet describes with alarm the dangerous influences at court who succeeded in converting Charles II to Catholicism and the dire consequences of French imperialism and French-style absolutism to which this conversion led. Cibber, by contrast, expresses pity for a man who had to perform the rituals of one religion while feeling another in his heart. In the first childhood memory recorded in the *Apology*, he recounts witnessing this conflict when his father once took him to the chapel in Whitehall, where he saw "the King and his royal Brother the then Duke of *York*, with him in the Closet, and present during the whole Divine Service. Such Dispensation, it seems, for his Interest, had that unhappy Prince from his real Religion, to assist at another to which his Heart was so utterly averse" (22). The theatricality of the king persuades others but demands constant performance that, Cibber relates with sympathy, must exact a toll.

By Cibber's own account, Charles II inspired his literary career. In his minimal account of his childhood, he credits his first foray into literary expression to an assignment by his schoolmaster for all of the children to compose a funeral oration for the king, "a higher kind of Exercise" that was so "new to us all" that his classmates universally pleaded their lack of capacity (22). Preadolescent Cibber, however, took on this task, "thoughtless of Consequences," and wrote an oration that focused on the "single Topick of his Affability," neglecting, in his youthful enthusiasm, to take into account the monarch's failings. Looking back, the adult Cibber is amused by his own former naïveté. He muses over "how very childish a Notion I had of [the king's] Character at that time." Cibber was the only boy in the class to complete the assignment, a feat that earned him a position at the head of the form. This youthful literary achievement, however, made his life worse rather than better, and foreshadowed his future self-described position as an object of envy when the other boys resented his success and jeered him relentlessly. A boy of "meek Spirit" might have backed down, but instead Cibber repeated his literary performance by composing an ode to celebrate the accession of

James II. Why, he asks his readers, should he conceal his talents now any more than he did as a child? Alexander Pope, he suggests, attacked him for the same reason.

The experience of naïvely elegizing Charles II and praising his brother James not only gave birth to Cibber's literary career, but also created his own most renowned version of theatricality: his fop performance. Others might envy him, make fun of him, and call him, with his youthful classmates, a "Pragmatical bastard," but, the author reminds us, he wrote the funeral oration when the other boys could not. To recall these accomplishments may seem vain, he admits, "but if all these Facts are true (as true they are) how can I help it?" (24). The incident not only led the author to discover his poetic talents, but to foppishly parade them in spite of criticism and his retrospective feeling that Charles might not have been so praiseworthy. By asking readers to focus only on the fine performance—his own literary skill and the merry monarch's affability—Cibber admits the misdirection of his youthful political naïveté while at the same time connecting himself to Charles II. The fop, like this monarch, powers through his errors.

In the *Apology*, Colley Cibber thus claims to be telling the story of his own life in the theater, but this is not exactly what he does. Instead, his theatrical history starts with the Restoration, eleven years before he was born. The author is conscious of this discrepancy: "Tho' I have only promis'd you an Account of all the material Occurrences of the Theatre during my own Time; yet there was one which happen'd not above seven Years before my Admission to it" (54). But in order to tell the story of the events shortly before he made his first appearance onstage, he must then go even further back to begin with the Restoration. Shakespeare's role in theater history in the *Apology* is mainly providing great roles for Thomas Betterton, the performer whom Cibber gives the most praise.[65] No doubt, Betterton deserved it: by all accounts, he moved audiences to laughter and to tears.[66] It seems possible, however, that Cibber was particularly intrigued by this actor not just for his skill but also for his close association with the Restoration. Betterton starred in the opening production of Sir William Davenant's *The Siege of Rhodes*, itself an iconic performance, as we saw in chapter 1. He played the role of Sulieman the Magnificent (Solyman, in Davenant's play), the first fully admiring representation of an Ottoman figure on the English stage, but also a figure associated with Charles II. The production launched Davenant's new theater company, one of the two patented theaters of the Restoration.

Cibber not only begins his account with Charles II, but persistently returns to the merry monarch and the Restoration throughout the *Apology* as a point of reference for all that theater has become. At one point, he interrupts the progress of his theatrical career to look back with envy for a stage that he argues flourished under advantages that "perhaps may never happen again in any Age" (54). These advantages included the personal involvement of the monarch in theatrical disputes and the patronage of the theater by Charles and his court. By attending performances so consistently, these nobles lent their power and their aura to the institution. Further, this theater benefited from the public's hunger following "so long a Fast." Also greatly to the advantage of the new theater was the fact that "before the Restoration, no Actresses had ever been seen upon the *English Stage*." Shakespeare, according to Cibber, understood the disadvantages of the boy actor, and "in few of his Plays" does he have any "greater Dependence upon the Ladies, than in the Innocence and Simplicity of a *Desdemona*, an *Ophelia*, or in the short Specimen of a fond and virtuous *Portia*. The additional Objects then of real, beautiful Women, could not but draw a proportion of new Admirers to the Theatre." Underscoring once more the close ties between the monarch and the theater, Cibber insists on the excellence of these first actresses, supporting this claim by pointing out that more than one of them "had Charms sufficient at their leisure Hours, to calm and mollify the Cares of Empire" (55).

In the next chapter, Cibber begins his discussion of performers by returning again to the Restoration to describe a period in which a sufficient number of actresses had not yet been cultivated, so that former boy actor Edward Kynaston continued to perform in women's parts. This leads him to an anecdote in which King Charles arrives at the theater early, only to find the performance delayed until the queen finishes shaving: "The King, whose good Humour lov'd to laugh at a Jest, as well as to make one, accepted the Excuse, which serv'd to divert him, till the male Queen cou'd be effeminated" (71). Cibber later recalls King Charles again when assessing the career of Samuel Sandford (1661–1698), "an excellent actor in disagreeable Characters" (77), and quotes with appreciation a quip from Charles, "who was black brow'd, and of a swarthy Complexion," objecting that whenever theaters wanted to represent a rogue they "*clap him on a black Perriwig*" when it was well known that "*one of the greatest Rogues in* England *always wears a fair one*," referring to Titus Oates (78). In a later chapter, Cibber again returns to the Restoration, although this time to tackle the problem of the immorality of the stage, which had been creeping in "ever since King *Charles* his Time." *The London Cuckolds*, "the most rank Play that ever succeeded," he writes, gained particular popularity at court, and Dryden's plays were "more fam'd for their Wit, than their Chastity" (147). He does not agree with Jeremy Collier, however, that this should lead to shutting down the theaters, as plays are "a delightful

Method of mending our Morals" (151); nevertheless, even though Collier, as he notes, attacked Cibber's own *Love's Last Shift, or the Fool in Fashion*, the critique overall led to a general improvement in the moral tone of the stage. Cibber has not abandoned the Restoration, but he has refined it.

While the *Apology* moves forward in a roughly linear history, then, Cibber continually circles back to the Restoration, as if he does not want his readers to forget this foundational moment, repeating as if remembering anecdotes about events that he could not possibly have observed. In the final chapter of his narrative, Cibber returns to this time once again to address the issue of immorality, in this case to establish the difference between his own account of the period and that of Gilbert Burnet. Here, he defends Nell Gwynn against disparaging comments from the bishop. First he tells a comic anecdote about Nell's having to pay for a performance when both the king and the duke had run out of cash. Then he turns to Burnet:

> Whether the reverend Historian of his *Own Time*, among the many other Reasons of the same Kind, he might have for stiling this Fair One the *indiscreetest, and wildest Creature, that ever was in a Court*, might know This to be one of them, I can't say: But if we consider her, in all the Disadvantages of her Rank, and Education, she does not appear to have had any criminal Errors more remarkable, than her Sex's Frailty to answer for: And, if the same Author, in his latter end of that Prince's Life, seems to reproach his Memory, with too kind a Concern for her Support, we may allow, that it becomes a Bishop to have no Eyes, or Taste for the frivolous Charms or playful *Bandinage* of a King's Mistress. (296)

Cibber elaborates on Gwynn's positive attributes: she never meddled in politics and never engaged in the amorous infidelities "which others, in that grave Author [Burnet] are accus'd of." Cibber notes that Burnet praised Mrs. Rogers, another mistress, for repenting at the end of her life, but that the "Mitred Historian, who seems to know more Personal Secrets, than any that ever write before this" fails to mention that Nell Gwynn did the same, a fact of which Cibber has been "unquestionably inform'd" (297). (Cibber was six years old when Gwynn died, so it's not clear who informed him.) He is not overly harsh in this disagreement with Burnet, though. Essentially he chalks up their differences to their professions: as a bishop, Burnet is being true to his vocation by his failure to see the charms in the king's mistress. (Given Burnet's reputation to the contrary, it seems possible that Cibber notes this with irony.) Yet he clearly represents himself as going over the same territory as Burnet, as telling the same story, although from the point of view of the institution of theater rather than the institution of the church. Both, Cibber's

Apology suggests, need to be recognized as part of the story of the nation, and for both men, something crucial about this story begins in the Restoration.

That the church provides the cornerstone of national identity is an assumption deeply ingrained in Burnet's *History*. That the theater represents the nation, however, is less obvious, and something Cibber establishes through his self-conscious revision of Burnet and a series of analogies threaded throughout his narrative. He discusses his experience in the army early in the *Apology*; he also notes that the actor Charles Hart had served as a soldier (96). The stage is like a nation, he writes: misbehavior in the theater created a "sort of Civil War" in which the author, "like a good Prince," loses by seeing his subjects as "mortal variance" when "the Commonwealth, his Play, is, during the Conflict, torn to Pieces" (100).[67] Theater managers need to take just as much care of their actors as monarchs do of their subjects. "I remember one of our Princes, in the last Century," he writes, "to have lost his Crown, by too arbitrary a Use of his Power, though he knew how fatal the same Measures had been to his unhappy Father before him; why should we wonder, that the same Passions taking Possession of Men, in lower Life, by an equally impolitick Usage of their Theatrical Subjects, should have involved the Patentees, in proportionable Calamities" (223). Cibber, in fact, brings up this theater–nation analogy so often that he worries that he has overused it (301). If the stage is like the nation, then its manager is like a monarch. The monarch of greatest significance, and with whom Cibber encourages identification in his *Apology*, is Charles II.

Cibber, then, represents the fate of the theater as deeply imbricated with and analogous to the fate of the nation. He rejects the absolutism and immorality of the Stuarts, but at the same time seeks to revive a sense of the period's aesthetic innovation, support of the stage, exploration of sexual possibilities, cosmopolitanism, and general theatricality. He embodies this Restoration revival, conversion, and revision with his career-long re-creation of the Restoration fop, the complex performance with which he became most associated, offstage and on. Cibber attempted other roles and dreamed, by his own account, of playing the lead opposite Anne Oldfield. He had, however, neither the looks nor the resonating voice of a leading man, and soon found a niche in this off-center identity. He made a particular splash in the role of Sir Novelty Fashion, a part he wrote for himself in his play *Love's Last Shift* (1696) who self-consciously echoes Etherege's iconic Sir Fopling Flutter. The stage, of course, produced a steady stream of fops between these two characters; yet there is reason to believe that Cibber's fops, and the persona that Cibber developed around them, specifically conjure the Restoration court. As Kristina Straub has noted, Cibber's fops self-consciously belong to an earlier era of theatricality, which contributes to their gender-bending queer suggestiveness.[68] Citing Stephen Orgel's work on early modern theatrical dynamics of looking, Straub notes how the figure positioned to draw visual attention to the theater once constituted the position of greatest power and would be reserved, in the audience, for the monarch. Early modern courtiers found no shame in being looked at, and instead displayed themselves through ever more elaborate means.[69] By the time of the publication of Cibber's *Apology*, however, the male flamboyance of the early seventeenth century had been replaced by greater demands for visual sobriety: "the great male renunciation," in the resonant phrase of J. C. Flügel, redefined sartorial style. Flügel places the change in which men sacrificed adornment for new forms of masculine power in the second half of the eighteenth century, but Thomas A. King documents evidence of this change by Cibber's time.[70] As Straub observes, then, there is something deliberately anachronistic about Cibber's fops, created at a time when power dynamics were shifting to suggest the greater vulnerability of the object of the gaze.[71] Cibber decorated his fop persona with huge wigs that had not been in style for years, with elaborate lace, and with an excess of ribbons. These performances present a figure comically out of touch with masculine style and affecting the look of a previous age: like male versions of Lady Wishfort, they are happily oblivious that an entire generation has passed.

Not only does the Cibberian fop suggest a man out of sync with current fashions—a flaw that becomes comically visible through his intensified efforts to keep up with them—but Sir Novelty Fashion, who later becomes Lord Foppington in John Vanbrugh's sequel (although still played by Cibber) deliberately echoes Sir Fopling Flutter from George Etherege's *The Man of Mode*, a play praised by the critic John Dennis as an accurate picture of the court of Charles II.[72] As in Etherege's play, the fop appears first in gossip about his appearance before the actor reveals himself to the audience. When he makes his entrance at the beginning of act 2, Cibber treats us to a scene that closely echoes Sir Fopling's catalogue of his apparel: Sir Novelty Fashion also gives details to slightly mocking spectators about everything he is wearing, encouraged, as in Etherege's play, by one of the women. Such a deliberate homage could not have been missed by audiences. As discussed in chapter 2, Sir Fopling Flutter has stood out among Restoration fops for the way this character both reveals the destabilization of rank through commerce and fashion and at the same time satirizes the cosmopolitan ambitions and comic cosmopolitan failures of the elite. Etherege staunchly supported the Stuarts, so much so that he followed James II into exile. Nevertheless, his iconic character satirized the cosmopolitan and imperial ambitions—and

empire envy—of the Stuart monarchs and their brilliant court. Lord Foppington, then, is a satire of a satire.

No doubt, Cibber adopted the fop role for the practical reasons he
describes in his *Apology*. Nevertheless, in his own performances he concentrates on figures of descent *within* Restoration cosmopolitics. When asked
where he is from, the fop Clodio in Cibber's *Love Makes a Man* boasts of his
cosmopolitan identity: "I am a stranger nowhere."[73] Cibber envelops himself
in these figures, ironizing his repetition of earlier fops by out-fopping them.
Through Sir Fopling Flutter, *The Man of Mode* satirizes cosmopolitan failure,
thus both observing and helping to create the implied alternative of the true
cosmopolite. Novelty Fashion and Lord Foppington, however, satirize Restoration cosmopolitanism itself, while at the same time exploiting its pleasures.
Thus, Cibber fashions his greatest characters and his authorial persona as
figures out of sync with time, as delightful comic remnants of a hopelessly
old-fashioned world.

Cibber's fop performances suggest not just the aesthetic style of a recently
passed era, but also a version—or multiple versions—of sexuality that had also
been rendered less fashionable by an age of reform.[74] Fops from Etherege to
Cibber present a wide range of sexual proclivities, although many, as Mark
Dawson points out, express unremarkable heterosexual inclinations, especially
when a desired marriage could bring an estate.[75] Cibber's fops, however, as
Kristina Straub has shown, consistently display "sexually suspicious" inclinations, even if they also seek to impress women. In *Love Makes a Man* (1700),
Clodio kisses men as a greeting: "I love to kiss a Man, in *Paris* we kiss nothing
else" (1.1.148–49). George Brilliant in *The Lady's Last Stake* (1708) also loves to
kiss men, remarking to Lord Wronglove after his greeting that "By *Ganymede*
there's Nectar on thy Lips. O the pleasure of a Friend to tell the Joy!" (1.1.17).
The homoeroticism of these scenes bears much consideration, but for current
purposes I wish only to suggest that it recalls an earlier moment of theatricality in which the queen needed to shave and in which Rochester declared his
page the equal of forty wenches.[76] In addition to invoking the sexual flexibility
before reform, Cibber's fops also combine unfortunate fashion choices with
the rakish heterosexual inclinations in Restoration plays that scandalized some
members of the post-1688 audience. In *Love's Last Shift*, Sir Novelty Fashion
pursues Narcissa while he keeps a mistress in the wings. In *The Lady's Last
Stake*, George Brilliant attempts to seduce Lady Gentle, keeps Miss Notable
on a string, and finally falls in love with Mrs. Conquest. Clodio in *Love Makes a
Man* boasts of all the women he has seduced in England, France, and Portugal
(4.4.202). In Cibber's performances, then, fops merge with rakes for maximum
Restoration repetition and satire.

That Cibber chose in his public persona to embody a figure that parodied, but nevertheless depicted multiple facets of the Restoration cosmopolite does not mean that he generated nostalgia for the political vision of the
time. In fact, much of his writing points in another direction: like Burnet and
in synch with the general shifting tides, as discussed by Gerald Newman, Cibber's plays track toward nationalism. The plays, however, frequently return
with ambivalence to Restoration-style cosmopolitanism. In Cibber's first
play, *Love's Last Shift* (1696), the central character Loveless has destroyed his
fortune and his health by his multiyear tour of Europe. His servant Snap
particularly objects to the "Pearl Necklace you gave that damned *Venetian*
strumpet," and chides that "you had better ha' laid out your money here in
London" (1.1.2). Thus Loveless not only violates domesticity by betraying
his wife, but he does so with foreign women. His wife, however, tempts
him back to her bed in the guise of a mysterious exotic lady: she seduces
by bringing cosmopolitan pleasures home. In his dedication to *The Provok'd
Husband* (1728), a play he adapted from John Vanbrugh's *A Journey to London*,
Cibber characterizes the role of the theater as an institution that can assert a
sophisticated national identity:

> As their Publick Diversions are a strong Indication of the Genius of
> a People; the following Scenes are an Attempt to Establish such, as
> are fit to Entertain the Minds of a sensible Nation; and to wipe off
> that Aspersion of Barbarity, which the *Virtuosi* among our Neighbours,
> have sometimes thrown upon our Taste. The *Provok'd Husband* is, at
> least, an Instance, that an *English* Comedy may, to an unusual Num-
> ber of Days, bring many Thousands of His Majesty's good Subjects
> together, to their Emolument and Delight, with Innocence.[77]

While Vanbrugh's original version leaves husband and wife beyond reconciliation, Cibber destines his sophisticated Lady Townley, whose name declares
her urbanity, for reform. The opening scene reveals that in spite of all her
other faults, the lady has retained her virtuous reputation, but she drives her
husband to distraction through her excessive cosmopolitan desires. She loves
everything fashionable and imported. A central scene reveals her delight in a
masquerade, with its rituals of exotic identity-shifting.[78] In fact, she confesses
to her husband that indulgence in such pleasures provided her main motiva-
tion for marriage in the first place:

> A married Woman may have Men at her Toilet, invite them to Dinner,
> appoint them a Party, in a Stage-Box at the Play; engross the Conver-
> sation there, call 'em by their Christian Names; talk lowder than the

Players;—From thence jaunt into the City—take a frolicksome Supper at an *India* House—perhaps, in her *Gayeté de Cœur* toast a pretty
Fellow—Then clatter again to this End of Town, break with the Morning into an Assembly, crowd to the Hazard Table, throw a familiar
levant upon some sharp lurching Man of Quality, and if he demands
his Money, turn it off with a loud Laugh, and cry—you'll owe it him,
to vex him! ha! ha![79]

In *Love Makes a Man*, Clodio, who "has seen the world" (1.1.146), reveals
his absurdity mostly through his excessive passion for everything French.
After an arduous sea voyage searching for his lost fiancée with her frantic
father, he frets that he has lost his snuffbox and must return to Paris to purchase another. He loves Paris in particular, but nevertheless fancies himself,
as mentioned, "a stranger nowhere." Cibber's fops, like their Restoration
models, generally make similar claims to world citizenship. Nevertheless,
Sir Novelty Fashion turns heroically to the products of his own nation,
making a case for luxury spending that Bernard Mandeville would later
make in all seriousness:

> I must confess, Madam, I am for doing good to my Country: For you
> see this Suit, Madam—I suppose you are not ignorant what a hard time
> the Ribbon-Weavers have had since the late Mourning: Now my design
> is to set the poor Rogues up again, by recommending this sort of Trim-
> ming: The Fancy is pretty well for second Mourning.—By the way,
> Madam, I had fifteen hundred Guineas laid in my Hand, as a Gratuity,
> to encourage it: But, i'gad, I refus'd 'em, being too well acquainted
> with the Consequences of taking a Bribe in a national Concern! (2.1.18)

Sir Novelty here makes a joke about corrupt politicians, but also proposes
that he turned down payment for this product placement. As a patriot, he
instead parades in the ribbons at no charge for the economic benefit of his
country. Cibber here plays against the understanding of the fop as a cosmopolitan consumer by having Sir Novelty Fashion make such a great sacrifice
for his country in bringing its ribbon-makers back into the market through
his own example.

Cibber's fops, then, parody cosmopolites. The playwright joins Gilbert
Burnet in the critique of Catholicism (in *King John*, for example) and also in
anti-Jacobitism in his play *The Non-Juror*. Nevertheless, Cibber, as we have
seen in the *Apology*, departs from Burnet by reviving rather than disparaging the theatrical aesthetics forged in the Restoration: as much as his fops
parody cosmopolitan identities, they also *indulge* them. By embodying the

Restoration in the figure of the fop in contrast to Burnet's Tiberius, Cibber's gender-bending performances defang (or, we are tempted to say, castrate) the Stuart threat. Fops concoct many plots and pose serious threats to the mainstream romantic characters, but they rarely succeed. They tend to begin the comic scramble for the heiress with the advantages of wealth and often rank, but someone else usually gets the girl and her money. Fops often, through the machinations of other characters, end up humiliated by marriages to women of lower rank,[80] or they remain uncoupled. If they represent the Restoration for later generations, then, they do not convey the period's absolutist violence or war capitalism, but its fashion victimization. Further, as Robert Heilman and Susan Staves have argued, while the figure of the fop satirizes personal and social foibles, his creator often grants him certain charms. Clodio's fretting over his snuffbox in the face of a mission to rescue his supposed fiancée from pirates lightens the mood. Sir Novelty Fashion provides an energetic counterpoint to Sir William Wisewoud, a kind of "anti-fop" with the ambition to avoid passion and frivolity, who is outraged that Sir Novelty courts his daughter. He refuses to consider this suitor, who has too great an interest in his own person "to have any for your Wife's" and such an "extravagant Care in cloathing" for his body that his understanding "goes naked" (3.1.32). Sir Novelty Fashion becomes the butt of humor in the play and the dupe of the more sophisticate characters; nevertheless, Sir William's rigid philosophy, which he himself cannot maintain in the face of a genuine disturbance, allows Sir Novelty to charm through his rejection of abstemiousness and his unbridled delight in dressing: "All men hate the Name of Fop," he confides, but "love the Pleasure of being so" (3.1.32). The character identifies this enjoyment as erotic: men hate being called fops but love foppery just as women hate being called whores but love whoring. He goes on to explain that just as some women, regardless of their inclinations, lack the youth and beauty needed to cuckold their husbands, so many men sadly lack the "fertile genius" for fashion. Sir Novelty intends to reveal this in a play he will write about a country booby who aspires to become a beau but lacks the "foreign education." Fashion will name his work "in imitation of another famous comedy, *He Would If He Could*," giving a shout-out to Etherege (author of the 1668 *She Would If She Could*) as the inspiration for Cibber's own fops and reasserting the erotic pleasure of male accessorizing. While the fop then usually fails in his own social and marital ambitions, he nevertheless offers nonjudgmental permission for erotic and sartorial pleasures. Go ahead, the fop tells his audience, and enjoy your exotic pleasures; you would have to pile on a lot more of them before you could become as ridiculous as I. Burnet and others condemned the decadent sensual and exotic pleasures of the Restoration court culture. Cibber, as we have seen, similarly supports the new reformist regime; he was, in fact, one of the earliest playwrights to recognize the potential popularity of this new style.[81] At the same time, however, he preserves a harmless version of the Restoration cosmopolite through his fop revivals.

For the most part, then, Cibber's fops contribute to the laureate's overall project of creating a comic version of the Restoration in counterbalance to Burnet's tragic one, with courtly versions of exotic consumerism now available for a wider audience. The plays do not advocate the fop's excessive consumer delight, but they nevertheless propose its erotic quality and acknowledge its joys. In fact, *Love's Last Shift* makes a nice wig a male requirement for sexual activity, as Amanda sets out fresh headgear for Loveless as a prelude to his seduction. Novelty Fashion and others thus encourage all spectators to get in touch with their inner fop, which they can do safely because it never will be as extravagant as his own.

But if Cibber lays the groundwork for *The Peckham Frolic*, his own fops nevertheless retain some of the Burnetian darkness. What the bishop wrote about Charles II could be said of Cibber's fops: nothing seems to touch their hearts. George Brilliant plots to exploit Lady Grace through her gambling debts. Sir Novelty Fashion, like Dorimant, wants to drop his mistress and marry an heiress. Clodio does not love Angelina, but tries to marry her and to dispossess his older brother. *The Relapse*, Vanbrugh's sequel to *Love's Last Shift*, which featured Cibber in the signature role of Lord Foppington, pits two fops against each other. Lord Foppington refuses to share his wealth with his brother, Young Fashion, so Young Fashion tricks Foppington out of the country heiress he intends to marry. Foppington satirizes sentimentalism, as C. R. Kropf points out, by his pitiless coldness.[82] Cibber's fops, then, have an dark edge; while they do not, like Burnet, recall the aggressive absolutism of the reign of Charles, they at least capture some of the brutality beneath the elegance.

While Cibber's fops, then, recall and render frivolous the Restoration, they too, like the *Apology*, return to Charles II in particular. Cibber became one of the most powerful cultural forces in the first half of the eighteenth century, controlling the theater and appearing onstage, as Elaine McGirr has calculated, more than six thousand times.[83] His *Apology* and his stage-fops paved the way for Jerningham's *Frolic* by offering an alternative narrative about the Restoration to Burnet's. Where Burnet gives his readers Tiberius, Cibber parodies Restoration excess with a degraded version of a man of the world, who nevertheless remains heartless. Cibber, then, might be credited with developing an alternative kind of cosmopolitan figure. In the opening to his *Cosmopolitanism: Ethics in a World of Strangers*, Kwame Anthony Appiah touches on the term's association with the frivolous: cosmopolitanism can suggest "an unpleasant posture of superiority toward the putative provincial. You imagine a Comme des Garçons–clad sophisticate with a platinum frequent-flyer card regarding, with kindly condescension, a ruddy-faced farmer in workman's overalls. And you wince."[84] Appiah and other theorists of contemporary cosmopolitan possibilities tend to avoid, reject, or dismiss the foppish variety. *The Stanford Encyclopedia of Philosophy* notes that in the Enlightenment, "the term [cosmopolitan] was sometimes used to indicate a person who led an urbane life-style, or who was fond of traveling, cherished a network of international contacts, or felt at home everywhere" but that "these usages are not of much philosophical interest."[85] We have seen more philosophical versions of cosmopolitanism threaded through some of the mixed-marriage plays and especially in Congreve; the epilogue will explore how Adam Smith folds philosophical ideals into cosmopolitics. Colley Cibber, however, trains his attention specifically on the problem and delights of the sophisticate with the platinum frequent-flyer card, although in this case it is a card that may have been maxed out years ago. If he, like Burnet, resisted the potential absolutism of the Stuarts, he nevertheless found, unlike the bishop, their worldly theater and theatricality intriguing, exciting, and profitable. Cibber's fops, with their dubious credit, enact a version of cosmopolitanism that has continued to unsettle discussions of world citizenship ever since the Restoration.

Epilogue
Mr. Spectator, Adam Smith, and
the New Global Citizenship

Throughout *Ways of the World*, I have been making the case for a privileged relationship between theater and cosmopolitanism in the Restoration. The relationship was not an accident, but deliberate: Charles II believed that a cosmopolitan theater culture was essential to an admirable nation and a powerful empire. I have argued that, as a result, in the Restoration the theater had a particular, almost idiosyncratic relationship with the court as both a social and political force. In the aftermath of civil wars with looming threats of renewed instability, Charles and his court saw the theater as an expression of national culture striving to escape its violent, barbaric past and inaugurate a new era of refinement, sophistication, scientific inquiry, and expansive global reach. As Eugenia Zuroski Jenkins has noted, these cosmopolitan ambitions did not conflict with a nationalist agenda: a powerful nation would be a global nation, both in its imperial authority and in its absorption of exotic pleasures, profits, and possibilities.[1] The legacy of Restoration cosmopolitan ambition is thus profoundly mixed. At the theater, audiences could explore remote locations and ponder the meaning of connections across the boundaries of culture. While theatergoing was out of reach for a large portion of the population, for the powerful and the fortunate, it merged this public confrontation with global traffic with the social pleasures of the court masque, becoming a cosmopolitan space in its own right and one of the very few spaces in which men and women mingled, flirted, and displayed their wit together in public. Visitors from the provinces and from foreign countries joined Londoners in viewing performances that explored and often violated the boundaries of propriety. Those explorations extended beyond the stage. London grew rapidly, and its denizens frequented coffeehouses managed by Turkish proprietors or turbaned English entrepreneurs trying to serve up as much Ottoman flavor as they could. The elite spoke French, attended Italian opera, and collected Asian porcelain. Sugar from the Caribbean sweetened tea from China, around which new domestic rituals developed. The newly founded Royal Society investigated the natural world and the human body; astronomers at the new Royal Observatory in Greenwich attempted to advance navigation. In many ways, then, the English in the Restoration embraced the new, the foreign, and the exotic in unprecedented ways. London had become, for better or worse, a global city.

Fueling this newly cosmopolitanized theater and culture was "war capitalism."[2] Charles II chartered the Royal African Company and benefited from its profits. He married Catherine of Braganza to improve such opportunities, acquiring Bombay and Tangier through her dowry, as well as access to coastal forts that would help secure the trade in enslaved Africans.[3] While, try as they might, the English could not hold Tangier and establish a colony in the Mediterranean—one key aspect of the Stuart strategic plan that failed—the brutal success of the Royal African Company, the cultivation of trade with Asia, and the "acquisition" of Bombay have been felt for centuries and shaped the Anglo-American world. Charles used the profits from one set of exploits to indulge in others, as many contemporaries complained, collecting mistresses and celebrating their beauty and his supremacy by posing them in portraits with enslaved African children. Restoration playwrights understood the ambitions of both Charles and James; they accommodated royal absolutism with elaborate displays of the exotic in tragedies and heroic plays. They also accommodated court libertinism with outrageous, often exploitative performances of sexual exploration and expressions of misogyny.

But theater artists—playwrights, managers, actors—had ideas as well. As I hope I have shown, sometimes they accommodated royal ambitions, but at other times they raised questions about imperial ruthlessness and sexual exploitation. While performances at this time may not have directly challenged human commodification in the form of chattel slavery, they did not always avoid confronting audiences with its contradictions and its costs. The theater embraced cosmopolitan style in its lavish visual effect, but at the same time mercilessly mocked the "empire envy" of individuals and of nations, including their own. Perhaps because of the king's love of theater and also the ephemerality of productions, certain forms of skepticism and even resistance became possible on stage that would have met with censorship (or worse) in other genres. Part of what enabled these expressions of skepticism, I have suggested throughout, are the subtle ways in which theater can appeal to, elicit, and manipulate emotions in public. Congreve's Zara may not be virtuous, but her pain demanded audience empathy and has literally remained part of our vocabulary of emotional distress. The Restoration chapters in *Ways of the World* have aimed to show the interplay between theater, feelings, and cosmopolitics; the post-Restoration chapters were intended to show the continuing influence of the electric relationship between theater and court in the Restoration, a moment that left enduring marks on theatrical practice and theater culture.

Restoration cosmopolitanism did not end in the Restoration: as we saw with Colley Cibber, it was detached from its original political urgency and repurposed by Whig writers for commercial, entertainment, and aesthetic purposes. I will close with three very different examples, turning to eighteenth-century writers who moved between the bracing violence and spectacular display of Restoration cosmopolitan drama and a newly normalized incorporation of globalized thinking and feeling. The worldliness of these writers is familiar: Joseph Addison and Richard Steele's Mr. Spectator models cosmopolitan taste; Adam Smith considers the emotional and economic possibilities of a world without absolutist monarchical control, with significant consequences; George Lillo, in his tragedy *The London Merchant*, imagines a humble apprentice rather than a heroic warrior as a consequential figure, with a military conflict with the Spanish Empire happening offstage and at a distance. The *Spectator*'s memorable urban cosmopolitanism and description of the global marketplace influenced Adam Smith and scaffold his understanding of human nature and the possibility of historical progress.[4] Both Smith and his precursor, Mr. Spectator, attempt in different ways to imagine a version of global commerce distinct from the war capitalism of the Restoration, while *The London Merchant* reminded captivated audiences of the persistence of violence.

Mr. Spectator, Man of the World

In their popular periodicals *The Tatler* and *The Spectator*, Joseph Addison and Richard Steele offer a cosmopolitan vision aligned in many ways with Gilbert Burnet's Whig principles, but with a notably more conciliatory tone. Burnet, inspired by standing before a statue of Tiberius, ends his history of the reign of Charles II with a comparison of this king to the notorious Roman emperor known for his debauchery and cruelty. Mr. Spectator also revisited the imperial ambitions of the Restoration by contemplating a statue. In the midst of reveling in the Royal Exchange, a marketplace of merchants from all over the world, Mr. Spectator "has often fancied one of our old Kings standing in Person, where he is represented in Effigy."[5] The king, Mr. Spectator imagines, marvels at how much London has changed, at how many languages are spoken, at how men who would once have been "vassals" now buy and sell with large sums of money. Mr. Spectator's readers would have known that statues of English kings decorated the perimeter of the Royal Exchange, with Charles II the most conspicuous. It was this statue, Natasha Glaisyer notes, "that received the most attention from engravers, guide-book writers and poets"; it dominated the Exchange by its prominent location in the middle of the square.[6] The stone Charles II loomed over this center of worldly commercial activity, and Mr. Spectator asks his readers to consider the difference between Restoration cosmopolitanism and the glorious activity of a public market in the 1711 Royal Exchange.[7] How would Charles II feel about all this, his progeny?

Addison thus looks back to the Restoration for the origin of the cosmopolitanism that Mr. Spectator embraces. The *Spectator* and the *Tatler* themselves were entertaining instruction manuals on cosmopolitan practice, explaining why readers should become citizens of the world, but also why some people should not. These periodicals explore and gently mock the exigencies of taste. They were among the earliest of an industry devoted to the sophistication of everyday life, consumed by country wives, men of mode, and dandies (as Kwame Anthony Appiah characterizes the frivolous versions of cosmopolitanism) with platinum credit cards.[8] Joseph Addison, the author of the essay on the Royal Exchange, was an innovator in his profitable impulse to disseminate models of worldliness, but his contemplation of the statue in the Royal Exchange suggests a conversation with an earlier generation as well. Addison had a personal connection not just to the king's statue but to one of Charles II's imperial projects on which considerable hope rested and for which the monarch sacrificed much treasure and good will. Addison's father Lancelot Addison (as noted in chapter 3) served for seven years as chaplain of the ill-fated and controversial outpost in Tangier, a project enabled by the king's marriage to Catherine of Braganza and defended by the king at great cost and ultimately to no avail. The senior Addison published from his experiences *West Barbary, or a Short Narrative of the Revolutions of the Kingdoms of Fez and Morocco* in 1671, a year before his son Joseph was born.[9] Joseph's younger brother Gulston served briefly as the governor of Madras, following

Thomas Pitt.[10] Addison's family, then, had a front-row seat at the theater of Stuart ambition and Stuart failure in major imperial projects enabled by the king's marriage to Catherine of Braganza. When Mr. Spectator starts a conversation with the statue of Charles, his creator would have understood that monarch's global investments and his stake in witnessing the bustle of merchants from all over the world. Mr. Spectator designates Charles as the avatar of this moment.

As Adam Smith would later agree, the circulation of so many commodities had filled the lives of many people—not just the elite—with satisfaction and delight. Addison presents the worldly city, now a hub of global exchange, to Charles II as a fulfillment of the old monarch's vision beyond his dreams. He suggests, however, that it has transformed English society into something more egalitarian, though launched by the tumultuous Restoration. In this essay and many others as well, Mr. Spectator reconfigures the elite cosmopolitanism of Charles II and his court for a broader audience. He does not just bring philosophy out of the closet and into the streets, as he claims; he also proposes that the global marketplace shifts political power from an absolutist monarch to a network of entrepreneurs. Mr. Spectator's character is founded on a cosmopolitanism that smoothly combines the two elements—embrace of the global and sophistication—that converged in the Restoration:

> Upon the Death of my Father I was resolved to travel into Foreign Countries, and therefore left the University, with the Character of an odd unaccountable Fellow, that had a great deal of Learning, if I would but show it. An insatiable Thirst after Knowledge carried me into all the Countries of *Europe*, in which there was any thing new or strange to be seen; nay, to such a Degree was my curiosity raised, that having read the Controversies of some great Men concerning the Antiquities of *Egypt*, I made a Voyage to *Grand Cairo*, on purpose to take the Measure of a Pyramid; and, as soon as I had set my self right in that Particular, returned to my Native Country with great Satisfaction.[11]

Thereafter, he haunts the coffeehouses, theaters, and other public spaces of London, answers letters from the curious, makes observations about manners, and renders judgments on current fashions. Crucial to the *Spectator* is the exploration of taste in multiple, sometimes incongruous, dimensions of culture: the periodical includes essays on contemporary manners, but also on Milton, on classical tragedy, on clothing, on behavior, on polite forms of interpersonal exchange, on wit, on theatrical performances, on marriage.

The *Spectator* proposes that a wide variety of people have the potential to become cosmopolites, and that they should embark on this journey by reading the *Spectator*. Mr. Spectator himself provides a model as he quietly and anonymously watches those around him and judges their actions on a scale of politeness, sophistication, and the appropriate level of global engagement. He does not lay out rules, but rather suggests that even though some people are born with better taste than others, his readers can improve theirs through good reading and good company. In *Spectator* 409, he recalls one man who could blindly identify not only ten different kinds of tea, but up to three different tea leaves that contributed to one cup. A man of great literary taste, by comparison, can identify not only faults and beauties, but also the "Foreign Infusions of Thought and Language" in a text, thus celebrating the appetite for the foreign and exotic in multiple realms.[12]

In *Spectator* 69, international merchants, rather than operating at the behest of a monarch, form their own sphere. Alison Games has suggested, we recall, how early modern English merchants succeeded in spite of their nation's relative weakness through absorption of local customs when abroad. In Addison's vision, the Englishman not only dresses like the other but *becomes* the other; the location of exchange, however, has moved to the heart of London: "I am a *Dane*, *Swede*, or *French-man* at different times; or rather fancy my self like the old Philosopher, who upon being asked what Country-man he was, replied, That he was a Citizen of the World."[13] Commerce has become its own world, distinct from regional politics and regional identities. While Stuart cosmopolitanism suggested that the capacity to possess and appreciate exquisite global objects distinguished the elite from the common and that such pleasures could best be acquired through absolutism, Mr. Spectator proposes that the project of circulating commodities catalyzes a transformation in political authority: "I must confess I look upon High-Change to be a great Council, in which all considerable Nations have their Representatives. Factors in the Trading World are what Ambassadors are in the Politick World; they negotiate Affairs, conclude Treaties, and maintain a good Correspondence between those wealthy Societies of Men that are divided from one another by Seas and Oceans, or live on the different Extremities of a Continent."[14]

While celebrating global exchange, Addison and his collaborator Richard Steele nevertheless often craft Restoration comedy–like narratives of failed cosmopolitanism, counterbalancing the exuberance over the market— it brings Mr. Spectator to tears—with ridicule of those with aspirations deemed inappropriate.[15] In *Tatler* 178, for example, an upholsterer becomes so obsessed with the succession in Sweden and other global events that he ignores his family and lets his business collapse. As a tradesman, the upholsterer foolishly becomes preoccupied with matters beyond his class, sophistication, and sphere of influence. Thus, the cosmopolitanism in the *Spectator* does not include everyone in the same way, although it proves broadly tempting. Women in general, as Erin Mackie has shown in her reading, seem to frequently run the risk of becoming overly sophisticated by indulging in dubious fashion trends.[16] Trade opens up new opportunities for men who otherwise would have been vassals; it gives women access to otherwise impossible forms of personal decoration. Mr. Spectator weeps at the beauty of the marketplace, but at the same time channels social anxieties that such a flood of people, products, and information will create chaos: tradesmen will neglect their workbenches and women their modesty. The negative examples suggest how attempts to become cosmopolitan can go terribly wrong: the upholsterer updates Wycherley's Don Diego. But while *The Gentleman Dancing-Master* satirizes expansionist desire itself, the *Spectator* turns its gaze instead to the refinements of usage, connoisseurship, and proper behavior in the midst of the plethora. It suggests that anyone can become a cosmopolitan, and that those interested should start by carefully reading the *Spectator*. At the same time, the comical stories about *failed* cosmopolitanism, inspired by Restoration theatrical predicaments, suggest that many readers, and all of those who are not reading, might want to leave this ambition to others. The *Spectator*'s sorting-out of potential cosmopolitans, comically failed cosmopolitans, and those who really should stick to the local entices readers into the cultivation of their own sophistication. This periodical, then, drew inspiration from the Restoration stage in its satire of those with an insufficiently nuanced understanding of the ways of the world even as it condemned that stage for its excessive sophistication.

Adam Smith

Adam Smith's *Wealth of Nations* (1776) echoes the delight expressed by the *Spectator* in a global market; for Smith, this circulation provides the philosophical foundations of commercial cosmopolitan modernity.[17] Smith, I will suggest, proposes an ambitious vision of world citizenship based on the rejection of Stuart-style absolutism and Stuart-style war capitalism almost a hundred years after the defeat of James II, but with some of the Restoration aspirations embedded in his project. Human potential and sophistication itself, schematized by Smith and others into four stages, depends in *Wealth of Nations* on a cosmopolitan vision of global circulation in the final and highest human expression. Slavery moves humanity away from this goal, he argues, because, like feudalism, it offers no incentive for creativity:

> If great improvements are seldom to be expected from great propri-
> etors, they are least of all to be expected when they employ slaves
> for their workmen. The experience of all ages and nations, I believe,
> demonstrates that the work done by slaves, though it appears to cost
> only their maintenance is in the end the dearest of any. A person who
> can acquire no property, can have no other interest but to eat as much,
> and to labour as little as possible. Whatever work he does beyond what
> is sufficient to purchase his own maintenance can be squeezed out of
> him by violence only, and not by an interest of his own.[18]

Smith does not here use the word "sophistication," which had acquired its modern meaning of welcome complexity and shed some of its earlier reference to contamination, but the stadial theory to which he subscribed proposes an entire scheme of human cultural development, from hunting to animal domestication to agriculture to commerce, in which societies achieve a higher level of complexity and stability at every economic stage. Slavery blocks this development, as it stifles the enslaved from inventiveness or aspiration.

Restoration comedy, as we have seen, thematizes the tensions between rustic girls like Margery and urban sophisticates like Horner, but Smith emphasizes throughout *Wealth of Nations* the interdependence of the coun-try and the city: "The inhabitants of the town and those of the country are mutually the servants of one another" (vol. 1, 481). He describes the city as a "continual fair or market" to which country people bring their agricul-tural products and from which they return home with manufactured goods made out of their essential raw materials. In the comic vision of the Restora-tion, Margery becomes "refined" through her urban experience, in positive and negative ways. *The Man of Mode* suggests that urban sophisticates rely on a steady stream of "raw" women from the country, as we learn when Dorimant consults with the Orange Woman about any new ladies who have come to London. Sophistication provides comic scandal in the Restoration; for Smith and other stadial theorists, however, such movement is necessary and welcome.

What Restoration drama represents as a new cosmopolitanizing force to be reckoned with satirically through comedy and philosophically through tragedy becomes in *The Wealth of Nations* a theory about human nature itself. In Smith's view, we should not be afraid of becoming consumers, and indeed the figure of the fop as fashion victim and empire envier fades in the eighteenth century, replaced by the fop as sexual suspect.[19] In keeping with this period's emergent sinophobia and proto-orientalism,[20] Smith's negative alternative example is China, described as a place of economic stagnation due to the rejection of foreign influence (vol. 1, 197) rather than a land of exquisite craftsmanship and sensual treasures. Still, global citizenship and sophistication, as in Restoration drama, remain explicitly linked. Importing global objects expands taste, which in turn leads to innovation in arts and manufacturing to imitate these expensive commodities (504). Smith's belief is that the British should aim to produce their own versions of the appealing products for which they trade abroad. So on the one hand, his influential project had the rejection of the Stuart global model of mercantilism at its heart (vol. 2, 80). On the other hand, *The Wealth of Nations* codifies into a theory of humanity the connections between global networks and sophistication analyzed, celebrated, and satirized in Restoration theater culture. Smith lays out a plan for a form of capitalism that could operate, he believes, without the mercantilism war machine, regulated instead by mutual interests in orderly exchange both at home and abroad.

Smith's book rejects the mercantile control of global trade—or, as I have been calling it, following Sven Beckert's apt corrective, "war capitalism"— with a *Spectator*-like vision of a global marketplace that would allow pleasing and useful goods to circulate more freely. At the final stage of societal development, however, this (impossibly) idealized capitalism would demand different skills and even different personalities. Scholars have long debated the relationship between *Wealth of Nations* and Smith's earlier discussion of emotions in *Theory of Moral Sentiments*, a point to which I will return. I want to suggest here, however, that *Wealth of Nations* depends on the kind of emotional and moral scheme laid out in the earlier work. At the risk of oversimplification, for Smith capitalism ultimately depends on a new kind of empathy, one in which it is crucial to understand motives from a range of different directions. One clear way that he expresses this need is through continually explaining to readers that others act on self-interest. (Smith's word for this in *Moral Sentiments* is "sympathy," but his usage suggests something closer to what we would call "empathy," as it implies understanding of the other's perspective without necessarily compassion or pity.) To return to the example of slavery: a slave master, Smith suggests, must understand that the enslaved person is motived to labor as little as possible, a perspective only attained by imagining what the world would look like from the self-interested position of the enslaved. He places so much emphasis on empathy because part of the project of these two major works is to move from one microstage to another: from mercantilism or war capitalism to a peaceful and open global marketplace. Rejecting Stuart absolutism here thus demands a more capacious sense of all stakeholders, including the people who labor and those who serve. For Smith, slavery will lead to violence that serves the economic interests of neither the slave master nor the enslaved. Self-interest suggests the benefit of moving to another stage of development.

Notably, labor is largely missing from the *Spectator's* celebration of the cosmopolitan marketplace. In *Spectator* 69, each region produces something unique and precious. The merchants, then, wonderfully transport these objects all around the globe, so that "Mohametans" wear British cloth and "The Brocade Petticoat rises out of the Mines of *Peru.*" But of course the silver threads woven into brocade petticoats did not *rise* out of the mines out of Peru; instead, they were extracted by native slave labor, or appropriated through torture by Spanish conquistadors. As an avid theatergoer, Mr. Spectator would have known this from watching the torture of Montezuma in Dryden's *The Indian Emperour,* which remained popular, although William Davenant's *The Cruelty of the Spaniards in Peru,* which makes the point even more explicitly, had fallen out of fashion. Mr. Spectator further observes that "The Fruits of *Portugal* are corrected by the Products of *Barbadoes,*" but does not mention the African slave labor that produced sugar to sweeten Portuguese fruit. He does celebrate that commerce "finds work for the poor," but neglects to mention the economic significance of unfree labor or to connect the exquisite products visible in the marketplaces to the hands and bodies that made them possible.

In both *Wealth of Nations* and *Theory of Moral Sentiment,* however, Smith argues for the strategic importance of empathy for the widest possible range of positions; in his foundational *Moral Sentiments,* as I will show, he reveals that he came to this insight through the theater.[21] He characterizes humans as exchangers by nature; commerce, in fact, defines the human against the animal. In the opening of *The Wealth of Nations,* Smith argues that it is part of human nature to "truck, barter, and exchange one thing for another" (vol. 1, 117). Animals can cooperate, but "nobody ever saw a dog make a fair and deliberate exchange of one bone for another with another dog" (118). It is not clear, by contrast, that moral sentiments are inherently human. In *Moral Sentiments,* Smith attempts to characterize the working of sympathy without any such routine assumptions, and relies on theater for his understanding of how humans treat each other and feel about each other in different stages of history. Theatrical performance becomes for him the index of the emotional and ethical development of human society, which he understands as constantly evolving. In these forays into drama, Smith identifies distinct "emotional regimes," to borrow William Reddy's framework for the history of emotions, appropriate to different phases of history.[22] Smith's generally over-looked discussions of theater also suggest that he was intensely interested in not just change over time in general but a particular transformation in cosmopolitanism—including both global relations and sophistication—that took place between the Restoration and his own moment. Smith turns to the theater to cast these changes in both ethical and political terms.

That one of the first political economists began his career analyzing feelings rather than profits has persistently raised interesting questions about the relationship between sympathy and exchange. Some critics have seen the projects of *The Wealth of Nations* and *Moral Sentiments* as separate and even contradictory: while one argues for compassion, the other justifies exploitation. Stewart Justman has proposed that the earlier project provides a counterbalance to the latter one; alternatively, Jonas Barish has suspected that *Moral Sentiments* presents the emotional structures that will keep the exploitation of capitalism in place. Skeptical of critical attraction to Smith for the study of the novel,[23] James Chandler argues that *Moral Sentiments* stabilizes and reinforces the hierarchies of a commodity culture through its central observation of the tendency to sympathize up.[24] The relationship between these two works by Smith comes into better focus, however, when we look at the evidence on which his theory of sympathy rests.

In the opening of *Moral Sentiments*, Smith explains the mechanics of sympathy by appealing to a dramatic public scene: viewing "our brother on the rack." We do not experience our brother's pain, but we imagine what it would be like to be in his position and "enter as it were into his body" and endure emotional distress, the intensity of which depends on "the vivacity or dullness of the conception." We know people sympathize, Smith suggests, by "many obvious observations."[25] These come from visceral experience: when we see a blow about to fall on the arm or leg of another person, we shrink back or draw in our own limbs; we twist our bodies to balance them when watching a rope dancer. Particularly delicate people feel itchy and uneasy when looking at the sores and ulcers of others. Even strong men can experience this unease in vulnerable body parts, such as their eyes. In seeking persuasive support for his opening claim about the human propensity to sympathize, Smith looks to immediate and observable bodily responses. The involuntary examples open the explanation because they suggest an unreflective response to the perceived feelings of others that can be observed, in public, by a third party.

When Smith moves away from "pain or sorrow" to the more conscious feelings of "pity and compassion," however, he turns from casual observation of unselfconscious bodies in public to the more organized form of public gazing in the theater. He writes, "Whatever is the passion which arises from any object in the person principally concerned, an analogous emotion springs up, at the thought of his situation in the breast of every attentive spectator. Our joy for the deliverance of those heroes of tragedy or romance who interest us, is as sincere as our grief for their distress, and our fellow-feeling with their misery is not more real than that with their happiness" (13).[26] Smith has moved through three categories of example in his opening explanation: (1) first, the brother on the rack, which is vivid but unlikely to be experienced by his readers; (2) visceral unpleasant examples from quotidian experiences observable in public that would persuade readers of their own involuntary tendency to sympathize; and (3) perhaps the payoff of sympathy that involves more sophisticated experiences. For the third category, Smith turns to the theater.

Smith's vision of commercial society is itself, as David Marshall has shown, fundamentally theatrical.[27] He depicts a world in which all actions and expressions take place in front of an audience, asking readers to imagine an "impartial spectator" judging their actions. Smith, Marshall argues, "is concerned with the inherent theatricality of both presenting a character before the eyes of the world and acting as a beholder to people who perform acts of solitude" (594). Jonas Barish argues that this theatricality reveals a weakness in Smith's argument, which oscillates between positing an actual spectating crowd that needs to be pleased and a theoretical "impartial spectator" with more perfect judgment.[28] Marshall, however, finds in this oscillation an expression of vulnerability. The impartial spectator with impeccable judgment offers the best hope for comfort against the persistent threat of being beheld by an unsympathetic gaze, a predicament in which actors continually find themselves. Thus we cling to the impartial spectator, in Marshall's reading, because sympathy in Smith only comes to us under certain circumstances. As Marshall observes, the motives for accumulating wealth in Smith can be explained by the terrifying specter of public exposure without sympathy suffered by the poor:[29] "[N]othing," Smith writes, "is so mortifying as to be obliged to expose our distress to the view of the public, and to feel, that though our situation is open to the eyes of all mankind, no mortal conceives for us the half of what we suffer" (61). This fear explains the otherwise mysterious motive behind seeking riches so far beyond what a person can actually manage to consume or enjoy.

While Barish and Marshall both point out the *theatricality* of Smith's vision of human experience, they both overlook the importance of the *theater*. In Smith's presentation of the three examples that demonstrate the tendency to sympathize, the spectator's feelings for the hero in the tragedy are the most

conscious and complex. These are the kind that Smith most wants to cultivate. When watching the hero, we do not simply cringe or draw back, but
feel grief for his distress and joy for his deliverance. But that's not all: we also
feel gratitude toward his loyal friends and resentment against the people who
injured him. This is a more complicated experience than cringing as a blow
approaches another's limb, not just for the multiplicity of feelings associated
with the sympathy for the hero, but for the intellectual effort demanded
by the production in sorting out of the nuances regarding which characters
deserve which feelings, and in what proportions, in the kinds of complicated
plays to which *Moral Sentiments* regularly refers. Before you sympathize with
the hero, you have to figure out who he or she is and what various claims
to heroism the production offers. Further, a collaboration of artists with a
sophisticated sense of how sympathy operates has already figured this out
and manipulated it for your entertainment and edification.

Theater potentially offers the richest forms of sympathy in Smith; some of
the simpler experiences of sympathy, however, have thespian origins as well.
Before turning to tragedy, Smith points out that spectators watching a dancer
on a slack rope twist in sympathy with his peril. This example resembles the
blow that threatens another's arm in the way it generates a visceral reaction; spectators move their bodies in an unconscious way without recognizing that their contortions will not be able to help the dancer. This example,
however, differs from the threatened limb in that it describes a consciously
contrived piece of theater rather than a spontaneous event. Rope-dancing
was a popular commercial form of entertainment in which the possibility of
the dancer's loss of balance and subsequent injury created part of the enjoyment. Surely the best rope dancers became adept at frightening their audiences by appearing to be about to fall and then recovering their balance. But
while this example implies that entertainers had long understood the emotional dynamics that Smith codifies, he here also distinguishes between *kinds*
of sympathy in terms of levels of refinement that would have been apparent
to eighteenth-century readers. Rope-dancing became the go-to example in
periodicals of this time period for the corruption of the stage. Most notably,
Joseph Addison and Richard Steele, who influenced Smith considerably,[30]
compare rope-dancing as a senseless form of entertainment to tragedy as the
more sophisticated one.[31] In Jonathan Swift's Lilliput, courtiers who want
to gain favor must dance on a rope before the king. The lowest point for
this art form may have been in 1766, when the Haymarket Theater created
a stir with a rope-dancing monkey, whose act provided the opportunity to
satirize the London theater world in *A Letter from the Rope-Dancing Monkey in
the Hay-market, to the Acting Monkey of Drury Lane*.[32] Satirists distinguish here

between rational propriety and sensational exploitation, a cultural hierarchy on which Smith draws when choosing his examples. Finally, even the opening example of the brother on the rack probably owes a debt to the theater. While eighteenth-century Britons certainly engaged in inhumane punishments, probably the only place that most people would have seen a rack of the kind used for torture would have been on stage in a tragedy (possibly in Dryden's still-popular *The Indian Emperour*). Our brother on the rack, then, is probably not really our brother and not really on the rack, but rather an actor on a prop.

Having established the human propensity to sympathize through theatrical examples, Smith considers which performances attract the strongest feelings of sympathy. Theater provides the answer here as well. Sympathy itself in Smith, as Alexander Broadie argues and as the example of the vulnerable limb suggests, is initially a mechanical process,[33] involuntary and brief. In Smith's words, "Mankind, though naturally sympathetic, never conceive, for what has befallen another, that degree of passion which naturally animates the person principally concerned. That imaginary change of situation, upon which their sympathy is founded, is but momentary" (26–27). Anyone seeking consolation must figure out how to sustain this attention. Smith proposes that the best way to attract the desired "concord of affection" would be to flatten the actual feeling so as not to alienate the sensitive spectator, who has a short attention span and no natural desire to feel your pain beyond the involuntary initial spasm (27); we are "disgusted with that clamorous grief, which, without any delicacy, calls upon our compassion with sighs and tears and importunate lamentation" (29). Sympathy for pain is real, but brief and limited. Here is the evidence: "The loss of a leg may generally be regarded as a more real calamity than the loss of a mistress. It would be a ridiculous tragedy, however, in which the catastrophe was to turn upon a loss of that kind" (35–36). Greek tragedy offers a possible counterexample: in *Philoctetes*, the title character cries out in constant pain. Hercules and Hippolytus also suffer in other plays. Smith explains, however, that the impact of these tragedies emerges not from the actual presumed physical suffering of the heroes, but for the solitude of Philoctetes and the impending doom of Hercules and Hippolytus.

Similarly, we cannot sympathize with a friend who is in love because, not being in love with the same object, we will always feel the beloved to be overvalued. Yet in some tragedies and romances, "this passion appears so wonderfully interesting" (38). But as Smith explains, the story of two people in love with no impediments to their happiness would make a terrible play. In tragedy, love needs to be improper—not to advocate for impropriety, but because the audience will foresee the "dangers and difficulties" of that love. Thus, women make particularly interesting heroines in these kinds of tragedies because the laws of society demand greater reserve from them. This explains how we can be "charmed" with the love of Phaedra in Racine's play—not because of her guilty passion, but the "secondary passions" of her "fear, her shame, her remorse, her horror, her despair" (40). While Thomas Otway's *The Orphan* confirms the impossibility of sympathizing with the emotion of love but the propensity nevertheless to sympathize with distress over obstacles in its way, *Othello* demonstrates that "[m]ankind, at the same time, have a very strong sense of the injuries that are done to another. The villain, in a tragedy or romance, is as much the object of our indignation, as the hero is that of our sympathy and affection. We detest Iago as much as we esteem Othello; and delight as much in the punishment of the one, as we are grieved at the distress of the other" (42).

Smith's crucial argument for the need to restrain emotion finds its best evidence at the theater, both through heroic suffering on stage and the demand to control one's own emotions as part of the audience:

> It is agreeable to sympathize with joy; and wherever envy does not oppose it, our heart abandons itself with satisfaction to the highest transports of delightful sentiment. But it is painful to go along with grief, and we always enter into it with reluctance. When we attend to the representation of a tragedy, we struggle against that sympathetic sorrow which the entertainment inspires as long as we can, and we give way to it at last only when we can no longer avoid it: we even then endeavor to cover our concern from the company. If we shed any tears, we carefully conceal them, and are afraid, lest the spectators, not entering into this excessive tenderness, should regard it as effeminacy and weakness. (55–56)

A reader would have no need to hide tears when indulging in a novel in private; it is only public experiences of sympathy that cultivate this crucial restraint while demanding complex moral judgments. Otway's *The Orphan* (1680) as well as *Oedipus* and Thomas Southerne's *The Fatal Marriage* (1694) demonstrate the distress that "an innocent person feels, who, by some accident, has been led to do something which, if it had been done with knowledge and design, would have justly exposed him to the deepest reproach" (126). Racine and Voltaire, among others, "best paint the refinements of delicacies of love and friendship, and of all other private and domestic affections." Voltaire's *Tragedy of Mahomet* (1741) supports Smith's claim that "it may sometimes happen, that with the most serious and earnest desire of acting so as to deserve approbation, we may mistake the proper rules of conduct, and thus be misled by that very principle which ought to direct us." Voltaire's plays show us "what ought to be our sentiments for crimes which proceed from such motives" (205, 206). Wisdom and virtue attract our favor, which is also something we know from the structure of tragedy in general but also, according to Smith, from Voltaire's *Orphan of China* (1755) in particular.

Smith seems aware that he draws his evidence for human behavior mostly from the stage, for at one point he concedes that tragedy and romance do not always align precisely with life. This acknowledgment, however, also reveals the importance to his thinking of debates raised by Stuart power and distinctive emotional regimes. In some tragedies, we "meet with many beautiful and interesting scenes, founded upon, what is called, the force of blood," the natural affection that related people supposedly have for each other. This force, however, exists only in these fictions, "nowhere but in tragedies and romances" (261). Even though Smith acknowledges here a distinction between tragedy and life, he nevertheless qualifies this observation in a way that both advocates for the wisdom of theater and the suspiciousness of hierarchies by blood: "Even in tragedies and romances, it [the force] is never supposed to take place between any relations, but those who are naturally bred up in the same house; between parents and children, between brothers and sisters. To imagine any such mysterious affection between cousins, or even between aunts or uncles, and nephews or nieces, would be too ridiculous" (261). Eighteenth-century drama often supports his suspicions of the "force of blood." In Richard Steele's *The Conscious Lovers* (1722), father and daughter reunite in the final scene through the accidental recognition of a bracelet. Before that moment, there is no "force of blood."

As we have seen, however, this force provides explanatory power in Restoration plays: Dryden's and Howard's *The Indian Queen* suggests that Zempoalla's self-destructive attraction to Montezuma can be explained by the royal blood that runs in his veins, one of many examples of royal magnetism, even when disguised. Smith's mockery of the "force of blood" in drama, however, aligns with his stadial theory, as different moments in history rely on different literary expressions, something explored most explicitly in his *Lectures on Rhetoric and Belles Lettres*.[34] All cultures, Smith argues, produce beautiful poetry; poetry is cultivated in "the most Rude and Barbarous nations, often to a considerable perfection."[35] Every culture has the need for leisure and diversion, and all indulge in singing, dancing, and verse. Prose, however, has only developed in commercial societies: "No one ever made a Bargain in verse" (137). The development of prose also demands greater time and leisure than "Savage" nations have available. Thus, while the *Lectures* say little about drama, they reveal Smith's understanding of particular literary genres as products of specific economic systems or historical stages. But if poetry emerges in all cultures as a form of entertainment and prose emerges as the necessary product of commerce, then what remains for drama? The answer, I want to suggest, is that it spans both forms of economic production (traditional and commercial); these two phases of history, however, have produced different kinds of theatrical productions and thus different kinds of emotional circulation that reveal two different emotional regimes.

Smith, James Chandler argues, aestheticizes the inequalities of a commercial society, beginning with the key observation in *Moral Sentiments* that "we sympathize more readily with those better off than ourselves" (561). This tendency to sympathize "up" has attracted much attention in readings of Smith; less attention has been paid to its foundational evidence in tragedy, which is where he turns to explain this key argument:

> It is the misfortunes of Kings only which afford the proper subject for tragedy. They resemble, in this respect, the misfortunes of lovers. Those two situations are the chief which interest us upon the theatre; because, in spite of all that reason and experience can tell us to the contrary, the prejudices of the imagination attach to these two states a happiness superior to any other. To disturb, or to put an end to such perfect enjoyment, seems to be the most atrocious of all injuries. The traitor who conspires against the life of his monarch, is thought a greater monster than any other murderer. All the innocent blood that was shed in the civil wars, provoked less indignation than the death of Charles I. A stranger to human nature, who saw the indifference of men about the misery of their inferiors, and the regret and indignation which they feel for the misfortunes and sufferings of those above them, would be apt to imagine, that pain must be more agonizing, and the conclusions of death more terrible to persons of higher rank, than to those of meaner stations. (63)

Chandler's astute observation of Smith's aesthetic point of reference comes through in this passage as well: the death of a king and lovers facing obstacles make compelling tragedies. What is less clear, however, is Smith's perspective on this harmony. Presumably, he believes that death comes to everyone of every rank with equal terror; thus, he *criticizes* the tendency to believe that people of higher rank suffer more. Smith is clearly also critical of the way so much "innocent blood" has been overlooked because of the fascination with the death of the king in the civil wars. Thus, we can see in this passage some tension between what tragedy teaches us and moral sentiments.

Smith briefly takes up the practice of featuring kings in tragedy in the *Lectures* as well, but in a way that is even more clearly critical. He observes, "Kings and Nobles are what make the best characters in a Tragedy. The misfortunes of the great as they happen less frequently affect us more. There is in human Nature a Servility which inclines us to adore our Superiors and an inhumanity which disposes us to contempt and trample under foot our inferiors. We are too much accustomed to the misfortunes of people below or equal with ourselves to be greatly affected by them."[36] Rather than advocating hierarchy as a natural order and thus aesthetically pleasing as presented on stage, Smith explains that kings work best in tragedy because of the human flaw of "servility" and the "inhuman" disposition to trample inferiors under foot. Thus, on the one hand, he assumes throughout that theater reveals the truth about human sentiments, and that some of those observations are more flattering than others. On the other hand, Smith consistently admires the stage, and even proposes in *The Wealth of Nations* that the state should encourage theater to mitigate the alienation of those in "low condition" and lessen the temptations of religious fanaticism.[37]

This apparent discrepancy can only be solved by thinking about Smith's understanding of theater, society, and emotional regimes as historically evolving. This is revealed by the mismatch between his discussions of drama in general, which tend to define the genres in highly traditional ways, and the plays that he discusses with admiration. While it is true that the misfortunes of a king provide the traditional structure of tragedy, most of the plays that Smith cites as evidence for his theory of moral sentiments do not follow this pattern. Certainly *Oedipus* traces the misfortunes of a king, but *Othello* does not. When we "esteem" Othello, we cannot be simply identifying "up," given the general's complicated position. Audiences admire him not for his rank, but for his eloquence and his accomplishments. Not all of the other characters in the play look up to Othello: some clearly look down on him and others certainly look at him askance, especially when he aspires to the hand of Desdemona. David Marshall puzzles over the "almost total absence of women from the world of *The Theory of Moral Sentiments*" in spite of having been written "in an age that closely associated both sympathy and sentiment with 'feminine' sensibilities."[38] And yet if we look at *theater* as well as theatricality, we can observe that several plays that Smith uses to explain sympathy place vulnerable women rather than monarchs at the center of tragic action. He turns to Thomas Southerne's *The Fatal Marriage; or, The Innocent Adultery*, in which Isabella marries Villeroy, believing that her husband has been killed in battle, for evidence of the way humans sympathize. In the play, Isabella's original husband, Biron, to the surprise of the other characters, returns alive, an event that precipitates the tragedy. The play was immensely popular. Elizabeth Barry played the original Isabella; in the mid eighteenth century, David Garrick adapted the play in a way that drew even more attention to the heroine, retitling it *Isabella; or, The Fatal Marriage*. Isabella became a signature role for the great Sarah Siddons, who heightened the pathos of the play by casting her own young son in the role of Isabella's son, the care and protection of whom becomes the motive for this second, unknowingly adulterous marriage. Thomas Otway's *The Orphan* features a similar "innocent adultery": here, Monimia, secretly married to one brother, is tricked into having sex with the other. Both of these plays encourage sympathy for a woman after her unwitting sexual missteps.

In this way, Smith offers his theory of upward identification not as a complacent view of human nature that demonstrates the effectiveness and appeal of a commercial market society through our constant tendency to want what others have, but as historically formulated critique. The impulse to sympathize "up" belongs primarily to an earlier, less enlightened moment—including the era of war capitalism—defined by classical rather than modern tragedy. Sympathy for the great in Smith follows from "those delusive colours in which the imagination is apt to paint" their condition. They are never what we think they are. The passage discussing this point becomes increasingly ironic, and is worth quoting at length. We admire the great and feel

> a particular sympathy with the satisfaction of those who are in it. We favour all their inclinations, and forward all their wishes. What pity, we think that any thing should spoil and corrupt so agreeable a situation! We could even wish them immortal; and it seems hard to us, that death should at last put an end to such perfect enjoyment. It is cruel, we think in Nature to compel them from their exalted stations to that humble, but hospitable home . . . Great King, live for ever! is the compliment, which, after the manner of eastern adulation, we should readily make them, if experience did not teach us its absurdity. (63)

Attachment to monarchs and the related default tendency to sympathize up emerge here as superstitious weakness. It is worth noting that in addition to admiring she-tragedies, which demand our sympathy for vulnerable and abused women,[39] Smith also holds up Samuel Richardson, in one of his very few references to a novel, as an expert in moral sentiments. Richardson, I believe, makes the grade for a similar reason to that of the authors of the she-tragedies: his most prominent novel tells the story of a virtuous woman who is raped by an aristocratic man who keeps her prisoner in a brothel. One of Lovelace's arrogant mistakes, we might say, is his assumption that everyone, including ultimately Clarissa, will sympathize up and forgive—even marry—him. *Clarissa* demands sympathy with the vulnerable, nonaristocratic woman before the titled male, a plot indebted to the she-tragedies of the previous century.

Smith associates the Stuarts with this misguided and outdated emotional regime that has been surpassed by modern (that is, post-1688) tragedies such as *The Orphan* and *The Fatal Marriage*. Because the people "cannot stand the mortification of their monarch," he writes in *Moral Sentiments*, compassion takes the place of resentment; past provocations are forgotten and "they run to re-establish the ruined authority of their old masters, with the same violence with which they had opposed it. The death of Charles I brought the restoration of the royal family. Compassion for James II almost prevented the Glorious Revolution" (65). The unreflective sympathy for the Stuarts corrupted a whole generation under Charles II, when licentiousness was equated with "generosity, sincerity, magnanimity, loyalty," and regularity of conduct became "altogether unfashionable." To "superficial minds," Smith warns, "the vices of the great seem at all times agreeable" and the "virtues of the inferior ranks of people" seem "mean and disagreeable" (235). In the Restoration, upward identification ruined the virtue of a generation. Some of the tragedies written soon after, however, point to many different directions in which sympathy needs to operate in a new political order.

A brief look at a very popular play will illustrate the importance of Smith's implicit distinction between tragedies that belong to an earlier emotional regime and more recent ones that demonstrate the significance of sympathizing in multiple directions. Because his desire for emotional regime change is bound up with political economy, it seems appropriate to turn to a play known for its vigorous defense of commerce: George Lillo's *The London Merchant* (1731). I make no claim here that Adam Smith was familiar with this play and am not aware of any writing in which he mentions it. Nevertheless, it was one of the most popular tragedies in the eighteenth century and shares Smith's dual interest in moral sentiments and political economy.[40] *The London Merchant* is also significant for its author's claim to having initiated a new kind of theater—in this case, in the play's turn from "Kings and nobles" to the tribulations of a humble apprentice.

The London Merchant tells the story of George Barnwell, apprentice to an Elizabethan-era merchant, who is seduced by a woman named Sarah Millwood. He resolves to break away from her, but is continually drawn back through her deceptions. First she persuades him to steal money from his master. Eventually she convinces him that he must kill his wealthy uncle and bring her the money. The titular London merchant is Thorowgood, the master who is ready to forgive George for his initial transgressions but can no longer defend him after he commits murder. The standard reading has been to treat the play as a fairly straightforward morality tale, although with complicated social implications. Critics had traditionally disdained the play as overly simplistic; more recent work, however, has discussed the negotiations of theatricality, class, labor, sexuality, and genre.[41] Most readers, however, have reasonably assumed that Thorowgood represents an ideal of the upstanding merchant—the name seems to be a dead giveaway—and that George serves as a lesson to the audience of the dangers of falling into temptation. It has also been widely observed with interest and curiosity, however, that Lillo allows Millwood to tell her side of the story in a series of powerful speeches. Some scholars have read this as a destabilizing force in the play, although others have suggested that this confession is part of the temptation that she represents. One critic has even fruitfully compared her language to that of Milton's Satan, suggesting that Lillo has her entice audiences to experience temptation as well.[42]

I would like to suggest an alternative to these views. *The London Merchant* demonstrates that Smith was right to see theater as already grappling with the ways that commercial society renegotiates affective relationships. Like the rope dancer, theater managers learn from immediate feedback. Their treatment of tragedy, in particular, reveals national political obsessions in the eighteenth century. While Jean Marsden and Lisa Freeman have shown the ways in which tragedy in this period expressed new relations of class and gender,[43] I would like to turn to the genre's negotiations of commerce and sympathy, in Smith's sense of the term. *The London Merchant*'s significance as a tragedy is not just that it replaces a king with an apprentice, as the author himself announces in the prologue, but that it represents a series of events that are beyond the characters' control. It is ultimately less a morality tale than a tragedy about failure of sympathy in commercial modernity.

It will be difficult to claim that the titular merchant Thorowgood is anything but thoroughly good, and yet that is what I am going to try to do. He is, of course, good in the sense that he uses his position to defend his country from a foreign threat (Spain), that he is willing to forgive George for his initial transgression, and that he wants his daughter to follow her heart in her marriage choice. At the same time, like those who weep over the executed Charles I but do not see the piles of dead bodies on the ground from the wars, Thorowgood can only sympathize up. The play opens, in fact, with his celebrating the military sea victory of the English over the Spanish Empire. Thorowgood explains his important part in this: he had served his queen (Elizabeth) by organizing his fellow merchants to limit the power of the Spanish to borrow money. At the end of the first part of *Wealth of Nations*, Smith actually warns against the potential political power of merchants, arguing that although they have a broader understanding of society than common workers, their judgments cannot be trusted because they will not be able to see beyond their own interest. They, like Thorowgood, are insufficiently capacious in their ability to sympathize. This opening seems to belie Smith's suggestions about merchants, but later events reveal the character's limitations. Thorowgood's daughter Maria rejects the titled gentlemen courting her because she loves her father's apprentice, which escapes his notice in spite of living with both of them. Obliviousness is not an act of will, of course, but later George gives him an explicit opportunity to sympathize that he refuses. When George first falls for Millwood's charms, he attempts to confess the reason for his overnight absence. Thorowgood immediately forgives him. This has been taken as more evidence of the master's generous virtue, rendering the apprentice's misdeeds all the more poignant. But George begs him again to hear his "confession." This is a crucial moment in the play, for here the tragic outcome could have been avoided. Sex with Millwood does not need to lead to murder. Thorowgood assumes the sexual nature of George's transgression and forgives him because sex, while a form of disobedience in his situation, is nevertheless not a fatal indulgence for a young man. George, however, is not looking for forgiveness but for *sympathy*: he wants his master to momentarily see the world as he does. Because Thorowgood lacks this crucial capacity and only sympathizes upward, he misses what George wants, even when George declares it unambiguously, begging, "Hear me, then, on my knees confess."[44] Had the master allowed the apprentice to tell his story, he would have been able to see how Millwood was manipulating George and prevented further mischief. Had he been able to sympathize down, he would have listened to George and figured out Millwood's plot, which George lacks the experience to understand.

The reason that sympathizing would have prevented the tragedy is because Millwood knows that she cannot tempt George to return through the promise of more sex. After the initial seduction, George vows to avoid her forever. She returns, however, with a story that her cruel guardian discovered their tryst. Previously, the cruel guardian has been demanding marriage, but she had managed to keep him at bay. Now, however, this (fabricated) guardian demands illicit sex because of the discovery; he will otherwise leave her impoverished. Thus she sets up for George a genuine ethical dilemma. He can rescue Millwood by stealing money from his master, which violates his duty to Thorowgood. But to turn her away at this point also seems wrong to him, given the (false) information that his night with her has ruined her. George instinctively sympathizes with Millwood, as Smith would predict; he is impressed with her beauty, her clothes, and her expensive lifestyle. She needs not actually experience the feelings that George attributes to her (distress, fear) in order for George to experience them in this act of sympathy. He knows that stealing from Thorowgood would be wrong, but he cannot sympathize with his master because the master has shut down the avenues for an exchange of feelings. Millwood has the greater success here: she sympathizes enough with George to recognize that sex will not tempt him to steal on her behalf. In both directions, we see a Smithian kind of sympathy that does not require an affective connection. It remains essentially theatrical on one side, because George sympathizes with Millwood's performance, and on the other side strategic, because Millwood, unlike Thorowgood, takes the trouble to figure out what makes George tick. Both count as sympathy for Smith, for in his vocabulary this reaction does not depend on compassion.

Millwood has a significant advantage over the other characters because she is not blinded by the tendency to only sympathize up. She succeeds in spite of her precarious position by sympathizing with George and even with Thorowgood. Her capacity to free herself from the limiting upward tendency of sympathy is displayed in a remarkable speech in which she suggests that all social rank is simply conventional (4.18.25–35). Thorowgood, by contrast, cannot understand George's predicament or even see the heartbreak of his own daughter. Maria and his other apprentice know, however, that he would only be able to detect a problem if the books do not balance, and so they scramble to prevent this from happening. George, unfortunately, only sympathizes upward, following Thorowgood's directive to keep his problems to himself. Even looking upward, he does not sympathize particularly well. Had he been aware of Maria's affection, he would never have been tempted by Millwood, but he lacks the capacity to see the world through her eyes and detect what she feels. The discovery of her affection shocks him; he dared not even consider that one so much above him would find him worthy. When George kills his uncle, his sympathy and awe for the uncle's greatness so overpower him that he becomes unable to rob the estate. Thus, it is no coincidence that Millwood is only caught when betrayed by people immediately beneath her: the servants, whose wavering loyalty she fatally misses.

For both Smith and Lillo, these hierarchies stand in the way of productive exchange, both financial and emotional. Thorowgood loses control of his apprentice, placing his business and the life of George's uncle in danger through his inability to sympathize down. He understands what he needs to do for his monarch, but not for those in his own household. Millwood does better through the advantage of her own degraded position, but she fatally overlooks the feelings of her servants. Apparently Lucy had been growing disgusted with her mistress's plots for quite some time: in private, she and her fellow servant Blunt discuss them in disapproving terms early in the play (1.6), a dynamic missed by the lady of the house.

For both Smith and Lillo, a cosmopolitan economy of exchange depends on emotional as well as financial circulation and sophistication unimpeded by blind spots produced by an outdated emotional regime. Neither makes this point out of revolutionary idealism, but instead at least partly out of the observation that exchange can open up new forms of vulnerability that neither is able to resolve. Whatever Lillo's intentions, the play allows us, however briefly, to glimpse the predicament of people such as Millwood, who are exploited by the commercial system. It also, however, shows that a clever victim of exploitation can exploit in return. Thus, we do not watch *The London Merchant* only as a warning against the temptation of bad women, but instead for the less comfortable insight that the maintenance of power depends on more than the hollow statements of morality that we get from Thorowgood. Instead, it demands the capacity to sympathize in many different directions, including down, for that is the direction from which future trouble will come.

As in *The London Merchant*, so in *The Wealth of Nations*, one must empathize in multiple directions, not just up. Unlike the authors of *The Spectator*, then, Smith pays attention to laborers as well as merchants. He begins *Wealth of Nations*, in fact, with a famous—or notorious—discussion of the division of labor, in which he describes the difference between one worker making a pin and a factory system in which "[o]ne man draws out the wire, another straights it, a third cuts it, a fourth points it, a fifth grinds it at the top for receiving the head."[45] There may be no sympathy here in the modern sense or, as Marx would point out, full recognition of the value of this labor, but in *The Wealth of Nations*, Smith attempts to account for all of the various moving parts of the vast system of global commerce that are not visible in the nevertheless likeminded cosmopolitanism of *The Spectator*. He ends the chapter on the pin factory by returning briefly, and disturbingly, to monarchy by way of an attempt at empathy with the workers: "Compared, indeed, with the more extravagant luxury of the great, his [the laborer's] accommodation must no doubt appear extremely simply and easy; and yet it may be true, perhaps, that the accommodation of a European prince does not always so much exceed that of an industrious and frugal peasant as the accommodation of the latter exceeds that of many an African king, the absolute master of the lives and liberties of ten thousand naked savages."[46] Smith, as we saw earlier, used China as his example of a static culture; here he characterizes Africans as naked bodies lacking in human worth.

In his *Theory of Moral Sentiments,* Smith at one point observes that most people would be more distressed by the loss of one finger than by news of an earthquake in which thousands of people in China perished.[47] Turning to his placement of racialized limitations in the face of his other intriguing suggestions for expanding the circle of sympathy benefits from comparison to the heroic plays of the Restoration. While certainly not free of ethnocentrism, these works, as we have seen, often express admiration for other empires and explore heroic friendships and heroic romances across the divide of nations. In the theater of the absolutism that Smith rejects, China represented the height of cosmopolitan fashion in *The Country Wife.* In *The Empress of Morocco* and *The Mourning Bride* and in *Oroonoko,* African courts enjoyed levels of sophistication and luxury that an English laborer would never see, as did Mesoamerican natives in *The Indian Queen* and *The Indian Emperour.*

Close attention to Smith, whose economic theories became orthodoxy, can help us see the strange and overlooked radicalism of the Restoration theater. If this era's plays universalize their own version of heroic cosmopolitans, Smith's comparison proposes a world in which "accommodation"— material plenty—surpasses both senses of honor: the pointless title, but also the universalized ethical practices believed to be found across all cultures. Restoration audiences consumed heroic cosmopolitanism in a lively, even chaotic performance space in which the action on stage competed with the gawking, flirting, and fighting in the audience. If the global tragedies of this period delicately explore the possibility of connection across the division of nation through romance and friendship, at the same time they took full advantage of the visual possibilities of extravagant costumes, strikingly decorated backdrops, and invented exotic dances. Like Defoe's later heroine Roxana, who would perform some unfamiliar French dance steps but convince her onlookers that they were witnessing an authentic Turkish performance, the Restoration stage offered a theatrical display of turbans, vests, folded fans, blackened skin, porcelain cups, feathered headpieces, and possibly, as I have suggested, enslaved African children. Thus these Restoration plays are forever balanced on the knife's edge between passionate expressions of love and friendship that cross cultural lines and a churning backdrop, regarded in the plays with various degrees of excitement, ambivalence, anxiety, and even outright distress about global violence, war capitalism, and slavery.

Legacies of the Restoration

In the study of British literature and culture, the Restoration has often been treated as an afterthought: too late for the early modern period and a preface to eighteenth century studies, representing the last surge of traditionalism about to be overtaken by capitalist modernity. Its reputation has not changed all that much from the images captured by *The Peckham Frolic*, Kathleen Winsor's *Forever Amber* (1944), and Jennifer Swale's 2015 play *Nell Gwynn*. Charles II's now-familiar appellation as the Merry Monarch, given to him in great bitterness by Rochester, had associated the period saliently with a playful libertinism. This libertinism is itself important and intriguing, both for the ways that the theater explored the boundaries of gender and desire, but also for the care with which characters must negotiate this world of complex social limits and new possibilities. Characters strive for seamlessly cosmopolitan social performances, earning admiration for their mastery and amused contempt for their failures. In 1959, Norman N. Holland declared these plays *The First Modern Comedies* for their psychological realism; in 1986, Harold Weber argued for Restoration comedies as the first English examples of literary works that detached sexuality from spirituality. The sophistication explored by and evident in the comedies has thus given them intermittent claims to modernity.

As I hope I have shown, however, there is an even broader claim to be made about this theater's and this period's relationship to modernity: while Charles II in many ways attempted to restore a traditional notion of the divine right of kings, at the same time he and his brother James embraced more modern methods of acquiring wealth. They did not stand in the way of an emergent system of global commerce; instead, they tried to monopolize it. As Steve Pincus has shown, the Restoration was not the last gasp of tradition, but rather the foundation of the eighteenth-century system of commercial modernity, including imperial expansion and the crucial chartering of the Royal African Company. The marriage of Charles II to Catherine of Braganza, the queen who brought the Indies, east and west, provided the opportunity for England to become a colonial power in India and a major force in the transatlantic slave trade, competing with the Spanish, French, and Dutch. This transformation involved cultural as well as economic investment, something that Charles II seems to have understood from the beginning. He was masterful in using visual displays to forward his agenda, as Paula Backscheider has shown in *Spectacular Politics* and Anna Keay in *The Magnificent Monarch*.[48] The cosmopolitan theater that he favored was central to this project. In *Ways of the World*, however, I have also tried to suggest how the lively theater culture that emerged during this period was not only a conduit for absolutist ideals but a space of complexity and contestation, where writers and performers pushed back in highly restricted circumstances. Theater professionals in the Restoration bore witness to crucial historical transformations and presented them back to their audiences as the drama of war capitalism, slavery, cosmopolitanism, and sophistication, seventeenth-century stage obsessions whose legacy continues to shape the ways of our world.

Notes

Preface

1. Between 1944 and 1946, *Forever Amber* sold 1,247,540 copies, turning its twenty-four-year-old author, Kathleen Winsor, into a celebrity. Lise Jaillant, "Subversive Middlebrow: The Campaigns to Ban Kathleen Winsor's *Forever Amber* in the US and Canada," *International Journal of Canadian Studies* 48 (2014): 33–52, 49 n. 26.

2. Quoted by Jaillant, 38.

3. Jaillant, 38.

4. Kathleen Winsor, *Forever Amber* (1944), (Chicago: Chicago Review Press, 2000), 237, 261, 263.

5. Jaillant, 42.

6. Jaillant, 43.

7. "Australia Bans 'Forever Amber,'" *New York Times*, August 1, 1945: 17.

8. Elaine Showalter, "Emeralds on the Home Front," *The Guardian*, August 9, 2002. Online. https://www.theguardian.com/books/2002/aug/10/featuresreviews.guardianreview19.

9. Winsor, 419.

10. Winsor, 307.

11. I borrow this term from Sven Beckert, *Empire of Cotton: A Global History* (New York: Alfred A. Knopf, 2014) and will return to it later.

12. I refer here to the scene from William Wycherley's *The Plain Dealer* in which characters discuss *The Country Wife*, suggesting that a woman who is offended by the play's "innocent" banter only reveals her own sexual knowledge.

Introduction

1. David Mazella, *The Making of Modern Cynicism* (Charlottesville: University of Virginia Press, 2007), 89–109.

2. Andrew Sofer, *Dark Matter: Invisibility in Drama, Theater, and Performance* (Ann Arbor: University of Michigan Press, 2013), 3–5.

3. Susan Staves, *Players' Scepters: Fictions of Authority in the Restoration* (Lincoln: University of Nebraska Press, 1979), chapter 1, esp. 41–42; Michael Neill, "Heroic Heads and Humble Tails: Sex, Politics, and the Restoration Comic Rake," *Eighteenth Century: Theory and Interpretation* 24 no. 2 (1983): 116–18.

4. See, for example, William M. Reddy, *The Navigation of Feeling: A Framework for the History of Emotions* (Cambridge: Cambridge University Press, 2001); Colin Jones, *The Smile Revolution in Eighteenth Century Paris* (Oxford: Oxford University Press, 2014); Daniel M. Gross, *The Secret History of Emotion: From Aristotle's Rhetoric to Modern Brain*

Science (Chicago: University of Chicago Press, 2006); Adela Pinch, *Strange Fits of Passion: Epistemologies of Emotion, Hume to Austen* (Stanford, CA: Stanford University Press, 1996). The phrase "emotional regimes" is from Reddy, 129: "The set of normative emotions and the official rituals, practices, and emotives that express and inculcate them; a necessary underpinning of any stable political regime."

5. Michael Dobson, *The Making of the National Poet: Shakespeare, Adaptation and Authorship, 1660–1769* (Oxford: Clarendon Press, 1992), esp. chapters 4 and 5.

6. On censorship during this period, see Harold Weber, *Paper Bullets: Print and Kingship under Charles II* (Lexington: University Press of Kentucky, 1996), 131–209.

7. Stuart Sherman, "'The General Entertainment of My Life': *The Tatler, The Spectator*, and the Quidnunc's Cure," *Eighteenth-Century Fiction* 27, no. 3–4 (2015): 343–71.

8. Mark Dawson makes the case that the Restoration fop marks the instability of gentility, an argument to which I will later return. See his *Gentility and the Comic Theatre of Late Stuart London* (Cambridge: Cambridge University Press, 2005), 145–63. On misguided heroes, see Neill, "Heroic Heads and Humble Tails."

9. On Catherine's dowry, see Gertrude Z. Thomas, *Richer Than Spices: How a Royal Bride's Dowry Introduced Cane, Lacquer, Cottons, Tea, and Porcelain to England, and So Revolutionized Taste, Manners, Craftsmanship, and History in Both England and America* (New York: Alfred A. Knopf, 1965). See also Edward Corp, "Catherine of Braganza and Cultural Politics," in *Queenship in Britain, 1660–1837: Royal Patronage, Court Culture, and Dynastic Politics*, ed. Clarissa Campbell (Manchester: Manchester University Press, 2002). For the role of Catherine's dowry in the slave trade, I am grateful to Holly Brewer for sharing her book manuscript "Inheritable Blood," chapter 2. See also her "Slavery, Sovereignty, and 'Inheritable Blood': Reconsidering John Locke and the Origins of American Slavery," *The American Historical Review* 122, no. 4 (October 2017): 1038–78.

10. On the English perception of their own barbarity, see Elliott Visconsi, *Lines of Equity: Literature and the Origins of Law in Later Stuart England* (Ithaca: Cornell University Press, 2008), esp. chapter 5.

11. I draw these arguments, respectively, from three excellent recent works on early cosmopolitanism: Alison Games, *The Web of Empire: English Cosmopolitans in an Age of Expansion, 1560–1660* (Oxford: Oxford University Press, 2008); Brian Lockey, *Early Modern Catholics, Royalists, and Cosmopolitans: English Transnationalism and the Christian Commonwealth* (Burlington, VT: Ashgate, 2015); and Margaret C. Jacob, *Strangers Nowhere in the World: The Rise of Cosmopolitanism in Early Modern Europe* (Philadelphia: University of Pennsylvania Press, 2006).

12. On this point, see Wolfram Schmidgen, *Exquisite Mixture: The Virtues of Impurity in Early Modern England* (Philadelphia: University of Pennsylvania Press, 2013).

13. On Charles's continuation of Cromwell's imperial projects, see Abigail Leslie Swingen, *Competing Visions of Empire: Labor, Slavery, and the Origins of the British Atlantic Empire* (New Haven, CT: Yale University Press, 2015), chapter 3. Indispensable recent studies of the English fascination with and humility before other empires include Robert Markley, *The Far East and the English Imagination, 1600–1730* (Cambridge: Cambridge University Press, 2006); Eugenia Zuroski Jenkins, *A Taste for China: English Subjectivity and the Prehistory of Orientalism* (New York: Oxford University Press, 2013); Gerald M. MacLean, *Looking East: English Writing and the Ottoman Empire before 1800*

(Basingstoke: Palgrave Macmillan, 2007); Alok Yadav, *Before the Empire of English: Literature, Provinciality, and Nationalism in Eighteenth-Century Britain* (New York: Palgrave Macmillan, 2004).

14. Sven Beckert, *Empire of Cotton: A Global History* (New York: Alfred A. Knopf, 2014).

15. E. P. Thompson, "Patrician Society, Plebeian Culture," *Journal of Social History* 7, no. 4 (1974): 382–405, 390.

16. One of the best discussions of this view remains Laura Brown, *English Dramatic Form, 1660–1760: An Essay in Generic History* (New Haven, CT: Yale University Press, 1981). See also J. Douglas Canfield, *Heroes & States: On the Ideology of Restoration Tragedy* (Lexington: University Press of Kentucky, 2000).

17. For this argument, I rely on Steven C. A. Pincus, *1688: The First Modern Revolution* (New Haven, CT: Yale University Press, 2009).

18. Marvin Carlson, *The Haunted Stage: The Theatre as Memory Machine* (Ann Arbor: University of Michigan Press, 2002), 8.

19. An excellent recent example of this reconstructive model is Tim Keenan, *Restoration Staging, 1660–74* (Abingdon: Routledge, 2017).

20. See, for example, Brown, *English Dramatic Form*; Canfield, *Heroes & States*; Nancy Klein Maguire, *Regicide and Restoration: English Tragicomedy, 1660–1671* (Cambridge: Cambridge University Press, 1992); and Susan J. Owen, *Restoration Theatre and Crisis* (Oxford: Clarendon Press, 1996).

21. The best works on imperialism in this period's drama remain Bridget Orr, *Empire on the English Stage, 1660–1714* (Cambridge: Cambridge University Press, 2001) and, more recently, Ayanna Thompson, *Performing Race and Torture on the Early Modern Stage* (New York: Routledge, 2008). See also Heidi Hutner, *Colonial Women: Race and Culture in Stuart Drama* (Oxford: Oxford University Press, 2001).

22. Important exceptions here are Joseph Roach's *Cities of the Dead: Circum-Atlantic Performance* (New York: Columbia University Press, 1996) and Thompson, *Performing Race and Torture*, although these works do not elaborate on the significant of the Royal African Company to Stuart rule. For the importance of the Royal African Company in the creation of the corporation itself, see John O'Brien, *Literature Incorporated: The Cultural Unconscious of the Business Corporation, 1650–1850* (Chicago: University of Chicago Press, 2016), chapter 4.

23. On the "political unconscious," see Fredric Jameson, *The Political Unconscious: Narrative as a Socially Symbolic Act* (Ithaca, NY: Cornell University Press, 1981). On "structures of feeling," see Raymond Williams, *The Long Revolution* (New York: Columbia University Press, 1961).

24. Pheng Cheah, Bruce Robbins, and the Social Text Collective, *Cosmopolitics: Thinking and Feeling beyond the Nation* (Minneapolis: University of Minnesota Press, 1998). I have also borrowed the term "cosmopolitics" from this volume.

25. See above, note 4.

26. I am grateful to Daniel O'Quinn for suggesting to me the title of this chapter.

27. Jeremy W. Webster, *Performing Libertinism in Charles II's Court: Politics, Drama, Sexuality* (New York: Palgrave Macmillan, 2005); Harold Weber, *The Restoration Rake-Hero: Transformations in Sexual Understanding in Seventeenth-Century England* (Madison: University of Wisconsin Press, 1986).

28. Marjorie B. Garber, *Vested Interests: Cross-Dressing and Cultural Anxiety* (New York: Routledge, 1992).

29. MacLean, *Looking East*, 20.

30. Orr, *Empire on the English Stage*; Hutner, *Colonial Women*; Roach, *Cities of the Dead*. The fullest discussion of this phenomenon is in Orr, chapters 1 and 2.

1. All Roads Lead to Rhodes

1. John Evelyn, *The Diary of John Evelyn*, ed. William Bray (New York: M. W. Dunne, 1901), 2, 26.

2. David Kuchta, *The Three-Piece Suit and Modern Masculinity: England, 1550–1850*. (Berkeley: University of California Press, 2002), 1.

3. Judy A. Hayden, "The Tragedy of Roxolana in the Court of Charles II," in *Roxolana in European Literature, History, and Culture*, ed. Galina I. Yermolenko (Burlington, VT: Ashgate, 2010), 75. On the fascination with Roxolana, see also Ros Ballaster, *Fabulous Orients: Fictions of the East in England, 1662–1785* (Oxford: Oxford University Press, 2005), 59–69.

4. Diana De Marly, "King Charles II's Own Fashion: The Theatrical Origins of the English Vest," *Journal of the Warburg and Courtauld Institutes* 37 (1974): 381.

5. Gerald MacLean, *Looking East: English Writing and the Ottoman Empire before 1800* (Basingstoke: Palgrave Macmillan, 2007), 55.

6. Coffee was still expensive, however, and thus remained a luxury limited to the elite. See Brian Cowan's excellent *The Social Life of Coffee: The Emergence of the British Coffeehouse* (New Haven, CT: Yale University Press, 2005).

7. MacLean, *Looking East*, 59.

8. Thomas St. Serfe, *Tarugo's Wiles; or, The Coffee-House* (London: Printed for Henry Herringman, 1668), Act 3, p. 17.

9. In 1663, Pepys purchased a globe and spent many hours mansplaining it to his wife. See his diary for September 8, October 21, December 6, and December 25. *The Diary of Samuel Pepys: A New and Complete Transcription*, ed. Robert Latham and William Matthews (Berkeley: University of California Press, 1970), vol. 4, 302, 343, 406, 433–34.

10. Cowan, *Social Life of Coffee*, 11, 14, 25, 32.

11. Cowan, *Social Life of Coffee*, 119.

12. Donna Landry, "Steal of a Turk: Restoration Horse-Trading and Eastern Bloodstock," *Prose Studies* 21, no. 9 (2007): 115–35.

13. On this point, see MacLean, *Looking East*, 175–85.

14. Richard Flecknoe is a good example of this, as we will see in the next chapter. See his *Relation of ten years in Europe, Asia, Affrique, and America: all by way of letters occasionally written to divers noble personages, from place to place, and continued to this present year* (London, 1655?).

15. Joseph Pitts, *A True and Faithful Account of the Religion and Manners of the Mohommetans* (Exon [Exeter], 1704), 70.

16. Linda Colley, *Captives: The Story of Britain's Pursuit of Empire and How Its Soldiers and Civilians Were Held Captive by the Dream of Global Supremacy, 1600–1850* (New York: Pantheon, 2002), 23–42; Tristan Stein, "Tangier in the Restoration Empire," *The Historical Journal* 54, no. 4 (2011): 985–1011.

17. Dale B. J. Randall, *Winter Fruit: English Drama 1642–1660* (Lexington: University of Kentucky Press, 1995), 170. For the stage innovations in Restoration theater, see

most recently Tim Keenan's excellent *Restoration Staging, 1660–74* (New York: Routledge, 2016). Davenant and his rival Richard Flecknoe also created the first operas in English.

18. Michael Guasco, *Slaves and Englishmen: Human Bondage in the Early Modern Atlantic World* (Philadelphia: University of Pennsylvania Press, 2014), 121–54. Holly Brewer also makes a compelling case for the influence of the Spanish on the Stuart monarchs' enthusiasm for slavery in her forthcoming book *Inheritable Blood*, chapter 1, which I have had the privilege to read in manuscript.

19. Thomas Killigrew was also a foundational figure. He spent the Interregnum in exile, writing about the experiences of cavaliers aboard in *Thomaso, or the Wanderer* (1663). He wrote plays set in Madrid, Naples, Rome, Paris, and Switzerland. I will discuss this briefly in chapter 3 in the context of Aphra Behn's *The Rover*. An edition of Killigrew's plays was published in 1664.

20. Richard Flecknoe, *Sr [sic] William D'avenant's Voyage to the Other World with His Adventures in the Poets Elizium: A Poetical Fiction* (London, 1668), 6–7.

21. On the English fascination with European refinement at this time, see Alok Yadav, *Before the Empire of English: Literature, Provinciality, and Nationalism in Eighteenth-Century Britain* (New York: Palgrave Macmillan, 2004), esp. 21–54.

22. As Lisa A. Freeman has argued, antitheatricality and protheatricality have historically been entangled in political alignments. See her *Antitheatricality and the Body Public* (Philadelphia: University of Pennsylvania Press, 2017), introduction.

23. For a recent overview of the influence of the "unities" on Restoration drama, see Christopher Wheatley, "Tragedy," in *The Cambridge Companion to English Restoration Theatre*, ed. Deborah Payne Fisk (Cambridge: Cambridge University Press, 2000), 70–85.

24. In one of the best recent formulations, Margaret Jacob shows that "by the second half of the eighteenth century, the word, and the ideal, had become commonplace." Jacob locates this cosmopolitan spirit in merchants, scientists, and radicals. In a related argument, Karen O'Brien has observed that while recent historians have focused on the emergence of nationalism in the eighteenth century, the major historians in England and France during the period instead conceived of history in cosmopolitan terms. Margaret C. Jacob, *Strangers Nowhere in the World: The Rise of Cosmopolitanism in Early Modern Europe* (Philadelphia: University of Pennsylvania Press, 2006); Karen O'Brien, *Narratives of Enlightenment: Cosmopolitan History from Voltaire to Gibbon* (Cambridge: Cambridge University Press, 1997). Other important accounts include Thomas J. Schlereth, *The Cosmopolitan Ideal in Enlightenment Thought: Its Form and Function in the Ideas of Franklin, Hume, and Voltaire, 1694–1790* (Notre Dame, IN: University of Notre Dame Press, 1977); David Adams and Galin Tihanov, eds., *Enlightenment Cosmopolitanism* (Leeds: Legenda, 2011); and Matthew Binney, *The Cosmopolitan Evolution: Travel, Travel Narratives, and the Revolution of the Eighteenth Century European Consciousness* (Lanham, MD: University Press of America, 2006.)

25. Alison Games, *The Web of Empire: English Cosmopolitans in an Age of Expansion, 1560–1660* (Oxford: Oxford University Press, 2008). For even earlier cosmopolitan possibilities within English culture, see John M. Ganim and Shayne Legassie, eds., *Cosmopolitanism and the Middle Ages* (New York: Palgrave Macmillan, 2013).

26. Brian Lockey, *Early Modern Catholics, Royalists, and Cosmopolitans: English Transnationalism and the Christian Commonwealth* (Burlington, VT: Ashgate, 2015). Religious

authority that transcended national boundaries emerged as a crucial point of contention in the Restoration. The Catholic cosmopolitan tradition had a significant influence on the restored Stuart court and formed a considerable political challenge.

27. On travel as state business that required royal permission, see Games, *Web
of Empire*, 22. On the Grand Tour, see Jeremy Black, *The British Abroad: The Grand
Tour in the Eighteenth Century* (New York: St. Martin's Press, 1992); Chloe Chard, *Pleasure and Guilt on the Grand Tour: Travel Writing and Imaginative Geography, 1600–1830*
(Manchester: Manchester University Press, 1999).

28. He argues that Davenant's epic poem *Gondibert* proposes a particular kind of
cosmopolitan vision by advocating for Christianity as the foundation for a transnational community. Lockey, *Early Modern Catholics*, 236. But the genre itself (with a few
major exceptions) was losing traction in the period. Susan Staves, in fact, has deemed
this period "the great age of the failed epic." Staves asserts that the functions once
fulfilled by the epic find their home instead in the theater, although the plays nevertheless exposed the "confusion of values left in the wake of fighting." See her *Players'
Scepters: Fictions of Authority in the Restoration* (Lincoln: University of Nebraska Press,
1979), 41–42. Theater flourished in the Restoration, and heroic plays and tragedies
clearly owed much to the traditional epic. But while Christian epics universalized
their religion and tradition epics expressed nationalism, Restoration plays presented
a wider range of possibilities.

29. Dror Wahrman, *The Making of the Modern Self: Identity and Culture in Eighteenth-
Century England* (New Haven, CT: Yale University Press, 2004). For Wahrman, the
period leading up to 1780 does not stretch back infinitely but marks a *particular* period
of fluidity between the early modern and the modern regimes of identity. His examples begin mostly after the Glorious Revolution, so I am backdating a little, but I think
it will be justified.

30. For a fuller discussion of identity on stage, see Cynthia Lowenthal, *Performing
Identities on the Restoration Stage* (Carbondale: Southern Illinois University Press, 2003).

31. These representations, of course, were not always sympathetic, but Orr persuasively demonstrates that the plays show a lot of detailed awareness of cultural and
political differences. She summarizes these tendencies in Bridget Orr, *Empire on the
English Stage, 1660–1714* (Cambridge: Cambridge University Press, 2001), chapters 1
and 2. See also Lowenthal, *Performing Identities* on this point.

32. Lockey, *Early Modern Catholics*, 223.

33. Dryden would later insist that the antitheatricality of the Cromwellian party
was so strong that they would "more easily dispossess their lawful Soveraign, than
endure a wanton jest." From "Of Heroique Playes, An Essay," preface to *The Conquest
of Granada* in *The Works of John Dryden*, vol. 11, ed. Edward Niles Hooker, H. T Swedenberg, and Vinton A. Dearing (Berkeley: University of California Press, 1956), 9.

34. Davenant and Flecknoe, however, both at first turned to opera to evade the
restriction on theater and as the kind of performance that would help the nation
overcome its barbarity. Flecknoe wrote the first opera in English (*Ariadne deserted by
Theseus and found and courted by Bacchus*, 1645), which he presented as refined entertainment fit for a court. Susan Wiseman, *Drama and Politics in the English Civil War*
(Cambridge: Cambridge University Press, 1998), 130–31. *Ariadne* was not performed.

35. On this point, see Wiseman, *Drama and Politics*, 137.

36. Alfred Harbage, *Sir William Davenant, Poet Venturer 1601–1668* (London: Oxford University Press, 1935), 75–119.

37. On Davenant's contributions to masques in Henrietta Maria's court, see Karen Britland, *Drama at the Courts of Queen Henrietta Maria* (Cambridge: Cambridge University Press, 2006), 141–49, 168–91.

38. On this debate, see Orr, *Empire on the English Stage*, 3.

39. Harbage, *Sir William Davenant*, 140. Cited from *The Dramatic Records of Sir Henry Herbert, Master of the Revels, 1623–1673*, ed. Joseph Quincy Adams (New Haven, CT: Yale University Press, 1917), 122–23.

40. Harbage, *Sir William Davenant*, 140.

41. Michael Neill, "Heroic Heads and Humble Tails: Sex, Politics, and the Restoration Comic Rake," *Eighteenth Century: Theory and Interpretation* 24, no. 2 (1983): 115–39.

42. J. Douglas Canfield, "Richard Flecknoe's Early Defense of the Stage: An Appeal to Cromwell," *Restoration and Eighteenth-Century Theatre Research* 2, no. 2 (Winter 1987): 1. Flecknoe would later praise Cromwell in his biography *The Idea of His Highness Oliver, Late Lord Protector* (1659).

43. Richard Flecknoe, *Love's Dominion, A Dramatique Piece, Full of Excellent Moralitie; Written as a Pattern for the Reformed Stage* (London, 1654), 9. Future references are to this edition and cited in the text.

44. C. H. Firth, "Elizabeth Claypole," rev. Peter Gaunt, *Oxford Dictionary of National Biography* (Oxford: Oxford University Press, 2004), http://www.oxforddnb.com/view/article/5566.

45. A letter from Captain Titus to Sir Edward Hyde (the Earl of Clarendon) about a wedding feast unattended by the wives of the major-generals captures these suspicions: "The feast wanting much of its grace by the absence of those ladies, it was asked by one where they were. Mrs Claypole answered, 'I'll warrant you washing their dishes at home as they use to do'. This hath been extremely ill taken, and now the women do all they can with their husbands to hinder Mrs Claypole from being a Princess, and her Highness." Quoted in Firth, "Elizabeth Claypole," from *State Papers Collected by Edward, Earl of Clarendon*, Vol. 3., ed. R. Scrope and T. Monkhouse (Oxford, 1767–1786).

46. J. Douglas Canfield points out that Flecknoe thus stunningly argues that theater is more important than the church.

47. "A Short Discourse of the English Stage," appended to Richard Flecknoe, *Love's kingdom a pastoral trage-comedy: not as it was acted at the theatre near Lincolns-Inn, but as it was written, and since corrected; with a short treatise of the English stage, &c. by the same author* (London: Printed by R. Wood for the author, 1664), N.p. Flecknoe later revised *Love's Dominion* as *Love's Kingdom*, but could not get it produced after the Restoration either. Dryden cites it in *Mac Flecknoe*, however, as the play that Father Flecknoe asks his son Shadwell to excel in dullness. "Heavens must bless my son, from *Ireland* let him reign / To far *Barbados* on the western main; / Of his Dominion may no end be known / And greater than his father's be his Throne. / Beyond love's Kingdom let him stretch his Pen." *Mac Flecknoe* in *The Works of John Dryden*, vol. 2, 139–143.

48. On Flecknoe and Davenant, see also Janet Clare, *Drama of the English Republic, 1649–60* (Manchester: Manchester University Press, 2002), 31.

49. [William D'Avenant], *A Proposition for Advancement of Moralitie* (London, 1654), 1. Future references are to this edition and cited in the text. According to Clare, this treatise was first published in 1653.

50. On the sensual quality of Davenant's theater, see Brandon Chua's excellent *The Ravishment of Reason: Governance and the Heroic Idioms of the Late Stuart Stage, 1660–1690* (Lewisburg, PA: Bucknell University Press, 2014), chapter 1.

51. Davenant's military heroic vision of an immersive theater won out over Flecknoe's dominion of love, and the poet-adventurer received permission to present a live semipublic entertainment at his residence, Rutland House (Clare, *Drama of the English Republic*, 31–32). See also on this point Wiseman, *Drama and Politics*, who notes that *The First Day's Entertainment at Rutland House* was the occasion for moving theatrical conventions associated with the court onto a public stage (144) and that Davenant argued that theater would help people avoid levity. Chua, *Ravishment of Reason* is right to point out that Davenant's model also includes love—although not erotic love, but rather love for the monarch.

52. Peter Stallybrass and Allon White, *The Politics and Poetics of Transgression* (London: Methuen, 1986), 84–85.

53. James R. Jacob and Timothy Raynor, "Opera and Obedience: Thomas Hobbes and 'A Proposition for Advancement of Moralitie' by Sir William Davenant," *The Seventeenth Century* 6, no. 2 (1991): 205–50.

54. C. H. Firth, "Sir William Davenant and the Revival of Drama during the Protectorate," *The English History Review* 18 (1903): 320. Firth includes the document in this brief article.

55. For Davenant as a flexible opportunist, see Kevin Cope, "The Glory That Was Rome—and Grenada, and Rhodes, and Tenochtitlan: Pleasurable Conquests, Supernatural Liaisons, and Apparitional Drama in Interregnum Entertainment," *Studies in the Literary Imagination* 32, no. 3 (1999): 1–17. For Davenant as a royalist ideologue, see Chad Thomas, "Negotiating the Interregnum: The Political Works of Davenant and Tatham," *1650–1850: Ideas, Aesthetics, and Inquiries into the Early Modern Era* 10 (2004): 225–44.

56. Clare, *Drama of the English Republic*, 3. On the politics of antitheatricality and competing claims on the public sphere, see Lisa A. Freeman, *Antitheatricality and the Body Public* (Philadelphia: University of Pennsylvania Press, 2017), chapter 1.

57. Wiseman, *Drama and Politics*, 144.

58. Britland, *Drama at the Courts of Queen Henrietta Maria*. See, for example, her reading of Davenant's *The Temple of Love*, 141–48.

59. [William Davenant], *The First Days Entertainment at Rutland-House, By Declamations and Musick* (London, 1656), 1. Future references are from this edition and cited in the text.

60. David Mazella, *The Making of Modern Cynicism* (Charlottesville: University of Virginia Press, 2007), 49.

61. Flecknoe, *Relation of Ten Years Travell*, 88.

62. Mazella, *Making of Modern Cynicism*, 85.

63. By continually returning to the dangers of assembly, Davenant also evokes the specter of a dangerous collectivity, feared, as Melissa Mowry notes, by the commonwealth men as well as by the royalists. Melissa Mowry, "'Past Remembrance or History': Aphra Behn's *The Widdow Ranter*, or, How the Collective Lost Its Honor," *ELH* 79, no. 3 (2012): 597–621.

64. Mazella, *Making of Modern Cynicism*, 84.

65. *The lives of the ancient philosophers, containing an account of their several sects, doctrines, Actions, and Remarkable Sayings. Extracted from Diogenes, Laertius, Causabon, Menagins, Stanley, Gassenaus, Charleton, and others, the best Authors upon that Subject* (London, 1702), 256, 268. Future references are to this edition and cited in the text.

66. Readings of *The Siege of Rhodes* focus on the potential allegories for domestic politics (Wiseman) or the play's participation in the rhetoric of British imperialism (Orr). In my own reading, I have tried to incorporate elements of both while exploring the play's cosmopolitan aspirations. Bridget Orr is right to describe the various ways in which the play repeats unflattering stereotypes about Turks. I hope to show, however, that in spite of these limitations, the admiration for the Ottomans is also visible and significant. On this point, see also Haitham Abdul Aziz Saab, "Davenant's *The Siege of Rhodes* and the New Attitude towards the Orient," *International Journal of Arabic-English Studies* 2, no. 1–2 (June 2001): 27–42 and Judy H. Park, "The Limits of Empire in Davenant's *The Siege of Rhodes*," *Mediterranean Studies* 24, no. 1 (2016): 47–76; Wiseman, *Drama and Politics*, 156–61; and Orr, *Empire on the English Stage*, 67–72. I am also indebted in my reading to Matthew Birchwood's insights. Birchwood argues that "Davenant's play takes the topical belief that England might 'Learne of a Turke' a crucial step further, performing an extraordinary refraction of identity upon the already complex and fragmented figure of the Muslim." In the play, Solyman "represents a groundbreaking inversion of ingrained notions of enmity and apostasy, engendering anxieties that have a clear resonance in the capricious political climate." Matthew Birchwood, *Staging Islam in England: Drama and Culture, 1640–1685* (Cambridge: D. S. Brewer, 2007), 96–128, 128.

67. Brandon Chua, "The Purposes of Playing on the Post–Civil War Stage: The Politics of Affection in William Davenant's Dramatic Theory," *Exemplaria* 26, no. 1 (2014): 51. On the pageantry of Davenant's Interregnum theater, see also Cope, "Glory That Was Rome."

68. Chua, "Purposes of Playing," 52.

69. The best and most recent development of this line of argument is found in Jean I. Marsden, *Fatal Desire: Women, Sexuality, and the English Stage, 1660–1720* (Ithaca, NY: Cornell University Press, 2006).

70. An earlier siege in 1480 had not succeeded.

71. Daniel Goffman, *The Ottoman Empire and Early Modern Europe* (Cambridge: Cambridge University Press, 2002), 100–1.

72. Caroline Finkel, *Osman's Dream: The History of the Ottoman Empire, 1300–1923* (New York: Basic Books, 2005), 118–19.

73. Historians disagree about Ottoman power at this time, but more recent work suggests that the traditional narrative of Ottoman decline in the seventeenth century was exaggerated. See Goffman, *Ottoman Empire*, 18.

74. Wiseman, *Drama and Politics*, 154.

75. Wiseman, *Drama and Politics*, 154. On Cromwell's Western Design, see Abigail Leslie Swingen, *Competing Visions of Empire: Labor, Slavery, and the Origins of the British Atlantic Empire* (New Haven, CT: Yale University Press, 2015), chapter 2.

76. On the connections between Cromwell's ambitions and Davenant's *Cruelty*, see Richard Frohock, "Sir William Davenant's American Operas," *Modern Language Review* 96, no. 2 (April 2001): 323–33.

77. Wiseman, *Drama and Politics*, 153. On depictions of Cromwell as the Sultan, see also Birchwood, *Staging Islam in England*, 3–4. Birchwood points out that "comparison between Cromwell's regime and Ottomans had become commonplace" (108). Umberto Garcia shows the associations in the seventeenth and eighteenth centuries between republicanism and Islam. See his *Islam and the English Enlightenment, 1670–1840* (Baltimore: Johns Hopkins University Press, 2011), esp. chapter 1.

78. [William Davenant], *The Siege of Rhodes. Made a Representation by the Art of Prospective in Scenes, And the Story sung in Recitative Musick. At the back part of Rutland-House in the upper end of Aldergate-Street, London* (London, 1656), 1. Future references to the one-part version are from this edition and cited in the text.

79. Nabil Matar, *Islam in Britain, 1558–1685* (Cambridge: Cambridge University Press, 1988), 20, 51.

80. Matar, *Islam in Britain*, 15.

81. On identity in this period, see Wahrman, *Making of the Modern Self*. Wahrman, as noted in note 29, argues that writers in the period before 1780 in England understood major aspects of identity, such as gender, race, class, and the difference between humans and animals, in much more fluid terms than by the end of the century, when they became more rigid in recognizably modern terms. He states that this sense is particular to the "short eighteenth century" (the eighteenth century before 1780). While a little before Wahrman's time frame, Davenant's *Siege* and, I will argue, other Restoration plays encourage a similar fluidity.

82. [Bartolomej Georgijević,] *The Rarities of Turkey, Gathered by One that Was Sold Several Times a Slave in the Turkish Empire* (London, 1661), 111–16, 117.

83. For women acting before 1660, see Pamela Allen Brown and Peter Parolin, eds., *Women Players in England, 1500–1660: Beyond the All-Male Stage* (Burlington, VT: Ashgate, 2005). While there were certainly women performing, as this collection demonstrates, there was still something groundbreaking about Mrs. Coleman's professional appearance on a commercial English stage. The 1661 performance adds an earlier scene for Ianthe, but in the 1656 edition, she does not appear before this moment.

84. The opera was, however, vetted and accepted by Cromwell's censors. See Wiseman, *Drama and Politics*, 140. Randall also discusses Davenant's evocation of Henrietta Maria with Ianthe in *Winter Fruit*, 173, as does Birchwood, *Staging Islam in England*, 111.

85. Britland, *Drama at the Courts of Queen Henrietta Maria*, 141–48.

86. This reading of Ianthe as Henrietta Maria casts Alphonso as Charles I, which has some support although also some limitations. In some ways, the implications would be overtly unflattering, given Alphonso's failure to control his emotions. At the same time, it recasts a political conflict as a tragic romance. Almahide in John Dryden's *Conquest of Granada*, as Brandon Chua shows, similarly becomes a civilizing force in the play and tries to temper the passions of her lover. See *Ravishment of Reason*, 60.

87. John Downes, *Roscius Anglicanus*, ed. Judith Milhous and Robert D. Hume (London: Society for Theatre Research, 1987 [1708]), 73.

88. *Diary of Samuel Pepys*, July 2, 1661.

89. *Diary of Samuel Pepys*, December 27, 1662.

90. Pepys calls Mary Betterton "Ianthe" in 1662 on April 2, September 30, October 22, and December 1; in 1664 on February 1, July 28, and August 13; and in 1665 on April 3.

91. Pepys saw the play again on Tuesday, May 21, 1667 and read it again on Sunday, August 5, 1666. Praise quoted from Sunday, October 1, 1665.

92. The text of the two-part version was first published in 1663. Pepys would have seen this new version, as he mentions Roxolana, who does not appear in the earlier text. For a textual history, see Ann-Mari Hedbäck, *The Siege of Rhodes: A Critical Edition* (Uppsala: Acta Universitatis Upsaliensis, 1973). According to Hedbäck, for the 1663 edition Davenant inserted pages into part 1 and added the second part, reflecting the performances of this play that began in 1661. It was reprinted in 1670 and again in 1672, with little change. I have used the 1672 text for its consistent pagination with an awareness of the emendations noted by Hedbäck; I have used the separate one-part and two-part versions rather than her composite.

93. Michelle Anne White, *Henrietta Maria and the English Civil Wars* (Burlington, VT: Ashgate, 2006), 192–93.

94. Galina I. Yermolenko introduction to *Roxolana in European Literature, History, and Culture*, ed. Galina I. Yermolenko (Burlington, VT: Ashgate, 2010), 2–3.

95. Yermolenko, introduction, 6.

96. I have discussed this at greater length in "Rebels for Love: Maternity, Absolutism, and the Earl of Orrery's *Mustapha*" in *Stage Mothers: Women, Work, and the Theater, 1660–1830*, ed. Laura Engel and Elaine M. McGirr (Lewisburg, PA: Bucknell University Press, 2014), 105–20.

97. See Ballaster, *Fabulous Orients*, esp. 64.

98. Orr, *Empire on the English Stage*, 61. The fascination with the East continued in the eighteenth century and appeared in narratives as well, as Ballaster, *Fabulous Orients* has shown.

99. See Wahrman, *Making of the Modern Self*, 177–79.

100. Ballaster, *Fabulous Orients*, 56–67.

101. For Bridget Orr, the play hinges on the contrast between the virtuous Ianthe and the vicious Roxolana, characterizing East and West. While certainly Roxolana claims greater political authority than Ianthe in ways that reveal her inappropriate passion, taking all four lovers into consideration points to a more complicated dynamic. See Orr, *Empire on the English Stage*, 70–71.

102. William Davenant, *The Siege of Rhodes. as they were lately represented at His Highness the Duke of York's Theatre in Lincolns-Inn Fields: the first part being lately enlarg'd*. London, 1663.

103. Clare, *Drama of the English Republic*, 181. Davenant would go on to adapt several Shakespeare plays.

104. See Jean I. Marsden, "Mary Pix's *Ibrahim:* The Woman Writer as Commercial Playwright," *Studies in the Literary Imagination* 32, no. 2 (1999): 33–44.

105. Felicity A. Nussbaum, *Torrid Zones: Maternity, Sexuality, and Empire in Eighteenth-Century English Narratives* (Baltimore: Johns Hopkins University Press, 1995), 33.

106. See, for example, Gabriel de Brémond, *Hattige, or, The Amours of the King of Tamaran* (Amsterdam: Printed for Simon the African, 1680); *The Amours of the Sultana of Barbary* (London, 1689); P. Belon, *The Court Secret* (London, 1689).

107. Nussbaum, *Torrid Zones*, 91.

108. Gilbert Burnet and Thomas Burnet, *Bishop Burnet's History of His Own Time*, ed. Martin Joseph Routh, vol. 1. (Oxford: Oxford University Press, 1833), 456.

109. For a fuller discussion of popular objections to the Catholic mistresses, see Alison Conway, *The Protestant Whore: Courtesan Narrative and Religious Controversy in England, 1680–1750* (Toronto: University of Toronto Press, 2010), chapter 1.

110. Catherine's pushback is described by Pepys on Saturday, July 26, 1662. *Diary of Samuel Pepys* vol. 3, 147.

111. See, for example, Henry Marsh's *A New Survey of the Turkish empire and government in a brief history deduced to this present time, and the reign of the now Grand Seignior, Mahomet the IV, the present and XIV emperor: with their laws, religion, and customs: as also an account of the siege of Newhausel* (London, 1663), esp. 47–53. On the Ottoman system of slavery, see Goffman, *Ottoman Empire*, 63–68. On the English fear of Ottoman slavery, see Games, *Web of Empire*, 68–72.

112. See Laura Lunger Knoppers, *Politicizing Domesticity from Henrietta Maria to Milton's Eve* (Cambridge: Cambridge University Press, 2011), chapter 2.

113. W. G. Parrott, "The Emotional Experiences of Envy and Jealousy," in *The Psychology of Envy and Jealousy*, ed. Peter Salovey (New York, Guildford Press, 1991), 3–30, esp. 19 and 21.

114. MacLean, *Looking East*, 20, 55.

115. David Quint, *Epic and Empire: Politics and Generic Form from Virgil to Milton* (Princeton, NJ: Princeton University Press, 1993), introduction. On the importance of epic in this period, see Anthony Welch, "Epic Romance, Royalist Retreat, and the English Civil War," *Modern Philology* 105, no. 3 (2008): 570–602.

116. Marlin E. Blaine, "Epic, Romance, and History in Davenant's 'Madagascar,'" *Studies in Philology* 95, no. 3 (Summer 1998), 293–319; Games, *Web of Empire*, 181–217.

117. Chua, 16. As Chua also notes in *Ravishment of Reason* (19), for Davenant such heroes will always be flawed due to their excessive passions.

2. Travesties

1. Harold Weber, *Paper Bullets: Print and Kingship under Charles II* (Lexington: University Press of Kentucky, 1996), esp. 172–208; Tim Harris, *Restoration: Charles II and His Kingdoms, 1660–1685* (New York: Penguin, 2006), 69–70, 142–43.

2. Colley Cibber, *An Apology for the Life of Colley Cibber: With an Historical View of the Stage during His Own Time*, ed. Byrne R. S. Fone (Ann Arbor: University of Michigan Press, 1968), 54.

3. Samuel Pepys, *The Diary of Samuel Pepys: A New and Complete Transcription*, ed. Robert Latham and William Matthews, vol. 2 (Berkeley: University of California Press, 1970), 139–40.

4. A very good example of this kind of reading can be found in J. Douglas Canfield, *Tricksters & Estates: On the Ideology of Restoration Comedy* (Lexington: University Press of Kentucky, 1997). See also Laura Brown, *English Dramatic Form, 1660–1760: An Essay in Generic History* (New Haven, CT: Yale University Press, 1981).

5. Robert D. Hume, "The Myth of the Rake in 'Restoration' Comedy," *Studies in the Literary Imagination* 10, no. 1 (1977): 25–55.

6. B. Eugene McCarthy, *William Wycherley: A Biography* (Athens: Ohio University Press, 1979), 13.

7. McCarthy, *William Wycherley*, 116–17.

8. McCarthy, *William Wycherley*, 25, 89–91.

9. John Dryden, "Mac Flecknoe," in *The Works of John Dryden*, vol. 2, ed. Edward Niles Hooker, H. T Swedenberg, and Vinton A. Dearing (Berkeley: University of California Press, 1956), 139–43, lines 150–60.

10. Dryden's objections to Flecknoe could certainly also have been personal, and may additionally have been political. Much of what is known about Flecknoe's network of associations, however, suggests his loyalty to the Stuart monarchs, although he also wrote a biography of Oliver Cromwell, *The Idea of His Highness Oliver, Late Lord Protector, &c.: with Certain Brief Reflexions on His Life* (London, 1659). On Flecknoe, see also Paul Hammond, "Flecknoe and Mac Flecknoe," *Essays in Criticism: A Quarterly Journal of Literary Criticism* 35, no. 4 (1985): 315–29. See also J. Douglas Canfield, "Richard Flecknoe's Early Defense of the Stage: An Appeal to Cromwell," *Restoration and 18th Century Theatre Research* 2, no. 2 (1987): 1–7, in which Canfield praises Flecknoe for his defense of the stage. For an analysis of Flecknoe's own view of raillery, see James Fitzmaurice, "Margaret Cavendish, Richard Flecknoe, and Raillery at the Salon of Beatrix de Cusance," *English Studies: A Journal of English Language and Literature* 92, no. 7 (2011): 771–85.

11. Maximillian Novak comes close to this explanation when he suggests that Dryden despised Flecknoe for the latter's arrogance, egotism, and admiration for French literary technique. He concludes, however, that Dryden mainly chose Flecknoe because of Flecknoe's earlier attack on Davenant in *Sir William D'avenant's Voyage to the Other World* (1668). In this pamphlet, other dead poets attack Davenant for his ineptitude and offensive adaptations of their work. Dryden, of course, collaborated with and admired Davenant. See Maximillian Novak, "Dryden's 'Ape of the French Eloquence' and Richard Flecknoe," *Bulletin of the New York Public Library* 72 (1968): 499–506.

12. Flecknoe's life, career, and writing have received scant scholarly attention, except in two contexts: as the paternal hero of *Mac Flecknoe*, and as the object of Andrew Marvell's satire in "Flecknoe: An English Priest at Rome." Marvell presents Flecknoe in exile during the Interregnum as a scrawny poetaster living in a tiny room and yearning for company, trapping the poem's speaker into listening to his tedious verse and lute-playing. For the intersections between Flecknoe and Marvell, see Nigel Smith, *Andrew Marvell, The Chameleon* (New Haven, CT: Yale University Press, 2010), 56–59. Smith suggests that Marvell satirized Flecknoe in part because he saw in his rival a Catholic version of himself. See also Nicholas Murray, *World Enough and Time: The Life of Andrew Marvell* (New York: St. Martin's Press, 1999), 28–31.

13. Joseph Gillow, *A Literary and Biographical Dictionary of the English Catholics from the Breach with Rome, in 1534, to the Present Time*, vol. 2 (London, 1885–1903), 293–95. Quoted in Murray, *World Enough and Time*, 31.

14. Michael Gavin, *The Invention of English Criticism, 1650–1760* (Cambridge: Cambridge University Press, 2015), 28.

15. While King demonstrates the importance of the fop in the history of masculinity, Straub has noted the sexual suspicion that the fop role raised. Kristina Straub, *Sexual Suspects: Eighteenth-Century Players and Sexual Ideology* (Princeton, NJ: Princeton University Press, 1992), 47–68; Thomas Alan King, *The Gendering of Men, 1600–1750* (Madison: University of Wisconsin Press, 2004), 228–56. King sees the fop as maintaining a residual refusal of the emergent split between the public and private. Robert B. Heilman provides a good catalogue of fops, arguing for their ultimate benignity, in

"Some Fops and Some Versions of Foppery," *ELH* 49 (1982): 363–95. Susan Staves argues that Restoration fops point to a more egalitarian version of gender in "A Few Kind Words for the Fop," *SEL* 22 (1982): 413–28. On the sexual variety of fop figures, see Andrew P. Williams, *The Restoration Fop: Gender Boundaries and Comic Characterization in Later Seventeenth Century Drama* (Lewiston, NY: Edwin Mellen Press, 1995), 39–59. For a recent intriguing account of the fop's gender identity, see Emma Katherine Atwood, "Fashionably Late: Queer Temporality and the Restoration Fop," *Comparative Drama* 47, no. 1 (2013): 85–111.

16. Mark S. Dawson, *Gentility and the Comic Theatre of Late Stuart London* (Cambridge: Cambridge University Press, 2005), 145–204.

17. The fop is tricked into this marriage, but upon the discovery, he declares, "I'gad I'm glad on't: it's a very pretty Boy by my Soul: come to my Arms, my dear little Ganymede." Thomas Dilke, *The Lover's Luck* (London, 1696), 46.

18. Dror Wahrman concentrates mostly on the early eighteenth century, but his insights hold up for the Restoration period as well, which, as we have seen, saw considerable experimentation with identity. Dror Wahrman, *The Making of the Modern Self: Identity and Culture in Eighteenth-Century England* (New Haven, CT: Yale University Press, 2004).

19. Alison Games, *The Web of Empire: English Cosmopolitans in an Age of Expansion, 1560–1660* (Oxford: Oxford University Press, 2008).

20. *The Man of Mode; or, Sir Fopling Flutter* in George Etherege, *The Plays of Sir George Etherege*, ed. Michael Cordner (Cambridge: Cambridge University Press, 1982), 4.1.238–39.

21. In *Vested Interests: Cross-Dressing & Cultural Anxiety* (New York: Routledge, 1992), Marjorie B. Garber explores how both in modern culture and historically, transvestism overlaps with, but is not coterminous with homosexuality. Her final chapter (353–90), addresses the "unmarked transvestite" discussed here. While Garber's account is limited by the heavy emphasis on psychoanalysis and would be complicated by more recent work on transgender identities, I find her unmarked transvestite cultural category to be a highly productive framework for thinking about the fop and other figures in Restoration theater.

22. Williams, *Restoration Fop*, 73.

23. Etherege, *Man of Mode*, Act 1, Scene 1, 404–6.

24. For a good discussion of cultural cross-dressing, see Tara Mayer, "Cultural Cross-Dressing: Posing and Performance in Orientalist Portraits," *Journal of the Royal Asiatic Society* 22, no. 2 (2012): 281–98.

25. Edward Howard, *Six Days Adventure, or the New Utopia* (London, 1671); Joseph Arrowsmith, *The Reformation* (London, 1673), 15; Aphra Behn, *Town-Fopp: Or, Sir Timothy Tawdry* (London, 1673), prologue.

26. Garber, *Vested Interests*, 40.

27. Garber, *Vested Interests*, 16.

28. On Flecknoe, see note 12.

29. Richard Fleckno[e], *Relations of Ten Years Travell in Europe, Asia, Affrique, and America. All by way of Letters occasionally written to divers noble Personages, from place to place* (London, n.d. [1656]), 11. Future references are from this edition and cited in the text.

30. For Benjamin Backbite's poem, see *The School for Scandal* in Richard Brinsley Sheridan, *The School for Scandal and Other Plays*, ed. Eric S. Rump (London: Penguin,

1988), 2.2.11–15: "Sure never were seen two such beautiful ponies; / Other horses are clowns, but these macaronies: / To give 'em this title I'm sure isn't wrong, / Their legs are so slim, and their tails are so long." While his beloved parrot deserves an epigram, the "savages" of Brazil strike Flecknoe as little more than animals, "only fit for toil and druggery, which is the reason Nature perhaps provided that Country with neither Horse nor Asse" (76).

31. Mispaginated; follows from page 95.

32. One critic who does make this connection is R. S. Cox in "Richard Flecknoe and *The Man of Mode*," *Modern Language Quarterly* 29 (1968): 183–89. Cox argues that the play invokes Flecknoe when Emilia mockingly refers to *Diversions of Brussels*, satirically invoking Flecknoe's *Treatise on the Sport of Wit*. The reference to Flecknoe returns when Dorimant becomes Flecknoe-like as part of his disguise as the foppish Cortage.

33. A play of this description seems to have either been lost or never written.

34. As Margery Kingsley argues, *Mac Flecknoe* has attracted surprisingly little criticism, given its important place in the literary canon. See her "'High on a Throne of His Own Labours Rear'd': *Mac Flecknoe*, Jeremiad and Cultural Myth," *Modern Philology* 93, no. 3 (1996): 327–51.

35. *The Gentleman Dancing-Master* in *The Plays of William Wycherley*, ed. Arthur Friedman (Oxford: Oxford at the Clarendon Press, 1979). Future references are from this edition and cited in the text.

36. Mark Dawson has objected to the characterization of fops as upstarts and is right in many cases, but in this play only Gerrard can claim true gentility. On the significance of the coach as a symbol of status, see Danielle Bobker, "Carriages, Conversation, and *A Sentimental Journey*," *Studies in Eighteenth-Century Culture* 35 (2006): 243–66.

37. Critics disagree, however, over how the play characterizes her social and sexual desires. Sam Terry in "The Comic Standard in Wycherley's *The Gentleman Dancing-Master*," *Enlightenment Essays* 6 (1975): 3–11, argues that Hippolita is meant to be a negative character for her lust and social climbing. Peggy Thompson expands on the play's misogyny in "'Why Say We No?': The Trope of Insincere Resistance in *The Gentleman Dancing-Master* and *The Plain Dealer*," *Papers in Language and Literature* 42, no. 4 (2006): 420–39. John Vance, by contrast, argues that the play represents Hippolita's desires as healthy in *William Wycherley and the Comedy of Fear* (Newark: University of Delaware Press, 2000), chapter 2, and J. Douglas Canfield sees her as a trickster figure through whom the landed aristocracy appropriate city wealth in *Tricksters & Estates: On the Ideology of Restoration Comedy* (Lexington: University Press of Kentucky, 1997), 34–35. In *Performing Libertinism in Charles II's Court: Politics, Drama, Sexuality* (New York: Palgrave Macmillan, 2005), 83–89, Jeremy Webster points out that this play includes a libertine who redirects his desires into marriage and reads Hippolita as a masterful manipulator. He argues that the play contrasts her own desire for freedom with her father's obsession with control. Robert Markley suggests that "Hippolita and Prue become verbal and sexual aggressors" in *Two-Edg'd Weapons: Style and Ideology in the Comedies of Etherege, Wycherley, and Congreve* (Oxford: Clarendon Press, 1988), 152. Aspasia Velissariou also explores these tensions in "Patriarchal Tactics of Control and Female Desire in Wycherley's *The Gentleman Dancing-Master* and *The Country Wife*," *Texas Studies in Literature and Language* 37, no. 2 (1995): 115–26. John Bryce Jordan, in "'Is He No Man?': Toward an Appreciation of Male Effeminacy in English Dance

History," *Studies in Eighteenth-Century Culture* 30 (2001): 201–22, suggests that Wycherley's play provides evidence of suspicions around male dancers in the seventeenth century. Focusing more on "Paris" and "Don Diego," W. Gerald Marshall suggests that the play depicts different versions of madness and theatricality in "The Idea of Theatre in Wycherley's *The Gentleman Dancing-Master*," *Restoration: Studies in English Literary Culture, 1660–1700* 6, no. 1 (1982): 1–10. While not specifically engaged in this question, my argument suggests that the play applauds Hippolita's escape from patriarchal control and empire envy.

38. Cynthia Lowenthal, *Performing Identities on the Restoration Stage* (Carbondale: Southern Illinois University Press, 2003), 92–103.

39. Lowenthal, *Performing Identities*, 96.

40. See Lowenthal, *Performing Identities* on this point, 92–103.

41. Susan Dwyer Amussen, *Caribbean Exchanges: Slavery and the Transformation of English Society, 1640–1700* (Chapel Hill: University of North Carolina Press, 2007).

42. Amussen, *Caribbean Exchanges*, 194–95.

43. Amussen, *Caribbean Exchanges*, 195.

44. Amussen, *Caribbean Exchanges*, 196.

45. Amussen, *Caribbean Exchanges*, 215.

46. Joseph Roach, *Cities of the Dead: Circum-Atlantic Performance* (New York: Columbia University Press, 1996), 128.

47. Simon Gikandi, *Slavery and the Culture of Taste* (Princeton, NJ: Princeton University Press, 2011) argues that in this period there was a general disavowal of the slave plantations owned by British subjects. I suggest in my argument that there was more engagement with the moral, political, and personal implications of slavery than has been recognized, even though much of it did not take the overt form that we see later in the abolitionist movement.

48. Sven Beckert, *Empire of Cotton: A Global History* (New York: Alfred A. Knopf, 2014), xvi.

49. Holly Brewer, "Slavery, Sovereignty, and 'Inheritable Blood': Reconsidering John Locke and the Origins of American Slavery," *The American Historical Review* 122, no. 4 (2017): 1038–78; 1047, https://doi.org/10.1093/ahr/122.4.1038.

50. Kenneth Gordon Davies, *The Royal African Company* (London: Longmans, Green, 1957), esp. 60; Abigail Leslie Swingen, *Competing Visions of Empire: Labor, Slavery, and the Origins of the British Atlantic Empire* (New Haven, CT: Yale University Press, 2015), esp. chapter 3; William A. Pettigrew, *Freedom's Debt: The Royal African Company and the Politics of the Atlantic Slave Trade, 1672–1752* (Chapel Hill, NC: Published for the Omohundro Institute of Early American History and Culture, Williamsburg, Virginia, by the University of North Carolina Press, 2013).

51. On the guinea coin, see John O'Brien, *Literature Incorporated: The Cultural Unconscious of the Business Corporation, 1650–1850* (Chicago: University of Chicago Press, 2016), 146–47, and Holly Brewer, "Slavery, Sovereignty, and 'Inheritable Blood.'" In chapter 2 of her manuscript work in progress, Brewer shows a pattern of enslaved children wearing silver collars in these paintings. I am grateful to the author for sharing this work with me.

52. Swingen, *Competing Visions of Empire*, 59–60.

53. Swingen, *Competing Visions of Empire*, 28–29.

54. Davies, *Royal African Company*, 240–64; Swingen, *Competing Visions of Empire*, chapter 3; Brewer, "Inheritable Blood." Brewer makes the particular point about the use of military power.

55. On Francophobia during the Restoration, see Tim Harris, "Hibernophobia and Francophobia in Restoration England," *Restoration* 41, no. 2 (2017): 5–32. Swingen writes, "It is telling that the Royal African Company was reorganized at the same time that plans were under way to embroil England in yet another war with the Dutch . . . Although the Third Anglo-Dutch War was fought primarily in European waters and not in West Africa, the new company's main commercial purpose was to remove the Dutch from supplying slaves to English and Spanish colonies." Swingen, *Competing Visions of Empire*, 87.

56. On the English fears of French ambitions, see Bridget Orr, *Empire on the English Stage, 1660–1714* (Cambridge: Cambridge University Press, 2001), 223, and also Steven C. Pincus, *1688: The First Modern Revolution* (New Haven, CT: Yale University Press, 2009), 146, 226, 313–14, 438–39, and throughout.

57. Tim Harris, *Restoration*, 71–84.

58. For royal control of the press, see Harris, *Restoration*, 68–70; also Harold Weber, *Paper Bullets: Print and Kingship under Charles II* (Lexington: University Press of Kentucky, 1996), esp. chapters 4 and 5.

59. [Sir William Coventry], *Englands appeal from the private cabal at White-Hall to the great council of the nation, the Lords and Commons in Parliament assembled by a true lover of his countrey* (London, 1673), 6, 7.

60. Aparna Gollapudi, "Where Have All the Children Gone? The (As Yet) Invisible Child-Actor on the Eighteenth-Century Stage," Roundtable Presentation, American Society for Eighteenth-Century Studies (ASECS) Conference, Pittsburgh, March 2016.

61. Or, as Srinivas Aravamudan has argued, as a version of a pet. See his *Tropicopolitans: Colonialism and Agency, 1688–1804* (Durham, NC: Duke University Press, 1999), chapter 1.

62. John Crowne, *Calisto, or the Chaste Nimph. The Late Masque at Court* (London, 1675), 80–81.

63. McCarthy discusses Wycherley's sources in depth; see *William Wycherley*, 46–115. To take one example of an English precursor: John Caryll's *Sir Salomon; Or, The Cautious Coxcomb* (1671), drawing on Molière's *L'École des Femmes*, even has its titular character anticipate Pinchwife's stratagem of seeking marriage with a country girl as a guarantee of innocence. Sir Salomon encounters Betty as a child in the country and has her raised in isolation as his intended wife, with predictably comic and disastrous results.

64. See Raymond Williams, *The Country and the City* (New York: Oxford University Press, 1975); Jean-Christophe Agnew, *Worlds Apart: The Market and the Theater in Anglo-American Thought, 1550–1750* (Cambridge: Cambridge University Press, 1986).

65. This play's modern editor suggests that there may have been an earlier production. *"The Woman Turned Bully": Textos y Comentarios*, ed. María José Mora, Manuel J. Gómez-Lara, Rafael Portillo, and Juan A. Prieto-Pablos (Barcelona: Universitat de Barcelona, 2007), 16–18. The authorship of this play remains unidentified, although some have speculated that Aphra Behn might have had a hand in it, given its remarkable heroine. For a discussion of this controversy, see *The Woman Turned Bully*, 18–28. References are from this edition and cited in the text.

66. For a discussion of the political implications of this play, especially regarding the figure of the lawyer, see Juan A. Prieto-Pablos, "Ignoramus, *The Woman Turned Bully*, and Restoration Satire on the Common Lawyer," *SEL* 48, no. 3 (2008): 523–46.

67. A search of the phrase "breeches part" in the combined databases of Eighteenth-Century Collections online and Early English Books online produces results only from the late eighteenth century, with the first usage of this phrase in its current sense in Joseph Haslewood's *The Secret History of the Green Room* (London, 1790), 1: 230.

68. On the eroticization of Restoration actresses, see, for example, Elizabeth Howe, *The First English Actresses: Women and Drama, 1660–1700* (Cambridge: Cambridge University Press, 1992).

69. As Mora and the other editors of *The Woman Turned Bully* point out, Docket's character also has political implications because "common lawyers were regarded by royalists as supporters of the parliamentary cause, since their defense of the supremacy of the law over the sovereign proved to be instrumental in the crisis that led to the Civil War" (32).

70. Congreve's *The Way of the World* (1700) also picks up this anxiety about a widow's remarriage potentially preventing the marriages and financial security of the next generation.

71. Christopher J. Wheatley, *Without God or Reason: The Plays of Thomas Shadwell and Secular Ethics in the Restoration* (Lewisburg, PA: Bucknell University Press, 1993), 129–30.

72. John Crowne, *The Countrey Wit. A Comedy Acted at the Dukes Theatre* (London: Printed for James Magnes and Richard Bentley, 1675), 89.

73. For example, S. L., *Remarques on the Humours and Conversations of the Town. Written in a Letter to Sir T. L.* (London: Printed for Allen Banks, 1673); *Remarks upon Remarques: or, A vindication of the Conversations of the Town, in another letter directed to the same Sir T. L.* (London: Printed for A. C. Hensman, 1673); and *Animadversions on two late Books, one called Remarques, &c. to which is added Notes on some Humours and Conversations of the Country. (The other called Reflections on Marriage, and Poetick Discipline)* (London: Printed for A. C. Hensman, 1673). See also on this point Williams, *Country and the City*, 51–53, and my essay "'All Injury's Forgot': Restoration Sex Comedy and National Amnesia," *Comparative Drama* 42, no. 1 (2008): 7–28.

74. For information here and throughout about actors and their roles, I have relied on the invaluable *The London Stage, 1660–1800: A Calendar of Plays, Entertainments & Afterpieces, Together with Casts, Box-Receipts and Contemporary Comment: Compiled from the Playbills, Newspapers and Theatrical Diaries of the Period*, ed. William Van Lennep, Emmett Langdon Avery, Arthur H. Scouten, George Winchester Stone, and Charles Beecher Hogan (Carbondale: Southern Illinois University Press, 1960). For a key discussion of the way Restoration theaters created characters by associating them with performers, see Peter Holland, *The Ornament of Action: Text and Performance in Restoration Comedy* (Cambridge: Cambridge University Press, 1979).

75. David Kathman, "Charles Hart," *Oxford Dictionary of National Biography* (Oxford: Oxford University Press, 2004), http://www.oxforddnb.com/view/article/12473.

76. John Downes, *Roscius Anglicanus*, ed. Judith Milhous and Robert D. Hume (London: Society for Theatre Research, 1987), 41.

77. For an excellent discussion of the Royalist themes of early Restoration drama, see Nancy Klein Maguire, *Regicide and Restoration: English Tragicomedy, 1660–1671* (Cambridge: Cambridge University Press, 1992).

78. Wycherley, *The Country Wife*, in *The Plays of William Wycherley*, 2.1.20–21. Future references are cited in the text.

79. For example, J. Douglas Canfield characterizes Horner as a trickster figure, whereas Michael Neill has suggested that the libertines in Restoration drama rebel against authority as much as their Cromwellian counterparts. Erin Mackie, arguing against Neill, states that libertines like Horner are not radical, but violently destructive. Eve Kosofsky Sedgwick argues that homosocial relations organize the play, with the women serving as tokens of exchange. Helen Burke has countered this argument, suggesting that the Fidget ladies turn Horner into their property rather than the other way around. Canfield, *Tricksters & Estates*, 126–30; Neill, "Heroic Heads and Humble Tails"; Erin Mackie, "Boys Will Be Boys: Masculinity, Criminality, and the Restoration Rake," *Eighteenth Century: Theory and Interpretation* 46, no. 2 (2005): 129–49, esp. 138; see also her *Rakes, Highwaymen, and Pirates: The Making of the Modern Gentleman in the Eighteenth Century* (Baltimore: Johns Hopkins University Press, 2009); Eve Kosofsky Sedgwick, *Between Men: English Literature and Male Homosocial Desire* (New York: Columbia University Press, 1985), chapter 3; Helen M. Burke, "Wycherley's 'Tendentious Joke': The Discourse of Alterity in *The Country Wife*," *The Eighteenth Century: Theory and Interpretation* 29, no. 3 (1988): 227–41. See also Velissariou, "Patriarchal Tactics"; H. W. Matalene, "What Happens in *The Country-Wife*," *SEL* 22, no. 3 (1982): 395–411; Harold Weber, "Horner and His 'Women of Honour': The Dinner Party in *The Country-Wife*," *Modern Language Quarterly* 43, no. 2 (1982): 107–20; Webster, *Performing Libertinism in Charles II's Court*, chapter 2; Maximillian E. Novak, "Margery Pinchwife's 'London Desease': Restoration Comedy and the Libertine Offensive of the 1670s," *Studies in the Literary Imagination* 10, no. 1 (1977): 1–23.

80. As Helen Burke argues in "Wycherley's 'Tendentious Joke.'"

81. From *The Way of the World*, in *The Works of William Congreve*, vol. 2, ed. D. F. McKenzie (Oxford: Oxford University Press, 2011), 206, 5.4.25.

82. *The Oxford English Dictionary* (Oxford: Oxford University Press), online edition.

83. Wycherley, of course, takes the eunuch deception plot from Terence's *The Eunuch*, although in Terence the character Chaerea disguises himself as a particular eunuch to infiltrate the household of the object of his desire.

84. Rosenthal, "All Injury's Forgot."

85. On parallels in Restoration drama between the political and the domestic, see Susan Staves, *Players' Scepters: Fictions of Authority in the Restoration* (Lincoln: University of Nebraska Press, 1979).

86. On the context for Pinchwife's violent threats, see James Turner, *Libertines and Radicals in Early Modern London: Sexuality, Politics, and Literary Culture, 1630–1685* (Cambridge: Cambridge University Press, 2002), 205. Turner points out that this would have been a familiar kind of attack on a sex worker.

87. For an extended reading of this dynamic, see my "All Injury's Forgot."

88. Alok Yadav's excellent *Before the Empire of English: Literature, Provinciality, and Nationalism in Eighteenth-Century Britain* (New York: Palgrave Macmillan, 2004) focuses on a slightly later period than the one under discussion in this chapter but draws much of its evidence from 1660–1700.

89. Yadav, *Before the Empire of English*, 37.

90. See for example, David B. Morris, "Language and Honor in *The Country Wife*," *South Atlantic Bulletin* 37, no. 4 (November 1972): 3–10, esp. 7–8.

260 NOTES TO PAGES 82-88

91. Elizabeth Kowaleski Wallace, *Consuming Subjects: Women, Shopping, and Business in the Eighteenth Century* (New York: Columbia University Press, 1996), 55–57.

92. David Porter, *Ideographia: The Chinese Cipher in Early Modern Europe* (Stanford, CA: Stanford University Press, 2001), 182.

93. Porter, *Ideographia*, 183.

94. Lisa Berglund, "The Language of the Libertines: Subversive Morality in *The Man of Mode*," *SEL* 30, no. 3 (1990): 369–86. Berglund is writing about *The Man of Mode* here, but her insights apply more broadly.

95. Simon Shepherd, "'The Body,' Performance Studies, Horner and a Dinner Party," *Textual Practice* 14, no. 2 (2000): 285–303.

96. On this point, see Eugenia Zuroski Jenkins, *A Taste for China: English Subjectivity and the Prehistory of Orientalism* (Oxford: Oxford University Press, 2013), 82–83. Jenkins thus suggests that China itself becomes associated with the imaginary.

97. In *The French Gardiner* (London: Printed by J. C. for John Crooke, 1658), Nicolas de Bonnefons explains that oranges need to be grown in hothouses (87–89). He lists "China-oranges" as one of several varieties. China-oranges are the sweet variety. According to Pierre Laszlo in *Citrus: A History* (Chicago: University of Chicago Press, 2007), what we now call "Valencia" oranges were a sweet variety brought back from China by Spanish or Portuguese explorers (46). Thus, Margery's "China orange" was not imported from China, but grown in a hothouse; nevertheless, its variety originated in China and still bore those associations. On the Chinese origin of the sweet orange, see also Clarissa Hyman, *Oranges: A Global History* (London: Reaktion, 2013), 7–22.

98. This is mitigated by the fact that in refusing to protect Alithea's reputation, he is watching out for Margery's. Still, it comes across to Harcourt as a betrayal.

99. Porter, *Chinese Taste*, 135.

100. John Webb, *An Historical Essay Endeavoring a Probability That the Language of the Empire of China Is the Primitive Language* (London: Printed for Nath. Brook, 1669), 210.

101. Webb, *Historical Essay*, 112.

102. For important discussions of the English fascination with China's commercial and aesthetic accomplishments in this period, see Robert Markley, *The Far East and the English Imagination, 1600–1730* (Cambridge: Cambridge University Press, 2006) and Maxine Berg, *Goods from the East, 1600–1800: Trading Eurasia* (Houndmills: Palgrave Macmillan, 2015).

103. For the changing meaning of "china" in the eighteenth century, see Jenkins, *A Taste for China*.

104. Elkanah Settle, *The Conquest of China by the Tartars: A Tragedy, Acted at the Duke's Theatre* (London, 1676), 67.

105. Markley, *Far East and the English Imagination*, 2. See also Kenneth Pomeranz, *The Great Divergence: China, Europe, and the Making of the Modern World Economy* (Princeton, NJ: Princeton University Press, 2000).

3. Indian Queens and the Queen Who Brought the Indies

1. Samuel Pepys, *The Diary of Samuel Pepys: A New and Complete Transcription*, vol. 3, ed. Robert Latham and William Matthews (Berkeley: University of California Press, 1970), 232.

2. On sexual fantasies about Queen Elizabeth, see Louis Adrian Montrose, "'Shaping Fantasies': Figurations of Gender and Power in Elizabethan Culture," *Representations* 2, no. 2 (1983): 61–94. On the sexual allure of the mistresses of Charles II, see, for example, Alison Conway, *The Protestant Whore: Courtesan Narrative and Religious Controversy in England, 1680–1750* (Toronto: University of Toronto Press, 2010), introduction.

3. The best study of Catherine's dowry remains Gertrude Z. Thomas, *Richer Than Spices: How a Royal Bride's Dowry Introduced Cane, Lacquer, Cottons, Tea, and Porcelain to England, and So Revolutionized Taste, Manners, Craftsmanship, and History in Both England and America* (New York: Alfred A. Knopf, 1965).

4. Bridget Orr, *Empire on the English Stage 1660–1714* (Cambridge: Cambridge University Press, 2001), 2–3.

5. Orr, *Empire on the English Stage*, 25.

6. Nancy Klein Maguire, *Regicide and Restoration: English Tragicomedy, 1660–1671* (Cambridge: Cambridge University Press, 1992); Brandon Chua, *Ravishment of Reason: Governance and the Heroic Idioms of the Late Stuart Stage, 1660–1690* (Lewisburg, PA: Bucknell University Press, 2014); Elaine McGirr, *Heroic Mode and Political Crisis, 1660–1745* (Newark: University of Delaware Press, 2009). See also Susan J. Owen, *Restoration Theatre and Crisis* (Oxford: Clarendon Press, 1996) and J. Douglas Canfield, *Heroes & States: On the Ideology of Restoration Tragedy* (Lexington: University of Kentucky Press, 2000). Canfield is additionally interested in the tensions of class and rank evident in the plays.

7. See also Paula Backscheider, *Spectacular Politics: Theatrical Power and Mass Culture in Early Modern England* (Baltimore: Johns Hopkins University Press, 1993) on nationalist displays in the Restoration and Restoration plays as expressions of nationalism.

8. On Portugal's imperial ambitions and practices, see Roger Crowley, *Conquerors: How Portugal Forged the First Global Empire* (New York: Random House, 2015); A. R. Disney, *A History of Portugal and the Portuguese Empire: From Beginnings to 1807* (New York: Cambridge University Press, 2009).

9. On the play's exploration of female authority, see also Orr, *Empire on the English Stage*, 199–200. Such tensions in the royal marriage were well known. On April 25th, 1663, Pepys noted, "I did hear that the Queen is much grieved of late at the King's neglecting her, he having not supped once with her this quarter of a year." *Diary*, vol. 4, 112.

10. Here is a fuller summary of the plot: *The Womens Conquest* opens with the Persian monarch Tysamnes married to the Scythian queen Parisatis. Perhaps influenced by its author's fragmentary understanding of Muslim marriage law, the Persian men in this play have the right to divorce their wives at will. Tysamnes takes advantage of this rule by divorcing his Persian wife Statyra in order to take up with the foreign Parisatis. Her subjects, however, do not want to be ruled by Tysamnes. Meanwhile, the Amazon queen Mandana sends an ambassador demanding that Tysamnes end this practice of divorce at male will. Parisatis sees their point, but Tysamnes is outraged and out of defiance to the Amazonian ambassadress casts off Parisatis to demonstrate his power (36). Parisatis gives out that she has died and disguises herself as a Moor to join forces with Mandana. The Amazon queen is "taken with this stranger" (59) and takes her into her confidence. The Amazons defeat the Persians on the battlefield, capturing Tysamnes and Statyra. Yet patriarchal authority is not crushed: in the end,

Parisatis reveals her identity after overhearing the regrets of her husband. When Mandana falls in love with a Scythian nobleman, she agrees to recognize the dominion of men; Tysamnes, in turn, agrees to give up arbitrary power. Statyra steps aside to allow Parisatis and Tysamnes to reunite. The play ends, then, with the happy reunion of the Persian king with his foreign bride. Howard was not a professional playwright and had close ties to the court. Parisatis serves as an intriguing pivotal figure: a foreign queen rudely rejected by her husband who waits patiently for his return to her. She also resembles Henrietta Maria in her love of masques, although Catherine also brought foreign entertainments to court. Parisatis presents an extended masque early in *The Womens Conquest* for the pleasure and instruction of the king in its lesson of constancy. Like Henrietta in Davenant's masque, Parisatis transforms herself into an Amazon. Henrietta's role in Davenant's entertainment, grafted onto her reputation for heroic service to her husband and sovereign during the civil wars, was not forgotten. A 1669 elegy for the queen mother recalls her courage "Crossing the dangerous Seas, that She might bring / Treasure t' accommodate *Her Lord the* KING . . . Th' undaunted Courage of *Her Mighty Blood* / So *Penthisilea* th' *Amazonian* Dame / Before the Trojans won Immortal Fame." *An Elegie on the Death of the Most Serene Majesty of Henrietta-Maria, the Queen-Mother of Great Britain, &c.* (London: Printed by and for Thomas Ratcliffe and Thomas Daniel, 1669).

11. Felicity Nussbaum, *The Limits of the Human: Fictions of Anomaly, Race, and Gender in the Long Eighteenth Century* (Cambridge: Cambridge University Press, 2003), 159–60.

12. Edward Howard, *The Womens Conquest* (London, 1671), 57–59. Future references are cited in the text by page number in the absence of act and scene divisions. First performed in 1670.

13. For discussions of Catherine's "swarthy" skin color, see H. Forneron, *The Court of Charles II, 1649–1734: Compiled from State Papers*, 5th ed. (London: S. Sonnenschein, 1897), 14, and Lillias Campbell Davidson, *Catherine of Bragança, Infanta of Portugal & Queen-Consort of England* (London: J. Murray, 1908), 44.

14. Edward Corp, "Catherine of Braganza and Cultural Politics," in *Queenship in Britain, 1660–1837*, ed. Clarissa Campbell Orr (Manchester: Manchester University Press, 2002), 62.

15. John Evelyn, *The Diary of John Evelyn*, vol. 1, ed. William Bray (New York: M. W. Dunne, 1901). Evelyn describes the Portuguese women as having "complexions olivader and sufficiently unagreeable," 383.

16. More images of Audrey Flack's statue of Queen Catherine can be found on her website: http://www.audreyflack.com/public-commissions/. For the controversy around the statue, see the *New York Times*, January 6 and September 13, 1998; June 4, 2000; January 21, 2001; January 27, 2002; and November 9, 2017. The statue was eventually melted down, but a smaller version was made for Portugal.

17. On the significance of skin color in early modern literature, see Kim F. Hall, *Things of Darkness: Economies of Race and Gender in Early Modern England* (Ithaca, NY: Cornell University Press, 1995). Hall makes the point that "evocations of blackness" occur with "startling regularity" in early modern literature. She argues that these evocations do not just signify Renaissance aesthetics, but engage the "notions of 'self' and 'other' so well known in Anglo-American discourse" (1–2).

18. Thomas Ireland, *Speeches Spoken to the King and Queen, Duke and Duchesse of York, in Christ-Church Hall, Oxford, Sept. 29, 1663* (London: Printed for Richard Royston, 1663), 5.

19. John Crouch, "Upon the Approach of the Illustrious Infanta, of Portugal, Donna Catharina, Queen of England," in *Census Poeticus: The Poets Tribute Paid in Eight Loyal Poems* (London: Printed for the Author, 1663), 70.

20. Crouch, "Upon the Approach," 73.

21. *The Several Declarations of the Company of Royal Adventurers of England Trading into Africa: Inviting All His Majesties Native Subjects in General to Subscribe and Become Sharers in Their Joynt-Stock . . .: As Also a List of the Royal Adventurers of England Trading into Africa* (London, 1667). I am grateful to Holly Brewer for directing me to this document. Founding subscribers included Thomas Killigrew and Charles Sedley. In order to subscribe, one needed to invest at least £400.

22. For a discussion of the marriage box, see Lorraine Madway, "Rites of Deliverance and Disenchantment: The Marriage Celebrations for Charles II and Catherine of Braganza, 1661–62," *The Seventeenth Century* 27, no. 1 (2012): 79–105.

23. Madway, "Rites of Deliverance and Disenchantment," 85.

24. For an account of Portugal's empire-building, see Crowley, *Conquerors*.

25. Evelyn, *Diary*, vol. 1, 359. See also Manuel Andrade e Sousa, *Catherine of Braganza: Princess of Portugal, Wife to Charles II* (Lisbon: Edições Inapa, 1994), 47.

26. See Thomas, *Richer Than Spices*.

27. On the imperialist policies of Charles II, see Abigail Swingen, *Competing Visions of Empire: Labor, Slavery, and the Origins of the British Atlantic Empire* (New Haven, CT: Yale University Press, 2015), chapter 3.

28. *The Consolidated Treaty Series*, vol. 6, ed. Clive Parry (Dobbs Ferry, NY: Oceana Publications, 1969–1981), 329–36.

29. In this interpretation, I am following Holly Brewer, "Slavery, Sovereignty, and 'Inheritable Blood': Reconsidering John Locke and the Origins of American Slavery," *American Historical Review* 122, no. 4 (2017): 1047. I am grateful to Professor Brewer for calling my attention to the significance of this marriage treaty.

30. On the "Elephant and Castle" and the guinea coin, see John O'Brien, *Literature Incorporated: The Cultural Unconscious of the Business Corporation, 1650–1850* (Chicago: University of Chicago Press, 2016), 146–47. O'Brien shows how the Royal African Company became a crucial model for the corporation itself.

31. W. W., *Britannia Iterum Beata: Or, A Poem-Narrative of Her Gracious Majesties Departure from Lisbone, with Her Thrice-Welcome Arrival at Portsmith* (London: Printed by James Cottrel, 1661).

32. J. L., *A Poem Royal to the Sacred Majesty of Charles the II, King of Great Britain. And the Illustrious Donna Catharina His Incomparable* CONSORT (London: Printed for Gilves Clavert, 1662).

33. Crouch, "Upon the Approach," 73.

34. Rajani Sudan, *The Alchemy of Empire: Abject Materials and the Technologies of Colonialism* (New York: Fordham University Press, 2016), 67. Indeed, as Sudan describes, the eighteenth-century merchant who gave his name to Yale College made his fortune in India on nutmeg.

35. Crouch, "Upon the Approach," 76.

36. Samuel Holland, *The Phœnix. Her Arrival and Welcome to England* (London: Printed for the Author, 1663), 6. "Rigous" is shortened from "irrigous," meaning moistened.

37. Ireland, "Speeches Spoken to the King and Queen," 6.

38. *Here Is Some Comfort for Poor Cavaleeres* (London: Printed for F. Grove, 1660). Charles II lacked money and persistently sought new sources of wealth, although in the end the Portuguese, depleted by war with Spain, could not afford to pay the full dowry. Clyde L. Grose, "The Anglo-Portuguese Marriage of 1662," *The Hispanic American Heritage Review* 10, no. 3 (1930): 313–52, esp. 349.

39. Grose, "Anglo-Portuguese Marriage of 1662," 349.

40. The first European slave traders, the Portuguese, built Elmina Castle, which became one of the most important slave-trading fortresses along the African coast, although by the time of the royal marriage it had been taken by the Dutch.

41. J. D., *An Hymenæan Essay, or an Epithalamy upon the Royall Match of his most Excellent Majesty CHARLES the Second with the most Illustrious KATHARINE, Infanta of PORTUGALL* (London, 1662).

42. J. D., *Hymenæan Essay*, 4.

43. *An Heroick Poem, Most Humbly Dedicated to the Sacred Majesty of Catharine, Queen Dowager* (London, 1685), 4.

44. On this point, see Grose, "Anglo-Portuguese Marriage of 1662."

45. For a good discussion of another play that touches on the royal marriages, see Candy Schille, "'The King His Play': Charles II, Christina of Sweden, and Dryden's *Secret Love, or The Maiden Queen*," *Restoration* 36, no. 1 (2012): 41–59.

46. Janet J. Mackay, *Catherine of Braganza* (London: John Long, 1937), 195.

47. Heidi Hutner, *Colonial Women: Race and Culture in Stuart Drama* (Oxford: Oxford University Press, 2001), chapter 3, and Elliot Visconsi, *Lines of Equity: Literature and the Origins of Law in Later Stuart England* (Ithaca, NY: Cornell University Press, 2008), chapter 2, see the Spanish as standing for all Europeans but draw different conclusions about this. Orr, *Empire on the English Stage*, 141–58; Ayanna Thompson, *Performing Race and Torture on the Early Modern Stage* (New York: Routledge, 2008), chapter 4.

48. For an excellent study of the ways that Restoration plays tackle contemporary issues around sovereignty, see Maguire, *Regicide and Restoration*.

49. Orr, *Empire on the English Stage*, 145.

50. *The Indian Queen*, in *The Works of John Dryden*, vol. 8, ed. Edward Niles Hooker, H. T. Swedenberg, and Vinton A. Dearing (Berkeley: University of California Press, 1956). Future references are from this edition and cited in the text.

51. Hutner, *Colonial Women*, 77; Joseph Roach, *Cities of the Dead: Circum-Atlantic Performance* (New York: Columbia University Press, 1996), 150; Orr, *Empire on the English Stage*, 150–51; Visconsi, *Lines of Equity*, 45.

52. Thompson, *Performing Race and Torture*, 75–78, 93.

53. *The London Stage, 1660–1800: A Calendar of Plays, Entertainments & Afterpieces, Together with Casts, Box-Receipts and Contemporary Comment: Compiled from the Playbills, Newspapers and Theatrical Diaries of the Period*, ed. William Van Lennep, Emmett Langdon Avery, Arthur H. Scouten, George Winchester Stone, and Charles Beecher Hogan (Carbondale: Southern Illinois University Press, 1960), vol. 1 part 1, 74. Killigrew is listed as one of the original investors in the Company of Royal Adventurers of England Trading into Africa in *The Several Declarations*, 12.

54. On Dryden's engagement with and departure from historical sources, English and Spanish, see *The Works of John Dryden*, vol. 9, 310–15. References to *The Indian Emperour* are from this edition and cited in the text.

55. For an excellent discussion of how this play and especially *The Indian Emperour* strain the genre of the heroic in an imperial context, see Orr, *Empire on the English Stage*, 139–56.

56. Thompson, *Performing Race and Torture*, 77, for example, puzzles over the play's failure to fulfill the demands of this genre.

57. Dryden's editors (in *Works of John Dryden*, vol. 9, 301) suggest alternatively that he took the name from a character named Mexiqua in Marin le Roy de Gomberville's romance *Polexandre*. But the battle of Ameixial was well-known at the time. On June 29, 1663, Pepys wrote about the English celebrations: "Up betimes and to my office, and by and by to the Temple, and there appointed to meet in the evening about my business. And thence I walked home, and up and down the streets is cried mightily the great victory got by the Portugalls against the Spaniards, where 10,000 slain, 3 or 4000 taken prisoners, with all the artillery, baggage, money, &c., and Don John of Austria forced to flee with a man or two with him, which is very great news." Pepys, *Diary*, vol. 4, 202–3. *A Relation of the Great Success of the King of Portugal's Army Had upon the Spaniards, the 29th of May (Engl. Stile) 1663* was published in London "By Authority." For a full account of this battle, see Jonathon Riley, *The Last Ironsides: The English Expedition to Portugal, 1662–1668* (West Midlands: Helion & Company, 2014).

58. See *Consolidated Treaty Series* vol. 6, 329–36.

59. See Swingen, *Competing Visions of Empire*, chapter 2.

60. Gerald L. Belcher, "Spain and the Anglo-Portuguese Alliance of 1661: A Reassessment of Charles II's Foreign Policy at the Restoration," *Journal of British Studies* 15, no. 1 (1975): 67–88.

61. On the importance of female characters in Dryden's heroic drama, see David R. Evans, "'Private Greatness': The Feminine Ideal in Dryden's Early Heroic Drama," *Restoration: Studies in English Literary Culture, 1660–1700* 16, no. 1 (1992): 2–19, which explores how these characters support heroic ideology.

62. Carmen Nocentelli, *Empires of Love: Europe, Asia, and the Making of Early Modern Identity* (Philadelphia: University of Pennsylvania Press, 2013), 10–11.

63. We later see a similar relationship in the more familiar *Oroonoko*, in which the Coramantien prince raises his captured enemy warrior Jamoan to the position of honored friend.

64. Maguire, *Regicide and Restoration*, 69.

65. Bridget Orr suggests that Dryden and Howard represent the Mesoamericans as semiprimitive in their violence and near-lawlessness, but it is not clear to me that these plays are any more violent than others of this time with European or English settings. Further, England itself had just survived a period of violence and, in the opinion of some, lawlessness. While the Mesoamerican setting certainly allows for more extreme representations (such as human sacrifice), it is at the same time not entirely dissimilar to experiences of recent English history.

66. For a fuller discussion of the particular gender fluidity of this period, see Dror Wahrman, *The Making of the Modern Self: Identity and Culture in Eighteenth-Century England* (New Haven, CT: Yale University Press, 2004), esp. 2–82. Amazonian women, for example, did not represent the violation of gender propriety that they would later in the century (7–11).

67. See, for example, *Fourty four queries to the life of Queen Dick. By one who will at any time work a job of journey-work, to serve his country* (London, 1659).

68. Dryden co-authored a version of *Oedipus* with Nathaniel Lee.

69. For a different reading that focuses on Dryden's interest in religion, see J. M. Armistead, *Otherworldly John Dryden: Occult Rhetoric in His Poems and Plays* (Burlington, VT: Ashgate, 2014), 25–40. Armistead suggests that Dryden represents the Native Americans as pre-Christian but moving toward an acceptance of Providence.

70. Alex Garganigo,"The Heroic Drama's Legend of Good Women," *Criticism* 45, no. 4 (2003): 483–505; 488.

71. Portugal was under Spanish rule from 1580 to 1640.

72. Evelyn, *Diary*, vol. 1, 372. Quoted in *London Stage* vol. 1, lxxxv.

73. Aphra Behn, *Oroonoko: An Authoritative Text, Historical Backgrounds, Criticism* (New York: W. W. Norton, 1997), 9.

74. *Works of John Dryden*, vol. 9, 282.

75. *London Stage*, vol. 1, xciii. For a brilliant reading of feathers in this play and in English imperialism in general, see Roach, *Cities of the Dead*, 130–31.

76. Madway, "Rites of Deliverance and Disenchantment," 84.

77. Madway, "Rites of Deliverance and Disenchantment," 85.

78. Gilbert Burnet and Thomas Burnet, *Bishop Burnet's History of His Own Time*, vol. 1, ed. Martin Joseph Routh (Oxford: Oxford University Press, 1833), 456.

79. Such plots overlap with aristocratic ideology, but are not identical with it. So, while the "noble" figures are usually noble by birth, the plays often contrast them with nobly born figures who are *not* noble by character.

80. See Tim Keenan, *Restoration Staging, 1660–74* (New York: Routledge, 2017), 127, who argues that the sequel was designed to use the expensive sets developed for the original play.

81. Near the end of *The Rehearsal*, the final plot of the play is communicated through a scrap of paper on the ground. A running joke throughout is that no one can understand the plot, but this incident might also be a satire of the author's passing out printed explanations at the playhouse.

82. In this detail and many others, the play is blatantly counterhistorical.

83. Pepys, *Diary*, vol. 9, 23–24.

84. Eleanore Boswell Murrie, *The Restoration Court Stage (1660–1702): With a Particular Account of the Production of "Calisto"* (London: Allen & Unwin, 1966 [1932]). At this court performance, the "impertinent slut" Miss Davis apparently flaunted her relationship with the King while Lady Castlemaine sulked (Pepys, *Diary*, vol. 9, 24). The play was revived on the public stage in 1674 and 1691, according to *The London Stage*.

85. He later kills him, however, in a duel over Cydaria.

86. For a discussion of Dryden's sources for Cortez and other elements of the play, and for the ways he transformed them, see *Works of John Dryden*, vol. 9, 298–318.

87. Jonathan Elmer, *On Lingering and Being Last: Race and Sovereignty in the New World* (New York: Fordham University Press, 2008), 31.

88. Elmer, *On Lingering and Being Last*, 33.

89. For the mockery of Settle by Dryden and others, see Maximillian E. Novak, *"The Empress of Morocco" and Its Critics: Settle, Dryden, Shadwell, Crowne, Duffet* (Los Angeles: William Andrews Clark Memorial Library, 1968).

90. Linda Colley, *Captives* (New York: Pantheon, 2002), 23–42; Tristan Stein, "Tangier in the Restoration Empire," *The Historical Journal* 54, no. 4 (2011): 895–1011.

91. E. M. G. Routh, *Tangier, England's Lost Atlantic Outpost, 1661–1684* (London: J. Murray, 1912), 343.

92. Routh, *Tangier*, 129.

93. Routh, *Tangier*, 71.

94. Grose, "Anglo-Portuguese Marriage of 1662"; see also Stein, "Tangier in the Restoration Empire" on this point.

95. Routh, *Tangier*, 340.

96. Routh, *Tangier*, 56.

97. Routh, *Tangier*, 245.

98. C. R. Boxer, "'Three Sights To Be Seen': Bombay, Tangier, and a Barren Queen, 1661–1684," *Portuguese Studies* 3 (1987): 77–83; 77.

99. Susan B. Iwanisziw, "Tortured Bodies, Factionalism, and Unsettled Loyalties in Settle's Morocco Plays," in *Staging Pain, 1580–1800: Violence and Trauma in British Theater* (Surrey: Ashgate, 2009), 111–36. See also Anne Hermanson, *The Horror Plays of the English Restoration* (Burlington, VT: Ashgate, 2014), 59–82. But as Bridget Orr points out, the productions and revivals of the Morocco plays "all date from periods of tension over Tangier" (*Empire on the English Stage*, 99).

100. Routh, *Tangier*, 23.

101. Elkanah Settle, *The Empress of Morocco: A Tragedy* (London: Printed for William Cademan, 1673), 70. Future references are from this edition and cited in the text by page number.

102. Preface. Quoted in Novak, *"Empress of Morocco" and Its Critics*.

103. See *The present state of the Jews (more particularly relating to those in Barbary) wherein is contained an exact account of their customs, secular and religious: to which is annexed a summary discourse of the Misna, Talmud, and Gemara* (London, 1675).

104. G. E. Aylmer, "Slavery under Charles II: The Mediterranean and Tangier," *The English Historical Review* 114, no. 456 (1999): 378–88.

105. Canfield raises, but does not develop the possibility of such a reading. See *Heroes and States*, 26.

106. In Novak, *"Empress of Morocco" and Its Critics*, 13.

107. Settle, *Empress*, dedication.

108. Adam R. Beach, "Baffled Colonial Discourse: Representing the First Decade of English Tangier," *Restoration* 31, no. 2 (2007): 21–41.

109. The most recent work at this date is Andrade e Sousa, *Catherine of Braganza*. Popular biographies of Catherine include Davidson, *Catherine of Bragança*; Mackay, *Catherine of Braganza*; and Hebe Elsna, *Catherine of Braganza: Charles II's Queen* (London: Hale, 1967).

110. Corp, "Catherine of Braganza and Cultural Politics," 67.

4. Restoration Legacies

1. For the play's relationship to reported historical events, see Wilber Henry Ward, "Mrs. Behn's 'The Widow Ranter': Historical Sources," *South Atlantic Bulletin* 41, no. 4 (1976): 94–98.

2. John Hodges, *William Congreve the Man* (New York: Modern Language Association of America, 1941), 29.

3. Steve C. A. Pincus, *1688: The First Modern Revolution* (New Haven, CT: Yale University Press, 2009), 323–65.

4. Pincus, *1688*, 150, 82.

5. Pincus, *1688*, 78.

6. Pincus, *1688*, 82; John O'Brien, *Literature Incorporated: The Cultural Unconscious of the Business Corporation, 1650–1850* (Chicago: University of Chicago Press, 2016), 106–35.

7. See Tony Claydon, *William III and the Godly Revolution* (Cambridge: Cambridge University Press, 1996).

8. On the emergence of sentimentalism on stage, see, for example, Peter Hynes, "Richard Steele and the Genealogy of Sentimental Drama: A Reading of *The Conscious Lovers*," *Papers on Language and Literature: A Journal for Scholars and Critics of Language and Literature* 40, no. 2 (2004): 142–66; and Lisa A. Freeman, *Character's Theater: Genre and Identity on the Eighteenth-Century English Stage* (Philadelphia: University of Pennsylvania Press, 2002), chapter 5. Aparna Gollapudi argues, in *Moral Reform in Comedy and Culture, 1696–1747* (Farnham: Ashgate, 2011), introduction, for a distinction between reformist theater and sentimental, seeing the emergence of reform first with Colley Cibber and others.

9. O'Brien, *Literature Incorporated*, 69–71.

10. Janet Todd examines all sides of the evidence in *The Secret Life of Aphra Behn* (New Brunswick, NJ: Rutgers University Press, 1997), 46–66, 411–23.

11. On Oroonoko as a figure for Charles I, see Laura Brown's influential "The Romance of Empire: *Oroonoko* and the Trade in Slaves," in *The New Eighteenth Century: Theory, Politics, English Literature*, ed. Laura Brown and Felicity Nussbaum (New York: Methuen, 1987), 41–61.

12. Richard Kroll, "'Tales of Love and Gallantry': The Politics of *Oroonoko*," *Huntington Library Quarterly* 67, no. 4 (2004): 573–605; 578.

13. On the wide availability of information about Bacon's rebellion and Behn's departure from historical events, see Jenny Hale Pulsipher, "*The Widow Ranter* and Royalist Culture in Colonial Virginia," *Early American Literature* 39, no. 1 (2004): 41–66; 42.

14. Quoted in *The Works of William Congreve*, vol. 2, ed. D. F. McKenzie (Oxford: Oxford University Press, 2011), 545. References to *The Mourning Bride* are from this edition and cited in the text.

15. Quoted in *Works of Congreve*, vol. 2, 544.

16. Elliott Visconsi, *Lines of Equity: Literature and the Origins of Law in Later Stuart England* (Ithaca, NY: Cornell University Press, 2008), 155–84.

17. Aphra Behn, *The Widow Ranter*, Act 2, Scene 1, in *Oroonoko, The Rover, and Other Works*, ed. Janet Todd (London: Penguin, 1992), 269.

18. Gertrude Z. Thomas, *Richer Than Spices: How a Royal Bride's Dowry Introduced Cane, Lacquer, Cottons, Tea, and Porcelain to England, and so Revolutionized Taste, Manners, Craftsmanship, and History in Both England and America* (New York: Alfred A. Knopf, 1965), 152. Jonas Hanway (1712–1786) is commonly identified as the first Englishman to use, and eventually popularize, the umbrella for protection from rain.

19. Richard Flecknoe, *A relation of ten years in Europe, Asia, Affrique, and America: all by way of letters occasionally written to divers noble personages, from place to place, and continued to this present year* (London, 1656), 77.

20. Samuel Pepys, *The Diary of Samuel Pepys: A New and Complete Transcription*, vol. 7, ed. Robert Latham and William Matthews (Berkeley: University of California Press, 1970), 335 (Oct. 22, 1666).

21. James Clifford, *Routes: Travel and Translation in the Late Twentieth Century* (Cambridge, MA: Harvard University Press, 1997), 17–46.

22. Behn, *Widow Ranter*, 1.3.273.

23. Visconsi, *Lines of Equity*, 155–84.

24. Thomas Southerne, *The Works of Thomas Southerne*, vol. 2, ed. Robert Jordan and Harold Love (Oxford: Clarendon, 1988). This reading of *Oroonoko* appeared in a very different form in my "Oroonoko's Cosmopolitans," in *Approaches to Teaching Behn's "Oroonoko,"* ed. Cynthia Richards and Mary Ann O'Donnell (New York: Modern Language Association of America, 2014), 136–42.

25. For a fuller discussion of the recent critical history of *Oroonoko*, see my essay "*Oroonoko*: Reception, Ideology, and Narrative Strategy," in *The Cambridge Companion to Aphra Behn*, ed. Derek Hughes and Janet Todd (Cambridge: Cambridge University Press, 2004), 151–65.

26. Monogamy, of course, is not more "advanced" than polygamy, but many writers in the period represent it as a form of modernity and Behn might have understood it that way.

27. John Dryden, "To My Dear Friend Mr. Congreve, on his Comedy called *The Double Dealer*," in *The Works of John Dryden*, vol. 4, ed. Edward Niles Hooker, H. T. Swedenberg, and Vinton A. Dearing (Berkeley: University of California Press, 1956), 432.

28. Elmer B. Potter, "The Paradox of Congreve's *Mourning Bride*," *PMLA* 58, no. 4 (1943): 977–1001; Emmett L. Avery, "The Popularity of *The Mourning Bride* in the London Theaters in the Eighteenth Century," *Research Studies* [State College of Washington] 9 (1941): 115–16.

29. Congreve gives the Spanish princess the same name—Almeria—as the new Indian queen in Dryden's sequel.

30. Jean I. Marsden, *Fatal Desire: Women, Sexuality, and the English Stage, 1660–1720* (Ithaca, NY: Cornell University Press, 2006), 94, 97.

31. Tony Aston, *A Brief Supplement to Colley Cibber, Esq; His Lives of the Famous Actors and Actresses* ([London]: Printed for the author, abt. 1747), 6–7.

32. On Congreve's love for Anne Bracegirdle, see Hodges, *William Congreve the Man*, 44–45.

33. Quoted in *A Biographical Dictionary of Actors, Actresses, Musicians, Dancers, Managers & Other Stage Personnel in London, 1660–1800*, vol. 12, ed. Philip H. Highfill Jr., Kalman A. Burnim, and Edward A. Langhans (Carbondale: Southern Illinois University Press, 1987), 93.

34. Quoted in *A Biographical Dictionary*, vol. 12, 94.

35. The following actresses chose the role of Zara for a benefit performance: Mrs. Knight, Mrs. Hallam, Mrs. Roberts, Mrs. Horton, Mrs. Pritchard, Miss Phillips, Mrs. Mayo, Miss Young, and Mrs. Pope, as noted in *The London Stage, 1660–1800: A Calendar of Plays, Entertainments & Afterpieces, Together with Casts, Box-Receipts and Contemporary Comment: Compiled from the Playbills, Newspapers and Theatrical Diaries of the Period*, ed. William Van Lennep, Emmett Langdon Avery, Arthur H. Scouten, George Winchester Stone, and Charles Beecher Hogan (Carbondale: Southern Illinois University Press, 1960). Thomas Davies adds that Kitty Clive also chose the role for

her benefit. Usually a comic actress, Clive did not succeed in the role. Thomas Davies, *Dramatic micellanies [sic]: consisting of critical observations on several plays of Shakspeare: with a review of his principal characters, and those of various eminent writers, as represented by Mr. Garrick, and other celebrated comedians*, vol. 3 (London, 1783–1784), 353. The following actresses chose the role of Almeria for their benefit: Mrs. Thurmond, Miss Macklin, and Mrs. Bellamy.

36. Davies, *Dramatic micellanies*, vol. 3, 343.

37. Bridget Orr, *Empire on the English Stage, 1660–1714* (Cambridge: Cambridge University Press, 2001), 174–77.

38. From the Folger Shakespeare Library's copy of *Collectanea: or, a Collection of Advertisements and Paragraphs from the Newspapers, relating to various Subjects* (Strawberry Hill: Printed by Thomas Kirgate for the Collector, Daniel Lysons, n.d.), vol. 2, 130.

39. Orr, *Empire on the English Stage*, 175.

40. This particular volume does not appear in John Hodges' catalogue of *The Library of William Congreve* (New York: New York Public Library, 1955). However, Congreve owned a substantial number of travel books, including *The Life of Almanzor*.

41. For another view, see Orr, *Empire on the English Stage*, 176–77.

42. Orr, *Empire on the English Stage*, 175. She also points out how, once again, the Spanish become the symbol for excess imperialist ambitions in English literature.

43. William A. Pettigrew, *Freedom's Debt: The Royal African Company and the Politics of the Atlantic Slave Trade, 1672–1752* (Chapel Hill, NC: Published for the Omohundro Institute of Early American History and Culture, Williamsburg, Virginia, by the University of North Carolina Press, 2013), 1–82.

44. John Cary, *An essay on the state of England in relation to its trade, its poor, and its taxes, for carrying on the present war against France by John Cary, merchant in Bristoll* (Bristol: Printed by W. Bonny for the author, 1695), 47.

45. Cary, *Essay on the state of England*, 65–86.

46. *Considerations relating to the African bill Humbly submitted to the honourable House of Commons* (London, 1698); Cary, *Essay on the state of England*.

47. *Considerations humbly offer'd to the Honourable House of Commons, by the planters, and others, trading to our British plantations, in relation to the African Company's petition, now before this Honourable House* (London, 1698).

48. William Wilkinson, *Systema Africanum, or, A treatise, discovering the intrigues and arbitrary preceedings of the Guiney Company and also how prejudicial they are to the American planters, the woollen, and other English manufactures, to the visible decay of trade, and consequently greatly impairing the royal revenue, which would be infinitely increased, provided merchants and mariners were encouraged, who can discover several places not yet known, or traded account of their fortifications, humbly submitted to Their Majesties, and to the consideration of both houses of Parliament* (London, 1690).

49. Miranda Kauffman, "English Common Law, Slavery and," in *The Encyclopedia of Blacks in European History and Culture*, vol. 1, ed. Eric Martone (Westport, CT: Greenwood, 2008), 200–3. Reproduced at http://www.mirandakaufmann.com/common-law.html. On the legal ramifications of these rulings, see Imtiaz H. Habib, *Black Lives in the English Archives, 1500–1677: Imprints of the Invisible* (Aldershot: Ashgate, 2008), 184–87.

50. *Works of Congreve*, vol. 2, 574.

51. Although, as argued in chapter 4, the Spanish are also recognized as distinct from the English.

52. Chi-Ming Yang has pointed out that eighteenth-century orientalist depictions were elided with African ones and even functioned as a sign of Africanness. See her "Asia Out of Place: The Aesthetics of Incorruptibility in Behn's *Oroonoko*," *Eighteenth-Century Studies* 42, no. 2 (2009): 235–53. Depictions of African characters often show them dressed in robes and turbans with protruding feathers, which appears to be the costume worn by David Garrick when he played Alphonso disguised as Osmyn.

53. See Potter, "The Paradox of Congreve's *Mourning Bride*," on this point.

54. Alexander Lindsay and Howard Erskine-Hill, *William Congreve: The Critical Heritage* (London: Routledge, 1989), 245.

55. *The Mourning Bride* in some ways revives the style of the Restoration "horror play," a fashion that, according to Ann Hermanson, had ended decades before. On this trend, see her *The Horror Plays of the English Restoration* (Burlington, VT: Ashgate, 2014).

56. Ian Baucom, *Specters of the Atlantic: Finance Capital, Slavery, and the Philosophy of History* (Durham, NC: Duke University Press, 2005), 33.

5. "Have You Not Been Sophisticated?"

1. Frances Burney, *Evelina: Or, The History of a Young Lady's Entrance into the World*, ed. Edward A. Bloom (Oxford: Oxford University Press, 2002), 78. Future references are from this edition and cited in the text.

2. See James E. Evans, "Evelina, the Rustic Girls of Congreve and Abington, and Surrogation in the 1770s," *The Eighteenth Century: Theory and Interpretation* 52, no. 2 (2011): 157–71; 162.

3. For the importance of cosmopolitanism to this play, see Elizabeth Kowaleski Wallace, "Theatricality and Cosmopolitanism in Hannah Cowley's *The Belle's Stratagem*," *Comparative Drama* 35 no. 3–4 (2001): 415–33.

4. I realize that this distinction is not absolute, and that women performed in various ways, even in public, before 1660. The Restoration theater, however, created a new kind of professional actress. For women acting before 1660, see Pamela Allen Brown and Peter Parolin, eds., *Women Players in England, 1500–1660: Beyond the All-Male Stage* (Burlington, VT: Ashgate, 2005).

5. While comical unsophistication plots often focus on women, Richard Cumberland's *The West Indian* (1771) is an interesting example of a male figure in such a role.

6. See Michael Dobson, *The Making of the National Poet: Shakespeare, Adaptation and Authorship, 1660–1769* (Oxford: Clarendon, 1992) on this point.

7. Gerald Newman, *The Rise of English Nationalism: A Cultural History, 1740–1830* (New York: St. Martin's Press, 1997).

8. Eugenia Zuroski Jenkins, *A Taste for China: English Subjectivity and the Prehistory of Orientalism* (New York: Oxford University Press, 2013), 152–213.

9. Katie Trumpener, *Bardic Nationalism: The Romantic Novel and the British Empire* (Princeton, NJ: Princeton University Press, 1997).

10. See, for example, Michael Ragussis, *Theatrical Nation: Jews and Other Outlandish Englishmen in Georgian Britain* (Philadelphia: University of Pennsylvania Press, 2010).

11. For an excellent discussion of the importance of actresses on the eighteenth-century stage, see Felicity Nussbaum, *Rival Queens: Actresses, Performance, and the Eighteenth-Century British Theater* (Philadelphia: University of Pennsylvania Press, 2010).

12. Nahum Tate, *The History of King Lear*, ed. James Black (Lincoln: University of Nebraska Press, 1975).

13. John C. Hodges, *William Congreve, the Man: A Biography from New Sources* (New York: Kraus Reprint Corp, 1966 [1941]), 44–45. For more on Bracegirdle and her influence on the theater, see Gilli Bush-Bailey, *Treading the Bawds: Actresses and Playwrights on the Late-Stuart Stage* (Manchester: Manchester University Press, 2006), Part 1.

14. "sophisticated, adj." OED Online.

15. Daniel Szechi, *The Jacobites: Britain and Europe, 1688–1788* (Manchester: Manchester University Press, 1994), 54–56. For the way this threat continued into the eighteenth century, see Linda Colley, *Britons: Forging the Nation, 1707–1837* (New Haven, CT: Yale University Press, 2009).

16. Nussbaum, *Rival Queens*. This point is made throughout her study, but chapter 2 in particular shows how deeply invested audiences became in actresses and their rivalries.

17. Colley Cibber, *Apology for the Life of Colley Cibber*, ed. Byrne Fone (Ann Arbor: University of Michigan Press, 1968), 55.

18. Evans, "Evelina," 164; Martin Postle, "'The Modern Apelles': Joshua Reynolds and the Creation of Celebrity," in *Joshua Reynolds: The Creation of Celebrity*, exhibition catalogue, ed. Martin Postle and Mark Hallett (London: Tate Gallery, 2005), 17, quoted in Evans, "Evelina," 164.

19. Evans, "Evelina," 163.

20. William Congreve, *Love for Love*, in *The Works of William Congreve*, vol. 1, ed. D. F. McKenzie and C. Y. Ferdinand (Oxford: Oxford University Press, 2011), 2.11.25–47. Future references are from this edition and cited in the text.

21. William Wycherley, *The Country Wife*, in *The Plays of William Wycherley*, ed. Arthur Friedman (Oxford: Oxford at the Clarendon Press, 1979), 2.1.19–23. Future references are from this edition and cited in the text.

22. Samuel Pepys, *The Diary of Samuel Pepys: A New and Complete Transcription*, vol. 8, ed. Robert Latham and William Matthews (Berkeley: University of California Press, 1970), 481, Tuesday, October 15, 1667. As discussed in chapter 2, this play also celebrates the coffeehouse as a center of cosmopolitan curiosity.

23. On the figure of the trickster, see J. Douglas Canfield, *Tricksters & Estates: On the Ideology of Restoration Comedy* (Lexington: University Press of Kentucky, 1997). Canfield sees the trickster figure as a staple of Restoration comedy.

24. Thomas St. Serfe, *Tarugo's Wiles; or, The Coffee-House* (London, 1668), 11.

25. Kirsten Pullen, *Actresses and Whores: On Stage and in Society* (Cambridge: Cambridge University Press, 2005), 46.

26. See Pullen, *Actresses and Whores*, 22–54.

27. Pullen, *Actresses and Whores*, 47.

28. Burney's fascination with the hazards of female performance is well-documented and appears even more powerfully in her later novel *The Wanderer*.

29. Cheryl Wanko, *Roles of Authority: Thespian Biography and Celebrity in Eighteenth-Century Britain* (Lubbock: Texas Tech University Press, 2003), 58.

30. Wanko, *Roles of Authority*, 76. Felicity Nussbaum notes that Fenton's "sexual behavior was made to seem an inevitable consequence of her profession." She also observes, however, that the biography acknowledges Fenton's popularity and her "considerable dramatic talent." *Rival Queens*, 100.

31. This argument is consistent with Felicity Nussbaum's insight about the actress as an *individual*—that is, as creating a persona with interiority and depth at a time when flatter forms of characterization dominated. *Rival Queens*, 19.

32. *The Life of Lavinia Beswick, Alias Fenton, Alias Polly Peachum* (London, 1728), 28.

33. *Life of Lavinia Beswick*, 29.

34. *The Whole Life of Polly Peachum, Written by One of Her Companions* (London: printed by M. Hind, abt. 1730).

35. *The Life of Nell Gwinn* (London?, abt. 1760), 6–7.

36. E. Ambross, *The Life and Memoirs of the Late Miss Ann Catley* (London: Printed for J. Bird, abt. 1789), 52.

37. Matthew C. Augustine and Steven N. Zwicker, eds. *Lord Rochester in the Restoration World* (Cambridge: Cambridge University Press, 2015), 3.

38. On this point, see, for example, Erin Skye Mackie, *Rakes, Highwaymen, and Pirates: The Making of the Modern Gentleman in the Eighteenth Century* (Baltimore: Johns Hopkins University Press, 2009), 83.

39. In doing so, Gay admittedly draws on an already extant romanticization of the highwayman; he does, however, contribute significantly to this figuration, which itself draws on the cultural memory of the Restoration rake.

40. See, for example, Jochen Petzold, "Polly Peachum, a 'Model of Virtue'? Questions of Morality in John Gay's *Polly*," *Journal for Eighteenth-Century Studies* 35, no. 3 (2012): 343–57; 345.

41. In his adaptation of this play as *The Threepenny Opera*, Bertolt Brecht, clearly dissatisfied with the oddity of this character's innocence, turns Polly into a woman of business on the model of her father.

42. Mackie, *Rakes, Highwaymen, and Pirates*, 26.

43. On the similarities between Macheath and the Restoration rake, see Misty G. Anderson, "Genealogies of Comedy," in *The Oxford Handbook of the Georgian Theatre, 1737–1832*, ed. Julia Swindells and David Francis Taylor (Oxford: Oxford University Press, 2014), 364.

44. On this incident from Boswell's *London Journal*, see David M. Weed, "Sexual Positions: Men of Pleasure, Economy, and Dignity in Boswell's *London Journal*," *Eighteenth-Century Studies* 31, no. 2 (1997): 215–34.

45. John Gay, *The Beggar's Opera*, in *John Gay, Dramatic Works*, vol. 1, ed. John Fuller (Oxford: Clarendon Press, 1983), 1.10.11. Future references are from this edition and cited in the text.

46. William Empson long ago identified Gay's "double irony"; see his *Some Versions of Pastoral* (London: Chatto and Windus, 1925, rpt. 1950), 210. For another view, see Toni-Lynn O'Shaughnessy, "A Single Capacity in *The Beggar's Opera*," *Eighteenth-Century Studies* 21, no. 2 (1987): 212–27.

47. J. Douglas Canfield, "The Critique of Capitalism and the Retreat into Art in Gay's *Beggar's Opera* and Fielding's *Author's Farce*," in *Cutting Edges: Postmodern Critical Essays on Eighteenth-Century Satire*, ed. James E. Gill (Knoxville: University of Tennessee Press, 1995), 320–34.

48. This is one of the central arguments of Susan Staves's foundational work *Players' Scepters: Fictions of Authority in the Restoration* (Lincoln: University of Nebraska Press, 1979).

49. Canfield, "Critique of Capitalism," 320; Clement Hawes, *The British Eighteenth Century and Global Critique* (New York: Palgrave Macmillan, 2005), 93–108.

50. *Thievery à-la-Mode: or, The Fatal Encouragement,* (London, 1728), 12.

51. *Thievery à-la-Mode,* 13.

52. *Thievery à-la-Mode,* 13.

53. *Thievery à-la-Mode,* 16.

54. On theatrical "ghosting," see Marvin Carlson, *The Haunted Stage: The Theatre as Memory Machine* (Ann Arbor: University of Michigan Press, 2002).

55. Isaac Jackman, *All the World's a Stage* (London, 1777), 11. Future references are from this edition and cited in the text by page number.

56. David Nokes, *John Gay: A Profession of Friendship* (Oxford: Oxford University Press, 1995), 464.

57. See Nokes, *John Gay,* who argues that this was not Gay's intention: 433–44. On the banning of *Polly,* see pp. 445–62 and also C. F. Burgess, "John Gay and Polly and a Letter to the King," *Philological Quarterly* 47 (1968): 596.

58. John Gay, *Polly,* in *John Gay, Dramatic Works,* vol. 1, 3.15.50–51. Future references are from this edition and cited in the text.

59. Elizabeth Maddock Dillon, *New World Drama: The Performative Commons in the Atlantic World, 1649–1849* (Durham: Duke University Press, 2014), 124–30.

60. Sven Beckert, *Empire of Cotton: A Global History* (New York: Alfred A. Knopf, 2014), xvi.

61. On the significance of Macheath's blackface in later performances of this play, see Peter P. Reed, "Conquer or Die: Staging Circum-Atlantic Revolt in 'Polly' and 'Three-Finger'd Jack,'" *Theatre Journal* 59, no. 2 (2007): 241–58. Reed suggests (248) that Gay's play, in its performed adaptation by George Colman (1777), "acts out the convergence of class resistance and emerging racial emancipation" in the eighteenth-century Atlantic world.

62. Gay takes full advantage of Polly's male costume: Jenny Diver, Macheath's former-prostitute betrayer but now adored lover, tries to seduce the masculinized Polly, treating the audience to a homoerotic kiss between the women. On warrior women in the eighteenth century, see Diane Dugaw, *Warrior Women and Popular Balladry, 1650–1850* (Chicago: University of Chicago Press, 1996).

63. Robert G. Dryden, "John Gay's *Polly*: Unmasking Pirates and Fortune Hunters in the West Indies," *Eighteenth-Century Studies* 34, no. 4 (2001): 539–57; 540.

64. Hans Turley, *Rum, Sodomy, and the Lash: Piracy, Sexuality, and Masculine Identity* (New York: New York University Press, 1999), 32–35.

65. Subsequent monarchs struck guineas with their own images, but the coins from the days of Charles II and James II, with the monarch on one side and the elephant and castle on the other, would still have been in circulation.

66. On the relationship to corporations and slave trade in particular, see John O'Brien, *Literature Incorporated: The Cultural Unconscious of the Business Corporation, 1650–1850* (Chicago: University of Chicago Press, 2016), 136–85; on coins, 146–48.

67. On Gay's beliefs about slavery, see John Richardson, "John Gay and Slavery," *Modern Language Review* 97, no. 1 (2002): 15–25. Richardson points to other literary works of Gay's and to the fact that Gay invested heavily in the South Sea Company (19) and socialized with the "keen slaver" the Duke of Chandos (19–20).

Such logic, however, has its limits: it would seem simplistic to read *The Beggar's Opera* as endorsing capitalism on the biographical information that Gay invested at all.

68. Dryden, "John Gay's *Polly*," 540.

69. It is, admittedly, an awkward ending. Critics generally assume that she will marry the Indian prince, but she does not actually give consent in the play. The marriage offer puts her in a contradictory position reminiscent of the one that Shakespeare's Isabella faces at the end of *Measure for Measure*: if she marries Cawwawkee, she compromises her virtue through disloyalty to Macheath, even though he is both dead and undeserving. Like Shakespeare, Gay leaves the heroine's consent unspoken. The marriage to Cawwawkee compromises her purity, since it must constitute an admission of the impurity of her previous attraction to Macheath, for otherwise, virtue would demand that she continue to mourn for his loss.

70. William Congreve, *The Way of the World*, in *The Works of William Congreve*, vol. 2, 3.4.22. Future references are from this edition and cited in the text.

71. Twenty-first-century criticism has recognized the importance of Congreve's sense of change over time. Kevin J. Gardner, "Patrician Authority and Instability in 'The Way of the World,'" *South Central Review* 19, no. 1 (2002): 53–75 argues that Mirabell emerges as "the representative man of a new patrician social order" (54) because he has mastered social performances. In "Lady Wishfort and the Will of the World," *Modern Language Quarterly* 45, no. 4 (1985): 338–49, Robert A. Erickson points to the gap in time suggested by the difference between Lady Wishfort's picture and her current self (341). In "Sexual Arithmetic: Appetite and Consumption in *The Way of the World*," *Eighteenth-Century Studies* 47, no. 3 (2014): 261–76, Scott R. MacKenzie suggests a metaphorical time gap between Mirabell and Millamant having to do with their attitudes toward contract: "Millamant positions herself rhetorically as an agent of modern, contractual social and property relations, against Mirabell's ludic impersonation of old-order patriarchal obligation" (262). Here, MacKenzie intervenes in classical arguments that identify contract itself as the new "way of the world." Several critics have explored how the emphasis on contract in the play marks a new economic system. On this point, see Vivian Davis, "Dramatizing the Sexual Contract: Congreve and Centlivre," *SEL: Studies In English Literature, 1500–1900* 51, no. 3 (2011): 519–43; Richard Braverman, "Capital Relations and *The Way of the World*," *ELH* 52, no. 1 (1985): 133–58; and Lauren Caldwell, "'Drink up all the Water in the Sea': Contracting Relations in Congreve's *Love for Love* and *Way of the World*," *ELH* 82, no. 1 (2015): 183–210. Contracts are certainly a crucial issue in this play. In my reading, however, I am more interested in its specific negotiation of the passage of time and in its revivals and revisions of Restoration cosmopolitanism, which has been overshadowed by this issue of contractarianism.

72. See, for example, Elizabeth Kraft, "Why Didn't Mirabell Marry the Widow Languish?," *Restoration: Studies in English Literary Culture, 1660–1700* 13, no. 1 (1989): 26–34.

73. Prynne and Collier both launched diatribes against the immorality of English theater in the seventeenth century; John Bunyan and Francis Quarles offer Christian parables.

74. "atlas, n.2". OED Online. June 2018. Oxford University Press.

75. Cibber, *Apology for the Life of Colley Cibber*, 93.

76. This was like the Restoration itself for Congreve: exterior glamor, but cracked and flawed up close.

6. Histories of Their Own Times

1. Jules Smith, "Jerningham, Edward (1737–1812), poet and playwright," *Oxford Dictionary of National Biography*, 2013.

2. In *The Story of Nell Gwyn*, ed. Gordon Goodwin (Edinburgh: J. Grant, 1908), 178, Peter Cunningham notes that the court resided part time at Peckham. There does not seem to be any evidence, however, that Gwynn spent time there.

3. Edward Jerningham, *The Peckham Frolic: or, Nell Gwyn* (London, 1799), 1. Future references are from this edition and cited in the text.

4. The real Anne Killigrew died young; the character in the play is over forty.

5. Lisa Berglund demonstrates how language in Restoration plays often distinguishes insiders and outsiders. See her "The Language of the Libertines: Subversive Morality in *The Man of Mode*," *SEL: Studies in English Literature, 1500–1900* 30, no. 3 (1990): 369–86.

6. In the *Spectator* essay that popularized this story, Yarico is a native Caribbean.

7. Matthew C. Augustine and Steven N. Zwicker, eds. *Lord Rochester in the Restoration World* (Cambridge: Cambridge University Press, 2015), 3.

8. On the new attitudes toward sexuality on the Restoration stage, see Harold Weber, *The Restoration Rake-Hero: Transformations in Sexual Understanding in Seventeenth-Century England* (Madison: University of Wisconsin Press, 1986). Weber argues that this was the first period in which the stage represented sexuality as its own arena, disentangled from religion in particular.

9. Jeremy Webster, *Performing Libertinism in Charles II's Court: Politics, Drama, Sexuality* (New York: Palgrave Macmillan, 2005), 3.

10. James Turner, *Libertines and Radicals in Early Modern London: Sexuality, Politics, and Literary Culture, 1630–1685* (Cambridge: Cambridge University Press, 2002); Pat Gill, *Interpreting Ladies: Women, Wit, and Morality in the Restoration Comedy of Manners* (Athens: University of Georgia Press, 1994); Peggy Thompson, *Coyness and Crime in Restoration Comedy* (Lewisburg, PA: Bucknell University Press, 2011).

11. J. Douglas Canfield, *Tricksters & Estates: On the Ideology of Restoration Comedy* (Lexington: University Press of Kentucky, 1997); and also *Heroes & States: On the Ideology of Restoration Tragedy* (Lexington: University Press of Kentucky, 2000).

12. Cynthia Richards, "Wit at War: The Poetry of John Wilmot and the Trauma of War," *Eighteenth-Century Fiction* 27, no. 1 (2014): 25–54.

13. Gilbert Burnet and Thomas Burnet, *Bishop Burnet's History of His Own Time*, edited by Martin Joseph Routh, vol. 1 (Oxford: Oxford University Press, 1833), 495. Future references are to this edition and cited in the text.

14. William Beatty Warner, *Licensing Entertainment: The Elevation of Novel Reading in Britain, 1684–1750* (Berkeley: University of California Press, 1998), 42.

15. Linda Colley, *Britons: Forging the Nation, 1707–1837* (New Haven, CT: Yale University Press, 1992). See also Tony Claydon and Ian McBride, *Protestantism and National Identity: Britain and Ireland, c. 1650–c. 1850* (Cambridge: Cambridge University Press, 1998), esp. the introduction.

16. Gilbert Burnet, *Dr. Burnet's Travels, or Letters Containing an Account of What Seemed Most Remarkable in Switzerland, Italy, France, and Germany, &c.* (Amsterdam: Printed for Peter Savouret and W. Fenner, 1687).

17. Martin Greig, "A Peculiar Talent in Writing History: Gilbert Burnet and his *History of My Own Time,*" *Archives* 32 (2007): 19–27.

18. Burnet, *History*, vol. 3, 130.

19. Burnet also endured attacks from the other side by Whigs who thought that he did not disparage the Stuarts enough. One pamphlet, for example, accused Burnet of covering up the murder of Lord Essex, imprisoned in the wake of the Popish Plot but found dead in the tower. Burnet conceded to the official coroner's inquiry that Lord Essex cut his own throat, but one Laurence Braddon insists that he has evidence that Charles II ordered the murder. See *Bishop Burnet's Late History Charg'd with Great Partiality and Misrepresentations* (London: Printed for Tho. Warner, 1725), esp. 133. Burnet supported the emerging Whig ideas but distanced himself from the more radical thinkers of the period. On recent thinking about radicalism at this time, see Gary S. De Krey, "Radicals, Reformers, and Republicans: Academic Language and Political Discourse in Restoration London," in *A Nation Transformed: England after the Restoration*, ed. Alan Houston and Steve Pincus (Cambridge: Cambridge University Press, 2001), 71–99.

20. Michelle A. White, *Henrietta Maria and the English Civil Wars* (Aldershot: Ashgate, 2006), 136–49.

21. For an excellent study of the significance of Nell Gwynn's position in the religious politics of the Restoration and, later, in eighteenth-century literature, see Alison Conway, *The Protestant Whore: Courtesan Narrative and Religious Controversy in England, 1680–1750* (Toronto: University of Toronto Press, 2010), esp. 34–40.

22. I have discussed the Catholic queen of Charles II already at length in chapter 3. She does not figure in this discussion, however, because Burnet, to the outrage of Catherine's later biographers, thought that Charles never cared for her, and that she did not exert any authority at court. He does remark, unsurprisingly, on the problem of her Catholicism, wondering why there had not been greater protest against this marriage after the experience of Henrietta Maria. He reports that Charles was weary of the queen and wanted to get rid of her (vol. 1, 365), but ultimately did not agree to the proposed plots, such as Lord Buckingham's idea of transporting her to one of the colonies. Burnet himself had such great concern over the succession of James that he considered polygamy a reasonable option, a position he later came to regret.

23. An even closer look, beyond the scope of this argument, would show the deep divisions between those opposed to the Stuarts.

24. Olive Baldwin and Thelma Wilson, "The Harmonious Unfortunate: New Light on Catherine Tofts," *Cambridge Opera Journal* 22, no. 2 (2010): 217–34; 220, 221.

25. T. E. S. Clarke, H. C. Foxcroft, and C. H. Firth, *A Life of Gilbert Burnet, Bishop of Salisbury* (Cambridge: Cambridge University Press, 1907), 379.

26. Burnet's treatises on polygamy and divorce appear in *Memoirs of the life and writings of Sir Richard Steele. Wherein are contained two curious dissertations written by the late bishop Burnet, viz. I. A Defence of Polygamy, proving that it is not contrary to the Law and Nature of Marriage; and that an express Prohibition of it is no where to be found in Scripture. II. The Lawfulness of Divorce on Account of Sterility in Women, proving that Defect a sufficient Reason for Separation. also some memoirs of the Earls of Nottingham,*

Portmore, and Lord Chief Baron Pengelly, with his Will (London: Printed for E. Curll and W. Leventhorp, 1731). The author of the *Memoirs* reports that manuscript versions of these treatises in Burnet's own hand had been given to Richard Steele for publication in *The Lover.* Later in his account of Rochester's conversion, Burnet argues for God's disapproval of polygamy because it causes so much pain for women and would lead to marital conflict (112–13). Manley also satirized Burnet's defense of polygamy and later retraction.

27. James Turner and, more recently, Erin Mackie certainly capture the potential for the gendered violence of libertinism. Burnet's story, however, recounts state violence, an aspect that tends to drop out of accounts of the libertine court culture.

28. Sara B. Varhus is persuasive when she argues that Burnet does his best writing in the form of biography, and that he should be considered a pioneer in developing the form. Burnet's discussion of Lord Russell's trial was later reprinted independent of the *History.* Varhus considers these pages "a memoir that approaches biography." "Lively Examples: Gilbert Burnet's Use of Biography," *Restoration* 11, no. 1 (1987), 18.

29. Lord Russell's gallows humor is repeated throughout the century in joke books and collections of witticisms.

30. Not all of these attacks were over this particular series of volumes, although they capture the political opposition to his stance. Dryden mocked him in "The Hind and the Panther," Manley includes him as a character in her roman à clef *Memoirs of Europe,* and Swift attacked him in *A preface to the B—p of S—r—m's introduction to the third volume of the History of the Reformation of the Church of England. By Gregory Misosarum* (Dublin: Printed for John Morphew, 1713). A London rector with Jacobite sympathies "ordered Burnet's likeness under the character of Judas to be embodied in the altar-piece of his church." Clarke, Foxcroft, and Firth, *Life of Gilbert Burnet,* 464.

31. Emily H. Patterson, "Swift's Marginalia in Burnet's *History of His Own Time,*" *Enlightenment Essays* 3, no. 1 (1972): 47–54.

32. John Wilmot, "A Satyr on Charles II," in *The Complete Poems of John Wilmot, Earl of Rochester,* ed. David M. Vieth (New Haven, CT: Yale University Press, 1968), 61–62.

33. On the violence of libertine culture, see Turner, *Libertines and Radicals in Early Modern London,* esp. 47–73 and 197–25.

34. Michael Neill, "Heroic Heads and Humble Tails: Sex, Politics, and the Restoration Comic Rake," *Eighteenth Century: Theory and Interpretation* 24, no. 2 (1983): 115–39.

35. Gilbert Burnet, *Some Passages of the Life and Death of the Right Honourable John, Earl of Rochester who died the 26th of July, 1680, written by his own direction on his deathbed by Gilbert Burnet* (London, 1680), 12. Future references are from this edition and cited in the text.

36. For an excellent discussion of this incident and a reading of Rochester's scandalous work as a result, in part, of the ensuing trauma, see Richards, "Wit at War."

37. See Nicholas Fisher, "'I Abhor What I So Long Loved': An Exploration of Rochester's Death Bed Repentance," *Seventeenth Century* 25, no. 2 (2010): 323–49.

38. Fisher, "I Abhor What I So Long Loved," 340.

39. On the uneven movement toward human rights in the eighteenth century, see Lynn Hunt, *Inventing Human Rights: A History* (New York: W. W. Norton, 2007). On the variety of universalizing cosmopolitanisms that emerge in this period, see Margaret C. Jacob, *Strangers Nowhere in the World: The Rise of Cosmopolitanism in Early Modern Europe* (Philadelphia: University of Pennsylvania Press, 2006).

40. For an excellent discussion of all the reform movements that emerged at this time, see Tony Claydon, *William III and the Godly Revolution* (Cambridge: Cambridge University Press, 1996).

41. Robert Hume, for example, argues that Restoration-style comedy was not pushed out by sentimental comedy. See his *Development of English Drama in the Late Seventeenth Century* (Oxford: Oxford University Press, 1976), 9. A very good overview of this debate can be found in Peter Hynes, "Richard Steele and the Genealogy of Sentimental Drama: A Reading of *The Conscious Lovers,*" *Papers on Language and Literature* 40, no. 2 (2004): 142–66, esp. 142–45. Hynes concludes that while no clear "before" and "after" of Restoration and sentimentalism can be established, Richard Steele and others invested in sentimental drama saw themselves as writing a different kind of comedy than in the past.

42. Samuel Johnson, for example, criticized Shakespeare for caring more about theatrical effect than morality. Aparna Gollapudi in *Moral Reform in Comedy and Culture, 1696–1747* (Farnham: Ashgate, 2011) makes the case for thinking about the new generation of playwrights at the end of the seventeenth century as engaged in reform rather than sentimentalism.

43. See, for example, John O'Brien's discussion of Addison in *Harlequin Britain: Pantomime and Entertainment, 1690–1760* (Baltimore: Johns Hopkins University Press, 2004), 73–76.

44. Colley Cibber, *An Apology for the Life of Colley Cibber: With an Historical View of the Stage during His Own Time*, ed. Byrne Fone (Ann Arbor: University of Michigan Press, 1968), 7. Future references are from this edition and cited in the text.

45. Brian Glover also notes this allusion to Burnet; see his "Nobility, Visibility, and Publicity in Colley Cibber's *Apology,*" *SEL* 42, no. 3 (2002): 523–39; 524.

46. On the emergence of autobiography as a genre, see Felicity Nussbaum, *The Autobiographical Subject: Gender and Ideology in Eighteenth-Century England* (Baltimore: Johns Hopkins University Press, 1989), 1–29.

47. Glover, "Nobility, Visibility, and Publicity," 525.

48. On the *Apology* as a career narrative rather than an autobiography, see Elaine McGirr, *Partial Histories: A Reappraisal of Colley Cibber* (London: Palgrave Macmillan, 2016), 2.

49. Clarke, Foxcroft, and Firth, *Life of Gilbert Burnet*, 359. On the theological disputes between Collier and Burnet, see Andrew Starkie, "Contested Histories of the English Church: Gilbert Burnet and Jeremy Collier," *Huntington Library Quarterly* 68, no. 1–2 (2005): 335–51.

50. For a discussion of comedy and reform, see Gollapudi, *Moral Reform in Comedy and Culture*.

51. Julia H. Fawcett, "The Overexpressive Celebrity and the Deformed King: Recasting the Spectacle as Subject in Colley Cibber's *Richard III,*" *PMLA* 126, no. 4 (2011): 950–56.

52. See Michael Dobson, *The Making of the National Poet: Shakespeare, Adaptation and Authorship, 1660–1769* (Oxford: Clarendon Press, 1992), 185–222.

53. Neil McKendrick, John Brewer, and J. H Plumb, *The Birth of a Consumer Society: The Commercialization of Eighteenth-Century England* (Bloomington: Indiana University Press, 1985), 9. See also Maxine Berg, *The Age of Manufactures, 1700–1820: Industry, Innovation, and Work in Britain* (London: Routledge, 1994).

54. I borrow the idea of a "transvestite continuum" from Marjorie Garber, *Vested Interests: Cross-Dressing and Cultural Anxiety* (New York: Routledge, 1992), 353–74, and also explore it in chapter 2 of this book. Elaine McGirr has complicated this view of Cibber as identified primarily with his fop role by adding the important point that he specialized in villains as well. Fops, however, were among his most famous portrayals. See her *Partial Histories*, 28–34.

55. Kristina Straub points out that Cibber's awareness of himself as a visual object was out of step with the new masculine style of acting. *Sexual Suspects: Eighteenth-Century Players and Sexual Ideology* (Princeton, NJ: Princeton University Press, 1992), 32–33. On "the great male renunciation," in which men gave up elaborate dress and settled for a plainer look, see John C. Flügel, *The Psychology of Clothes* (London: Hogarth Press, 1930).

56. See, for example, John Brown, *Estimate of the Manners and Principles of the Times* (London, 1757). Bernard Mandeville satirizes the antiluxury argument in his *Fable of the Bees* (1714).

57. Straub, *Sexual Suspects*, 55.

58. See Dobson, *Making of the National Poet*, 134.

59. Joseph Roach, *Cities of the Dead: Circum-Atlantic Performance* (New York: Columbia University Press, 1996), 85.

60. See Roach's discussion of Thomas Betterton in *Cities of the Dead*, 73–118.

61. On this performance, see Fawcett, "Overexpressive Celebrity and the Deformed King."

62. Straub, *Sexual Suspects*, 24.

63. Critics, of course, saw Burnet as an unscrupulous operator; either way, he did not shy away from taking controversial stands and declaring unmitigated loyalties.

64. On the "public intimacy" created by Charles, see Erin Keating, "The Role of Manuscript Newsletters in Charles II's Performance of Power," *Restoration* 41, no. 2 (2017): 33–51. Keating borrows the idea of public intimacy from Joseph Roach, *It* (Ann Arbor: University of Michigan Press, 2007), 3. For Roach, Charles II serves as a prototype for a celebrity able to create this public intimacy (34–36).

65. On Betterton's association with Shakespeare roles, see Roach, *Cities of the Dead*, 116.

66. On Betterton's remarkable career, see David Roberts, *Thomas Betterton: The Greatest Actor of the Restoration Stage* (Cambridge: Cambridge University Press, 2010).

67. And again, later, a conflict between companies turns into a "Civil War, of the Theatre" (Cibber, *Apology*, 112).

68. Straub, *Sexual Suspects*, 32, 54–56. For a more recent and intriguing arguing exploring the queerness of the fop, see Emma Katherine Atwood, "Fashionably Late: Queer Temporality and the Restoration Fop," *Comparative Drama* 47, no. 1 (2013): 85–111.

69. Similarly, Amanda Bailey has shown how a subculture of young men engaged in pleasurable forms of self-display grew up around the early seventeenth-century theater. See her *Flaunting: Style and the Subversive Male Body in Renaissance England* (Toronto: University of Toronto Press, 2007).

70. Thomas Alan King, *The Gendering of Men, 1600–1750* (Madison: University of Wisconsin Press, 2004), 175–81.

71. Straub, *Sexual Suspects*, 54–56.

72. John Dennis, *A Defence of Sir Fopling Flutter, A comedy Written by Sir George Etheridge* (London: Printed for T. Warner, 1722).

73. Colley Cibber, *Love Makes the Man*, in *The Plays of Colley Cibber*, vol. 1, ed. Rodney L. Hayley (New York: Garland, 1980), 44.4.201. Future references to Cibber's plays are from this edition unless otherwise indicated and are cited in the text by act, scene, and page number.

74. On reform in this age, see Claydon, *William III and the Godly Revolution*.

75. Mark S. Dawson, *Gentility and the Comic Theatre of Late Stuart London* (Cambridge: Cambridge University Press, 2005), 164–82.

76. Song ("Love a woman, you're an ass!"), in Rochester, *Complete Poems*, 51.

77. Colley Cibber and John Vanbrugh, *The Provok'd Husband; or A Journey to London* (London 1728).

78. On personal identity and the masquerade, see Terry Castle, *Masquerade and Civilization: The Carnivalesque in Eighteenth-Century English Culture and Fiction* (Stanford, CA: Stanford University Press, 1986) and Dror Wahrman, *The Making of the Modern Self: Identity and Culture in Eighteenth-Century England* (New Haven, CT: Yale University Press, 2004), 157–65.

79. *Provok'd Husband*, 4.

80. See Dawson, *Gentility and the Comic Theatre* on this point, 154–82.

81. See Gollapudi, *Moral Reform*, 19–38, 43–108.

82. C. R. Kropf, "The Relapse and the Sentimental Mask," *Journal of Narrative Technique* 1 (1971): 193–99.

83. McGirr, *Partial Histories*, 11.

84. Kwame Anthony Appiah, *Cosmopolitanism: Ethics in a World of Strangers* (New York: W. W. Norton, 2006), xiii.

85. Pauline Kleingeld and Eric Brown, "Cosmopolitanism," *The Stanford Encyclopedia of Philosophy* (Fall 2014 edition), https://plato.stanford.edu/archives/fall2014/entries/cosmopolitanism/.

Epilogue

1. Eugenia Zuroski Jenkins, *A Taste for China: English Subjectivity and the Prehistory of Orientalism* (New York: Oxford University Press, 2013), 16–65.

2. As in other chapters, I borrow the phrase "war capitalism" from Sven Beckert, *Empire of Cotton: A Global History* (New York: Alfred A. Knopf, 2014), xvi, as a more accurate descriptive term than "mercantilism."

3. Holly Brewer, "Slavery, Sovereignty, and 'Inheritable Blood': Reconsidering John Locke and the Origins of American Slavery," *The American Historical Review* 122, no. 4 (2017): 1038–78, https://doi.org/10.1093/ahr/122.4.1038.

4. *The Spectator*, one of Smith's recent biographers argues, was an important influence and part of Smith's early education. See Nicholas Phillipson, *Adam Smith: An Enlightened Life* (New Haven, CT: Yale University Press, 2010), 19–23.

5. Joseph Addison and Sir Richard Steele, *The Spectator*, vol. 1, ed. Donald Frederic Bond (Oxford: Clarendon Press, 1965), 296 (no. 69, March 19, 1711). Bond notes (vol. 1, 296, n.1) that most of these statues were carved by the father of Colley Cibber, sculptor Caius Gabriel Cibber.

6. Natasha Glaisyer, *The Culture of Commerce in England, 1660–1720* (Woodbridge: Royal Historical Society/Boydell Press, 2006), 67.

7. The *Spectator* does not identify the particular monarch with whom its eidolon converses, but as Glaisyer's description suggests, Charles II would have come to mind.

8. See Kathryn Shevelow. *Women and Print Culture: The Construction of Femininity in the Early Periodical* (London: Routledge, 1989). Shevelow traces the *Spectator* and other periodicals as the origins of the women's magazine. For an excellent discussion of the way the *Spectator* shaped taste in the eighteenth century, see Erin Skye Mackie, *Market à la Mode: Fashion, Commodity, and Gender in the "Tatler" and the "Spectator"* (Baltimore: Johns Hopkins University Press, 1997). See also Manushag N. Powell, *Performing Authorship in Eighteenth-Century English Periodicals* (Lanham, MD: Bucknell University Press, 2012), which traces the rise and fall of the eidolon in eighteenth-century periodicals.

9. Lancelot also wrote about the Jews living on the Barbary Coast in *The Present State of the Jews* (London: Printed by J. C. for William Crooke, 1675).

10. On Addison's life, see Peter Smithers, *The Life of Joseph Addison* (Oxford: Clarendon, 1968). Gulston died shortly after receiving this appointment.

11. *Spectator*, vol. 1: 2–3.

12. *Spectator*, vol. 3: 528 (July 19, 1712).

13. *Spectator*, vol. 1: 294.

14. *Spectator*, vol. 1: 293.

15. On the limits of the *Spectator*'s encouragement of participation in the public sphere, see Anthony Pollock, *Gender and the Fictions of the Public Sphere, 1690–1755* (New York: Routledge, 2009). On the public sphere, see also Brian Cowan, *The Social Life of Coffee: The Emergence of the British Coffeehouse* (New Haven, CT: Yale University Press, 2005).

16. Mackie, *Market à la Mode*.

17. This implication runs throughout the *Spectator*, but see no. 69 in particular.

18. Adam Smith, *The Wealth of Nations*, vol. 1, ed. Andrew S. Skinner (London: Penguin, 1999 [1776]): 488–89. Future references are to this edition and cited in the text.

19. Kristina Straub, *Sexual Suspects: Eighteenth-Century Players and Sexual Ideology* (Princeton, NJ: Princeton University Press, 1992), chapter 3.

20. Jenkins, *Taste for China*, 188–213.

21. Smith spent much of his life in Glasgow, which did not have a theater until after the first edition of *Theory of Moral Sentiments* appeared. He did, however, see plays during his stay in France and possibly also in London and in Edinburgh. Theater was an important part of this early education, as acting out plays was part of the curriculum (Phillipson, *Adam Smith*, 18–19). Much of Smith's knowledge about drama probably came from reading. There is some evidence that he opposed the building of a theater in Glasgow. His eighteenth-century biographer, however, believed that Smith was writing a book about theater at the time of his death.

22. William M. Reddy, *The Navigation of Feeling: A Framework for the History of Emotions* (Cambridge: Cambridge University Press, 2001), 129.

23. See, for example, Ann Jessie Van Sant, *Eighteenth-Century Sensibility and the Novel: The Senses in Social Context* (Cambridge: Cambridge University Press, 1993); Gillian Skinner, *Sensibility and Economics in the Novel, 1740–1800: The Price of a Tear* (New York: St. Martin's Press, 1999); Markman Ellis, *The Politics of Sensibility: Race, Gender, and Commerce in the Sentimental Novel* (Cambridge: Cambridge University Press, 1996); and Claudia L. Johnson, *Equivocal Beings: Politics, Gender, and Sentimentality in the 1790s: Wollstonecraft, Radcliffe, Burney, Austen* (Chicago: University of Chicago Press, 1995).

24. Stewart Justman, "Regarding Others," *New Literary History* 27, no. 1 (1996): 83–93; Jonas A. Barish, *Anti-Theatrical Prejudice* (Berkeley: University of California Press, 1982); James Chandler, "The Politics of Sentiment: Notes toward a New Account," *Studies in Romanticism* 49 (2010): 553–75.

25. Adam Smith, *The Theory of Moral Sentiments*, ed. Knud Haakonssen (Cambridge: Cambridge University Press, 2002 [1759]), 12. Future references are from this edition and cited in the text.

26. Romance, of course, can also refer to the prose form as well as drama, but the emphasis here is theatrical.

27. David Marshall, "Adam Smith and the Theatricality of Moral Sentiments," *Critical Inquiry* 10, no. 4 (1984): 592–613; see also his *The Figure of Theater: Shaftesbury, Defoe, Adam Smith, and George Eliot* (New York: Columbia University Press, 1986). On the theatricality of sympathy beyond Smith, see Elizabeth D. Samet, "Spectacular History and the Politics of Theater: Sympathetic Arts in the Shadow of the Bastille," *PMLA* 118, no. 5 (2003): 1305–19. While Smith, as we will see, takes the sympathy generated in the theater very seriously, Samet notes how by contrast Mandeville, whom Smith attempts to refute, saw this kind of sympathy as similar to "an imitation spawned by imagination and enthusiasm" (1305). See also Jean-Christophe Agnew, *Worlds Apart: The Market and the Theater in Anglo-American Thought, 1550–1750* (Cambridge: Cambridge University Press, 1986).

28. Barish, *Anti-Theatrical Prejudice*.

29. Marshall, "Adam Smith and the Theatricality," 605.

30. Phillipson, *Adam Smith*, 21–23.

31. See *The Tatler*, 12, 99, and 108.

32. *A Letter from the Rope-Dancing Monkey in the Hay-market, to the Acting Monkey of Drury Lane* (London, 1767). On the monkey's performance, see *The London Stage, 1660–1800: A Calendar of Plays, Entertainments & Afterpieces, Together with Casts, Box-Receipts and Contemporary Comments*, Part 4, *1747–1776*, ed. George Winchester Stone, Jr. (Carbondale: Southern Illinois University Press, 1960).

33. Alexander Broadie, "Sympathy and the Impartial Spectator," in Knud Haakonssen, *The Cambridge Companion to Adam Smith* (Cambridge: Cambridge University Press, 2006), 158–88.

34. In a few places, Smith comments on Shakespeare's metaphors; in lecture 21, he discusses which modern playwrights have followed the three unities, although he ultimately, like Samuel Johnson, diminishes their significance because the audience knows from start to finish that they are observing a performance rather than real life (122). With two notable exceptions (lectures 21 and 23), Smith mostly leaves out theater in favor of prose and poetry.

35. Adam Smith, *Lectures on Rhetoric and Belles Lettres*, ed. J. C. Bryce (Indianapolis: Liberty Fund, 1985), 137; a reproduction of the Glasgow Edition of the *Works and Correspondence of Adam Smith*, vol. 4 (Oxford: Clarendon Press, 1983). Future references are from this edition and cited in the text.

36. Smith, *Lectures on Rhetoric and Belles Lettres*, lecture 21, 124.

37. The first remedy is an education in science and philosophy and the second "is the frequency and gaiety of public diversions. The state, by encouraging, that is by giving entire liberty to all those who for their own interest would attempt without scandal or indecency, to amuse and divert the people by painting, poetry, music, dancing; by all sorts of dramatic representations and exhibitions, would easily dissipate, in the greater part of them, that melancholy and gloomy humour which is almost always the nurse of popular superstition and enthusiasm. Public diversions have always been the objects of dread and hatred to all the fanatical promoters of those popular frenzies. The gaiety and good humour which those diversions inspire were altogether inconsistent with that temper of mind which was fittest for their purpose, or which they could best work upon. Dramatic representations, besides, frequently exposing their artifices to public ridicule, and sometimes even to public execration, were upon that account, more than all other diversions, the objects of their peculiar abhorrence." Smith, *Wealth of Nations*, vol. 2, 384.

38. Marshall, "Adam Smith and the Theatricality," 604. For Smith's presumed masculine orientation, see also Stewart Justman, *The Autonomous Male of Adam Smith* (Norman: University of Oklahoma Press, 1993).

39. The appeal of the she-tragedies cannot be explained simply by Smith's other traditional category of a couple in love facing some kind of block. These plays instead focus specifically on the suffering of a vulnerable woman rather than a couple in love. On this point, see Jean Marsden, *Fatal Desire: Women, Sexuality, and the English Stage, 1660–1720* (Ithaca, NY: Cornell University Press, 1996), chapters 3 and 5.

40. As Jean Marsden argues, tragedies moved toward sentimentality long before Richard Steele made this claim for his comedy *The Conscious Lovers* (1722). See Marsden, *Fatal Desire*, chapter 3.

41. Excellent readings of the play in this vein include Lucinda Cole, "*The London Merchant* and the Institution of Apprenticeship," *Criticism: A Quarterly for Literature and the Arts* 37, no. 1 (1995): 57–84; Lisa A. Freeman, "Tragic Flaws: Genre and Ideology in Lillo's *London Merchant*," *South Atlantic Quarterly* 98, no. 3 (1999): 539–61; and Lee Morrissey, "Sexuality and Consumer Culture in Eighteenth Century England: 'Mutual Love from Pole to Pole' in *The London Merchant*," *Restoration and 18th Century Theatre Research* 13, no. 1 (1998): 25–39. See also Laura Mandell, *Misogynous Economies: The Business of Literature in Eighteenth-Century Britain* (Lexington: University of Kentucky Press, 1999).

42. Clay Daniel, "The Fall of George Barnwell," *Restoration and Eighteenth-Century Theatre Research* 2, no. 2 (1987): 26–37.

43. Freeman, "Tragic Flaws"; Marsden, *Fatal Desire*.

44. George Lillo, *The London Merchant*, ed. William H. McBurney (Lincoln: University of Nebraska Press, 1965), 2.6.24. Future references are from this edition and cited in the text.

45. Smith, *Wealth of Nations*, 110.

46. Smith, *Wealth of Nations*, 117.

47. Smith, *Theory of Moral Sentiments*, 157.

48. Paula R. Backscheider, *Spectacular Politics: Theatrical Power and Mass Culture in Early Modern England* (Baltimore: Johns Hopkins University Press, 1993); Anna Keay, *The Magnificent Monarch: Charles II and the Ceremonies of Power* (London: Continuum, 2008).

SELECTED BIBLIOGRAPHY

Addison, Joseph, and Richard Steele. *The Spectator.* 5 vols. Ed. Donald Frederic Bond. Oxford: Clarendon Press, 1965.

Ambross, E. *The Life and Memoirs of the Late Miss Ann Catley.* London: Printed for J. Bird, ca. 1789.

Amussen, Susan Dwyer. *Caribbean Exchanges: Slavery and the Transformation of English Society, 1640–1700.* Chapel Hill: University of North Carolina Press, 2007.

Andrade e Sousa, Manuel. *Catherine of Braganza, Princess of Portugal, Wife to Charles II.* Lisbon: Inapa, 1994.

Appiah, Anthony. *Cosmopolitanism: Ethics in a World of Strangers.* New York: W. W. Norton, 2006.

Aravamudan, Srinivas. *Tropicopolitans: Colonialism and Agency, 1688–1804.* Post-Contemporary Interventions. Durham, NC: Duke University Press, 1999.

Armistead, J. M. *Otherworldly John Dryden: Occult Rhetoric in His Poems and Plays.* Burlington, VT: Ashgate, 2014.

Augustine, Matthew C., and Steven N. Zwicker, eds. *Lord Rochester in the Restoration World.* Cambridge: Cambridge University Press, 2015.

Aylmer, G. E. "Slavery under Charles II: The Mediterranean and Tangier." *The English Historical Review* 114, no. 456 (1999): 378–88.

Backscheider, Paula R. *Spectacular Politics: Theatrical Power and Mass Culture in Early Modern England.* Baltimore: Johns Hopkins University Press, 1993.

Baldwin, Olive, and Thelma Wilson. "The Harmonious Unfortunate: New Light on Catherine Tofts." *Cambridge Opera Journal* 22, no. 2 (2010): 217–34.

Ballaster, Ros. *Fabulous Orients: Fictions of the East in English 1662–1785.* Oxford: Oxford University Press, 2005.

Barish, Jonas. *The Anti-Theatrical Prejudice.* Berkeley: University of California Press, 1981.

Baucom, Ian. *Specters of the Atlantic: Finance Capital, Slavery, and the Philosophy of History.* Durham, NC: Duke University Press, 2005.

Beach, Adam R. "Baffled Colonial Discourse: Representing the First Decade of the English Tangier." *Restoration* 31, no. 2 (2007): 21–41.

Beckert, Sven. *Empire of Cotton: A Global History.* New York: Alfred A. Knopf, 2014.

Behn, Aphra. *Oroonoko.* Edited by Joanna Lipking. Norton Critical Editions. New York: W. W. Norton, 1997.

———. *The Widow Ranter.* In *Oroonoko, the Rover, and Other Works.* Edited by Janet Todd. London, England: Penguin Books, 1992.

Berglund, Lisa. "The Language of the Libertines: Subversive Morality in *The Man of Mode.*" *SEL: Studies in English Literature, 1500–1900* 30, no. 3 (1990): 369–86.

Birchwood, Matthew. *Staging Islam in England: Drama and Culture, 1640–1685*. Studies in Renaissance Literature 21. Cambridge: D. S. Brewer, 2007.

Blaine, Marlin E. "Epic, Romance, and History in Davenant's 'Madagascar.'" *Studies in Philology* 95, no. 3 (1998): 293–319.

Brewer, Holly. "Slavery and Sovereignty in Early America and the British Empire." Unpublished manuscript.

———. "Slavery, Sovereignty, and 'Inheritable Blood': Reconsidering John Locke and the Origins of American Slavery." *American Historical Review* 122, no. 4 (2017): 1038–78.

Britland, Karen. *Drama at the Courts of Queen Henrietta Maria*. Cambridge: Cambridge University Press, 2006.

Broadie, Alexander. "Sympathy and the Impartial Spectator." In *The Cambridge Companion to Adam Smith*, ed. Knud Haakonssen, 158–88. Cambridge: Cambridge University Press, 2006.

Brown, Laura. *Ends of Empire: Women and Ideology in Early Eighteenth-Century English Literature*. Ithaca, NY: Cornell University Press, 1993.

———. *English Dramatic Form, 1660–1760: An Essay in Generic History*. New Haven, CT: Yale University Press, 1981.

Burke, Helen M. "Wycherley's 'Tendentious Joke': The Discourse of Alterity in *The Country Wife*." *The Eighteenth Century: Theory and Interpretation* 29, no. 3 (1988): 227–41.

Burnet, Gilbert, and Thomas Burnet. *Bishop Burnet's History of His Own Time*. Edited by Martin Joseph Routh. 6 Vols. Oxford: Oxford University Press, 1833.

Burney, Frances. *Evelina: Or, The History of a Young Lady's Entrance into the World*. Edited by Edward A. Bloom. Oxford: Oxford University Press, 2002.

Canfield, J. Douglas. "The Critique of Capitalism and the Retreat into Art in Gay's *Beggar's Opera* and Fielding's *Author's Farce*." In *Cutting Edges: Postmodern Critical Essays on Eighteenth-Century Satire*, ed. James E. Gill, 320–34. Knoxville: University of Tennessee Press, 1995.

———. *Heroes & States: On the Ideology of Restoration Tragedy*. Lexington: University Press of Kentucky, 2000.

———. "Richard Flecknoe's Early Defense of the Stage: An Appeal to Cromwell." *Restoration and Eighteenth-Century Theatre Research* 2, no. 2 (1987): 1–7.

———. *Tricksters & Estates: On the Ideology of Restoration Comedy*. Lexington: University Press of Kentucky, 1997.

Carlson, Marvin. *The Haunted Stage: The Theatre as Memory Machine*. Ann Arbor: University of Michigan Press, 2002.

Cary, John. *An essay on the state of England in relation to its trade, its poor, and its taxes, for carrying on the present war against France by John Cary, merchant in Bristoll*. Bristol: Printed by W. Bonny for the author, 1695.

Cheah, Pheng, Bruce Robbins, and the Social Text Collective. *Cosmopolitics: Thinking and Feeling beyond the Nation*. Minneapolis: University of Minnesota Press, 1998.

Chua, Brandon. *The Ravishment of Reason: Governance and the Heroic Idioms of the Late Stuart Stage, 1660–1690*. Transits: Literature, Thought & Culture, 1650–1850. Lewisburg, PA: Bucknell University Press, 2014.

Cibber, Colley. *An Apology for the Life of Colley Cibber: With an Historical View of the Stage during His Own Time*. Edited by Byrne Fone. Ann Arbor: University of Michigan Press, 1968.

———. *The Plays of Colley Cibber*. Edited by Rodney L Hayley. 2 vols. New York: Garland, 1980.

Clare, Janet. *Drama of the English Republic, 1649–60*. Manchester: Manchester University Press, 2002.

Clarke, T. E. S., H. C. Foxcroft, and C. H. Firth. *A Life of Gilbert Burnet, Bishop of Salisbury*. Cambridge: Cambridge University Press, 1907.

Claydon, Tony. *William III and the Godly Revolution*. Cambridge: Cambridge University Press, 1996.

Colley, Linda. *Britons: Forging the Nation, 1707–1837*. Revised edition. New Haven, CT: Yale University Press, 2009.

———. *Captives*. New York: Pantheon, 2002.

Congreve, William. *The Works of William Congreve*. Edited by D. F. McKenzie. 3 vols. Oxford: Oxford University Press, 2011.

Considerations humbly offer'd to the Honourable House of Commons, by the planters, and others, trading to our British plantations, in relation to the African Company's petition, now before this Honourable House. London, 1698.

Conway, Alison. *The Protestant Whore: Courtesan Narrative and Religious Controversy in England, 1680–1750*. Toronto: University of Toronto Press, 2010.

Corp, Edward. "Catherine of Braganza and Cultural Politics." In *Queenship in Britain, 1660–1837*, ed. Clarissa Campbell Orr, 53–73. Manchester: Manchester University Press, 2002.

Cowan, Brian. *The Social Life of Coffee: The Emergence of the British Coffeehouse*. New Haven, CT: Yale University Press, 2005.

Cox, R. S. Jr. "Richard Flecknoe and *The Man of Mode*." *Modern Language Quarterly* 29 (1968): 183–89.

Crouch, John. *Census Poeticus: The Poets Tribute Paid in Eight Loyal Poems Three Upon the Arrival of the King, Queen, Queen-Mother. Two Upon the Coronation, Portugal Match. Two Elegies Upon the Duke of Glocster, Princess of Aurange. a Fancy Upon the Royal Oke with Its Accidental Lopping Upon Which Waite Two Other Poems*. London: Printed for the Author by H. Brugis, 1663.

Crowley, Roger. *Conquerors: How Portugal Forged the First Global Empire*. New York: Random House, 2015.

Crowne, John. *Calisto, or the Chaste Nimph. The Late Masque at Court*. London, 1675.

Davenant, William. *The First Days Entertainment at Rutland-House, By Declamations and Musick*. London, 1656.

———. *A Proposition for Advancement of Moralitie*. London, 1654.

———. *The Siege of Rhodes: A Critical Edition*. Edited by Ann-Mari Hedbäck. Uppsala: Acta Universitatis Upsaliensis, 1973.

———. *The Siege of Rhodes: As they were lately represented at His Highness the Duke of York's Theatre in Lincolns-Inn Fields: the first part being lately enlarg'd*. London, 1663.

———. *The Siege of Rhodes: As they were lately represented at His Highness the Duke of York's Theatre in Lincolns-Inne Fields: written by Sir William D'Avenant the first part being lately enlarg'd*. London, 1672.

———. *The Siege of Rhodes: Made a Representation by the Art of Prospective in Scenes, and the Story sung in Recitative Musick: At the back part of Rutland-House in the upper end of Aldergate-Street, London*. London, 1656.

Davies, Kenneth Gordon. *The Royal African Company*. London: Longmans, Green, 1957.

Dawson, Mark S. *Gentility and the Comic Theatre of Late Stuart London*. Cambridge Social and Cultural Histories 5. Cambridge, UK: Cambridge, 2005.

De Marly, Diana. "King Charles II's Own Fashion: The Theatrical Origins of the English Vest." *Journal of the Warburg and Courtauld Institutes* 37 (1974): 378–82.

Dilke, Thomas. *The Lover's Luck*. London, 1696.

Dillon, Elizabeth Maddock. *New World Drama: The Performative Commons in the Atlantic World, 1649–1849*. New Americanists. Durham, NC: Duke University Press, 2014.

D. J. "Hymenaea an Essay or an Epithamlamy, upon the Royall Match of his most Excellent Majesty CHARLES the Second with the most Illustrious CATHERINE, infant of PORTUGAL." London, 1662.

Dobson, Michael. *The Making of the National Poet: Shakespeare, Adaptation and Authorship, 1660–1769*. Oxford: Clarendon Press, 1992.

Downes, John. *Roscius Anglicanus*. Edited by Judith Milhous and Robert D. Hume. London: Society for Theatre Research, 1987.

Dryden, John. *The Works of John Dryden*. Edited by Edward Niles Hooker, H. T Swedenberg, and Vinton A. Dearing. Berkeley: University of California Press, 1956.

Dryden, Robert G. "John Gay's *Polly*: Unmasking Pirates and Fortune Hunters in the West Indies." *Eighteenth-Century Studies* 34, no. 4 (2001): 539–57.

Elmer, Jonathan. *On Lingering and Being Last: Race and Sovereignty in the New World*. New York: Fordham University Press, 2008.

Erickson, Robert A. "Lady Wishfort and the Will of the World." *Modern Language Quarterly: A Journal of Literary History* 45, no. 4 (1984): 338–49.

Etherege, George. *The Plays of Sir George Etherege*. Edited by Michael Cordner. Cambridge: Cambridge University Press, 1982.

Evans, James E. "Evelina, the Rustic Girls of Congreve and Abington, and Surrogation in the 1770s." *The Eighteenth Century: Theory and Interpretation* 52, no. 2 (2011): 157–71.

Evelyn, John. *The Diary of John Evelyn* Edited by John Bray. New York: M. N. Dunne, 1901.

Fawcett, Julia H. "The Overexpressive Celebrity and the Deformed King: Recasting the Spectacle as Subject in Colley Cibber's *Richard III*." *PMLA: Publications of the Modern Language Association of America* 126, no. 4 (2011): 950–65.

Finkel, Caroline. *Osman's Dream: The History of the Ottoman Empire, 1300–1923*. New York: Basic Books, 2005.

Flecknoe, Richard. *Love's Dominion, A Dramatique Piece, Full of Excellent Moralitie, Written as a Pattern for the Reformed Stage*. London, 1654.

———. *A relation of ten years in Europe, Asia, Affrique, and America: all by way of letters occasionally written to divers noble personages, from place to place, and continued to this present year*. London, ca. 1656.

———. *Sir William D'avenant's Voyage to the Other World with His Adventures in the Poets Elizium: A Poetical Fiction*. London, 1688.

Freeman, Lisa A. *Antitheatricality and the Body Public*. Philadelphia: University of Pennsylvania Press, 2017.

———. *Character's Theater: Genre and Identity on the Eighteenth-Century English Stage*. Philadelphia: University of Pennsylvania Press, 2002.

Games, Alison. *The Web of Empire: English Cosmopolitans in an Age of Expansion, 1560–1660*. Oxford: Oxford University Press, 2008.

Garber, Marjorie B. *Vested Interests: Cross-Dressing and Cultural Anxiety*. New York: Routledge, 1992.

Garganigo, Alex. "The Heroic Drama's Legend of Good Women." *Criticism* 45, no. 4 (2003): 483–505.

Gay, John. *John Gay, Dramatic Works*. 2 vols. Ed. John Fuller. Oxford: Clarendon Press, 1983.

Gikandi, Simon. *Slavery and the Culture of Taste*. Princeton, NJ: Princeton University Press, 2011.

Glaisyer, Natasha. *The Cultural of Commerce in England, 1660–1720*. Rochester, NY: Boydell Press, 2006.

Glover, Brian. "Nobility, Visibility, and Publicity in Colley Cibber's *Apology*." *SEL: Studies in English Literature, 1500–1900* 42, no. 3 (2002): 523–39.

Goffman, Daniel. *The Ottoman Empire and Early Modern Europe*. New Approaches to European History 24. Cambridge: Cambridge University Press, 2002.

Gollapudi, Aparna. *Moral Reform in Comedy and Culture, 1696–1747*. Performance in the Long Eighteenth Century: Studies in Theatre, Music, Dance. Farnham: Ashgate, 2011.

Greig, Martin. "A Peculiar Talent in Writing History: Gilbert Burnet and his *History of My Own Time*." *Archives* 32, no. 116 (2007): 19–27.

Grose, C. L. "The Anglo-Portuguese Marriage of 1662." *Hispanic American Historical Review* 10 (1930): 313–52.

Guasco, Michael. *Slaves and Englishmen: Human Bondage in the Early Modern Atlantic World*. Philadelphia: University of Pennsylvania Press, 2014.

Hall, Kim F. *Things of Darkness: Economies of Race and Gender in Early Modern England*. Ithaca, NY: Cornell University Press, 1995.

Harris, Tim. *Restoration: Charles II and His Kingdoms, 1660–1685*. London: Penguin, 2006.

Hawes, Clement. *The British Eighteenth Century and Global Critique*. New York: Palgrave Macmillan, 2005.

Heilman, Robert B. "Some Fops and Some Versions of Foppery." *ELH* 49 (1982): 363–95.

Hermanson, Anne. *The Horror Plays of the English Restoration*. Burlington, VT: Ashgate, 2014.

Hill, Aaron. *A Full and Just Account of the Present State of the Ottoman Empire in All Its Branches: With the Government, and Policy, Religion, Customs, and Way of Living of the Turks in General. Faithfully Related from a Serious Observation Taken in Many Years Travels through Those Countries. by Aaron Hill, Gent*. London: Printed by G. Parker, 1733.

Hodges, John. *Congreve the Man*. New York: Modern Language Association of America, 1941.

Howard, Edward. *Six Days Adventure, or the New Utopia*. London, 1671.

Howe, Elizabeth. *The First English Actresses: Women and Drama, 1660–1700*. Cambridge: Cambridge University Press, 1992.

Hume, Robert D. *The Development of English Drama in the Late Seventeenth Century*. Oxford: Clarendon Press, 1976.

Hutner, Heidi. *Colonial Women: Race and Culture in Stuart Drama*. Oxford: Oxford University Press, 2001.

Hynes, Peter. "Richard Steele and the Genealogy of Sentimental Drama: A Reading of *The Conscious Lovers*." *Papers on Language and Literature* 40, no. 2 (2004): 142–66.

Ireland, Thomas. *Speeches Spoken to the King and Queen, Duke and Duchesse of York, in Christ-Church Hall, Oxford, Sept. 29, 1663.* London: Printed for Richard Royston, 1663.

Iwanisziw, Susan. "Tortured Bodies, Factionalism, and Unsettled Loyalties in Settle's Morocco Plays." In *Staging Pain, 1580–1800: Violence and Trauma in British Theater*, ed. James Robert Allard and Mathew R. Martin, 111–36. Farnham: Ashgate, 2009.

Jackman, Isaac. *All the World's a Stage.* London, 1777.

Jacob, James R., and Timothy Raynor. "Opera and Obedience: Thomas Hobbes and 'A Proposition for Advancement of Moralitie' by Sir William Davenant." *The Seventeenth Century* 6, no. 2 (1991): 205–50.

Jacob, Margaret C. *Strangers Nowhere in the World: The Rise of Cosmopolitanism in Early Modern Europe.* Philadelphia: University of Pennsylvania Press, 2006.

Jaillant, Lise. "Subversive Middlebrow: The Campaigns to Ban Kathleen Winsor's *Forever Amber* in the US and Canada." *International Journal of Canadian Studies* 48 (2014): 33–52.

Jenkins, Eugenia Zuroski. *A Taste for China: English Subjectivity and the Prehistory of Orientalism.* New York: Oxford University Press, 2013.

Jerningham, Edward. *The Peckham Frolic: or, Nell Gwyn.* London, 1799.

Keay, Anna. *The Magnificent Monarch: Charles II and the Ceremonies of Power.* London: Continuum, 2008.

Keenan, Tim. *Restoration Staging, 1660–74.* Studies in Performance and Early Modern Drama. Abingdon: Routledge, 2017.

King, Thomas Alan. *The Gendering of Men, 1600–1750.* Madison: University of Wisconsin Press, 2004.

Kingsley, Margery A. "'High on a Throne of His Own Labours Rear'd': *Mac Flecknoe*, Jeremiad and Cultural Myth." *Modern Philology: A Journal Devoted to Research in Medieval and Modern Literature* 93, no. 3 (1996): 327–51.

The Life of Lavinia Beswick, Alias Fenton, Alias Polly Peachum. London, 1728.

The Life of Nell Gwinn. London, ca. 1760.

Lillo, George. *The London Merchant.* Ed. William H. McBurney. Lincoln: University of Nebraska Press, 1965.

Lindsay, Alexander, and Howard Erskine-Hill. *William Congreve: The Critical Heritage.* London: Routledge, 1989.

Lockey, Brian. *Early Modern Catholics, Royalists, and Cosmopolitans: English Transnationalism and the Christian Commonwealth.* Transculturalisms, 1400–1700. Burlington, VT: Ashgate, 2015.

Lowenthal, Cynthia. *Performing Identities on the Restoration Stage.* Carbondale: Southern Illinois University Press, 2003.

Mackie, Erin Skye. *Market à La Mode: Fashion, Commodity, and Gender in the "Tatler" and the "Spectator."* Baltimore: Johns Hopkins University Press, 1997.

———. *Rakes, Highwaymen, and Pirates: The Making of the Modern Gentleman in the Eighteenth Century.* Baltimore: Johns Hopkins University Press, 2009.

MacLean, Gerald M. *Looking East: English Writing and the Ottoman Empire before 1800.* Basingstoke: Palgrave Macmillan, 2007.

Madway, Lorraine. "Rites of Deliverance and Disenchantment: The Marriage Celebrations for Charles II and Catherine of Braganza, 1661–62." *The Seventeenth Century* 27, no. 1 (2012): 79–105.

Maguire, Nancy Klein. *Regicide and Restoration: English Tragicomedy, 1660–1671.* Cambridge: Cambridge University Press, 1992.

Markley, Robert. *The Far East and the English Imagination, 1600–1730.* Cambridge: Cambridge University Press, 2006.

Marsden, Jean I. *Fatal Desire: Women, Sexuality, and the English Stage, 1660–1720.* Ithaca, NY: Cornell University Press, 2006.

Marshall, David. "Adam Smith and the Theatricality of Moral Sentiments," *Critical Inquiry* 10, no. 4 (June 1984), 592–613.

Matar, Nabil. *Islam in Britain, 1558–1685.* Cambridge: Cambridge University Press, 1988.

Mayer, Tara. "Cultural Cross-Dressing: Posing and Performance in Orientalist Portraits." *Journal of the Royal Asiatic Society* 22, no. 2 (2012): 281–98.

Mazella, David. *The Making of Modern Cynicism.* Charlottesville: University of Virginia Press, 2007.

McCarthy, B. Eugene. *William Wycherley: A Biography.* Athens: Ohio University Press, 1979.

McGirr, Elaine. *Heroic Mode and Political Crisis, 1660–1745.* Newark, NJ: University of Delaware Press, 2009.

———. *Partial Histories: A Reappraisal of Colley Cibber.* London: Palgrave Macmillan, 2016.

Morris, David B. "Language and Honor in 'The Country Wife.'" *South Atlantic Bulletin* 37, no. 4 (1972): 3–10.

Mowry, Melissa. "'Past Remembrance or History': Aphra Behn's *The Widdow Ranter,* or, How the Collective Lost Its Honor." *ELH* 79, no. 3 (2012): 597–621.

Neill, Michael. "Heroic Heads and Humble Tails: Sex, Politics, and the Restoration Comic Rake." *Eighteenth Century: Theory and Interpretation* 24, no. 2 (1983): 115–39.

Newman, Gerald. *The Rise of English Nationalism: A Cultural History, 1740–1830.* Revised edition. New York: St. Martin's Press, 1997.

Nokes, David. *John Gay: A Profession of Friendship.* Oxford: Oxford University Press, 1995.

Novak, Maximillian E. *"The Empress of Morocco" and Its Critics: Settle, Dryden, Shadwell, Crowne, Duffet.* Los Angeles: William Andrews Clark Memorial Library, 1968.

———. "Margery Pinchwife's 'London Desease': Restoration Comedy and the Libertine Offensive of the 1670s." *Studies in the Literary Imagination* 10, no. 1 (1977): 1–23.

Nussbaum, Felicity. *The Limits of the Human: Fictions of Anomaly, Race, and Gender in the Long Eighteenth Century.* Cambridge: Cambridge University Press, 2003.

———. *Rival Queens: Actresses, Performance, and the Eighteenth-Century British Theater.* Philadelphia: University of Pennsylvania Press, 2010.

———. *Torrid Zones: Maternity, Sexuality, and Empire in Eighteenth-Century English Narratives.* Parallax: Re-Visions of Culture and Society. Baltimore: Johns Hopkins University Press, 1995.

O'Brien, John. *Harlequin Britain: Pantomime and Entertainment, 1690–1760.* Baltimore: Johns Hopkins University Press, 2004.

————. *Literature Incorporated: The Cultural Unconscious of the Business Corporation, 1650–1850*. Chicago: University of Chicago Press, 2016.

Orr, Bridget. *Empire on the English Stage, 1660–1714*. Cambridge: Cambridge University Press, 2001.

Orr, Clarissa Campbell. *Queenship in Britain, 1660–1837: Royal Patronage, Court Culture, and Dynastic Politics*. Manchester: Manchester University Press, 2002.

Owen, Susan J. *Restoration Theatre and Crisis*. Oxford: Clarendon Press, 1996.

Parrott, W. G. "The Emotional Experiences of Envy and Jealousy." In *The Psychology of Envy and Jealousy*, ed. Peter Salovey, 3–30. New York: Guildford Press, 1991.

Pepys, Samuel. *The Diary of Samuel Pepys: A New and Complete Transcription*. Edited by Robert Latham and William Matthews. Berkeley: University of California Press, 1970.

Pettigrew, William A. *Freedom's Debt: The Royal African Company and the Politics of the Atlantic Slave Trade, 1672–1752*. Chapel Hill, NC: Published for the Omohundro Institute of Early American History and Culture, Williamsburg, Virginia, by the University of North Carolina Press, 2013.

Phillipson, N. T. *Adam Smith: An Enlightened Life*. Lewis Walpole Series in Eighteenth-Century Culture and History. New Haven, CT: Yale University Press, 2010.

Pincus, Steven C. A. *1688: The First Modern Revolution*. Lewis Walpole Series in Eighteenth-Century Culture and History. New Haven, CT: Yale University Press, 2009.

Pitts, Joseph. *A True and Faithful Account of the Mahommetans*. London, 1704.

Pollock, Anthony. *Gender and the Fictions of the Public Sphere, 1690–1755*. Routledge Studies in Eighteenth-Century Literature 4. New York: Routledge, 2009.

Pomeranz, Kenneth. *The Great Divergence: China, Europe, and the Making of the Modern World Economy*. Princeton, NJ: Princeton University Press, 2000.

Porter, David. *The Chinese Taste in Eighteenth-Century England*. Cambridge: Cambridge University Press, 2010.

Powell, Manushag N. *Performing Authorship in Eighteenth-Century English Periodicals*. Transits: Literature, Thought & Culture. Lanham, MD: Bucknell University Press, 2012.

Prieto-Pablos, Juan A. "*Ignoramus, The Woman Turned Bully*, and Restoration Satire on the Common Lawyer." *SEL Studies in English Literature, 1500–1900* 48, no. 3 (2008): 523–46.

Pullen, Kirsten. *Actresses and Whores: On Stage and in Society*. Cambridge: Cambridge University Press, 2005.

Reddy, William. *The Navigation of Feeling: A Framework for the History of Emotions*. Cambridge: Cambridge University Press, 2001.

Riley, Jonathon. *The Last Ironsides: The English Expedition to Portugal, 1662–1668*. West Midlands: Helion, 2014.

Roach, Joseph. *Cities of the Dead: Circum-Atlantic Performance*. The Social Foundations of Aesthetic Forms. New York: Columbia University Press, 1996.

Rosenthal, Laura J. "'All Injury's Forgot': Restoration Sex Comedy and National Amnesia." *Comparative Drama* 42, no. 1 (2008): 7–28.

————. "*Oroonoko*: Reception, Ideology, and Narrative Strategy." In *The Cambridge Companion to Aphra Behn*, ed. Derek Hughes and Janet Todd, 151–65. Cambridge: Cambridge UP, 2004.

———. "Rebels for Love: Maternity, Absolutism, and the Earl of Orrery's *Mustapha.*" In *Stage Mothers: Women, Work, and the Theater, 1660–1830*, ed. Laura Engel and Elaine M. McGirr, 105–20. Lewisburg, PA: Bucknell University Press, 2014.

Routh, E. M. G. *Tangier, England's Lost Atlantic Outpost, 1661–1684*. London: J. Murray, 1912.

Royal African Company. *The Several Declarations of the Company of Royal Adventurers of England Trading into Africa: Inviting All His Majesties Native Subjects in General to Subscribe and Become Sharers in Their Joynt-Stock . . . As Also a List of the Royal Adventurers of England Trading into Africa*. 1667.

Sedgwick, Eve Kosofsky. *Between Men: English Literature and Male Homosocial Desire.* New York: Columbia University Press, 1985.

Settle, Elkanah. *The Empress of Morocco: A Tragedy.* London: Printed for William Cademan, 1673.

Shepherd, Simon. "'The Body,' Performance Studies, Horner and a Dinner Party." *Textual Practice* 14, no. 2 (2000): 285–303.

Sherman, Stuart. "'The General Entertainment of My Life': *The Tatler, The Spectator*, and the Quidnunc's Cure." *Eighteenth-Century Fiction* 27, no. 3–4 (2015): 343–71.

Shevelow, Kathryn. *Women and Print Culture: The Construction of Femininity in the Early Periodical.* London: Routledge, 1989.

Smith, Adam. *Lectures on Rhetoric and Belles Lettres.* Edited by J. C. Bryce. Indianapolis: Liberty Fund, 1985.

———. *The Theory of Moral Sentiments.* Edited by Knud Haakonssen. Cambridge: Cambridge University Press.

———. *The Wealth of Nations.* Edited by Andrew S. Skinner. 2 vols. London: Penguin, 1999.

Smithers, Peter. *The Life of Joseph Addison.* 2nd ed. Oxford: Clarendon Press, 1968.

Sofer, Andrew. *Dark Matter: Invisibility in Drama, Theater, and Performance.* Ann Arbor: University of Michigan Press, 2013.

Staves, Susan. "A Few Kind Words for the Fop," *SEL* 22 (1982): 413–28.

———. *Players' Scepters: Fictions of Authority in the Restoration.* Lincoln: University of Nebraska Press, 1979.

Stein, Tristan. "Tangier in the Restoration Empire." *The Historical Journal* 54, no. 4 (2011): 895–1011.

Straub, Kristina. *Sexual Suspects: Eighteenth-Century Players and Sexual Ideology.* Princeton, NJ: Princeton University Press, 1992.

St. Serfe, Thomas. *Tarugo's Wiles; or, The Coffee-House.* London, 1668.

Sudan, Rajani. *The Alchemy of Empire: Abject Materials and the Technologies of Colonialism.* New York: Fordham University Press, 2016.

Swingen, Abigail Leslie. *Competing Visions of Empire: Labor, Slavery, and the Origins of the British Atlantic Empire.* New Haven, CT: Yale University Press, 2015.

Tate, Nahum. *The History of King Lear.* Edited by James Black. Lincoln: University of Nebraska Press, 1975.

Thievery à-la-mode: or, The Fatal Encouragement, London, 1728.

Thomas, Gertrude Z. *Richer than Spices: How a Royal Bride's Dowry Introduced Cane, Lacquer, Cottons, Tea, and Porcelain to England, and so Revolutionized Taste, Manners, Craftsmanship, and History in Both England and America.* New York: Alfred A. Knopf, 1965.

Thompson, Ayanna. *Performing Race and Torture on the Early Modern Stage*. Routledge Studies in Renaissance Literature and Culture 9. New York: Routledge, 2008.

Thompson, Peggy. *Coyness and Crime in Restoration Comedy: Women's Desire, Deception, and Agency*. Lewisburg, PA: Bucknell University Press, 2012.

Todd, Janet. *The Secret Life of Aphra Behn*. New Brunswick, NJ: Rutgers University Press, 1997.

Trumpener, Katie. *Bardic Nationalism: The Romantic Novel and the British Empire*. Literature in History. Princeton, NJ: Princeton University Press, 1997.

Turley, Hans. *Rum, Sodomy, and the Lash: Piracy, Sexuality, and Masculine Identity*. New York: New York University Press, 1999.

Turner, James. *Libertines and Radicals in Early Modern London: Sexuality, Politics, and Literary Culture, 1630–1685*. Cambridge: Cambridge University Press, 2002.

Van Lennep, William, Emmett Langdon Avery, Arthur H. Scouten, George Winchester Stone Jr., and Charles Beecher Hogan, eds. *The London Stage, 1660–1800: A Calendar of Plays, Entertainments & Afterpieces, Together with Casts, Box-Receipts and Contemporary Comment: Compiled from the Playbills, Newspapers and Theatrical Diaries of the Period*. Carbondale: Southern Illinois University Press, 1960.

Velissariou, Aspasia. "Patriarchal Tactics of Control and Female Desire in Wycherley's *The Gentleman Dancing-Master* and *The Country Wife*." *Texas Studies in Literature and Language* 37, no. 2 (1995): 115–26.

Visconsi, Elliott. *Lines of Equity: Literature and the Origins of Law in Later Stuart England*. Ithaca, NY: Cornell University Press, 2008.

Wahrman, Dror. *The Making of the Modern Self: Identity and Culture in Eighteenth-Century England*. New Haven, CT: Yale University Press, 2004.

Wallace, Elizabeth Kowaleski. *Consuming Subjects: Women, Shopping, and Business in the Eighteenth Century*. New York: Columbia University Press, 1996.

Wanko, Cheryl. *Roles of Authority: Thespian Biography and Celebrity in Eighteenth-Century Britain*. Lubbock: Texas Tech University Press, 2003.

Warner, William Beatty. *Licensing Entertainment: The Elevation of Novel Reading in Britain, 1684–1750*. Berkeley: University of California Press, 1998.

Webb, John. *An Historical Essay Endeavoring a Probability That the Language of the Empire of China Is the Primitive Language*. London: Printed for Nath. Brook, 1669.

Weber, Harold. "Horner and His 'Women of Honour': The Dinner Party in *The Country-Wife*." *Modern Language Quarterly: A Journal of Literary History* 43, no. 2 (1982): 107–20.

———. *Paper Bullets: Print and Kingship under Charles II*. Lexington: University Press of Kentucky, 1996.

———. *The Restoration Rake-Hero: Transformations in Sexual Understanding in Seventeenth-Century England*. Madison: University of Wisconsin Press, 1986.

Webster, Jeremy W. *Performing Libertinism in Charles II's Court: Politics, Drama, Sexuality*. New York: Palgrave Macmillan, 2005.

Wheatley, Christopher J. *Beneath Iërne's Banners: Irish Protestant Drama of the Restoration and Eighteenth Century*. Notre Dame, IN: University of Notre Dame Press, 2000.

White, Michelle A. *Henrietta Maria and the English Civil Wars*. Aldershot: Ashgate, 2006.

Wilkinson, William. *Systema Africanum, or, A treatise, discovering the intrigues and arbitrary preceedings of the Guiney Company and also how prejudicial they are to the*

American planters, the woollen, and other English manufactures, to the visible decay of trade, and consequently greatly impairing the royal revenue, which would be infinitely encreased, provided merchants and mariners were encouraged, who can discover several places not yet known, or traded accound of their fortifications, humbly submitted to Their Majesties, and to the consideration of both houses of Parliament. London, 1690.

Williams, Andrew P. *The Restoration Fop: Gender Boundaries and Comic Characterization in Later Seventeenth Century Drama.* Lewiston, NY: Edwin Mellen Press, 1995.

Winsor, Kathleen. *Forever Amber* (1944). Chicago: Chicago Review Press, 2000.

Wiseman, Susan. *Drama and Politics in the English Civil War.* Cambridge: Cambridge University Press, 1998.

The Woman Turned Bully. Ed. María José Mora, Manuel J. Gómez-Lara, Rafael Portillo, Juan A. Prieto-Pablos Textos Y Comentarios. Barcelona: Universitat De Barcelona, 2007.

Wycherley, William. *The Plays of William Wycherley.* Edited by Arthur Friedman. Oxford: Oxford at the Clarendon Press, 1979.

Yadav, Alok. *Before the Empire of English: Literature, Provinciality, and Nationalism in Eighteenth-Century Britain.* New York: Palgrave Macmillan, 2004.

Yang, Chi-ming. "Asia out of Place: The Aesthetics of Incorruptibility in Behn's *Oroonoko.*" *Eighteenth-Century Studies* 42, no. 2 (2009): 235–53.

✍ INDEX

Abington, Frances, 156–57, 161
absolutism, 69–70, 131, 144, 166, 182–83, 186, 189–93, 215
actresses, 152–56
    Anne Bracegirdle, 95, 135, 136f, 142, 155
    boy actors replaced with, 5, 160
    in Davenant plays, 45–46
    Elizabeth Barry, 142, 162, 232
    Elizabeth Boutell, 157–58, 160–61, 163
    as force of refinement, 42, 43
    Frances Abington, 156–57, 161
    Kitty Clive, 269–70n35
    Lavinia Fenton, 161–62, 272n30
    in male clothing, 59, 74, 159, 160
    Mrs. Coleman, 41–42, 250n83
    and narrative of evolution from provincialism to sophistication, 7
    playing Miss Prue and Mrs. Pinchwife, 156–61
    playing Polly Peachum, 161–73
    Sarah Siddons, 142–43, 147, 148f, 149f, 232
    in The Siege of Rhodes, 37, 44–45
    in The Way of the World, 173–80
Addison, Gulston, 217–18
Addison, Joseph
    on rope-dancing, 226
    The Spectator, 216–20, 223, 282nn7–8
    The Tatler, 216–20
Addison, Lancelot, 119, 124, 217
All the World's a Stage (Jackman), 167–69
Amazons, 62, 90–91, 100, 104–5, 116, 135, 261–62n10, 265n66
Ameixial, battle of, 104, 265n57
Americas / New World, 5, 26–27, 100–101, 103, 134–39, 167, 170–71
Amussen, Susan Dwyer, 66–67
antitheatricality, 32, 178, 179, 245n22
Apology for the Life of Colley Cibber (Cibber), 185–86, 197–213
Appiah, Kwame Anthony, 212–13, 217
Aristophanes, 32–36

Arrowsmith, Joseph, 59
Aston, Anthony, 142
Augustine, Matthew, 182
autobiography, 198, 201

Backscheider, Paula, 240
Bailey, Amanda, 280n69
Baldwin, Olive, 189
Ballaster, Ros, 45
Barish, Jonas, 224, 225
Barry, Elizabeth, 142, 162, 232
Baucom, Ian, 151
Beach, Adam R., 126
Beckert, Sven, 6, 67, 170, 222
Beggar's Opera, The (Gay), 153, 161–69, 274–75n67
Behn, Aphra
    career of, 131
    commonalities between Congreve and, 139–40
    on Marshall's costume in The Indian Queen, 109
    Oroonoko, 129, 131–32, 137–39
    The Rover, 59, 194
    Town-Fopp: or, Sir Timothy Tawdry, 59
    The Widow Ranter, 129, 132, 134–37
    and The Woman Turned Bully, 257n65
Berglund, Lisa, 83, 276n5
Berkeley, George Monk, 39
Betterton, Mary, 44, 47, 90–91
Betterton, Thomas, 47, 90, 203
Birchwood, Matthew, 249n66, 250n77
black actors, 72–73
black children, 65–68, 71–72, 215
blackface performances, 90–91, 124
Blount, Henry, 21
Bouhours, Dominique, 39
boundary confusion, fops and, 57–60, 62
Boutell, Elizabeth, 157–58, 160–61, 163
boy actors, replaced with women, 5, 160
Boyle, Roger, 19–20

Bracegirdle, Anne, 95, 135, 136f, 142, 155
Brecht, Bertolt, 273n41
"breeches part," 59, 74
Brewer, Holly, 68, 245n18, 256n51
Britannia Iterarum Beata, 97–98
Britland, Karen, 43
Broadie, Alexander, 227
Brown, Laura, 67, 243n16
Buckingham, Duke of, 113, 117, 194–95,
    266n81
Burke, Helen, 259n79
Burnet, Gilbert
    on Catherine of Braganza, 277n22
    Cibber's invocation of, 198–99
    criticism of, 277n19, 278n30
    History of His Own Time, 183–85, 186–92,
        202, 205–6
    on polygamy, 48, 278n26
    and Protestant nationalism, 185–86
    *Some Passages of the Life and Death of John
        Wilmot, Earl of Rochester*, 193–96
    use of biography, 278n28
Burney, Frances, 152, 155, 156
Butts vs Penny (1677), 145

Calisto (Crowne), 72
Canfield, J. Douglas, 27, 166, 167, 183,
    259n79
capitalism
    Smith on, 222–23
    war capitalism, 6, 7, 67, 153, 170, 171–72,
        215, 222
Carlson, Marvin, 7
Cary, John, 144–45
Caryll, John, 257n63
category crises, 60, 84
Catherine of Braganza
    Burnet on, 277n22
    complexion of, 90–93, 96
    connection to slave trade, 95, 96, 99–100,
        110, 124–26
    cultural influence of, 5, 96–97, 100,
        127–28, 177
    dowry of, 14, 21, 50, 91, 93, 96–99, 104,
        116, 135, 215, 264n38
    and *The Empress of Morocco*, 116, 121–22
    fashion of, 135
    and *The Indian Queen*, 100–111
    marriage to Charles II, 21, 48–49, 88–89,
        96–100, 102–5, 108–9, 117, 126–27,
        239
    relationship with Henrietta Maria, 104
    statue of, in Queens, 91, 93f, 110
    and Tangier project, 117

and *The Widow Ranter*, 135
and *The Womens Conquest*, 90–100
Catherine of Braganza (Gennari), 91, 92f
Catholicism, 60, 69–70, 100, 104, 111, 114,
    121, 185, 186–89, 193, 202
Catley, Ann, 163
Chandler, James, 224, 230
Charles I, 26, 50, 62, 186–87, 188, 233,
    250n86
Charles II
    attends *The Siege of Rhodes*, 43–44
    Burnet on, 188, 189–91, 194–96, 277n22
    Cibber on, 199, 200–204
    connection to slave trade, 125–26
    control over print media, 55
    cultural significance of theater under, 4–6
    death of, 131
    image of, as "Great Turk," 48
    impact on theater, 184–85
    imperialistic ambitions of, 2
    and *The Indian Queen*, 100–111
    and libertine court culture, 183
    marriage to Catherine of Braganza,
        48–49, 88–89, 96–100, 102–5, 108–9,
        117, 126–27, 239
    mistresses of, painted with black servants,
        67
    Ottomanphilia of, 19–20, 21
    in *The Peckham Frolic: or Nell Gwyn*, 181,
        182
    and relationship between theater and
        cosmopolitanism, 214
    and Restoration's relationship to
        modernity, 239–40
    Rochester on, 194
    and slave trade, 68–69, 171–72, 215
    sympathy for, 233
    and Tangier project, 116
    and Third Dutch War, 69–70
    and *The Womens Conquest*, 90–100
    Wycherley's relationship with, 55–56
Chetwood, William, 142
child actors, 71–72
China, 85–87, 154
china orange, 84–85, 260n97
Chinese language, 85
chinoiserie, 1–2, 56, 81–87, 96
Christians, convert to Islam, 41
Chua, Brandon, 37, 89
Cibber, Colley
    Apology for the Life of Colley Cibber, 185–86,
        197–213
    influence of, 184
    The Lady's Last Stake, 208

Love Makes a Man, 208, 210
Love's Last Shift, 207–8, 209, 211–12
  on professional actresses, 156
  The Provok'd Husband, 209–10
  on royal patronage, 55
citizens of the world, 31–35
Clare, Janet, 30
Clarendon, Earl of, 117, 247n45
Claypole, Lady Elizabeth, 27–28
Clifford, James, 135
Clive, Kitty, 269–70n35
clothing
  of Charles II, 11
  and performance of fops, 12, 58–60
  transvestism, 58–60, 74, 84–85, 86, 159,
    160, 170, 254n21, 274n62
  See also fashion
coffee and coffeehouses, 20–21, 131
Coleman, Mrs., 37, 41–42, 250n83
Colley, Linda, 21, 116, 185
Collier, Jeremy, 133, 151, 196, 199, 204–5
Colman, George, 169, 274n61
comedies
  The Country Wife, 1–2, 56, 72–87, 157,
    158–61, 241n12
  The Gentleman Dancing-Master, 63–72
  Mac Flecknoe, 56–63, 255n34
  political meaning in, 54–55
  provincialism in, 55, 152–53, 155, 158–59,
    167–69
commercial modernity, 32, 172, 234, 239
Congreve, William
  background of, 131
  commonalities between Behn and,
    139–40
  Dryden on, 140
  Love for Love, 143, 152, 156–61
  The Mourning Bride, 129, 133–34, 139–51
  roles for women, 155
  The Way of the World, 155, 173–80, 275n71
Conquest of China by the Tartars (Settle), 85,
  86
Conquest of Grenada, The (Dryden), 38–39,
  250n86
Conscious Lovers, The (Steele), 182
conversion
  of Charles II, 202
  of Christians to Islam, 41
  of Rochester, 183–84, 195–96, 278n26
Corp, Edward, 128
corporations, 171
cosmopolitanism
  alteration of standard narratives of, 6–7
  Burnet and paradox for history of, 196

and "china scene" in *The Country Wife*, 1–2
Cibber's rebranding of, 197–213
Cibber's satirization of, 208, 210–11
and commercial and imperial strategy of
  English monarchs, 5
and Davenant's protheatricality, 23–24
discrepant cosmopolitanisms, 135–36
eighteenth-century anxieties about,
  153–54
in eighteenth-century mainstream,
  245n24
emergence of, 2
as engaged, critiqued, and embodied by
  theater, 2–5, 7, 10–11
and evolution of theater, 154, 155–56
failure of, 54, 57, 60
following Restoration, 216
and global commerce in *Wealth of Nations*,
  220–39
and imperialism, 172
and *The Indian Emperour*, 111
in *The Indian Queen*, 101
of Lavinia Fenton, 162–63
mixed implications of, 5–6
and mixed marriage, 105
in *Oroonoko*, 138
Ottomanphilia as rooted in, 20–21, 51
in *Polly*, 171, 172–73
and protheatricality and sophistication in
  *The First Day's Entertainment at Rutland
  House*, 31–37
and provincialism in Restoration
  comedies, 152–53, 155, 158–59, 167–69
rejection of foppish variety of, 213
relationship between theater and,
  214–16
of *Relations of Ten Years Travell*, 62–63
Rhodes as figure for Christian, 40
scholarship on, 7–8
in *The Spectator* and *The Tatler*, 216–20
in *The Way of the World*, 173–80
See also refinement; sophistication
cosmopolitan merchants
  flexible identities of, 24, 58
  networks of, 6
  resemblance of fops to, 58
cosmopolitics, 1, 10–11, 133, 137, 139, 156,
  208, 213, 216
Countrey Wit, The (Crowne), 75
Country Wife, The (Wycherley), 1–2, 56,
  72–87, 157, 158–61, 241n12
court culture, 183–84
court masques, 187
Coventry, Sir John, 189–90

Coventry, Sir William, 70
Cowan, Brian, 20
Cromwell, Oliver, 26–27, 39, 250n77
Crowne, John, 72, 75
Cruelty of the Spaniards in Peru, The
    (Davenant), 26–27, 109, 111, 223

Davenant, Sir William
    The Cruelty of the Spaniards in Peru, 26–27,
        109, 111, 223
    on dangers of assembly, 248n63
    The First Day's Entertainment at Rutland
        House, 22, 31–37
    Gondibert, 26, 246n28
    Henrietta Maria as patron of, 187
    The History of Sir Francis Drake, 26–27
    Madagascar, 52
    Proposition for Advancement of Moralitie,
        28–29
    protheatricality of, 23–31
    The Siege of Rhodes, 21–22, 25, 26, 37–53,
        139, 203, 249n66
    Some Observations Concerning the People of
        this Nation, 30
    travels of, 23, 24
    turns to opera, 246n34
Davies, Thomas, 269–70n35
Davis, John, 117
Dawson, Mark, 57, 208, 242n8, 255n36
Defoe, Daniel, 99
De Marly, Diana, 20
Dennis, John, 207
detachment, encouraged by Diogenes the
    Cynic, 34, 35
Dillon, Elizabeth, 170
Diogenes Laertes, 33–34
Diogenes of Sinope, 2, 31–36
discrepant cosmopolitanisms, 135–36
divine right, 101, 201, 239
Dobson, Michael, 3, 200
Downes, John, 44, 76–77
Dryden, John
    on antitheatricality of Cromwellian party,
        246n33
    on Congreve, 140
    The Conquest of Grenada, 38–39, 250n86
    Davenant's influence on, 109
    on Flecknoe, 253nn10–11
    The Indian Emperour, 102, 111–16, 119,
        121, 129, 172–73, 223
    The Indian Queen, 100–112, 116, 121, 229,
        265n65
    Mac Flecknoe, 56–63, 255n34

Notes and Observations on the Empress of
    Morocco, 121, 122–23
Dryden, Robert G., 170, 172

East Indies, 5, 88, 103, 105
Elmer, Jonathan, 115
emotional regimes, 3, 223–24, 229, 230, 231,
    233, 237, 242n4
empathy, 222–38
Empress of Morocco (Settle), 72, 116–26
Enlightenment, and cosmopolitanism, 24
enslaved children, 65–68, 71–72, 215
enslaved monarchs
    in *The Mourning Bride*, 129, 133–34, 139–51
    in *Oroonoko*, 129, 131–32, 137–39
    in *The Widow Ranter*, 129, 132, 134–37
envy
    in *The Country Wife*, 81
    in *The Gentleman Dancing-Master*, 64–65,
        68, 70–71
    imperial, 51, 81, 215–16
    in *The Siege of Rhodes*, 51, 52
Epsom Wells (Shadwell), 75
Erickson, Robert, 175, 275n71
Essex, Lord, 190, 193, 202, 277n19
Etherege, George, 56, 57, 59, 207–8
eunuchs, 2, 44, 79–80, 85, 259n83
Evelina (Burney), 152, 155, 156
Evelyn, John, 19, 20, 91, 97, 109
exchange, sympathy and, 223–24, 237
exile, 26, 32–34, 60–61
exoticism, 22, 126

"Fall of Mexico, The" (Jerningham), 182
fans, folded, 177, 238
fashion
    and black slaves as symbols of wealth, 66,
        70, 135
    of Catherine of Braganza, 14, 88, 96–97,
        135, 177
    of fops, 12, 58–60, 207–8, 210
    in *Love's Dominion*, 28
    and Ottomanphilia, 19–20, 165
    women and, 220
    See also clothing
Fatal Marriage: or, The Innocent Adultery, The
    (Southerne), 231–32
feet, exposure of, 135
feminism, in Congreve's comedies, 143
Fenton, Lavinia, 161–62, 272n30
Finkel, Caroline, 38
First Day's Entertainment at Rutland House,
    The (Davenant), 22, 31–37

Firth, C. H., 27–28
Fischer, Nicholas, 195
Flack, Audrey, 91, 93f, 110
Flecknoe, Richard
  Dryden's objections to, 253nn10–11
  on exile, 32
  on Portuguese umbrella use, 135
  protheatricality of, 23, 27–30
  scholarship on, 253n12
  travels of, 23, 60–63
  turns to opera, 246n34
  See also Mac Flecknoe (Dryden)
Flügel, J. C., 207
fop(s)
  changing perception of, 221–22
  characterized as upstart, 255n36
  Cibber's performances as, 199–200, 203,
    206–12, 280n54
  clothing of, 12, 58–60
  and failure of Restoration
    cosmopolitanism, 54
  gender fluidity of, 57–59, 62
  globally oriented, in The Gentleman
    Dancing-Master, 63–72
  importance and aesthetics of, in Mac
    Flecknoe, 56–63
  as marker of instability of gentility, 242n8
  in Restoration comedies, 55, 56
  scholarship on, 253–54n15
Forever Amber (Winsor), xi–xiv, 241n1
France
  and Charles II's absorption of French
    style, 69–70
  depiction of, in The Country Wife, 79
  and Francophobia, 257n55
  and Third Dutch War, 69
  See also Paris
Freeman, Lisa, 234, 245n22

Games, Alison, 24, 34, 40, 58, 219
Garber, Marjorie, 58, 59, 60, 254n21
Garcia, Umberto, 250n77
Garganigo, Alex, 108
Garrick, David, 142, 153, 200, 232
Gay, John
  The Beggar's Opera, 153, 161–69, 273n39,
    274–75n67
  Polly, 153, 163–64, 169–73, 274n62, 275n69
  gender fluidity, of fops, 57–59, 62
Gennari, Benedetto II, 91, 92f
Gentleman Dancing-Master, The (Wycherley),
    63–72
Gikandi, Simon, 67, 256n47

Gildon, Charles, 133
Gill, Pat, 183
Glaisyer, Natasha, 217
globalization and global relations
  and cosmopolitanism in The Spectator, 220
  and The Country Wife, 72–87
  and fops in The Gentleman Dancing-Master,
    63–72
  and marriage of Charles II and Catherine
    of Braganza, 88–89
  and mixed implications of Restoration
    cosmopolitanism, 6
  and relationship between theater and
    cosmopolitanism, 215
  and The Siege of Rhodes, 37–38
  Smith on cosmopolitanism and, 220–39
  understanding theater culture in context
    of, 8–10
Glorious Revolution of 1688, 140, 144, 186,
    233
Glover, Brian, 198
Goffman, Daniel, 38
golilla, 71
Gondibert (Davenant), 26, 246n28
Greig, Martin, 186
Guasco, Michael, 22
Gwynn, Nell, 112, 163, 188, 205

Hall, Kim F., 262n17
Harbage, Alfred, 27
Hart, Charles, 76–77
Hawes, Clement, 167
Hedbäck, Ann-Mari, 251n92
Heilman, Robert, 211
Henrietta (Minette), 188
Henrietta Maria, 26, 27, 31, 43, 44, 50, 90,
    104, 187–88, 250n86
Herbert, Sir Henry, 27
heroic drama, 52–53
  Davenant's popularization of, 26–27
  death of, 129, 134, 246n28
  love in formula of, 148
  The Mourning Bride, 129, 133–34, 139–51
  Oroonoko, 129, 131–32, 137–39
  The Widow Ranter, 129, 132, 134–37
History of His Own Time (Burnet), 183–85,
    186–93, 202, 205–6
History of Sir Francis Drake, The (Davenant),
    26–27
Hobbes, Thomas, 30
Hogarth, William, 164, 165f
Holland, Norman N., 239
homosexuality, 208, 254n21

Howard, Edward, 59, 90–100, 261–62n10
Howard, Sir Robert, 100–112, 116, 121, 229,
    265n65
Hume, Robert, 55
Hurrem, 44–45
Hutner, Heidi, 102
Hynes, Peter, 279n41

imperial envy, 51, 81, 215–16
imperialism
    Catherine of Braganza's connection to,
        97–100, 103
    and cosmopolitanism, 172
    and *The Empress of Morocco*, 117–18,
        121–22, 124, 126–27
    and *The Indian Queen*, 100–111
    as intertwined with sovereignty, 89
    James II's vision of, 131
    Jerningham on, 182
    and *The Mourning Bride*, 143, 144
India, 5, 7, 52, 96–97, 98, 103, 128, 215, 239
Indian Emperour, The (Dryden), 102, 111–16,
    119, 121, 129, 172–73, 223
Indian Queen, The (Dryden and Howard),
    100–112, 116, 121, 122, 229, 265n65
Isabella; or The Fatal Marriage (Garrick), 232
Islam, Christian conversion to, 41
Iwanisziw, Susan, 117, 120–21

Jackman, Isaac, 167–69
Jacob, James R., 30
Jacob, Margaret, 245n24
Jacobitism, 155–56
James I, 186
James II, 5, 69, 131, 132, 144, 183, 191–93,
    202–3, 233
jealousy, in *The Siege of Rhodes*, 51, 52
Jeffreys, George, 192–93
Jenkins, Eugenia Zuroski, 6, 154, 214
Jerningham, Edward
    The Peckham Frolic: or Nell Gwyn, 181–83,
        186, 193
    "The Fall of Mexico," 182
    "Yarico to Inkle," 182
Johnson, Samuel, 146
Journey to London, A (Vanbrugh), 209
Justman, Stewart, 224

Keay, Anna, 240
Kéroualle, Louise de, Duchess of
    Portsmouth, 66f, 67, 70, 188, 189
Killigrew, Thomas, 47, 102, 245n19, 264n53
King, Thomas A., 57, 207
Kingsley, Margery, 255n34

Kirke, Percy, 192
Kowalski-Wallace, Elizabeth, 81–82
Kroll, Richard, 132
Krop, C. R., 212

Lady's Last Stake, The (Cibber), 208
Lectures on Rhetoric and Belles Lettres (Smith),
    229–31
Leigh, Elinor, 178
libertinism, 182–84, 189, 191, 194–96, 215,
    239, 259n79, 278n27
*Life of Lavinia Beswick, Alias Fenton, Alias
    Polly Peachum, The*, 161–62, 163
Lillo, George, 233–37
Lockey, Brian, 24, 25
London, debate on Paris and, in *The First
    Day's Entertainment at Rutland House*,
    36–37
London Merchant, The (Lillo), 233–37
Louise de Kéroualle, Duchess of Portsmouth
    (Mignard), 66f, 67, 70
Louis XIV, 188, 189, 198
love, in formula of heroic drama, 148
Love for Love (Congreve), 143, 152, 156–61
Love Makes a Man (Cibber), 208, 210
*Love's Dominion, A Dramatique Piece, Full of
    Excellent Moralitie; Written as a Pattern
    for the Reformed Stage* (Flecknoe), 27–28,
    247n47
Love's Last Shift (Cibber), 207–8, 209,
    211–12
Lowenthal, Cynthia, 64
luxury, 32, 34, 137, 167, 170, 200, 210

Mac Flecknoe (Dryden), 56–63, 255n34
MacKenzie, Scott R., 275n71
Mackie, Erin, 165, 220, 259n79, 278n27
MacLean, Gerald, 6, 20, 51
Madagascar (Davenant), 52
Madway, Lorraine, 96
Maguire, Nancy, 89, 106
Man of Mode, The (Etherege), 59, 207–8
Markley, Robert, 6, 86–87
Marsden, Jean, 142, 234, 284n40
Marshall, Anne, 106–7, 109
Marshall, David, 225, 231
Marvell, Andrew, 62
masques, 187
Matar, Nabil, 40–41
Mazella, David, 2, 32, 33
McGirr, Elaine, 89, 212, 280n54
McKenzie, D. F., 145
mercantilism, 6, 34, 68, 222–23, 281n2
Mignard, Pierre, 66f, 67, 70

mixed marriages
  in *The Empress of Morocco*, 116, 119, 121,
    122
  in *The Indian Emperour*, 102, 111, 112–13,
    114, 116
  in *The Indian Queen*, 103, 105–6
  in *The Mourning Bride*, 141–42, 150
  in *Polly*, 170, 173
  in Restoration tragedies and heroic plays,
    89–90
  in *The Widow Ranter*, 134–35, 137
mole (Tangier), 116–17, 122–24
Monmouth's rebellion, 191–92
Moors, 72, 91–93, 117, 122, 124, 146, 192, 193
Morgan, Henry, 171
Mourning Bride, The (Congreve), 129,
    133–34, 139–51
Mowry, Melissa, 248n63
Mustapha (Boyle), 19–20

nation, theater as representing, 206, 209
national identity
  and complexities of purity and
    sophistication in *The Country Wife*,
    79–81
  of Flecknoe, 62–63
nationalism, 154, 185–86, 196
Neill, Michael, 3, 27, 195, 259n79
new historicism, 9
Newman, Gerald, 154
*Notes and Observations on the Empress of
  Morocco* (Dryden et al.), 121, 122–23
Novak, Maximillian, 253n11
Nussbaum, Felicity, 48, 90, 156, 272n30

Oates, Titus, 117, 190, 204
O'Brien, John, 171
O'Brien, Karen, 245n24
On Lingering and Being Last (Elmer), 115
Orgel, Stephen, 207
Oroonoko (Behn), 129, 131–32, 137–39
Orphan, The (Otway), 228, 232
Orr, Bridget, 25, 26, 45, 89, 101, 102, 143,
    246n31, 249n66, 251n101, 265n65, 267n99
Osborne, Francis, 21
Othello (Shakespeare), 47, 228, 231
Ottoman Empire
  eunuchs as palace guards in, 79–80
  and imperial envy, 51
  siege of Rhodes, 37–39
  theatrical representation of, 40–41
Ottomanphilia
  and characterization of Stuart court, 48
  of Charles II, 19–20

and Davenant's protheatricality, 23–31
and *The Siege of Rhodes*, 21–22, 37–39, 45
and *Tarugo's Wiles: or, The Coffeehouse*,
    20–21
Otway, Thomas, 228, 232

Palmer, Barbara, Countess of Castlemaine,
    48–49, 55, 108
Paris
  debate on London and, in *The First Day's
    Entertainment at Rutland House*, 36–37
  Flecknoe on, 60
Parrott, W. Gerrod, 51
patriarchy, 64, 68, 80, 82, 143, 144, 164, 167,
    178
Peckham Frolic: or Nell Gwyn, The
    (Jerningham), 181–83, 186, 193
Pepys, Samuel
  on battle of Ameixial, 265n57
  on Catherine's exposed foot, 135
  fantasizes about Queen of England, 88
  on *The Indian Emperour*, 112
  on royal patronage, 55
  and sexual allure of transvestism, 74
  on *The Siege of Rhodes*, 44
  on *Tarugo's Wiles*, 159
  on tensions in royal marriage, 261n9
Philoctetes, 227
Pincus, Steve, 69, 131, 239
piracy, 171
Pitts, Joseph, 21
Pix, Mary, 48
Plain Dealer, The (Wycherley), 56, 160,
    241n12
poetry, Smith on, 229–30
Polly (Coleman), 169, 274n61
Polly (Gay), 153, 163–64, 169–73, 274n62,
    275n69
polygamy, 48, 278n26
Pope, Alexander, 197–98, 203
Popish Plot (1678–1681), 117, 186, 190, 191,
    277n19
porcelain, 1–2, 56, 81–87, 88, 96
Porter, David, 81–82, 85
Porter, Mrs., 142
portraits, 62, 66–67, 70–72, 91, 147, 215
Portugal
  alliance between England and, 98–99, 100,
    102, 104, 108–9
  role in slave trade, 91–92, 99, 103
  trade with Africa, 96
  war capitalism of, 96–97
  See also Catherine of Braganza
Postle, Martin, 156

print culture and media
    Charles II's control over, 55
    impact on theater, 4
Pritchard, Hannah, 141, 142
Proposition for Advancement of Moralitie
    (Davenant), 28–29
Protestantism, 131, 185–86, 187–88, 193, 200
Protestant nationalism, 185–86, 196
protheatricality, 23–37, 43, 245n22
proto-feminism, in Congreve's comedies,
    143
provincialism
    and evolution of theater, 154
    and failure of Restoration
        cosmopolitanism, 54
    in Restoration comedies, 55, 152–53, 155,
        158–59, 167–69
    and sophistication and global commerce
        in *The Country Wife*, 72–87
    in *The Way of the World*, 175–76
Provok'd Husband, The (Cibber), 209–10
Prynne, William, 187
Pullen, Kirsten, 160

Quint, David, 52

rack, 227
Raynor, Timothy, 30
Reddy, William, 223–24, 242n4
Reed, Peter P., 274n61
refinement, 22, 25, 28–30, 35, 36, 42, 60,
    159, 228. *See also* cosmopolitanism;
    sophistication
Reformation, The (Arrowsmith), 59
Rehearsal, The (Buckingham), 113, 266n81
Relapse, The (Vanbrugh), 212
Relations of Ten Years Travell (Flecknoe),
    60–63
Reynolds, Joshua, 156, 157f
Rhodes, Ottoman siege of, 37–39. See also
    Siege of Rhodes, The (Davenant)
Richards, Cynthia, 184
Richardson, Samuel, 232–33
Roach, Joseph, 67, 102, 200–201
Rochester, John Wilmot, Earl of, 162, 163,
    193–96
rope-dancing, 226
Routh, E. M., 116–17
Rover, The (Behn), 194
Roxolana, 44–45
Royal African Company, 5, 68–69, 132, 139,
    144–45, 147, 171, 215
Russell, Lord, 190–91, 202
rustic, the. *See* provincialism

sacrifice, Aristophanes on, 35
Samet, Elizabeth D., 283n27
Sandford, Samuel, 204
Second Dutch War, 65, 68–69
Sedgwick, Eve Kosofsky, 259n79
self-interest, 222–38
Settle, Elkanah, 72, 85, 86, 116–26
sexuality
    of Charles II, 189
    fops and conventions of, 57–59, 208
    Restoration literary experiments with
        sexual norms, 183
Shadwell, Thomas, 56–57, 75
Shakespeare, William, 3, 59, 154–55, 199,
    200, 203, 284n34
    Othello, 47, 228, 231
Shepherd, Simon, 83
Sheridan, Richard, 181
Sherman, Stuart, 4
she-tragedies, 232–33, 284n39
Shevelow, Kathryn, 282n8
*Short View of the Prophaneness and Immorality
    of the English Stage* (Collier), 151
Siddons, Sarah, 142–43, 147, 148f, 149f, 232
Siege of Rhodes, The (Davenant), 21–22, 25,
    26, 139, 203, 249n66
    1656, 37–43
    1661, 43–53
Sir Salomon; Or, The Cautious Coxcomb
    (Caryll), 257n63
*Sir William Davenant's Voyage to the Other
    World* (Flecknoe), 23
Six Days Adventure, or the New Utopia
    (Howard), 59
skepticism, 216
slavery and slave trade
    Adam Smith on, 221
    Behn's association of Stuarts with, 132
    and black actors, 72–73
    Catherine of Braganza's connection to,
        95, 96, 99–100, 110, 124–26
    under Charles II, 68–69, 171–72, 215
    debates concerning, 144–45, 147
    English contact with Ottoman Empire
        and naturalization of, 22
    enslaved children, 65–68, 71–72, 215
    The Mourning Bride's relationship to,
        145–47
    in *Oroonoko*, 137–39
    Portugal's role in slave trade, 92, 99–100
    Smith on capitalism and, 222–23
    and Tangier project, 122
    in *Tarugo's Wiles: or, The Coffeehouse*, 159
    See also enslaved monarchs

Slighted Maid, The, 159

Smith, Adam, 17, 220–39, 282n21, 283nn27,34

Smith, John Raphael, 147

Sofer, Andrew, 3

Some Observations Concerning the People of this Nation (Davenant), 30

Some Passages of the Life and Death of John Wilmot, Earl of Rochester (Burnet), 193–96

sophistication
  of actresses, 162
  changing aspirations to, in *The Way of the World*, 173–80
  and Davenant's protheatricality, 22
  and *The First Day's Entertainment at Rutland House*, 31–37
  and global commerce in *The Country Wife*, 72–87
  and global commerce in *Wealth of Nations*, 221–22
  in *Polly*, 172–73
  and protheatricality, 23–31
  and Restoration cosmopolitanism, 1–6
  Restoration definition of, 78–79, 155
  See also cosmopolitanism; refinement

Southerne, Thomas, 137, 231–32

Spanish Empire, in *The Gentleman Dancing-Master*, 63–65, 67–68, 71

Spectator, The, 216–20, 223, 282nn7–8

Stallybrass, Peter, 30

Staves, Susan, 3, 211, 246n28

Steele, Richard
  The Conscious Lovers, 43
  as influence on Smith, 226
  The Spectator, 216–20, 223, 282nn7–8
  The Tatler, 216–20
  The Tender Husband, 168

Stein, Tristan, 21, 116

Straub, Kristina, 57–58, 200, 201, 206–7, 208, 280n55

St. Serfe, Thomas, 20–21, 159

Sudan, Rajani, 98

Suleiman the Magnificent, 19–20, 38, 39, 41–50, 52, 139, 203, 249n66

Swift, Jonathan, 226

Swingen, Abigail, 6, 68–69, 257n55

sympathy, 222–38

Tangier, 21, 50, 96, 116–18, 121–22, 126, 215

Tarugo's Wiles: or, The Coffeehouse (St. Serfe), 20–21, 159

Tatler, The, 216–20

tea, 5, 88, 96, 177–78, 219

Tender Husband, The (Steele), 168

Teviot, Earl of, 126

theater
  antitheatricality, 32, 178, 179, 245n22
  change in theatrical style, 131
  Charles II's impact on, 184–85
  and Cibber's rebranding of cosmopolitanism, 197–213
  as civilizing force, 47–48, 73
  cultural significance of, 4–5
  Davenant's support for, 22
  debate on, in *The First Day's Entertainment at Rutland House*, 31–37
  evolution of, 154, 155–56
  flourishing of, in Restoration, 246n28
  as force of harmonization, 31
  global encounters through, 24–25
  impact of Restoration, 11
  and nationalist Protestant reform, 196
  proposed tax on playhouses, 190
  protheatricality, 23–31, 43, 245n22
  relationship between cosmopolitanism and, 214–16
  as representing nation, 206, 209
  Restoration cosmopolitanism as engaged, critiqued, and embodied by, 2–5, 7, 10–11
  and Smith's views on emotional and ethical development of society, 223–38
  underestimation of Restoration, 17–18

theater aesthetics, 23, 32, 137, 156, 199–200, 208, 210–11, 231

theater culture, 3–4, 8–10

theater studies, 8

theatricality, 34, 155, 159–60, 167–68, 170, 179, 182–83, 199, 202–3, 206–8, 225

Theory of Moral Sentiments (Smith), 222–30, 231–33, 238

Thievery A-la-mode: or, The Fatal Encouragement, 167

Third Dutch War (1672), 69–70, 257n55

Thomas, Gertrude, 97, 100, 135

Thompson, Ayanna, 101, 102, 109, 111

Thompson, E. P., 6

Thompson, Peggy, 183

tobacco, 134

Todd, Janet, 132

Tofts, Catherine, 189

torture, 111, 113, 114, 116, 119–20, 172–73, 223, 227

Town-Fopp: or, Sir Timothy Tawdry (Behn), 59

tragedies
  Empress of Morocco, 72, 116–26
  The Indian Emperour, 102, 111–16, 119, 121, 129, 172–73, 223

tragedies (*continued*)
 The Indian Queen, 100–112, 116, 121, 122,
  229, 265n65
 mixed marriages in, 89–90
 The Mourning Bride, 129, 133–34, 139–51
 Oroonoko, 129, 131–32, 137–39
 The Widow Ranter, 129, 132, 134–37
 The Womens Conquest, 90–100, 261–62n10
Tragedy of Mahomet (Voltaire), 228–29
transvestism, 58–60, 74, 84–85, 86, 159, 160,
 170, 254n21, 274n62
travel
 of Davenant, 23, 24
 as encouraged for young men, 25
 of Flecknoe, 23, 60–63
 and global encounters through theater,
  24–25
 and protheatricality and sophistication in
  *The First Day's Entertainment at Rutland
  House*, 31–37
travesty roles, 12, 58, 74, 84, 161
Trumpener, Katie, 154
Turner, James Grantham, 183, 278n27

umbrellas, 135, 268n18
urbanity, 6, 15, 73, 76, 81, 152, 170, 175,
 209

Vanbrugh, John, 209, 212
Varhus, Sara B., 278n28
Venetians, Ottoman attacks on, 39
Visconsi, Elliott, 102, 134
Voltaire, 228–29

Wahrman, Dror, 25, 45, 58, 246n29, 250n81,
 254n18
Walpole, Horace, 142
Wanko, Cheryl, 162
war capitalism, 6, 7, 67, 153, 170, 171–72,
 215, 222
Warner, William, 185
Way of the World, The (Congreve), 155,
 173–80, 275n71

Wealth of Nations (Smith), 220–24, 231, 235,
 237–38
Webb, John, 85
Weber, Harold, 55, 239, 276n8
Webster, Jeremy, 183
West Barbary (Addison), 119, 124, 217
West Indies, 97, 103, 105, 159
Wheatley, Christopher, 75
White, Allon, 30
Widow Ranter, The (Behn), 129, 132, 134–37
Wilkinson, William, 145
William of Orange, 131
Williams, Andrew, 59
Wilson, Thelma, 189
Winsor, Kathleen, xi–xiv, 241n1
Wiseman, Susan, 31, 39, 43
Woman Turned Bully, The, 73–75, 257n65,
 258n69
women
 and changed manners in Restoration, 75
 Congreve's roles for, 155
 cosmopolitanism and over sophistication
  of, 220
 Flecknoe's preference for company of, 60
 she-tragedies, 232–33, 284n39
 and transvestism, 59, 74, 84–85, 159, 160,
  170, 274n62
 See also actresses
Womens Conquest, The (Howard), 90–100,
 261–62n10
world citizenship, 31–35
Wycherley, William
 The Country Wife, 1–2, 56, 72–87, 157,
  158–61, 241n12
 The Gentleman Dancing-Master, 63–72
 The Plain Dealer, 56, 160, 241n12
 relationship with Charles II, 55–56

Yadav, Alok, 6, 80–81, 259n88
Yang, Chi-Ming, 271n52
"Yarico to Inkle" (Jerningham), 182

Zwicker, Steven, 182

CPSIA information can be obtained
at www.ICGtesting.com
Printed in the USA
LVHW111748081020
668327LV00004B/45/J

9 781501 751585